Lecture Notes in Computer Science 14722

Founding Editors

Gerhard Goos
Juris Hartmanis

Editorial Board Members

The series Lecture Notes in Computer Science (LNCS), including its subseries Lecture Notes in Artificial Intelligence (LNAI) and Lecture Notes in Bioinformatics (LNBI), has established itself as a medium for the publication of new developments in computer science and information technology research, teaching, and education.

LNCS enjoys close cooperation with the computer science R & D community, the series counts many renowned academics among its volume editors and paper authors, and collaborates with prestigious societies. Its mission is to serve this international community by providing an invaluable service, mainly focused on the publication of conference and workshop proceedings and postproceedings. LNCS commenced publication in 1973.

Panayiotis Zaphiris · Andri Ioannou
Editors

Learning and Collaboration Technologies

11th International Conference, LCT 2024
Held as Part of the 26th HCI International Conference, HCII 2024
Washington, DC, USA, June 29 – July 4, 2024
Proceedings, Part I

 Springer

Editors
Panayiotis Zaphiris ⓘ
Department of Multimedia and Graphic Arts
Cyprus University of Technology
Limassol, Cyprus

Andri Ioannou ⓘ
Department of Multimedia and Graphic Arts
Cyprus University of Technology
Limassol, Cyprus

Research Center on Interactive Media, Smart
Systems and Emerging Technologies
(CYENS)
Nicosia, Cyprus

ISSN 0302-9743   ISSN 1611-3349 (electronic)
Lecture Notes in Computer Science
ISBN 978-3-031-61671-6   ISBN 978-3-031-61672-3 (eBook)
https://doi.org/10.1007/978-3-031-61672-3

This Springer imprint is published by the registered company Springer Nature Switzerland AG
The registered company address is: Gewerbestrasse 11, 6330 Cham, Switzerland

If disposing of this product, please recycle the paper.

Foreword

This year we celebrate 40 years since the establishment of the HCI International (HCII) Conference, which has been a hub for presenting groundbreaking research and novel ideas and collaboration for people from all over the world.

The HCII conference was founded in 1984 by Prof. Gavriel Salvendy (Purdue University, USA, Tsinghua University, P.R. China, and University of Central Florida, USA) and the first event of the series, "1st USA-Japan Conference on Human-Computer Interaction", was held in Honolulu, Hawaii, USA, 18–20 August. Since then, HCI International is held jointly with several Thematic Areas and Affiliated Conferences, with each one under the auspices of a distinguished international Program Board and under one management and one registration. Twenty-six HCI International Conferences have been organized so far (every two years until 2013, and annually thereafter).

Over the years, this conference has served as a platform for scholars, researchers, industry experts and students to exchange ideas, connect, and address challenges in the ever-evolving HCI field. Throughout these 40 years, the conference has evolved itself, adapting to new technologies and emerging trends, while staying committed to its core mission of advancing knowledge and driving change.

As we celebrate this milestone anniversary, we reflect on the contributions of its founding members and appreciate the commitment of its current and past Affiliated Conference Program Board Chairs and members. We are also thankful to all past conference attendees who have shaped this community into what it is today.

The 26th International Conference on Human-Computer Interaction, HCI International 2024 (HCII 2024), was held as a 'hybrid' event at the Washington Hilton Hotel, Washington, DC, USA, during 29 June – 4 July 2024. It incorporated the 21 thematic areas and affiliated conferences listed below.

A total of 5108 individuals from academia, research institutes, industry, and government agencies from 85 countries submitted contributions, and 1271 papers and 309 posters were included in the volumes of the proceedings that were published just before the start of the conference, these are listed below. The contributions thoroughly cover the entire field of human-computer interaction, addressing major advances in knowledge and effective use of computers in a variety of application areas. These papers provide academics, researchers, engineers, scientists, practitioners and students with state-of-the-art information on the most recent advances in HCI.

The HCI International (HCII) conference also offers the option of presenting 'Late Breaking Work', and this applies both for papers and posters, with corresponding volumes of proceedings that will be published after the conference. Full papers will be included in the 'HCII 2024 - Late Breaking Papers' volumes of the proceedings to be published in the Springer LNCS series, while 'Poster Extended Abstracts' will be included as short research papers in the 'HCII 2024 - Late Breaking Posters' volumes to be published in the Springer CCIS series.

I would like to thank the Program Board Chairs and the members of the Program Boards of all thematic areas and affiliated conferences for their contribution towards the high scientific quality and overall success of the HCI International 2024 conference. Their manifold support in terms of paper reviewing (single-blind review process, with a minimum of two reviews per submission), session organization and their willingness to act as goodwill ambassadors for the conference is most highly appreciated.

This conference would not have been possible without the continuous and unwavering support and advice of Gavriel Salvendy, founder, General Chair Emeritus, and Scientific Advisor. For his outstanding efforts, I would like to express my sincere appreciation to Abbas Moallem, Communications Chair and Editor of HCI International News.

July 2024   Constantine Stephanidis

HCI International 2024 Thematic Areas
and Affiliated Conferences

- HCI: Human-Computer Interaction Thematic Area
- HIMI: Human Interface and the Management of Information Thematic Area
- EPCE: 21st International Conference on Engineering Psychology and Cognitive Ergonomics
- AC: 18th International Conference on Augmented Cognition
- UAHCI: 18th International Conference on Universal Access in Human-Computer Interaction
- CCD: 16th International Conference on Cross-Cultural Design
- SCSM: 16th International Conference on Social Computing and Social Media
- VAMR: 16th International Conference on Virtual, Augmented and Mixed Reality
- DHM: 15th International Conference on Digital Human Modeling & Applications in Health, Safety, Ergonomics & Risk Management
- DUXU: 13th International Conference on Design, User Experience and Usability
- C&C: 12th International Conference on Culture and Computing
- DAPI: 12th International Conference on Distributed, Ambient and Pervasive Interactions
- HCIBGO: 11th International Conference on HCI in Business, Government and Organizations
- LCT: 11th International Conference on Learning and Collaboration Technologies
- ITAP: 10th International Conference on Human Aspects of IT for the Aged Population
- AIS: 6th International Conference on Adaptive Instructional Systems
- HCI-CPT: 6th International Conference on HCI for Cybersecurity, Privacy and Trust
- HCI-Games: 6th International Conference on HCI in Games
- MobiTAS: 6th International Conference on HCI in Mobility, Transport and Automotive Systems
- AI-HCI: 5th International Conference on Artificial Intelligence in HCI
- MOBILE: 5th International Conference on Human-Centered Design, Operation and Evaluation of Mobile Communications

List of Conference Proceedings Volumes Appearing
Before the Conference

1. LNCS 14684, Human-Computer Interaction: Part I, edited by Masaaki Kurosu and Ayako Hashizume
2. LNCS 14685, Human-Computer Interaction: Part II, edited by Masaaki Kurosu and Ayako Hashizume
3. LNCS 14686, Human-Computer Interaction: Part III, edited by Masaaki Kurosu and Ayako Hashizume
4. LNCS 14687, Human-Computer Interaction: Part IV, edited by Masaaki Kurosu and Ayako Hashizume
5. LNCS 14688, Human-Computer Interaction: Part V, edited by Masaaki Kurosu and Ayako Hashizume
6. LNCS 14689, Human Interface and the Management of Information: Part I, edited by Hirohiko Mori and Yumi Asahi
7. LNCS 14690, Human Interface and the Management of Information: Part II, edited by Hirohiko Mori and Yumi Asahi
8. LNCS 14691, Human Interface and the Management of Information: Part III, edited by Hirohiko Mori and Yumi Asahi
9. LNAI 14692, Engineering Psychology and Cognitive Ergonomics: Part I, edited by Don Harris and Wen-Chin Li
10. LNAI 14693, Engineering Psychology and Cognitive Ergonomics: Part II, edited by Don Harris and Wen-Chin Li
11. LNAI 14694, Augmented Cognition, Part I, edited by Dylan D. Schmorrow and Cali M. Fidopiastis
12. LNAI 14695, Augmented Cognition, Part II, edited by Dylan D. Schmorrow and Cali M. Fidopiastis
13. LNCS 14696, Universal Access in Human-Computer Interaction: Part I, edited by Margherita Antona and Constantine Stephanidis
14. LNCS 14697, Universal Access in Human-Computer Interaction: Part II, edited by Margherita Antona and Constantine Stephanidis
15. LNCS 14698, Universal Access in Human-Computer Interaction: Part III, edited by Margherita Antona and Constantine Stephanidis
16. LNCS 14699, Cross-Cultural Design: Part I, edited by Pei-Luen Patrick Rau
17. LNCS 14700, Cross-Cultural Design: Part II, edited by Pei-Luen Patrick Rau
18. LNCS 14701, Cross-Cultural Design: Part III, edited by Pei-Luen Patrick Rau
19. LNCS 14702, Cross-Cultural Design: Part IV, edited by Pei-Luen Patrick Rau
20. LNCS 14703, Social Computing and Social Media: Part I, edited by Adela Coman and Simona Vasilache
21. LNCS 14704, Social Computing and Social Media: Part II, edited by Adela Coman and Simona Vasilache
22. LNCS 14705, Social Computing and Social Media: Part III, edited by Adela Coman and Simona Vasilache

47. LNCS 14730, HCI in Games: Part I, edited by Xiaowen Fang
48. LNCS 14731, HCI in Games: Part II, edited by Xiaowen Fang
49. LNCS 14732, HCI in Mobility, Transport and Automotive Systems: Part I, edited by Heidi Krömker
50. LNCS 14733, HCI in Mobility, Transport and Automotive Systems: Part II, edited by Heidi Krömker
51. LNAI 14734, Artificial Intelligence in HCI: Part I, edited by Helmut Degen and Stavroula Ntoa
52. LNAI 14735, Artificial Intelligence in HCI: Part II, edited by Helmut Degen and Stavroula Ntoa
53. LNAI 14736, Artificial Intelligence in HCI: Part III, edited by Helmut Degen and Stavroula Ntoa
54. LNCS 14737, Design, Operation and Evaluation of Mobile Communications: Part I, edited by June Wei and George Margetis
55. LNCS 14738, Design, Operation and Evaluation of Mobile Communications: Part II, edited by June Wei and George Margetis
56. CCIS 2114, HCI International 2024 Posters - Part I, edited by Constantine Stephanidis, Margherita Antona, Stavroula Ntoa and Gavriel Salvendy
57. CCIS 2115, HCI International 2024 Posters - Part II, edited by Constantine Stephanidis, Margherita Antona, Stavroula Ntoa and Gavriel Salvendy
58. CCIS 2116, HCI International 2024 Posters - Part III, edited by Constantine Stephanidis, Margherita Antona, Stavroula Ntoa and Gavriel Salvendy
59. CCIS 2117, HCI International 2024 Posters - Part IV, edited by Constantine Stephanidis, Margherita Antona, Stavroula Ntoa and Gavriel Salvendy
60. CCIS 2118, HCI International 2024 Posters - Part V, edited by Constantine Stephanidis, Margherita Antona, Stavroula Ntoa and Gavriel Salvendy
61. CCIS 2119, HCI International 2024 Posters - Part VI, edited by Constantine Stephanidis, Margherita Antona, Stavroula Ntoa and Gavriel Salvendy
62. CCIS 2120, HCI International 2024 Posters - Part VII, edited by Constantine Stephanidis, Margherita Antona, Stavroula Ntoa and Gavriel Salvendy

https://2024.hci.international/proceedings

Preface

In today's knowledge society, learning and collaboration are two fundamental and strictly interrelated aspects of knowledge acquisition and creation. Learning technology is the broad range of communication, information, and related technologies that can be used to support learning, teaching, and assessment, often in a collaborative way. Collaboration technology, on the other hand, is targeted to support individuals working in teams towards a common goal, which may be an educational one, by providing tools that aid communication and the management of activities as well as the process of problem solving. In this context, interactive technologies not only affect and improve the existing educational system but become a transformative force that can generate radically new ways of knowing, learning, and collaborating.

The 11th International Conference on Learning and Collaboration Technologies (LCT 2024), affiliated with HCI International 2024, addressed the theoretical foundations, design and implementation, and effectiveness and impact issues related to interactive technologies for learning and collaboration, including design methodologies, developments and tools, theoretical models, and learning design or learning experience (LX) design, as well as technology adoption and use in formal, non-formal, and informal educational contexts.

Learning and collaboration technologies are increasingly adopted in K-20 (kindergarten to higher education) classrooms and lifelong learning. Technology can support expansive forms of collaboration; deepened empathy; complex coordination of people, materials, and purposes; and development of skill sets that are increasingly important across workspaces in the 21st century. The general themes of the LCT conference aim to address challenges related to understanding how to design for better learning and collaboration with technology, support learners to develop relevant approaches and skills, and assess or evaluate gains and outcomes. To this end, topics such as extended reality (XR) learning, embodied and immersive learning, mobile learning and ubiquitous technologies, serious games and gamification, learning through design and making, educational robotics, educational chatbots, human-computer interfaces, and computer-supported collaborative learning, among others, are elaborated in the LCT conference proceedings. Learning (experience) design and user experience design remain a challenge in the arena of learning environments and collaboration technology. LCT aims to serve a continuous dialog while synthesizing current knowledge.

Three volumes of the HCII 2024 proceedings are dedicated to this year's edition of the LCT 2024 conference. The first focuses on topics related to Designing Learning and Teaching Experiences, and Investigating Learning Experiences. The second focuses on topics related to Serious Games and Gamification, and Novel Learning Ecosystems, while the third focuses on topics related to VR and AR in Learning and Education, and AI in Learning and Education.

The papers of these volumes were accepted for publication after a minimum of two single-blind reviews from the members of the LCT Program Board or, in some cases, from members of the Program Boards of other affiliated conferences. We would like to thank all of them for their invaluable contribution, support, and efforts.

July 2024

Panayiotis Zaphiris
Andri Ioannou

11th International Conference on Learning and Collaboration Technologies (LCT 2024)

Program Board Chairs: **Panayiotis Zaphiris**, *Cyprus University of Technology, Cyprus*, and **Andri Ioannou**, *Cyprus University of Technology, Cyprus* and *Research Center on Interactive Media, Smart Systems and Emerging Technologies (CYENS), Cyprus*

- Miguel Angel Conde Gonzalez, *University of Leon, Spain*
- Fisnik Dalipi, *Linnaeus University, Sweden*
- Camille Dickson-Deane, *University of Technology Sydney, Australia*
- David Fonseca, *La Salle, Ramon Llull University, Spain*
- Alicia Garcia-Holgado, *Universidad de Salamanca, Spain*
- Francisco Garcia-Penalvo, *University of Salamanca, Spain*
- Aleksandar Jevremovic, *Singidunum University, Serbia*
- Elis Kakoulli Constantinou, *Cyprus University of Technology, Cyprus*
- Tomaz Klobucar, *Jozef Stefan Institute, Slovenia*
- Birgy Lorenz, *Tallinn University of Technology, Estonia*
- Nicholas H. Müller, *Technical University of Applied Sciences Würzburg-Schweinfurt, Germany*
- Fernando Moreira, *Universidade Portucalense, Portugal*
- Anna Nicolaou, *Cyprus University of Technology, Cyprus*
- Antigoni Parmaxi, *Cyprus University of Technology, Cyprus*
- Dijana Plantak Vukovac, *University of Zagreb, Croatia*
- Maria-Victoria Soule, *Cyprus University of Technology, Cyprus*
- Sonia Sousa, *Tallinn University, Estonia*

The full list with the Program Board Chairs and the members of the Program Boards of all thematic areas and affiliated conferences of HCII 2024 is available online at:

http://www.hci.international/board-members-2024.php

HCI International 2025 Conference

The 27th International Conference on Human-Computer Interaction, HCI International 2025, will be held jointly with the affiliated conferences at the Swedish Exhibition & Congress Centre and Gothia Towers Hotel, Gothenburg, Sweden, June 22–27, 2025. It will cover a broad spectrum of themes related to Human-Computer Interaction, including theoretical issues, methods, tools, processes, and case studies in HCI design, as well as novel interaction techniques, interfaces, and applications. The proceedings will be published by Springer. More information will become available on the conference website: https://2025.hci.international/.

General Chair
Prof. Constantine Stephanidis
University of Crete and ICS-FORTH
Heraklion, Crete, Greece
Email: general_chair@2025.hci.international

https://2025.hci.international/

Contents – Part I

Investigating Learning Experiences

Contents – Part II

Novel Learning Ecosystems

Contents – Part III

AI in Learning and Education

Designing Learning and Teaching Experiences

Digital Nudging in Online-Learning Environments: Enhancing Self-regulation and Decision Through Usability-Centric Design

Thorleif Harder$^{(\boxtimes)}$ ⓘ and Monique Janneck$^{(\boxtimes)}$ ⓘ

Institute for Interactive Systems, Technische Hochschule Lübeck, Lübeck, Germany
{thorleif.harder,monique.janneck}@th-luebeck.de

Abstract. Self-directed learning and the ability to self-regulate are crucial for success in online studies. This study focuses on the development and evaluation of digital nudges in learning management systems (LMS) to strengthen these key competencies in online students. Based on design recommendations, we designed specific interventions and analyzed their impact on students' decision-making quality. A usability study using the Thinking Aloud approach allowed the study of user reactions and interactions in different scenarios and a follow-up interview provided more in-depth insights into user perceptions. The results show that elements such as progress bars, notifications and call-to-action phrases significantly influence students' decisions. While progress bars had a motivating effect and notifications increased interaction, call-to-actions led to direct requests for action, but also created pressure in some cases. The study emphasizes that well-considered digital nudges can effectively improve the self-regulation skills of online students, with adjustments in certain areas further increasing their effectiveness and acceptance.

Keywords: Self-regulation · Digital Nudging · Online Learning · User Interface · Decision making and decision support · Usability study

1 Introduction

Self-directed learning and the ability to self-regulate are key success factors in online studies. Online students need a high level of organizational skills and self-discipline to meet the specific challenges of virtual learning [4]. Important aspects such as intrinsic motivation, self-directed goal setting and self-management are crucial factors for the successful completion of online courses or study modules [1]. However, the support of teaching staff is often required to maintain student motivation. In these cases, limitations such as a lack of self-control or limited ability to concentrate can affect the quality of students' decisions and in some cases even lead to students dropping out [5].

Supporting online students through specific interventions is an important aspect of improving their self-regulation skills and the quality of their decision-making in their studies. In this context, nudging interventions have shown promise in influencing behavior without limiting choice or economic incentives [29]. However, evidence for

P. Zaphiris and A. Ioannou (Eds.): HCII 2024, LNCS 14722, pp. 3–18, 2024.
https://doi.org/10.1007/978-3-031-61672-3_1

the concrete application of such digital nudges is limited despite some positive effects in education [7]. To close this gap, Harder [13] developed specific design recommendations for nudges that can serve as a conceptual basis for interventions to support self-regulation in learning management systems (LMS) such as Moodle. However, these recommendations are so far only of a theoretical basis and require further research to confirm their effectiveness in practical settings.

This article will therefore present the process of developing and evaluating such nudges. These nudges will be integrated into a learner dashboard (LD), which will be implemented as a plug-in in Moodle. This LD will be used in a university network with over 4,000 enrolled online students and aims to promote self-directed learning and student self-organization through visual representations of learning progress and insightful perspectives on further development [8]. The nudges are designed not only to strengthen self-regulation, but also to meet high usability standards and ensure intuitive integration into the everyday use of the LMS.

A mixed-method approach was used to evaluate the effectiveness of these nudges, combining quantitative data from a usability study with qualitative findings from post-interviews. The objective was to gain a deeper understanding of how usability nudges can effectively support the self-regulation and learning behavior of online students.

2 Theoretical Background

2.1 Nudging in Education

The concept of nudging, based on the principles of behavioral economics, is becoming increasingly relevant in education. Through subtle nudges that respect individuals' freedom of choice, an environment is created that helps learners to make better decisions [29]. The lecturers act as a "decision architect" who supports the learning process by structuring the learning environment and offering various learning options [19].

In this context, Harder [13] offers specific design recommendations that aim to support the self-regulation of online students through targeted nudging interventions. These recommendations address important aspects such as *designing information, supporting self-control, enhancing self-efficacy, enhancing social support,* and *dealing with cognitive and attention-related limitations.* These recommendations are based, among other aspects, on the use of availability heuristics, anchoring or other psychological principles to positively influence decision quality and learning behavior.

However, both lecturers and learners are susceptible to cognitive biases that can affect the learning process. These biases range from confirmation bias to over-generalization and can arise, for example, from a one-sided presentation of information or through preconceived opinions [14]. To make the learning process effective, it is therefore crucial to consider learning behavior and its various influencing factors.

In digital learning environments, nudging mechanisms offer additional opportunities to positively influence the learning process. For example, reminders and interactive elements can help to keep learners' attention and motivate them to continue learning [13]. Understanding psychological effects, such as self-efficacy expectation or reward bias, is crucial for the effective application of nudging techniques in education [7].

The integration of the suggested design recommendations into nudging interventions, considering ethical considerations, and respecting the autonomy of online students, is a central point of discussion in current research. These approaches are particularly relevant to address cognitive and attentional limitations, which is of particular importance in digital learning environments.

2.2 Influence of Usability and Design on Nudging

Nudging is becoming increasingly important in the education sector. A crucial factor for the success of these nudging interventions is the consideration of usability during the design process. Research shows that the way learning platforms are designed has an impact on the effectiveness of nudging interventions [34].

Research such as that by Ardito et al. [3] emphasizes the importance of user-centered design in e-learning applications. An intuitive and accessible design of the LMS makes it easier for students to navigate and interact, which can overcome potential barriers such as lack of self-control or limited ability to concentrate [13]. This is particularly relevant as interfaces that are poorly designed can hinder effective learning [3].

Furthermore, the design of nudging interventions must be tailored to the needs and preferences of the students. Caraban et al. [6] uses the "Nudge Deck" to show how thoughtful design leads to more effective and creative nudging interventions. This tool illustrates the importance of carefully designing nudges for maximum effectiveness.

Designing nudges in online learning environments that focus on usability and engaging design is an important step to support self-regulation and self-directed learning of online students. By considering these aspects, educational institutions and lecturers can create a learning environment that is not only usable but also positively influences learning behavior.

3 Objective

Considering the importance of self-directed learning in online environments, this paper focuses on the design and evaluation of nudges to enhance online students' self-regulation. Our primary concern is to get a clear understanding of how to best use digital nudges in LMS by answering the following research questions (RQ):

RQ1. How should digital nudges in LMSs be designed to enhance learning decisions of online students?

RQ2. How do online students perceive digital nudges in LMS?

The study addresses the question of which specific design elements best support the active participation and decision-making of online students. This includes examining different types of digital nudges, how they affect online students' self-regulation and how the students themselves view these nudges.

4 Method

The methodology of this study was carefully developed to comprehensively answer the research questions. It is based on a combination of the design-oriented development of digital nudges and a following evaluation consisting of usability tests and post-interviews.

Initially, the focus was on the development of nudges aimed at enhancing the self-regulation of online students. These nudges were therefore designed based on current design recommendations and theoretical concepts that specifically address the needs and requirements of the target group [13]. The nudges were then thoroughly tested in a usability study. This study followed the "Thinking Aloud" approach to gain an in-depth understanding of user behavior and user decisions. Finally, post-interviews were conducted with the participants to gather direct feedback and evaluate the effectiveness of the nudges from the user's perspective. In the following illustration, the left-hand side shows the methodology used to collect the requirements and develop the design recommendations. The right-hand side presents the development and evaluation of the nudges (Fig. 1).

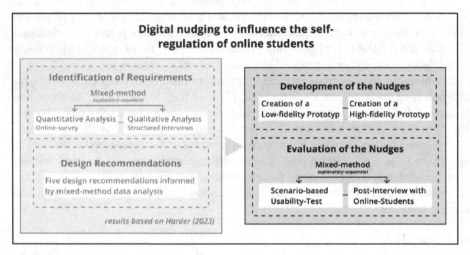

Fig. 1. Process diagram of the use of digital nudging to influence the self-regulation of online students.

4.1 Design-Oriented Development of the Nudges

The development phase started with a focus on user needs and requirements, combined with Harder's design recommendations [13]. Using the Schneider et al. framework [28], we analyzed which decision situations should be influenced, which decision types should be addressed, and which heuristics should be applied to enhance the desired user decisions. Based on this, a targeted conceptualization of nudges was developed to support defined objectives and decisions. These conceptual considerations were visualized and further developed in an iterative process, starting with sketches on paper.

In the design phase, the focus was on the development of wireframes. Accordingly, the wireframes focused on the structural layout of the elements, with functional and aesthetic aspects being dispensed with for the time being to emphasize the core functionalities [27]. The objective of the nudge design was to initiate positive behavioral changes through subtle cues and motivational messages based on established theories of behavioral economics and motivational psychology [30]. In addition, the integration of elements of cognitive psychology into the design was essential. This included the consideration of attention control and information processing of the user to ensure that the nudges effectively enhance the desired behaviors without overwhelming or distracting the user [32].

Once the wireframe had been defined, high-fidelity prototypes were created. In the visual design, especially the color scheme, care was taken to subtly attract the user's attention, which is in line with the principles of emotional design [24].

4.2 Usability Tests

The effectiveness of the designed nudges was analyzed using a scenario-based usability study based on the "Thinking Aloud" approach according to Nielsen [23]. This approach allowed an authentic view of the mental processes of the users to be captured and provided important insights into the perception and decision-making behavior of online students. Students' interactions with the nudges were observed to determine which incentives were most effective in enhancing their learning decisions. These findings are crucial to design digital nudges that support students' self-regulation in online studies. This addresses the central question of RQ1 and at the same time provides relevant information for RQ2. Participants were guided through three carefully designed scenarios that simulated real-life conditions to provide detailed insights into their behaviors and reactions:

- **Scenario 1** focused on the improvement of studies through goal orientation and reflection to analyze the setting and reflection of learning goals.
- **Scenario 2** focused on improving social contacts during studies by evaluating the possibility of group communication and social interaction.
- **Scenario 3** aimed to ensure the accessibility of teaching materials and communication with lecturers to examine interaction with teaching materials and communication options.

The number of participants was focused on the online students at the university network. Ten students from different study programs participated in the study. This included five students from the master's program in media informatics, three from the bachelor's program in media informatics, and two from the bachelor's program in business administration. Additionally, six of the students were female and four were male. The number of participants addresses the recommendations of Nielsen [23] and Faulkner [11], who emphasize that such a group size is suitable for identifying most usability problems.

The usability tests were conducted remotely and emphasized the integration of the participants in the Thinking Aloud process. In addition, attention was drawn to compliance with ethical guidelines, with particular emphasis placed on informed consent from participants before the study began. This included data privacy and confidentiality, which was reflected in the careful handling of the audiovisual data. The tests deliberately took 25 to 30 min to ensure a balance between depth of examination and comfort.

4.3 Post Interviews

After completing the usability tests, we conducted structured interviews with the participants. As part of this, the participants were presented with a detailed definition of the nudging concept, followed by an overview of all the scenarios involved and the associated nudges. This approach aimed to bring the individual elements back into focus and make it easier to answer the questions. The interviews concentrated on evaluating the immediate impact of the nudges, recording subjective perceptions, and identifying possible weaknesses or potential for improvement (RQ2). The following specific questions were addressed to the participants:

1. How did the nudges influence your decision?
2. How possible are you to carry out the recommended activity?
3. How did you perceive the nudges?
4. How could the nudges be improved to be even more effective?
5. What about the nudge made you uncomfortable or confused?
6. Did anything about the nudge make you want to ignore it?

The targeted questions encouraged participants to share their direct experience and impressions, allowing a thorough evaluation of the effectiveness of the nudges from the user's perspective.

5 Results

The results of this study are divided into three main chapters: First, the developed nudges are presented, and their psychological background is explained. The usability test findings are then examined, including the participants' reactions to the different nudges and their influence on the objectives of the usage scenarios. The following post-interview will consider the participants' feedback to understand the impact of the nudges on decision-making.

5.1 Presentation of the Developed Nudges

Five specific nudges were developed in total based on Harder's design recommendation [13]. The nudges developed can be divided into two categories according to their integration and activation mode. The first category comprises nudges that are integrated as permanent visual components of the LD. These are designed to ensure continuous and unobtrusive support of the learning process. The second category includes nudges that are activated in response to specific actions or behaviors of students within the LD. These are designed to ensure immediate feedback and motivate students to take specific actions that enhance learning.

In order not to put pressure on online students through the nudges, the nudges included an option to quit or close in the shape of a close icon. This supports the principle of libertarian paternalism [29] by allowing students freedom of choice and always offering them a way out. The careful choice of color scheme for the nudges was an important aspect of the nudge, as color plays a key role in the perception and impact of these elements. The specific choice of a subtle shade such as beige emphasizes the importance of a balanced visual presentation. The goal was to choose a color that would attract enough attention to subtly call students' attention to the nudges without being too dominant or distracting.

Nudge to Set Individual Learning Goals. Nudge to set individual learning goals. Setting personal learning goals is an essential component of effective learning and is also a crucial element in enhancing self-control [25]. This nudge takes up this recommendation and shows how online students can be supported in the process of goal setting. In contrast to the other nudges, this element will be a permanent part of the LD and will not be activated with the help of a trigger.

The illustration in Fig. 2 uses the anchor effect to recommend, for example, the catching up of learning materials. In addition, two heuristics - the bias of self-control and the status quo bias - are addressed by integrating a date picker. This function makes it possible to set deadlines and suggests through a default end date that a specific learning progress has already been achieved. The focus was on the color scheme of the date picker and the drop-down menu. The selected colors indicate that the system has made a pre-selection. This implicitly sets a deadline for the online students and thus supports self-control.

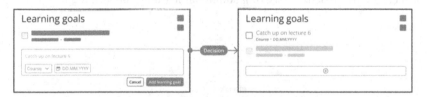

Fig. 2. Element for setting learning goals

Nudge to Enhance the Creation of Learning Groups. In line with the design recommendation to "design information", this nudge enhances the creation of learning groups (Fig. 3). Therefore, this nudge is activated as soon as the last student in the LMS completes the group search process, which is considered complete. By using the availability heuristic, this information is placed prominently in the dashboard after activation to catch the eye immediately. A heading lists all group members, with the names highlighted to draw the focus to the people (framing). Under the heading, the profile picture, name, and university show which people the student is in a group with. In the university network analyzed, there is the special feature that students can also be enrolled at different universities. The "Go to group chat" button at the end of the nudge is intended to encourage students to get in touch with them.

Nudge for Contacting Lecturers. The efficient use of contacting the lecturers is a crucial factor for learning success [12]. In line with the recommendations on "addressing cognitive and attentional limitations", this nudge aims to support online students in contacting lecturers and requesting information material (Fig. 4). By emphasizing the availability of consultation hours and the ability to ask for further materials, the proactive

Fig. 3. Information element to enhance creation a group.

use of teaching resources is enhanced. The notification is triggered when a lecturer announces new consultation hours and automatically during the semester to remind students of the contact options.

Since it cannot be guaranteed that all students have access to the relevant information, the notification is informational rather than a strict reminder. This considers the cognitive load of the students and avoids pressure, especially given the voluntary participation in consultation hours. The focus is on the options 'ask questions' and 'ask for further learning materials' to draw attention to these options. This emphasizes the framing effect and makes it clear to students that they can actively use these resources for their learning processes. Learners' autonomy is enhanced, and they can use their cognitive resources more effectively by proactively seeking additional learning support.

Fig. 4. Notification of individual consultation hours and learning materials

Nudge to Check the Lecturer Feedback. Based on the recommendation to " enhance self-efficacy", this nudge reminds the online students to check the feedback from the lecturers (Fig. 5). For this purpose, a notification system has been integrated into the LD based on the way the moodle system works.

The notification is triggered 24 h after the feedback is available, provided it has not yet been viewed by the students. To ensure a clear assignment, the header of the notification contains a picture of the course, the module name, and the time of the notification. In addition, a question is asked to motivate students to check the feedback. A 'Feedback' button takes students directly to the feedback. This notification function is accessible via a bell symbol in the header of the LD. This nudge not only supports students in checking the feedback in a timely manner, but also enhances their self-efficacy by encouraging them to learn from the feedback and improve their educational performance [2, 31].

Fig. 5. Notification of new feedback on the assignment

Nudge to Track the Learning Progress. A crucial factor in increasing the social support of online students is the enhancement of social interaction and connectedness among fellow students [13]. By combining progress indicators and social comparison information, this nudge motivates students to continuously follow their learning process and actively keep up with their fellow students (Fig. 6). A progress bar was adapted as a gamification element for this purpose. In this nudge, the learning progress is linked to a social aspect to support the online students. This behavioral incentive is not permanently present in the dashboard but appears based on specific criteria - a combination of the progress status in the semester week and the percentage of tasks completed. If a student is falling behind their fellow students, this incentive is activated. The nudge consists of several components:

- Progress bar: A progress bar is placed at the top of the nudge to increase student motivation. The visual illustration of their progress increases students' self-confidence as they recognize their own progress and feel closer to their learning goal [10].
- Incentive to Act: A percentage shows your own progress on the left. A heading opposite invites you to complete the current task. A section underneath emphasizes this request with the help of the social norm and framing. The social norm indicates the average progress of fellow students, which is intended to motivate students to become active and catch up. The framing reinforces the message by emphasizing the calculated progress once again.
- Call-to-Action-Button: A button at the bottom of the nudge encourages students to continue their tasks in the LMS.

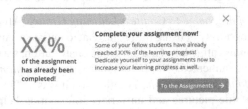

Fig. 6. Information element for requesting the completion of an assignment.

5.2 Results of the Usability Test

These results focus on the integration and user behavior in relation to the nudges developed within the LMS. To this end, an overview is given of the students' reactions to various nudges relating to the objectives of their studies, social interaction, the use of teaching materials and communication with lecturers.

Scenario 1 – Enhancing Studies Through Goal Orientation and Reflection. In scenario 1, students were confronted with three nudges: The setting of individual learning goals, the tracking of learning progress and the notification to check lecturer feedback. The findings are systematically structured according to the understandability, usability, and relevance of the notifications.

Setting Learning Goals. A significant number of the participants identified the plus icon as an effective tool for adding learning goals. Nevertheless, there was some confusion regarding the default placeholder text that was intended to act as an anchor. Some participants misunderstood this as a concrete learning goal instead of identifying it as a recommendation. The option to add deadlines was also used by five participants, but it was not clear that this was already a default field. Furthermore, most participants stated that adding a learning goal was an intuitive process and easy to do.

Understanding of the Tracking of Learning Progress. The progress bar and the element for tracking learning progress were perceived to be present and understandable by all participants. The comparison with the learning progress of other students triggered mixed reactions. While seven out of ten participants found this motivating, the remaining three found it rather stressful. One participant expressed his surprise at the comparison: *"Oh, other students are further ahead than me?"* and explained that a competitive impulse was triggered in a percentage of his fellow students.

Reactions of Feedback Notifications. All participants recognized the notification immediately. Four participants also expected the notification according to the task and the scenario and stated that they would also appreciate such feedback notifications in the future. One participant described her positive reaction to the scenario: *"Feedback on the task: Oh, I've been waiting for this."* Some participants noted that the icon for the notification is too small and suggested enlarging it to make it more visible. The use of a polite tone in the notification was also appreciated by some participants. Here, one participant mentioned that the notification sounds *"[...] friendly and not so matter of fact"*.

Scenario 2 – Enhancing Social Contacts at University. In scenario 2, the nudge for creating a learning group was tested on the students. The results are particularly structured around the recognition and use of the nudge to create a learning group.

Recognition and Use of the Nudge to Create a Learning Group. All participants immediately identified the possibility of using the group chat to initiate group work. The simple access, through the prominently placed „to the group chat" button, was positively emphasized. One participant commented: *"It gives incentive or motivation, because it's very easy to get straight into the conversation. "*Another felt it was an "invitation" to contact other students. The profile pictures and university information helped participants to better identify with their fellow students, which increased their willingness to exchange ideas. However, there was a desire to see the online status of other students. There were also uncertainties regarding the communication channel used. Questions such as *"Which chat is being used here? The one in Moodle?"* or *"Do you have to specify an application beforehand through which the communication takes place?"* indicated a lack of clarity and transparency of the nudge.

Scenario 3 – Ensuring the Accessibility of Teaching Materials and Communication with Lecturers. Scenario 3 focused on the nudge to contact lecturers. Based on the results, these were divided into three sections. Firstly, the perception and reaction to the specific notification of the request for contact was considered. Furthermore, the communication and appointment agreement as such was analyzed and then the interaction and feedback on notifications within the scenario was discussed.

Perception and Reaction to Notification of Communication with Lecturers. All participants were aware of the notifications about contacting the lecturer and rated them as useful for their studies. Four participants reacted instinctively to the system's notifications, to which one person commented: "I am generally someone who has to click on the notifications directly.". However, some participants were surprised and had questions about the information provided by the system, again highlighting the need for more transparency. The presentation of the notifications was rated positively overall, although the context was sometimes missed.

Communication with Lecturers and Making Appointments. Participants offered various ideas about the desire for a calendar for consultation appointments and a list of preferred appointments. However, participants expressed concerns that certain factors could affect the effectiveness of the nudge, e.g. differences between students and lecturers or doubts about their competence. Despite the different views, the majority showed a strong motivation to get in touch with lecturers, which was enhanced by both the scenario and personal study goals.

Interaction and Feedback on Notifications. The notifications of the system were generally perceived as helpful, but some participants expressed concerns about a possible overload of notifications. One of the participants argued that an overload of notifications could lead to students ignoring them, as their importance would be influenced.

5.3   Results of the Post-interviews

In the post interviews of the usability test, the results were analyzed in detail regarding the developed nudges. The results were summarized in three categories: Effectiveness and impact of the nudges, perception and acceptance, potential for improvement and challenges. In addition, the results were supported by selected quotes from the participants to provide a realistic insight into the impact and possible improvement of the nudges.

Effectiveness and Impact. The results on the impact of the nudges on the decision show clearly that the nudges had a significant influence on the participants' decisions. The progress bar (incl. Social norm), notifications, call-to-action formulations, and the option to open a group chat led to positive reactions. Most participants found the progress bar motivating, as *"they could visualize their progress and felt inspired to catch up with their fellow students"*. The notifications and the call-to-action button motivated participants to act and generated curiosity. The option to start a group chat was also seen as influential as it allowed students to connect directly with other Students. Some participants commented that they would *"do the recommended actions 100%"* as the nudges were displayed prominently.

Perception and Acceptance. The participants generally found the nudges pleasant and unobtrusive. The design also contributed to the nudges being perceived as highlighting important information and thus setting the right context. One participant noted that the nudges were perceived as a *"very nice hint"* and emphasized that there was no obligation to respond to a nudge. Three other participants shared this view and added that the presence of a close symbol reduces the pressure to respond to a nudge. However, there were also critical voices. One participant noted that the visible learning progress of fellow students could put pressure on other students.

Potential for Improvement and Challenges. The participants made various suggestions for improvement. Six participants wanted the learning progress bar and consultation hours to be highlighted more prominently in the notification system. In addition, two participants criticized the functionality of the learning goals. The green-colored dropdown menu, which is intended to convey a status quo bias, caused confusion among the participants. As a result, the desire for more clarity and comprehensibility was expressed. In addition, one participant expressed the wish to be able to look at past nudges again if necessary.

Regarding the ignoring of nudges, it was noted that too many notifications could lead to notices being ignored. One person said: *"The nudges shouldn't appear too often. Otherwise, I would be annoyed and ignore them."* However, specific triggers could also be a potential reason. One such reason could be that consultation hours are not used due to differences between students and teachers or due to doubts about the competence of the lecturer.

6 Discussion

This study analyzed the development and evaluation of nudges in an LD. The results show that these nudges have a significant influence on students' decision-making. These findings are based on dual process theory, which understands human behavior as an interconnection of conscious and unconscious processes [15]. The participants' quick perception and reaction to the nudges, highlighted by the thinking-aloud method, was striking [30].

The participants showed different reactions to the individual nudges. Some participants found the setting of individual learning goals intuitive and reacted positively to the possibility of setting personal deadlines. This finding reflects the effect of the self-control bias, influenced by the anchor effect and the status quo bias. However, it is important to remember that these behaviors may be influenced by subjective perceptions. Personal experience and attitudes towards learning could bias the evaluation of the nudges, which is a limitation in the interpretation of the results.

The progress bar and the comparison with the learning progress of other students led to mixed reactions. The prominent placement of the element in the LD increased user interaction, which can be attributed to the availability heuristic [21]. Furthermore, it was shown that tracking learning progress is helpful for self-regulation and can be further enhanced by peer and self-assessment. Ndoye [22] showed that this enhances students' engagement in their own learning process and encourages them to take responsibility for it. The visualization was also perceived positively by the students, however, some students expressed that the resulting pressure could have a negative impact on the well-being of some students. Based on the results, closing nudges showed a mitigating effect on this pressure by offering students more control and autonomy, which Keller [17] highlights as a key mental factor. These findings suggest the need to further investigate the influence of this nudge in future studies to fully understand its impact on students' wellbeing and learning experience and to adequately address it in future iterations of LD.

In the lecturer feedback, all participants focused their attention on the notification icon and interacted immediately after activating it. This behavior confirms that the notification function increases the salience of action options [33]. It also supports the findings of Marques et al. [20], which show that notification systems help students to work more efficiently and overcome challenges, which could help to reduce dropout rates.

In our study, the nudge contributed to the creation of learning groups to improve social contacts. The results show that the attention and interaction of users can be increased with the help of the highlighted elements. The group chat button enhanced rapid social interaction in new groups and has the potential to increase social contact - an aspect that is particularly relevant in online study programs because isolation and insufficient social integration can often contribute to dropouts [9].

The evaluation of contact with lecturers showed active participation by the participants. A study by Kraft & Rogers [18] showed that such nudges can lead to a significant increase in contact between teachers and students. However, participants expressed concerns that certain factors could impair the effectiveness of the nudge, e.g. differences between students and teachers or doubts about their competence.

Overall, the nudges were received positively and motivationally and design aspects such as the visual design and color scheme had a significant influence on online students' decisions. They helped to draw attention to relevant scenarios and improve the self-regulation of online students. The calming color scheme and shape of the visual cues helped to support relevant areas in the LMS for online students for the learning process (RQ1). Most of the nudges were considered useful, but there was also a need for improvement, such as the desire for a way to review nudges that had already been removed or completed. In terms of the perception of the recommended measures, nudges that focus on social interaction, personal feedback or the learning process were most likely to lead to a change in behavior (RQ2). However, factors that favor ignoring nudges were also identified, such as the quality of the relationship with lecturers or being overwhelmed by too many notifications. These findings emphasize the need to consider subjective perceptions and the long-term effects of nudges. Participants may have made their assessments based on personal preferences and experiences. In addition, it remains uncertain whether the positive effects of the nudges will persist over a longer period. Optimizations in these areas could therefore further increase the effectiveness and acceptance of the nudges and make their long-term effects on the self-regulation of online students more effective.

7 Conclusion and Future Work

Our study on the development and evaluation of nudges in LMS and further research on nudging systems offer a future-oriented outlook. Particularly revealing was the finding that different nudges evoke different reactions in students, which emphasizes the importance of personalized approaches. Based on these findings, the implementation of intelligent and adaptive technologies can be identified as the next stage in the development of nudging.

In this context, the concept of "smart nudging" becomes relevant [16]. It influences user behavior through customized digital nudges that are tailored to the specific needs of everyone [16]. These intelligent systems could be implemented in learning environments to optimize learning support.

Another important aspect is the objective measurement of the effectiveness of these nudges. The analysis of data from LMS provides a way to evaluate the impact of the nudges without directly influencing learning behavior. In their study, Rodriguez et al. [26] demonstrate the positive effects of personalized nudges on learner performance and satisfaction and on the reduction of dropout rates.

This combination of personalized nudges and data-driven evaluation promises to make digital learning more efficient and effective. Intelligent nudging systems that consider both the individual needs and behavior of learners and whose effectiveness is objectively evaluated could represent a major advance in personalized learning support and thus significantly improve the learning experience.

Acknowledgments. This work was funded by the German Federal Ministry of Education. (grant No. 01PX21001B).

References

1. Abuloha, S., Sharaydih, R., Wazaify, M.: Exploring the needs, barriers, and motivation of Jordanian pharmacists towards continuing education, p. 7 (2019)
2. Adams, A.M., Wilson, H., Money, J., Palmer-Conn, S., Fearn, J.: Student engagement with feedback and attainment: the role of academic self-efficacy. Assess. Eval. High. Educ. **45**(2), 317–329 (2020). https://doi.org/10.1080/02602938.2019.1640184
3. Ardito, C., et al.: Towards guidelines for usability of e-learning applications. In: Stary, C., Stephanidis, C. (eds.) UI4ALL 2004. LNCS, vol. 3196, pp. 185–202. Springer, Heidelberg (2004). https://doi.org/10.1007/978-3-540-30111-0_16
4. Barak, M., Hussein-Farraj, R., Dori, Y.J.: On-campus or online: examining self-regulation and cognitive transfer skills in different learning settings. Int. J. Educ. Technol. High. Educ. **13**(1), 35 (2016). https://doi.org/10.1186/s41239-016-0035-9
5. Bäulke, L., Eckerlein, N., Dresel, M.: Interrelations between motivational regulation, procrastination, and college dropout intentions. Unterrichtswissenschaft **46**(4), 461–479 (2018). https://doi.org/10.1007/s42010-018-0029-5

6. Caraban, A., Konstantinou, L., Karapanos, E.: The nudge deck: a design support tool for technology-mediated nudging. In: Proceedings of the 2020 ACM Designing Interactive Systems Conference, pp. 395–406. ACM, Eindhoven Netherlands (2020). https://doi.org/10.1145/3357236.3395485

7. Damgaard, M.T., Nielsen, H.S.: Nudging in education. Econ. Educ. Rev. **64**, 313–342 (2018). https://doi.org/10.1016/j.econedurev.2018.03.008

8. Drzyzga, G., Harder, T.: A three level design study approach to develop a student-centered learner dashboard. In: da Silva, H.P., Cipresso, P. (eds.) CHIRA 2023. LNCS, vol. 1996, pp. 262–281. Springer, Cham (2023). https://doi.org/10.1007/978-3-031-49425-3_16

9. Erichsen, E.A., Bolliger, D.U.: Towards understanding international graduate student isolation in traditional and online environments. Educ. Tech. Res. Dev. **59**(3), 309–326 (2011). https://doi.org/10.1007/s11423-010-9161-6

10. Falakmasir, M.H., Hsiao, I.H., Mazzola, L., Grant, N., Brusilovsky, P.: The impact of social performance visualization on students. In: 2012 IEEE 12th International Conference on Advanced Learning Technologies, Rome, Italy, pp. 565–569. IEEE (2012). https://doi.org/10.1109/ICALT.2012.218

11. Faulkner, L.: Beyond the five-user assumption: benefits of increased sample sizes in usability testing. Behav. Res. Methods Instrum. Comput. **35**(3), 379–383 (2003). https://doi.org/10.3758/BF03195514

12. Harbour, K.E., Evanovich, L.L., Sweigart, C.A., Hughes, L.E.: A brief review of effective teaching practices that maximize student engagement. Preventing School Failure Alternat. Educ. Child. Youth **59**(1), 5–13 (2015). https://doi.org/10.1080/1045988X.2014.919136

13. Harder, T.: Selbstreflexion bei Online-Studierenden fördern: Implikationen einer quantitativen und qualitativen Befragungsstudie zur effektiven Gestaltung von Nudges. In: Gemeinschaften in Neuen Medien. Inklusiv Digital: Gemeinschaft offen gestalten (2023, in Press)

14. Jonas, E., Schulz-Hardt, S., Frey, D., Thelen, N.: Confirmation bias in sequential information search after preliminary decisions: an expansion of dissonance theoretical research on selective exposure to information. J. Pers. Soc. Psychol. **80**(4), 557–571 (2001). https://doi.org/10.1037/0022-3514.80.4.557

15. Kahneman, D.: Thinking, Fast and Slow, 1st edn. Farrar, Straus and Giroux, New York (2011)

16. Karlsen, R., Andersen, A.: Recommendations with a Nudge. Technologies **7**(2), 45 (2019). https://doi.org/10.3390/technologies7020045

17. Keller, H.: Autonomie und Verbundenheit sind menschliche Grundbedürfnisse, pp. 15–21 (2011). https://doi.org/10.1007/978-3-642-15303-7_4

18. Kraft, M.A., Rogers, T.: The underutilized potential of teacher-to-parent communication: evidence from a field experiment. Econ. Educ. Rev. **47**, 49–63 (2015). https://doi.org/10.1016/j.econedurev.2015.04.001

19. Liening, A.: Ökonomische Bildung: Grundlagen und neue synergetische Ansätze. Springer Fachmedien Wiesbaden, Wiesbaden (2019). https://doi.org/10.1007/978-3-658-24731-7

20. Marques, J.M., Calvet, L., Arguedas, M., Daradoumis, T., Mor, E.: Using a notification, recommendation and monitoring system to improve interaction in an automated assessment tool: an analysis of students' perceptions. Int. J. Hum.-Comput. Interact. **38**(4), 351–370 (2022). https://doi.org/10.1080/10447318.2021.1938400

21. Mirsch, T., Lehrer, C., Jung, R.: Digital Nudging: Altering User Behavior in Digital Environments (2017)

22. Ndoye, A.: Peer/self-assessment and student learning. Int. J. Teach. Learn. Higher Educ. **29**, 255–269 (2017). https://api.semanticscholar.org/CorpusID:148689179

23. Nielsen, J.: Usability Engineering. Morgan Kaufmann Publishers Inc., San Francisco (1994)

24. Norman, D.A.: Emotional Design: Why We Love (or Hate) Everyday Things. Basic Books (2004)

25. Pompian, M. (ed.): Self-Control Bias. John Wiley & Sons, Inc., Hoboken (2015). https://doi.org/10.1002/9781119202400.ch19
26. Rodriguez, M.E., Guerrero-Roldán, A.E., Baneres, D., Karadeniz, A.: An intelligent nudging system to guide online learners. Int. Rev. Res. Open Distrib. Learn. **23**(1), 41–62 (2022). https://doi.org/10.19173/irrodl.v22i4.5407
27. Rudd, J.R., Stern, K.R., Isensee, S.: Low vs. high-fidelity prototyping debate. Interactions **3**, 76–85 (1996). https://api.semanticscholar.org/CorpusID:207195099
28. Schneider, C., Weinmann, M., vom Brocke, J.: Digital nudging: guiding online user choices through interface design. Commun. ACM **61**(7), 67–73 (2018). https://doi.org/10.1145/3213765
29. Thaler, R.H., Sunstein, C.R.: Nudge: Improving Decisions About Health, Wealth, and Happiness. Yale University Press (2008)
30. Tversky, A., Kahneman, D.: Judgment under Uncertainty: heuristics and Biases: Biases in judgments reveal some heuristics of thinking under uncertainty. Science **185**(4157), 1124–1131 (1974). https://doi.org/10.1126/science.185.4157.1124
31. Van De Ridder, J.M.M., Peters, C.M.M., Stokking, K.M., De Ru, J.A., Ten Cate, O.T.J.: Framing of feedback impacts student's satisfaction, self-efficacy, and performance. Adv. Health Sci. Educ. **20**(3), 803–816 (2015). https://doi.org/10.1007/s10459-014-9567-8
32. Van De Sand, F., Frison, A.K., Zotz, P., Riener, A., Holl, K.: The role of information processing for product perception. In: User Experience Is Brand Experience, pp. 17–35. Springer, Cham (2019). https://doi.org/10.1007/978-3-030-29868-5_2
33. Von Grafenstein, M., Hölzel, J., Irgmaier, F., Pohle, J.: Nudging - Regulierung durch Big Data und Verhaltenswissenschaften (2018). https://www.abida.de/de/blog-item/gutachten-nudging
34. Weijers, R.J., De Koning, B.B., Paas, F.: Nudging in education: from theory towards guidelines for successful implementation. Eur. J. Psychol. Educ. **36**(3), 883–902 (2021). https://doi.org/10.1007/s10212-020-00495-0

Pedagogical Foundations of a Short Term Intensive Online Course for Businessmen on Development of Negotiating Skills in English

Marina S. Kogan(✉) ⑩, Maria A. Ievleva, and Anna V. Gavrilova ⑩

Peter the Great St Petersburg Polytechnic University, Polytechnicheskaya Str. 29, 195251 St. Petersburg, Russia
kogan_ms@spbstu.ru

Abstract. English language has conquered the world as the instrument to communicate ideas across different cultures and contexts, every day it is used by innumerable people to do business. To succeed in business communication and negotiations businessmen have to possess negotiating skills or be able to acquire or develop them very quickly. The lack of ready-made resources for the purpose requires tailoring an intensive online course to meet the needs of adult learners. The paper explains how to integrate well-known principles of intensive language learning and effective English teaching approaches (lexical, concept-based, and communicative) into a short term 20h length online course helping businessmen to develop their negotiating skills, justifies the choice of digital tools and online platforms for the course design, and describes the results of implementation of the course in teaching several groups of business people. The subjects of the first experimental group participated in pre- and end- course surveys and the final oral test and showed quite high total score in the final oral test (4.45 vs 3.65 of the control group); speech fluency growth by 7.6%; and remarkable growth in confidence in business negotiations in English according to the learners' self-esteem. The learners in all groups achieved the set goals and were satisfied with the course. The designed intensive course seems to be quite effective in terms of development of students' fluency, confidence, and understanding the nature of a dialog communication. Further research steps are outlined.

Keywords: Intensive Online Course · Negotiating Skills · Business English · Digital Tools and Platforms

1 Introduction

The ever increasing unparallel pace of modern life requires that professionals master new soft skills, e.g., negotiating in a foreign language very quickly. Though the methods of intensive teaching foreign languages were developed in the XX century [see e.g., 1, 2], their application in modern conditions requires considering several issues. They are as follows:

P. Zaphiris and A. Ioannou (Eds.): HCII 2024, LNCS 14722, pp. 19–37, 2024.
https://doi.org/10.1007/978-3-031-61672-3_2

- The organization of the course in the online format that appeared at the beginning of the XXI c. and became a leading format of teaching professionals during in-service training after Coronavirus pandemic [3].
- Developed in the XX c, such approaches to foreign language teaching as communicative [4], lexical [5], concept-based (based on the teaching of the outstanding Soviet psychologist P.Ya. Gal'perin on orientation and formation of thought activities [6, 7]) have not been fully integrated into coursebooks focusing on teaching specific aspects of business communication, e.g., negotiating [8].
- The selection of vocabulary items and grammar structures for an intensive course is a dynamic process. It should take into account the results of research of professional discourse [9–11], which differs from an academic discourse in the same specialist domain in a number of parameters as Conrand highlighted [12].

Any negotiating process is a dialogue or polylogue. Therefore, it is obvious that first of all it is necessary to teach students dialogical speech. Using ready-made teaching materials is not always acceptable. According to Nicholas, most teaching materials tend to be oversimplified as a result not all the skills necessary for conducting a dialogue can be practiced [8]. In addition, any educational complex is designed for a course length of 60 to 120 h, e.g. *In Company* Intermediate course book[1], which is not relevant for the task of preparing a group for business negotiations for a limited time from two weeks to a couple of months. This is exactly the problem that the second author of our research team faced.

Creating a short-term course on developing business negotiating skills involves the use of intensified learning techniques exploiting psychological reserves of learners' personalities, which are better manifested if learning takes place in a joyful and non-stressful environment on both conscious and subconscious levels [1, 13]. This is the main difference between intensive methods and traditional ones. Other fundamental principles of intensive methods formulated by famous founders of the accelerated approaches in language teaching and learning are:

- the principle of communicative and speech activity;
- the principle of a step-by-step-concentric organization of an educational subject;
- personal-role principle.

In the Soviet Union and post-Soviet Russia, leading specialists in intensive methods of teaching foreign languages were academicians Galina A. Kitaygorodskaya, teacher of foreign languages, and Alexey A. Leontyev, a psychologist, both are followers of Lozanov's ideas.

G.A. Kitaigorodskaya developed a method for activating the reserve capabilities of the individual and the team. She considered it fundamentally important during classes to seat students in a semicircle to create natural communication conditions, facilitate visual contacts and use suggestion techniques in teaching. All classes are united by one plot. At the first lesson, all students receive foreign names, which become their names for the entire course. This helps remove barriers of various kinds: psychological, psychotherapeutic, methodological, linguistic. Role-playing and playful activities make classes lively, interesting, and involving. The first two days of the intensive course

---

[1] Powel, M.: In company 3.0. Intermediate student's book pack. Macmillan London (2019).

are extremely important, when a large amount of thematic vocabulary (150–200 new words) and 30–50 speech cliches and several typical speech phenomena are introduced and practiced in a polylogue format. In the process of intensive training, a flexible skill of transferring learned vocabulary into varying communication situations is formed [2].

A.A. Leontiev noted that intensive methods of teaching foreign languages allow 1) combining optimal techniques and personality development in the learning process harmoniously; 2) creating momentary (here and now) motivation for learning and communication close to the real thing; 3) overcoming psychological barriers; 4) mastering the maximum amount of educational material in the minimum time; 5) actively using the learned material in oral communication, demonstrating high and immediate learning effectiveness [14, 15].

Among modern popular intensive methods of teaching English researchers point out linguistic coaching and the lexical approach. Linguistic coaching is a method that is based on presenting material in a form most easily processed by the students. This helps not only to learn new material more efficiently and quickly, but also to overcome psychological barriers. Paling defines linguistic coaching as a system for transferring language skills from coach to student quickly and effectively through methods built on the principles of coaching and knowledge of brain activity [16].

In order to intensify the development of skills within short-term courses, it is advisable to use various tools: a communicative way of presenting materials and organizing work within the course; creating a comfortable and friendly atmosphere; goal setting and making notes to support motivation, analyze progress and mistakes; studying language material within lexical blocks. Learning goals should be as detailed as possible, achievable, assessable, related to the course calendar and relevant to the course objectives, prioritizing practical skills that students must master by the end of the course [17]. Grammatical material should correlate with specific speech tasks; the course should be organized in learning blocks. The objectives of such courses also include the formation of individual linguistic and extralinguistic skills. In order to optimize their formation, it is advisable to use techniques formed within the framework of the lexical approach suggested by Lewis [5]. Developing the approach the following stages in improving lexical competence necessary for the formation of fluent speech are highlighted in multiple studies [e.g., 18–21]:

- presenting meaning of a lexical unit and formation of semantic knowledge;
- giving examples of using the lexical unit in context in audio or printed text;
- developing the skill of pronunciation and intonation of a lexical unit depending on the context and illocutionary purpose of the utterance;
- analysis of lexical and grammatical patterns of using a lexical unit,
- using a lexical unit in its own context.

One must also bear in mind the important part that conceptual metaphors play in business discourse. Research shows that modern business communication media are full of metaphors used to present abstract economic notions through specific images [22].

Besides lexical and grammatical awareness, pronunciation, intonation and listening skills, fluent speech is characterized by the following indicators: decreasing the number of questions and clarifications associated with insufficient understanding of the partner's statement; increasing the number of stimulus questions that allow the speaker to control the progress of the dialogue; decreasing repetitions; increasing the duration of the utterance with a proportional increase in the speed of speech [23].

When developing negotiating skills, it is necessary to provide exercises allowing learners to develop pragmatic, discursive, sociocultural, social and strategic competencies [17]. Burns and Goh argue that speech and communication competencies are formed during the implementation of a special system of exercises aimed at developing basic speech skills; the ability to implement a speech task in various ways, i.e. strategic competence; the ability to use grammar and lexis to perform a speaking task more accurately; skills in using different registers of speech; skills in using various discourse strategies; skills to recognize genre differences; independent study skills [24]. A famous Russian scholar in methodology of foreign language teaching, the pioneer of the communicative approach in Russia, prof. E.I. Passov proposed two series of exercises: *conditional speech* and *speech* exercises. Conditional speech exercises are specially organized for the formation of a communicative skill through imitation, transformation, substitution, and reproduction exercises. They have the same repeatability, lexical units, discontinuity in time. Speech exercises aim to prepare a learner to production of prepared or spontaneous speech through retelling a text, a description of a picture or a series of pictures, objects, commenting, debating, and role playing. The ratio of both types of exercises is selected individually [25].

Depending on the form, purpose, format of interaction and degree of formality business communication is distinguished as business conversation, interview, dispute, business meeting, presentation, bargaining, business correspondence, press conference, business negotiations. Negotiations are an integral part of our life. We negotiate every day, discussing everyday issues; business people negotiate prices, delivery dates or execution of contracts, guarantees, etc. [17]. During the negotiations, the short stage of establishing and maintaining contact is crucial. Therefore, from the first minutes of the meeting, it is important to impress your partner and show him your interest through active listening techniques, namely: echo-questions, paraphrasing, clarifying questions [26, 27]. All these techniques are ultimately used to realize win-win negation scenario of achieving mutual benefits, i.e. a situation in which the win of one participant does not necessarily mean the loss of the other [28].

Obviously, to help students to acquire and consolidate what they learnt during online classes of the short-term course, relevant interactive tasks have to be developed with help of available digital tools.

Requirements to pedagogical design of the online course for teaching adult learners are considered by Cercone in the context of different andragogical theories. The author distinguishes 13 characteristics of adult learners accompanying each of them with a list of detailed recommendations (varying from 4 to 20 per each) on how to implement them in the online course. The characteristics/needs include physical limitations that some adults might have; the individualization of learning experiences as learning styles might differ; active involvement in the learning process; providing scaffolding, support, and facilitation by the instructor; need to link new knowledge to past experience; immediate application of their new knowledge to their lives; providing problem-centered and learner-centered learning and teaching; clear idea of how the learning will be conducted;

need to test their learning as they go along, rather than receive background theory; collaborative, respectful, mutual, and informal climate for learning and social interaction; need to self-reflect on the learning process, support for transformational learning [29, p.: 140, 142, 154–159]. Meeting these requirements will contribute to achieving the set goals of the intensive online course on development of negotiating skills in adult professionals.

2 Creating a Short-Term Intensive Course for Businessmen on Development of Negotiating Skills in English

2.1 Pedagogical Goals and Means for Their Implementation

The course was designed in order to facilitate students' preparation to conduct negotiations in English in a short period of time. Within the frame of the course the main goal was to increase students' active pool of functional vocabulary which is necessary for business communication. It was supposed that an active pool of functional vocabulary may improve students' fluency and at the same time increase their cultural awareness which in turn can significantly boost the ability to negotiate in English. The course included 10 classes, 2 academic hours each.

For **independent work** between classes students had access to the *Quizlet* platform and to the *Online Test Pad* platform. Tasks for revising the vocabulary items introduced during the class were created on the *Quizlet* platform. The *Online Test Pad* platform contained training tasks for consolidating grammar structures and functional language aspects introduced during class sessions as well as relevant videos highlighting specific aspects of business negotiations in English.

Synchronous classes of the course were organized on the *Zoom* platform for it has a wide variety of tools to organize modes of the group work. Each lesson was designed according to the basic principles of the communicative approach and included the following stages:

Warm-up activities stage took up to 15% of all the classroom time aiming at improving memorization of the target vocabulary and its retrieval, enriching students' awareness of communication patterns within the context of business negotiating, and developing their ability to paraphrase.

Lead-in stage included interactive exercises on the lesson's vocabulary and grammar items created at the Learning App platform organized in the all-group work format.

Controlled and semi-controlled practice was implemented through pairs of exercises. One of which was aimed to increase awareness of how learned vocabulary items can be combined in chunks of functional phrases while the other was aimed to develop understanding of how these chunks can be used in a conversation taking into account the appropriateness of the chunk for a particular situation and response it can result in.

Free practice took up to 40% of all classroom time and was organized as a business simulation as it was seen as the most important task of the course to give students an opportunity to practice all learned material in communication situations as close to real as it was possible. All activities described above were designed with online instruments to be used in an online class.

2.2 Choosing Online Instruments for Creating the Online Course

While designing this course a number of different online instruments were used to facilitate both students' independent work and work in the online classroom.

For independent work platforms such as the following were chosen:

Quizlet, created in 2005 by an American sophomore to memorize French words, has become the undoubted leader in its class of digital tools with 30 million monthly users from 130 countries[2]. It is no coincidence that this resource was chosen by the creators of the New General Service List (NGSL), the New Academic Word List (NAWL), TOEIC Service List (TSL) и Business Service List (BSL) to help English language learners master the most frequent vocabulary in each category [30]. It allows students to revise vocabulary using a number of exercises involving those which develop writing, reading and pronunciation skills.

Online Test Pad[3], which is a free universal constructor that allows one to create 18 types of test questions, logic games and crosswords. Being a development of Russian specialists, the platform is popular among developers of digital educational content in Russia [31]. This platform allows instructors to organize all course material provided for independent students' work in blocks, enrich course material with videos, texts and audios to offer students additional input and consequently maximize exposure to language items learned within the course; another benefit of this platforms is a wide range of exercise types for vocabulary and grammar revision.

Google slides tool[4] was used as the main online instrument for organizing classroom work. It was selected for the following reasons:

- It is easy to use for both a teacher and students;
- It does not require registration for students.
- It can be used as an online board which is not inferior to such popular online boards as *Miro, Stormboard*, and *Limnu.*
- It allows arranging material on a screen in a friendly way.
- It can be used quite sustainably even in case of poor Internet connection.
- It can be used simultaneously by several people, which allows a teacher to organize pair work of students where necessary to provide each student with different information, e.g. for business simulations or exercises developing paraphrasing and mediating skills.

LearningApps[5] - another popular website specialised in online learning offering a great variety of task templates including millionaire game, select quiz, word grill, cloze test, fill table, mindmap, pinboard, write together, etc. It was used during online class sessions in a synchronous mode.

2.3 The Course Syllabus

The course material was devised with use of course pack *English for Negotiating* [32]. As it was important to deliver the course in an intensive form material was arranged in 6

---

[2] https://quizlet.com/latest

[3] https://onlinetestpad.com/ru/

[4] https://docs.google.com/presentation/u/0/?ec=asw-slides-hero-goto.

[5] http://learningapps.org

modules where each module contained 20–30 functional phrases, and a grammar topic which can be implemented in negotiations. The syllabus of the course is presented in Table 1.

Table 1. The course syllabus

Topics (hours allocated)	Subtopics	Lexical and grammatical material	Functional language
Preparation for negotiations (4)	Setting and prioritizing goals Skills of a successful negotiator Agenda Gathering information about the negotiating partner company	The structure of the interrogative sentence	–Indirect question –Formal and informal interrogative structures –Explanatory constructions –Expressions to explain their tasks and intentions
Business meeting in an intercultural context (2)	Invitation to a business meeting; Latest clarifications to the agenda; Greetings in an intercultural context	Prepositions of time	–Greetings –Small talk –Expressions for explanation of one's tasks and intentions
Making a proposal during negotiations / response / counter-proposal (2)	Making a proposal for negotiations; Response to the proposals Putting forward a counter-proposal	Modal verbs Zero and the first type conditionals	–Expressions for making assumptions and suggestions –Expressions for expressing an opinion about what is not possible; Expressions for discussing conditions and possible outcomes
Types of negotiations (4)	Different negotiation styles; Leadership strategies; Active listening techniques	Special questions	–Expressions for responding to suggestions; –Expressions to express your opinion; –Expressions for suggesting alternative solutions to the problem

(continued)

Table 1. (*continued*)

Topics (hours allocated)	Subtopics	Lexical and grammatical material	Functional language
Resolving/Dealing with a conflict situation (4)	Negotiation tactics; Win-win strategy; Dealing with objections and conflicts	Modal verbs of politeness Hedging	–Expression of disagreement of varying degrees of politeness; –Expressions for gaining time; –Expressions for inviting the interlocutor to make suggestions; –Expressions of partial consent; –Evasive expressions
Finalising negotiations (4)	Discussion of guarantees Development of a plan for further actions	Grammar for discussing current actions and immediate plans	–Expressions of gratitude; –Expressions for summarizing

3   Research Questions

1. Does the course increase students' active pool of functional vocabulary?
2. Does the students' increased pool of functional vocabulary help them in improving speech fluency?
3. Does the course increase students' confidence in ability to conduct business negotiations?
4. Do students consider their independent work with the course materials efficient?

4   Procedure

4.1   The Organization of the Intensive Course Implementation

The implementation of the course was organized in three runs. Each run was organized around specific needs of the course participants who had a common need to improve their business negotiating skills very quickly.

4.2   The Selection of Participants for the First Course Run Through the Pre-Course Survey

As the course was designed for adults with pre-intermediate level of English language proficiency, candidates were tested for their language proficiency before they could subscribe for the course. The questionnaire used to survey applicants included five questions:

- How long have you studied English?
- What apps and platforms have you already used for studying the English language?
- Which language skills are most difficult for you?
- What is more difficult to memorize: words, phrasal verbs, chunks?
- Grade from 1 to 10 how comfortable for you to communicate in English on business topics.

The survey involved 15 candidates aged from 21 to 52 years. Most of the respondents answered that they had learnt English since childhood. All of them except one used different apps, namely *Quizlet, Duolingo*, and *Lingualeo* in their studies. Among other resources *YouTube* videos and classes from a famous Russian online school *Skyeng* were mentioned. More than a half of respondents find listening the most difficult skill; 88,8% of respondents stated that phrasal verbs and chunks were more difficult to remember. Their confidence of talking in English on business topics 33% of respondents graded 6, 22% graded 5, and 44% graded below 5.

In order to evaluate students' speaking skills before the course, an oral interview was organized. It included 10 questions that allowed the instructor not only to determine oral language proficiency level, but also to understand experience in negotiating in both languages English and Russian. The majority of the interviewed applicants claimed that they had an experience in negotiating in English; however, they evaluated it as more negative than positive and attributed their failure mostly to insufficiency of vocabulary knowledge and lack of confidence in the choice and usage of English vocabulary items and grammar structures.

As the result of the entrance survey, 8 candidates out of 15 applicants were shortlisted for taking part in the course.

4.3 The Characteristics of the Participants of the First Course Run

The subjects were 8 students aged from 21 to 52, with the pre-intermediate level of language proficiency according CEFR selected according to the results of the entrance survey. Most students had previous experience in using online instruments for foreign language learning. Though the students were from different backgrounds, most of them worked in different departments in IT companies where English was used in everyday communication. Nevertheless, they stated both in the questionnaire and interview that they felt insecure when speaking English at work. All of them decided to take up the course on their own initiative.

There also was the control group in the first course run. It consisted of 8 adult students working for the same IT company with the headquarters residing in the Arab Emirates enrolled to the course by their employer. Both groups were taught by the same teacher.

4.4 Data Collection in the First Run of the Course

In order to analyze the outcomes of the course implementation as well as results of the experimental group the following data was collected:

- Entrance testing and oral interview to assess the applicants' language proficiency level, learn about their previous experience in foreign language studying and analyze their needs.

- Quizlet and Online Test Pad's analytics was checked to control students' involvement in independent work during the course.
- End-course oral assessment in a format of business negotiation simulations was conducted according to the criteria of the Cambridge BEC preliminary exam. The oral assessment was conducted by an English language teacher not affiliated with this course to ensure impartiality. To evaluate the progress in speech pace the oral part of the entrance and final tests was audio-recorded for both groups.
- The end-course questionnaire comprised 4 questions offering to evaluate: efficacy of the course in terms of developing negotiating skills in English; progress in language proficiency achieved within the course; the increase in the participants' confidence when talking in English on business topics; and their overall opinion about the course (assuming an answer in a free form). This questionnaire was filled in by the members of the experimental group.

4.5 Teaching in the First Run of the Course Implementation

The **control group** studied Business English using the *In Company 3.0* Intermediate coursebook[6]. This coursebook designed for 120 academic hours was taught for 40 h without using additional electronic resources. The thematic content focused on developing skills necessary for negotiations, namely units 7 and 8 focused on grammar and vocabulary for agreeing / disagreeing and influencing an opponent; units 12, 15, and 16 focused on delivering a presentation as well as on suggesting solutions to different problems using modal verbs etc.; unit 19 as it is devoted to a negotiating process. The course material was delivered within the frame of communicative approach with a fair share of free practice alongside with controlled practice. Synchronous classes were conducted online via Zoom platform. In addition to the coursebook Google slides were used as an online board. Exercises from the coursebook were assigned for students' independent work. In contrast to the experimental course syllabus, the course syllabus for the control group involved the formation and development of grammatical and receptive skills, as well as business writing skills.

The **experimental group** was trained according to the program presented in Table 1 (Subsect. 2.3) based on the principles described in Subsect. 2.1.

4.6 The Second and Third Runs of the Course Implementation

The second run of the course implementation was aimed at preparing students for negotiating with a potential investor. It constituted a series of three consequent course launches. Two of them were organized as the first run of the course implementation described above: length of the course was 20 h (10 classes) each. The number of participants – 8 people aged from 25 to 35 in the first launch, and 8 people aged from 21 to 52 in the second launch. The level of English proficiency in all groups was pre-intermediate.

The third launch was different in the number of participants – only 2 students aged about 40 and the course length reduced to 6 h (3 online classes). In addition to

---

[6] Powell, M.. Clarke, S., Allison J., Pegg, Ed, de Chazal, Ed. In company 3.0. Intermediate student's book pack. Macmillan, London (2014).

course materials students of each course launch actively used Quizlet modules during independent work.

The third run of the intensive course was organized for training 9 IT professionals from different departments of an IT company aged from 35 to 45 during 20 h (10 online classes). The course was adapted to meet the requirements of the client company to prepare its employees for conducting technical job interviews with potential candidates as interviewers.

The data came from the observation of the learning process during the course and the feedback about the course collected by the client company.

5 Results and Discussion

5.1 The Use of Online Instruments by Students from the Experimental Group During Independent Work

As mentioned above in order to enhance acquisition of the course material students were assigned to revise target vocabulary of the course using *Quizlet*. The majority of students used it regularly during the course. The most popular modes appeared to be: Flashcards, Learn, Test, and Match. On the other hand, students were unwilling to use such learning modes as spelling and writing, presumably as they required more time and effort. According to the platform's statistics the level of vocabulary acquisition in each unit varies from 66% to 79%. The statistics from *Online Test Pad* platform used to consolidate students' knowledge of grammar and functional language during the independent work shows that the students were not eager to fulfil the assigned exercises in due time except for watching videos; though scoring up to 100% correct answers when they completed the tasks.

We will risk suggesting the following explanation of the phenomenon in the perspective of P.Ya. Gal'perin theory of *orientation in thought* [6, 7]. Watching videos with articulate aspects of business negotiations might be a sort of orientation stage framing learners' behavior during negotiations in different situations while vocabulary and grammar exercises on the same platform could be perceived as tools for performance stage less important at the time of watching a video and more associated with class work. Probably, tasks accompanying the videos should consolidate the *orientation* (through the analysis of factors helping the negotiators to achieve their goals, noticing their postures, body language, facial expression, eye contact, intonation, language used etc.) rather than *performance* (through grammar and vocabulary revision exercises) as the orientation stage of action forms a psychological mechanism of the action [7].

All in all, the statistics provided by the chosen platforms shows that students eagerly use online instruments provided for independent learning; however, they tend to choose the tasks that are less time and effort consuming.

Students from the control group who were assigned exercises from the coursebook for independent word, didn't show willingness to contribute their free time for it. They also were less motivated to perform free practice activities suggested by the coursebook during online classes because they were not specially tailored to address students' specific needs.

5.2 Assessment of Oral Speech Improvement

In order to ensure objectives of the assessment, the final oral test of both groups was conducted by an English teacher non-affiliated to the course designing process. The oral test was designed to be a business simulation game, during which the assessor awarded grades according to the following criteria:

- Grammar and Vocabulary;
- Discourse Management;
- Pronunciation;
- Interactive Communication

based on performance descriptors from the analytical assessment scales for the BEC preliminary exam[7].

In addition to this, oral speech of the experimental and control groups was recorded to check the change of speech fluency throughout the first run of the course. The results are presented in Tables 2 and 3.

Table 2. Average results of the final oral test in the experimental and control groups

Participants	Grammar and Vocabulary	Discourse Management	Pronuncia-tion	Interactive Communication	Global achievement	Total score
Experimental group	4,0	4,5	4,63	4,75	4,38	4,45
Control group	3,25	3,13	4,38	4,0	3,5	3,65

Table 3. Average results in fluency progress in the experimental group

	1-st class Words per minute	10-th class Words per minute	Fluency progress %
Experimental group	34.25	36.63	7,86
Control group	34.42	34. 85	Almost no progress

In all aspects of the BEC preliminary exam criteria the experimental group showed better results than the control group (Table 2), which proves the efficacy of the developed electronic resources boosting speaking and negotiating skills as supplement to the main coursebook while teaching negotiating skills in the intensive course.

Considering the progress in speech fluency, it can be claimed that students in the experimental group managed to increase fluency by 7,86% (on average) owing to active

---

[7] https://www.cambridgeenglish.org/images/business-english-certificates-handbook-for-tea chers.pdf (p. 44).

use of functional vocabulary learned within the course while the control group did not demonstrate a measurable progress (Table 3). Also, increased awareness of business negotiation structure and strategies allowed students to use more appropriate language means to succeed in the simulation negotiation game. In contrast, at the beginning of the course the students often had to resort to their native language due the shortage of business vocabulary. The examples of using Russian expressions include *pogasit' odnim platezhom* (pay in one lump sum); *oplatit' chastjami* (pay in installments); *tsenju* (appreciate); *smeny* (shifts); *procentnaja* stavka (interest rate); *nepolnaja rabochaja stavka* (part time job). At the end of the course no one had an urge to use their native language to achieve the communication goal.

The choice of a business simulation game as the final oral test format was determined by the following considerations: students should become familiar with the exam format during the learning process and the exam format should correspond as much as possible to the use of the foreign language in practice beyond the classroom. The advantages and drawbacks associated with the use of role-playing games as a testing tool for different categories of students are discussed in a number of papers [33–35].

Much attention in the intensive course program was paid to business games as a language teaching and learning tool. Business games were organized as part of pair work for 7–10 min in zoom breakout rooms using google slides documents with individual tasks for learners and the teacher's monitoring. After returning to the main zoom room, the teacher provided feedback on mistakes and usage of target vocabulary for about 4 min. In organizing role-playing, possible causes that prevent students from speaking were taken into account. The most typical causes highlighted by researchers [34, 36] are the following: inadequate vocabulary, inadequate control of grammar, lack of fluency, mispronunciation, uninteresting role play, and lack of peer´s support.

In our opinion, role plays contributed a lot in students' fluency improvement because they were designed in accordance with Nation and Newton's requirements for fluency development. These include meaningful activities; students centered classes helping students develop fluency from previous knowledge; and encouraging students to be creative and move beyond what is being taught in class [36]. Demanding that students should use patterned phrases in role plays we followed Selivan who believes reproducing short phrases involving more words is easier and less time consuming than constructing them from individual words, which results in increasing the speed of utterance [37].

Figure 1 shows examples of cards for a role-playing situation that testees had to present in the format of a business game "Role play a meeting with your colleague to discuss… (possibilities of renting a new office)." Vocabulary items the use of which the examiner paid special attention are in bold as they were in the study cards; however, they were not highlighted in the exam tasks.

All in all, our research confirmed that a role play regarded as a versatile tool for language teaching [35] can be successfully used in an intensive online course for practicing and using the language for meaningful communication. It is also a valuable and adaptable assessment tool that allows teachers to effectively organize an oral examination at the end of the intensive course providing important diagnostic information about learners' development.

ST A
You are going to rent a new office and right now you are preparing for the meeting with a potential landlord.
Talk to your colleague to exchange useful information.
You have already 5 quotations all offer you an office in the city center.
Before sharing your info ask to specify
1.   the price range within which the offer is acceptable
2.   How big should be the office
3.   Prefered location
4.   any special requirements that you need to take into account.
But actually, you like only two of them. One is 1500 $ per m2 but they can give you a discount about 20 % if you pay for a year, but the location is perfect for your business and it is not very big just 120 m2. The landlord is a nice person who is easy to have a rapport with him.
The second is a bit further from city center you need to go about 15 min from a metro station there is no good parking zone, but price is perfect 1000 $ and you can persuade the landlord to concede up to 10%, you should pay monthly

ST B
You are going to rent a new office and right now you are preparing for the meeting with a potential landlord.
talk to your colleague to exchange useful information.
You are ready to pay not more than 1000 $ per square meter. You need the office about 150- 200 m2
You suppose that the office should be not far from the city center.
You need a landlord you can get on with
You think that there should be a canteen or a cafe near the office

1.   How many quotations do you have at the moment?
2.   Which landlords offer the best price and payment terms?
3.   How much each landlord is ready to concede?
4.   which option is the best one from your colleagues prospective

Fig. 1. Role play exam cards for students A and B. "Role play a meeting with your colleague to discuss possibilities of renting a new office"

5.3   End-Course Questionnaire

All the experiment participants took part in the final survey. 75% of students evaluated the effectiveness of the course as 9 out of 10 and 25% as 10 out of 10; 75% ranked the level of comfort higher than 7 out of 10; 87,5% ranked their progress higher than 6 out of 10. In the open question the majority of students mentioned that they feel much more confident when communicating in English on business topics not only because their language proficiency had increased slightly, but also because they had an opportunity to use all the knowledge they were getting in simulations of business negotiation which, in turn, gave them feeling of successful experience. A few students mentioned the role of their independent work on the *Quizlet* platform and videos on the *Online Test Pad* platform for achievements of the course goals.

The growth in confidence in business negotiations in English among the students from the experimental group based on their answers to the pre-course and post-course questionnaires is visualized in the bar chart (Fig. 2).

For any task, including a negotiation, an actor has some level of confidence in his/her ability to perform that task that experts in the field of social sciences refer to as self-efficacy [39]. Long-term research indicates that better results are observed in people with higher levels of self-efficacy. Someone who is confident in their abilities to perform a specific task, is focused on ways to achieve success, and overcomes difficulties confidently. In contrast, people with low levels of task-specific self-efficacy anticipate

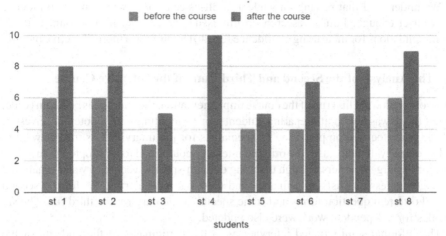

Fig. 2. Level of confidence diagram when communicating in English on business topics based on pre- and post-course surveys

failure, focus their thoughts on potential problems, react to difficulties, and reduce their performance.

According to Bandura self-efficacy affects the choices people make about how to spend their time: people tend to avoid tasks for which they have a low level of self-efficacy, preferring those for which they have higher levels [39]. Social cognitive theory allows concluding that self-efficacy predicts negotiators' choice of tactics. Sullivan and his co-authors claim that negotiators' confidence with respect to specific negotiation strategies influences their use of particular tactics [38]. Negotiation is a complex cognitive task made more difficult by being interdependent, resulting in, sometimes, the indirect effect of self-efficacy on performance [38].

Unfortunately, special studies on the role of confidence in negotiations do not discuss the aspect of proficiency in a foreign language (English) separately, if it is not native to the negotiators. Our respondents indicated an increase in this particular aspect, which correlates well with the results of the final oral test. This is also consistent with Bandura's conclusion that self-efficacy is best measured with respect to the specific task at hand (in our case – the final test) [39].

Self-efficacy is a dynamic construct that can change in response to task successes and failures. Therefore, our subjects have to continually develop their language skills, which they acquired in the intensive course, so that their confidence in their negotiation abilities does not let them down in the future. The researchers of negotiator confidence stress that the success of negotiations depends a lot on how to initiate the process [38, p.579]. In this respect, confident (ideally automatic) mastery of the relevant English clichés could be crucial for the subsequent course of negotiations. Our study also shows that increased self-confidence could be an important/sensitive indicator of learners' satisfaction with an intensive online course.

We understand that relying on students' self-esteem in growth in their confidence is not strict enough. Future research on this issue should take into account existing recommendations for measuring confidence [38, 40] to provide a more objective picture.

5.4 The Analysis of the Second and Third Runs of the Intensive Course

After completion the first run of the course implementation, the course has been run twice. One of those was aimed at preparing students for negotiating with a potential investor, and the other focused on preparing IT specialists for job interviews as interviewers to the IT company. In both cases the original intensive course had to be adopted to meet the needs of the target learners through updating domain-specific vocabulary and functional language expressions lists with finance and banking vocabulary items for the second run and different question forms and some special vocabulary for the third run. *Quizlet* modules for independent work were also updated.

The informal semi-structed interview with the participants of the 2nd run of the course expressed their satisfaction with the course. Even more important is the fact that soon after all three students of the mini-group received promotion in their company due to successfully conducted negotiation with the company partners and signed job contracts with the company on more beneficial conditions.

At the end of the third run of the course, the client company surveyed its employees that had taken the course. The feedback was positive, with the respondents scoring the usefulness of the course with 9 out 10 and readiness to recommend it to their colleagues with 8 out of 10 (on average).

6   Conclusions and Further Work

According to data collected from the *Quizlet* and *Online Test Pad* platforms students are quite willing to use online instruments that offer a variety of exercises as well as their mobile versions (apps), which makes the learning process not just much easier, but also more flexible in terms of time and place for learning. On the contrary, the exercises for independent work devised on *Online Test Pad* platform were not as popular as the *Quizlet's*. Thus, it could be concluded that *Quizlet* and the like platforms focusing on vocabulary memorization are more important among adult learners of the intensive course than those with a wider range of types of exercises covering different grammar and language aspects.

The designed intensive course seems to be quite effective in terms of development of students' fluency, confidence, understanding the nature of a dialog communication, cultural awareness thus contributing to conducting successful negotiations with foreign partners.

The course requires adaptation depending on the learners' needs. Its online format makes the instructor's work easier and less time and labour consuming allowing them to keep all materials in the same place.

Going far beyond the scope of the paper for detailed analysis, our observations allow us to conclude that most recommendations about the organization of online teaching adult learners described by Cercone [26] were implemented in our short term intensive online course.

The study convincingly showed that an effective online short term intensive course might not be based on a single textbook. However, further research is required to decide how to organize different developed electronic resources in a more efficient way: if it is worth developing a single course on LMS such as *Moodle, Stepik* or *Schoology* or it is better to exploit educational resources using templates on different platforms such as *LearningApps* and *Quizlet,* which gives more flexibility in integrating the resources into teaching and learning process, e.g. separating classroom activities and independent work for students and in updating the resources.

The question about the impact of relevance of a set of exercises to the orientation and performance stages of the action in Gal'perin's sense on the willingness of learners to complete the exercises also needs further research.

Disclosure of Interests.   The authors have no competing interests to declare that are relevant to the content of this article.

References

1. Lozanov, G.: Suggestology and Suggestopedia: Theory and practice. Ministerstvo na narodnata prosveta, Bulgaria (1984)
2. Kitaigorodskaya, G.A.: Metodika intensivnogo obuchenija [Methodology of intensive teaching]. Vysshaja shkola, Moscow (1986). (in Russian)
3. Haleem, A., Javaid, M., Qadri, M.A., Suman, R.: Understanding the role of digital technologies in education: a review. Sustainable Operations and Computers 3, 275–285 (2022). https://doi.org/10.1016/j.susoc.2022.05.004
4. Canale, M., Swain, M.: Theoretical bases of communicative approaches to second language teaching and testing. Appl. Linguis. 1, 1–47 (1980)
5. Lewis, M.: Lexical Approach: The State of ELT and the Way Forward. Thomson Heinle: Language Teaching Publications, Boston (2008)
6. Gal'perin, P. Y.: The role of orientation in thought. Soviet Psychol. 18(2), 19–45 (1979) https://doi.org/10.2753/rpo1061-0405180284
7. Stepanova, M.A.: Galherin's Theory of orientation and methods of psychological research. Vestnik Moskovskogo Universiteta. Seriya 14. Psikhologiya [Moscow University Psychology Bulletin] 1, 289–311 (2021). https://doi.org/10.11621/vsp.2021.01.12
8. Nicholas, A.: A concept-based approach to teaching speech acts in the EFL classroom. ELT J. 69(4), 383–394 (2015). https://doi.org/10.1093/elt/ccv034
9. Chan, C.S.: Long-term workplace communication needs of business professionals: Stories from Hong Kong senior executives and their implications for ESP and higher education. Engl. Specif. Purp. 56, 68–83 (2019). https://doi.org/10.1016/j.esp.2019.07.003
10. Chan, C.S.: Helping university students discover their workplace communication needs: an eclectic and interdisciplinary approach to facilitating on-the- job learning of workplace communication. Engl. Specif. Purp. 64, 55–71 (2021). https://doi.org/10.1016/j.esp.2021.07.002
11. Jaworska S.: Corporate discourse In: De Fina, A., Georgakopoulou, A. (eds.) The Cambridge Handbook of Discourse Studies, pp. 666 – 687. Cambridge University Press, Cambridge (2022) https://doi.org/10.1017/9781108348195.031

12. Conrad, S.: A comparison of practitioner and student writing in civil engineering. J. Eng. Educ. **106**(2), 191–217 (2017). https://doi.org/10.1002/jee.20161

13. Lozanov, G.: Suggestopedia pri obuchenii inostrannym jazykam [Suggestopedia in teaching foreign languages]. Metody intensivnogo obuchenija inostrannym jazykam [Methodology of intensive foreign language teaching] **1**, 9–17 (1973). (in Russian)

14. Leontyev, A.A.: Myslitel'nye processy v usvoenii inostrannogo jazyka [Thought processes in foreign language acquisition]. Inostrannye jazyki v shkole [Foreign languages at school]. **5**, 72–76 (1975). (in Russian)

15. Leontyev, A.A.: Psychology and the language learning process/A.A.Leontyev/Language teaching methodology series. – Oxford etc.: Pergamon Press (1981). – XIII+ 159 p

16. Paling, R.: Neurolanguage Coaching: Brain Friendly Language Learning. The Choir Press, New York (2017)

17. Frendo, E.: How to Teach Business English. Pearson Education Limited, London (2005)

18. Dellar, H., Walkley, A.: Teaching lexically. Delta publishing, London (2016)

19. Webb, S., Nation, P.: How Vocabulary is Learned. Oxford University Press, Oxford (2017)

20. Shamov, AN.: Tehnologii obuchenija leksicheskoj storone inojazychnoj rechi [Technology of teaching lexis of foreign language]. FLINTA, Moscow (2021). (in Russian)

21. Passov, E.I., Solovtsova, J.I.: Vyzov slova: mehanizmy i sledstvija [Challenge of word: mechanisms and consequences] In: Problemy Kommunikativnogo metoda obuchenija inojazychnoj rechevoj dejatel'nosti [Problems of Communicative method of teaching foreign language production/activities]. Proceedings. pp. 58–66. Voronezh (1981). (in Russian)

22. Melnichuk, M.V., Osipova, V.M.: Metaphor in English business discourse. Nauchnyj Dialog **11**(47), 31–41 (2015). (In Russian)

23. Thorbury, S., Slade, D.: Conversation: From Description to Pedagogy. Cambridge University Press, Cambridge (2006)

24. Goh, C.C.M., Burns, A.: Teaching Speaking: A Holistic Approach. Cambridge University Press, New York (2012)

25. Passov, E.I.: Osnovy kommunikativnoj metodiki obuchenija inojazychnomu obshheniju [Basis of the communicative approach to teaching communication in foreign language]. Russkij jazyk, Moscow (1989). (in Russian)

26. Hoppe, M.H.: Lending an ear: why leaders must learn to listen actively. Leadersh. Action. **27**, 11–14 (2007). https://doi.org/10.1002/lia.1215

27. Royce, T.: The negotiator and the bomber: analyzing the critical role of active listening in crisis negotiations. Negot. J. **21**, 5–27 (2005). https://doi.org/10.1111/j.1571-9979.2005.000 45.x

28. Fisher, R., Ury, W.L.: Getting to Yes: Negotiating Agreement Without Giving in, 2nd edn. Penguin Books, New York (1991)

29. Cercone, K.: Characteristics of adult learners with implications for online learning design. AACE J. **16**(2), 137–159 (2008)

30. Browne, C.: A new general service list: the better mousetrap we've been looking for? Vocabulary Learn. Instruct. **3**(2), 1 (2014). https://doi.org/10.7820/vli.v03.2.browne

31. Evdokimova, V.E., Kirillova, O.A., Zhdanova, E.A.: Online Test Pad as one of the modern means of evaluating learning results. J. Shadrinsk State Pedagogical University **3**(55), 32–41 (2022). (in Russian). https://doi.org/10.52772/25420291_2022_3_32

32. Lafond, C., Vine, S., Welch, B.: English for Negotiating. Oxford University Press, Oxford (2014)

33. Littlejohn, A.: The use of games-simulations as a language testing device. In: Crookall, D., Oxford, R.L. (eds.) Simulation, Gaming and Language Learning, pp. 125–134. Newbury House, New York (1990)

34. Rojas, M.A.: Role-play as an assessment tool in English as a foreign language (EFL) Class. In: Soto, S.T., Intriago, P., Villafuerte, J.S. (eds.) Beyond Paper-and-Pencil Tests: Good Assessment Practices for EFL Classes, pp. 49–73. Editorial Universidad Técnica de Machala, Machala – Ecuador (2019). https://doi.org/10.48190/9789942241115.2

35. Courtney, L.: Role Plays: A Versatile tool for assessing young learners. In: Santovac, D.P. Rixon, S. (eds.) Integrating Assessment into Early Language Learning and Teaching. pp. 155–169 MULTILINGUAL MATTERS, Bristol (2019). https://doi.org/10.21832/978178892482 5-013

36. Nation, I.S.P., Newton, J.: Teaching ESL/EFL Listening and Speaking. Routledge, Taylor & Francis, New York (2009)

37. Selivan, L.: Lexical Grammar Activities for Teaching Chunks and Exploring Patterns. Cambridge University Press, Cambridge (2018)

38. Sullivan, B.A., O'Connor, K.M., Burris, E.R.: Negotiator confidence: the impact of self-efficacy on tactics and outcomes. J. Exp. Soc. Psychol. **42**, 567–581 (2006). https://doi.org/ 10.1016/j.jesp.2005.09.006

39. Bandura, A.: Self-efficacy: The Exercise of Control. W.H. Freeman, New York (1997)

40. Stajkovic, A.D., Luthans, F.: Self-efficacy and work-related performance: a meta-analysis. Psychol. Bull. **124**(2), 240–261 (1998). https://doi.org/10.1037/0033-2909.124.2.240

Interface Design for Educational Chatbot to Increase Engagement for Online Learning: A Conceptual Design

Chi Lok Lei[✉] and Camille Dickson-Deane

University of Technology Sydney, P.O. Box 123, Broadway 2007, Australia
jasperlei5@gmail.com

Abstract. As students in online learning spaces find it difficult to stay engaged with content, the integration of chatbots can be seen as a promising solution (Tsivitanidou & Ioannou, 2021). Engagement in an online learning environment typically occurs through an interface that outlines the functionality. As a learner interacts with a chatbot, its functionality can lead to them having an experience that assists with learning or one that is hindered by the design of the interface. This study uses design-based research as a way to partner with authors of extant literature to model what an ideal chatbot's interface should look like. The findings outline nine key features that can increase engagement for students. When modelled, the features create a design that, by description, can be deemed complex but based on the learning need.

Keywords: Chatbot · engagement · user interface design · design-based research · research partnership

1 Introduction

The Covid-19 Pandemic has required the online learning space to have more ways to engage students, thus wanting to increase the interactivity in the online environment to mirror that of the face-to-face environment (Moore & Hodges, 2020). Students in online learning spaces find it difficult to stay engaged with content, and the learning experience can be unenjoyable and inefficient. In recent years, the integration of chatbots in learning environments has emerged as a promising solution (Tsivitanidou & Ioannou, 2021). Chatbots in online learning have the potential to provide personalised, interactive, and engaging learning to students. However, engagement and the potential enhanced learning outcomes are strongly influenced by the design of these educational chatbots (Hobert et al., 2023). This paper will discuss the significance of user interface design in educational web-based chatbots and outline strategies for designing elements to optimise chatbots potentially towards increasing engagement in online learning environments (OLEs).

1.1 Chatbots as a Way to Increase Engagement

The term chatbots can be defined as a computer program that uses dialogue to provide a service (Hwang & Chang, 2023). As Hwang and Chang (2023) mentions, chatbots can be used for a variety of purposes such as chatting, entertainment, data query, agent execution tasks, answering questions, and dialogue exercises - all of these promoting engagement. While engagement can be defined as "the basic processing operations that describe how students react and interact with the learning materials and environments", cognitive engagement is described as thoughtfulness and willingness to exert effort in learning or problem-solving (Hwang & Chang, 2023). It is found that interactive designs of chatbots may influence engagement, and thus, a chatbot, though its design can require more time for users to complete the overall tasks where they may report a higher knowledge gain (Hobert et al., 2023). This study uses the need to increase engagement in an online learning environment to investigate the medium through which a student can improve such by interacting with a chatbot - through its interface. To do this, we as investigative designers ask "What design elements are key for interface design for educational chatbots?".

1.2 Interface Design as a Problem Space

The value of a chatbot in an educational environment is the convenience and the relevant feedback it gives to the student at a specific time. In traditional online learning platforms, students go through asynchronous learning, where students interact with content and instructors deliver content at different times. In these types of environments, when there is no synchronous activity, students receive minimal to no immediate feedback from resources and may require additional yet timely assistance. Tsivitanidou et al. (2021) note that chatbots can encourage cognitive engagement proactively, during or retrospective to the learning process. In asynchronous environments, a chatbot can be activated based on a student-led action, but from a design perspective how the chatbot functions and thus interacts with the student in the using and learning process is also important (Dickson-Deane & Chen, 2018). As very few acknowledge that how the chatbot is designed is key to that integration towards measuring impact, access and usability, this study seeks to use extant literature to create design models that will discuss how well common features are used to create a functioning chatbot. Through the use of these models we believe we can use a design-based research methodology which can be used to investigate chatbot interface designs. Thus, planning how it is used and designed is key.

2 Literature Review

The field of conversational chatbots has been a rapidly growing field in all industries and revolutionised how we interact with technology. With the increased popularity of online learning, the educational industry is looking for innovative and effective strategies to aid with the learning process. As this review explores the range of designs of chatbots, it becomes apparent that designs that are more interactive chatbot designs could lead to better results and increase user engagement (Hobert et al., 2023).

Currently, most chatbots use predetermined conversational paths, and only a quarter utilise a personalised learning approach (Kuhail et al., 2023). Kuhail et al. (2023) also mentions there are two main uses of a chatbot, which are frequently asked questions(FAQ) and conducting short quizzes. It was also found that a chatbot system in education can also personalise online learning and make learning materials more accessible from anywhere at any time (Kuhail et al., 2023; Okonkwo & Ade-Ibijola, 2021). The presented benefits of implementing a chatbot system in education include content integration, quick access, motivation and engagement, allowing multiple users and immediate assistance (Kuhail et al., 2023; Okonkwo & Ade-Ibijola, 2021). As online learning can sometimes lack key features of face-to-face learning such as personalised feedback (Fidan & Gencel, 2022), chatbots can be used to personalise OLEs by catering to student's learning needs. Chatbots can also be used for experimental and collaboration learning design principles where they have the ability to provide a cost-effective method to increase student engagement (Kuhail et al., 2023). This means considering chatbots as a way to adopt engaging methods can be an important way forward for the field.

Current literature focuses on user experience, AI models and benefits and challenges in chatbots. For learning environments, the focus is quite similar - learner experience design. Within this research space, not much research has been conducted on the functionality of the chatbots to interact with the user/learner - chatbot interface design (Dickson-Deane & Chen, 2018; Hobert et al., 2023). Interface design, a more tangible and static outcome in user experience, is more important than just investigating the perception of utility, ease of use and efficiency, a more intangible and dynamic outcome. By using a design-based investigative approach to convey function, using extant literature as the foundation for designs, this approach can document what the current literature believes a functioning chatbot should look like and thus allow all to ensure that there is sufficient critique towards how integration in OLE's can occur.

3 Methods

This research adopts a comprehensive and systematic approach to survey the current literature on educational chatbots, focusing specifically on the interface design elements. We first conducted a literature collection utilising academic databases and Google Scholar to gather relevant papers related to educational chatbots. There is a variety of terminology used for chatbots and its user interfaces, and our search included the following keywords: "educational chatbots", "user experience", "cognitive engagement", "conversational agent", "online learning" and "user interface" to reflect such. Because there is limited literature describing the interface designs of conversational agents, we wanted to make sure we are able to cover all areas where interface designs of chatbots are possible, so all types of learning are included (ie., industry, higher education, etc.). Secondly, we want to focus on how these design elements can increase the user's engagement, specifically in an online learning space. We then analysed each of the research articles to identify where the design elements and features of a chatbot were discussed. By using these descriptions, we interpreted the descriptions and iteratively put all the features together to create a conceptual yet functional model of each article's view for the interface of an educational chatbot.

Each article's conceptual-functional model, illustrated in a design mockup, was then compared and contrasted to create a complete conceptual-functional model of an ideal chatbot's interface. This method, a design-based investigative approach to interface design, uses and interprets each original author's words in the form of a partnership to create the final mock-ups (Amiel & Reeves, 2008). The design-researchers then translated these interpretations iteratively and collaboratively into one final design - the design of each article includes the previous articles' designs. We see this approach as grounded in systematic inquiry by achieving iterative designs to develop a collaborative understanding of how current literature views this educational practice and technology. We, the design-researchers are in partnership whereby we are in dual mode wearing two hats, the researchers and the designers, with the outcomes of the investigation of the research - the designs- being used as the data for this study (LeMahieu et al., 2017).

4 Conceptual Findings

Answers to the research question allowed for different effects of interface design in chatbot. There were 212 original articles found when the search criteria were entered into databases. Of those articles only five (5) had descriptions of interface designs of chatbots, each of these articles and their descriptions are explained below. The five articles are in order of publication dates:

1. Bers, J., Miller, S., & Makhoul, J. (1998). Designing conversational interfaces with multimodal interaction. DARPA Workshop on Broadcast News Understanding Systems,
2. Plantak Vukovac, D., Horvat, A., & Čižmešija, A. (2021). Usability and user experience of a chat application with integrated educational chatbot functionalities. International Conference on Human-Computer Interaction,
3. Senevirathne, G., & Manathunga, K. (2021, September). Impact of E-Learning system user interface design on user satisfaction. In *2021 IEEE 9th Region 10 Humanitarian Technology Conference (R10-HTC)* (pp. 01–06). IEEE.
4. Iniesto, F., Coughlan, T., Lister, K., Devine, P., Freear, N., Greenwood, R., Holmes, W., Kenny, I., McLeod, K., & Tudor, R. (2023). Creating 'a Simple Conversation': Designing a Conversational User Interface to Improve the Experience of Accessing Support for Study. ACM transactions on accessible computing, 16(1), 1–29. https://doi.org/https://doi.org/10.1145/3568166
5. Jamil, M. B. A., & Shahzadi, D. (2023). A systematic review A Conversational interface agent for the export business acceleration. Lahore Garrison University Research Journal of Computer Science and Information Technology, 7(2), 37–49.

The findings were organised based on the simplicity of design description towards the complexity of the design description. This means that the findings are presented in the following order.

1. Jamil and Shahzadi (2023)
2. Bers et al. (1998)
3. Plantak Vukovac et al. (2021)
4. Senevirathne and Manathunga (2021)

5. Iniesto et al. (2023)

Design 1 - Jamil and Shahzadi (2023). In their paper, Jamil and Shahzadi (2023) discuss a conversational interface agent for business acceleration. The paper focuses on the broader application and potential of conversational agents across different industries, emphasising the importance of user-centred design and continuous improvement based on user feedback and technological advancements. The authors did not consider a specific context outside of the discipline space and coupled interface design features with user experience requirements. these features and requirements are (Jamil & Shahzadi, 2023):

1. Input Handling: How the chatbot processes and interprets user inputs.
2. Dialogue Management: Chatbot's ability to lead and continue a meaningful discussion in a context-appropriate manner.
3. Language Understanding: The capability of the chatbot to understand natural language inputs from users.
4. Response Generation: The process by which the chatbot generates responses to user inputs.
5. Security: Measures to ensure the chatbot's interactions and data handling are secure.
6. Personality and Tone: The chatbot's style of interaction, including its personality traits and the tone of its responses.

In reviewing these features and requirements, features 1 to 4 can be translated to design features, and features 5 and 6 are more user experience and are more relegated to the backend of the chatbot. By looking directly at each feature and translating it into an interface design, the first point is Input handling, which the designers-researchers assume is an input dialogue box used for anyone to enter information. Then the second and third points are Dialogue management and Language understanding, which, when translated, can reference the instructions for how the chatbot should be used. Finally, response generation speaks directly to the output from the chatbot. These features can thus be interpreted in Fig. 1.

Figure 1 shows a potential design that implements the requirements mentioned by Jamil and Shahzadi (2023). The design was able to handle input, lead and manage the dialogue and generate a response and sets a good baseline for the next few designs and feature implementations.

Design 2 – Bers et al. (1998). Bers et al. (1998) introduced VoiceLog, a system combining voice and pen input for web-based applications designed for mobile and pen-based computers. It discussed VoiceLog's innovative client-server architecture for its speech recognition and also its multimodal interface. The system emphasises a user-friendly multimodal interface that combines visual and audio feedback for efficient operation. The paper focuses on enhancing the user's interaction in various device environments and potential future improvements. The requirements and features are summarised as (Bers et al., 1998):

1. Simplicity and Efficiency: The interface uses Java applets, which were widely used in web browsers in the early 2000s, in an effort to achieve efficiency and simplicity.
2. Multimodal Input: The system incorporates a dual-input technique to increase the interface's adaptability and accessibility. Users can use voice instructions or a pen to communicate with the system, which supports both pen and speech input.

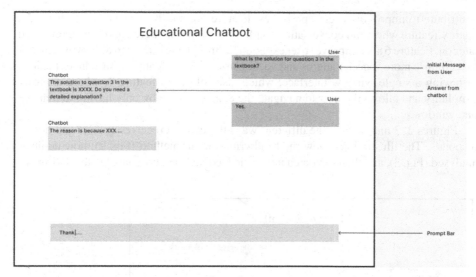

Fig. 1. Interpreted chatbot interface design as described by Jamil & Shahzadi, 2023)

3. Feedback Mechanisms: There are two types of feedback presented in response to user input: basic visual feedback for straightforward interactions and more complex, integrated feedback for multimodal inputs. This feedback mechanism makes sure that user inputs are responded to promptly and appropriately

4. Dialogue Management: System controls dialogue in a variety of conditions, including Idle, Object_input, Action_input, and Both_input, with time-outs to maintain flow. This structure allows dynamic interaction and accommodates user preferences and the delay characteristics of different input modalities.

5. Modular Multimodal Architecture: The backend architecture's modular design makes it easier to improve and reuse its constituent parts. Because of its architecture, the system is versatile and can be used for a variety of purposes.

6. Centralised Speech Recognition Server: A centralised voice recognition server optimises performance and resource utilisation by allowing the use of huge vocabulary on lightweight client devices.

7. Single-Window Interface: Users do not need to exert much cognitive effort when navigating and using the system because of the single-window interface design.

8. Web-Based Architecture: The system's backend web-based architecture, which centrally maintains all application code and data on the web server, provides broad accessibility and makes maintenance and updates easier.

Feature 1 can be seen as UI/UX design, simplicity of the interface design, and how well the system performs and is integrated into the website. Feature 2 is a feature providing multiple types of media inputs into the chatbot. In the example, it was by voice and handwritten words that the chatbot recognised other than text. Feature 3 relates to the output, where Bers et al. (1998) introduce two types of feedback depending on the input. A simple visual output for the straightforward inputs and more complex, integrated feedback for multimodal inputs. Features 4, 5, 6 and 8 are all related to the backend and contribute to improving user experiences. Feature 5 could be translated into having a history feature where old conversations with the chatbots are saved and can be reviewed later on. Feature 6 also improves user experience through the input and allows the chatbot to recognise more speech patterns and vocabularies. Lastly, feature 7 introduces the idea of having a single window interface, which also relates to feature 1, where it shows simplicity and allows the user to navigate the chatbot easily by only having to manage one window.

Figures 2, 3 and 4 show the different ways the chatbot receives queries and how it responds. The illustrations show the handwritten input method (Fig. 2), how audio is analysed (Fig. 3), and then separated into basic feedback and complex feedback (Fig. 4).

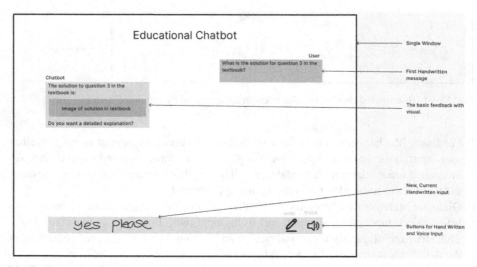

Fig. 2. 2: Interpreted chatbot interface design receiving written input as described by previous designs, including Bers et al. (1998)

Design 3 - Plantak Vukovac et al. (2021). Plantak Vukovac et al. (2021) evaluates the usability and user experience of an educational chatbot called 'Differ'. Differ provides information on courses and communication features with other students and teachers, acting as a chat platform. Differ's purpose is to help students make friends and create the feeling of a university environment, and increase their engagement with their studies. Plantak Vukovac et al. (2021) introduce a few key user experiences that allow the success of Differ. Firstly, Differ categorises the user's needs into three categories: learning and teaching, research and social bonding. This can be translated into a design where the chatbot can include multiple views for the three very different needs. It is also suggested by Plantak Vukovac et al. (2021) that a successful chatbot should be able to handle complex conversations, offer personalised feedback, understand different user needs and have a friendly personality. These are all user experience features that could all potentially increase the user's engagement. Complex conversation as interpreted by the authors could mean handling different media types such as audios and writings. Personalised feedback

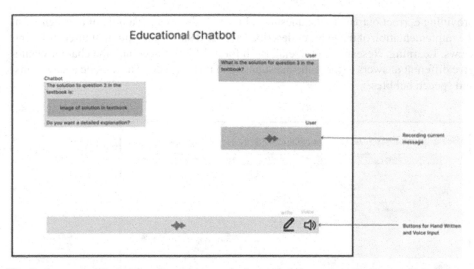

Fig. 3. Interpreted chatbot interface design analysing audio input as described by previous designs including Bers et al. (1998)

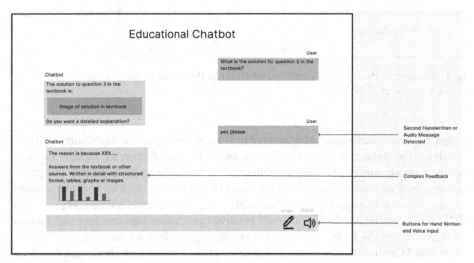

Fig. 4. Interpreted chatbot interface design responding to prompts using a complex mixture of text and graphics as described by previous designs, including Bers et al. (1998)

is very important as suggested by literature (Fidan & Gencel, 2022), in increasing the engagement of students in an online environment where classrooms are large.

A second suggestion is that a chatbot should include an introduction about itself and their capabilities and features. This allows the user to understand its purpose and how they are able to navigate through the chatbot features. They should provide clear interactions between the users and provide a pleasant communication experience while providing correct outputs to the questions. Figure 5 shows an example of a design with the implementation of the features described above. It shows the option of three different views, Learning, Research and Social. Each for a different need and the chatbot would give different answers to the same questions. The interface designs include avatar icons and speech bubbles.

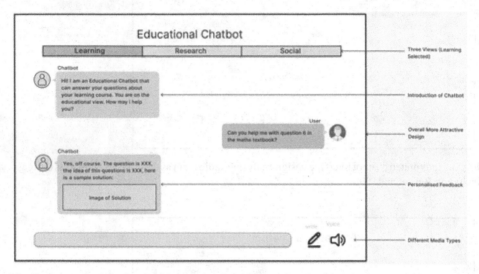

Fig. 5. Interpreted chatbot interface design for Differ as described by previous designs including Plantak Vukovac et al. (2021).

Design 4 - Senevirathne and Manathunga (2021). Senevirathne & Manathunga (2021) investigate the impact of user interface design on the satisfaction of learners by conducting a questionnaire and then implementing a prototyping accordingly. The paper evaluates user interaction designs such as ease of navigation, ease of resource discoverability, ease of configuring integrated tools, etc. As Senevirathne and Manathunga (2021) have mentioned, there is a strong positive correlation between user satisfaction and interactivity; the higher the satisfaction, the higher the user engagement. Senevirathne and Manathunga (2021) have also discovered a variety of challenges faced by students and lecturers when using an online learning platform. The challenges faced by students when using online learning platforms were a lack of computer literacy, lack of proficiency with the English language and lack of good internet facilities. From the lecturer's perspective, some of the challenges were a lack of student motivation and technical problems. Challenges are important to the final result of the chatbot design as it will have to consider solving these common challenges.

Solutions can be integrated into the design of the chatbot to solve the challenges. Lack of computer literacy and language problems can be solved by implementing more images and signs instead of writing. Alternatively, an option to change languages would also solve the language barrier problem. Lack of a good internet connection would still be a challenge as long as the chatbot is running on a website. Lastly, Senevirathne and Manathunga (2021) have also received suggestions from the participants for future improvements, including creating an interactive interface design; using pictures to convey messages and integrating speech recognition options. These features can also be translated into designs whereby responses from the chatbot could include images as feedback, use of multiple languages, managing message design and secondly, integrating a speech recognition method of input.

Figure 6 shows the design elements suggested by Senevirathne and Manathunga (2021). It included more icons and the option to change the language. The chatbot will also separate long messages into separate short messages if necessary for viewability. The design also added a Frequently Asked Question (FAQ) button for guides and answers to common questions (see Fig. 6).

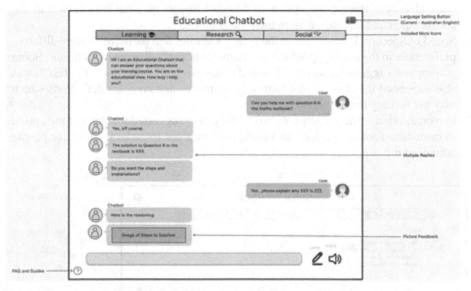

Fig. 6. Interpreted chatbot interface design as described by previous designs including Senevirathne and Manathunga (2021)

Design 5 - Iniesto et al (2023). Iniesto et al. (2023) discusses a virtual assistant project which focuses on conversation user interfaces that aids students with accessibility needs. It focuses on administrative processes such as disclosing disabilities and access support. Iniesto et al (2023) designed the chatbot to simplify processes through dialogue instead of traditional forms. Its results indicate a preference over the chatbot, highlighting its potential in enhancing user experience in administrative tasks. Some key user experience requirements and elements mentioned:

1. Tolerance for Spelling Error - It was shown that young adults with dyslexia may struggle with typing accurate spellings and more complex messages in a chatbot. This could be improved by building a tolerance for spelling errors, which may require a better trained and designed chatbot.

2. Linguistic Understanding - Improving the linguistic understanding of these chatbots can eliminate problems with grammar and people with minimal English levels. The chatbot would also ideally be able to to understand emotions in statements from the user.
3. Multimodality - Users will have the option of communication channels to make the interaction more accessible. Such as voice and text as input and output, or a mixture of both. The author mentions the potential benefits of voice assistants to people with physical disabilities as chatbots become more mainstream and being able to perform more complex tasks.
4. Multi Language - The authors have also found that non-native English speakers also experienced many more barriers compared to people with disabilities. Therefore implementing multi-language features to alter between languages would benefit such users.
5. Chat History - Having the option to search through the chat history within the conversation and find information mentioned before.
6. Speed of Speech - It was found in the author's studies that participants have different preferences in the talking speed of that chatbot when it is giving voice outputs. Some participants suggested it was too slow and others suggested that it was too fast. It was also suggested the chatbot uses confusing sentences and complex definitions which may not be easy to understand.
7. Personalisation - The participants in the study also suggested that having the option to customise font size, colour, and background colour to make it easier for people who need it.

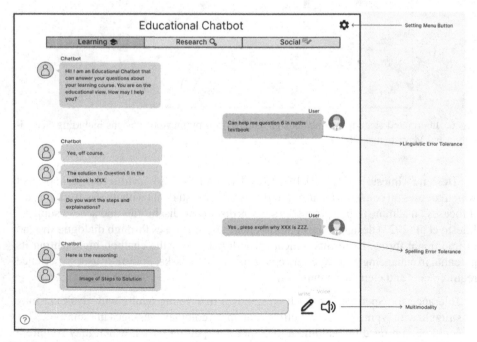

Fig. 7. : Interpreted chatbot interface design recognising spelling errors as described by Iniesto et al (2023)

Figure 7 incorporates the design elements suggested by Iniesto et al. (2023). The chatbot in Fig. 7 can understand inputs with sentences in broken grammar and words with the wrong spellings to a certain degree. We also implemented a settings button when clicked, will open a menu, which can be seen in Fig. 8.

Figure 8 has the chatbot settings menu opened. In the settings menu, there are multiple things you can change. First, we can change the language so people with minimal English literacy can change to their preferred language. Flags are used to guide users to the language they want without having to read. The other settings contribute to personalisation, changing the speed of speech of the chatbot, changing the size of the text, changing the background colour and lastly, the text font.

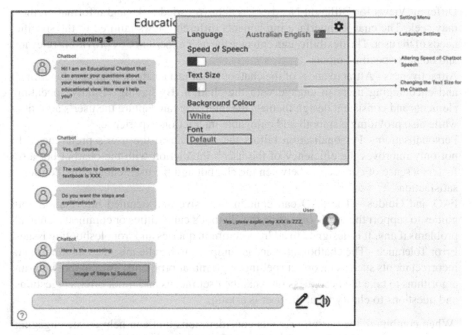

Fig. 8. Interpreted chatbot interface design recognising language and formatting options as described by previous designs including Iniesto et al (2023).

5 Design Discussion and Conclusion

Through the design-based investigative approach, we have an interface design for a chatbot with all the suggested requirements and design elements from different authors (see Fig. 8). Some key elements and restrictions shown are:

1. Simplicity - It is shown that simplicity guides the design to ensure that all experience levels can navigate and interact with the chatbot effortlessly. Minimising clutter and focusing on an intuitive interface can promote ease of use. The simple design choice also means increased user acceptance and continuous engagement with a straightforward design.

2. Multimodal Input and Output - A multimodal input and output can help broaden the chatbot's accessibility and enhance the interaction experience by allowing users to have the option of their preferred mode of communication.
3. Complex Feedback - Having complex feedback can ensure users receive a meaningful and contextually fitting response. Involving detailed explanations and suggestions to graphs, charts and images when needed. Complex feedback is important for users to understand and increase the interaction with the chatbot and, therefore, better engagement.
4. Chatbot Introduction - An integrated, clear introduction familiarises users with the chatbot's capabilities and interaction modalities. This process is crucial for setting user expectations and decreasing initial barriers when interacting.
5. Different Views for Different Needs - Users have varied tasks and information they may seek. The chatbot interface implements different views tailored to the specific needs of the user. The flexibility can enhance the user experience by providing relevant and context-specific outputs.
6. Attractiveness - Attractiveness of the chatbot is not just aesthetics but also functional and encouraging users to engage with the chatbot. By having visually appealing elements and consistent design themes, the interface can capture the user's attention while also providing a smooth and enjoyable interaction experience.
7. Personalisation - Personalisation tailors the interface to the user's preferences. It not only improves the efficiency of the user's interaction with the chatbot but also fosters a sense of connection between the chatbot and the user, enhancing the user's satisfaction.
8. FAQ and Guides - The FAQ can contain extensive and detailed information and guides to support the user's regarding the chatbot's capabilities or common technical problems if any. It is designed to address common queries and troubleshooting issues
9. Error Tolerance - The chatbot interface is equipped to handle misunderstandings and incorrect inputs such as incorrect spelling or grammar problems. The chatbot will run algorithms to take the best guess on what the user means and if not offer suggestions and questions to clarify what the user is asking.

When combined, the design presents considerations that can help create engaging interactions in an online learning environment. The focus on engagement with the under-standing of the needs towards functionality allows for the completed design presented in Fig. 8. Depending on design descriptions to interpret features using a simplistic approach was key to the outcomes of the interface design. The synthesis of the different design principles taken from literature aimed at creating an engaging interface. Through the investigative design approach, some key elements address a wide range of user needs. It enhances the functionality but also sets a foundation for future improvements and adaptations.

Our use of descriptions in articles as an interpretation of the designs has not been validated by each of the authors. This would be one of the next steps to improve the research process. This approach helped to illuminate a gap, being that they are not inter-face design focus, which means that the lack of inclusion in the papers has contributed to and prohibited the outcomes. As such, the interpretation of the design may not be as what the authors themselves may envision but draws on what the design-researchers believe are commonly seen/used examples. As such, looking at the aesthetics (look and feel) for each of the interface designs is a big implication for this study as the functionality is normally tied to perceived ease of use. This, along with questions that pose what these designs may look like, especially in an OLE in terms of placement and sizing of the chatbot within the environment, would be next to complete this study.

Disclosure of Interests. The authors have no competing interests to declare that are relevant to the content of this article.

References

Amiel, T., Reeves, T.C.: Design-based research and educational technology: rethinking technology and the research agenda. J. Educ. Technol. Soc. **11**(4), 29 (2008)

Bers, J., Miller, S., Makhoul, J.: Designing conversational interfaces with multimodal interaction. In: DARPA Workshop on Broadcast News Understanding Systems, pp. 319–321 (1998). https://citeseerx.ist.psu.edu/document?repid=rep1&type=pdf&doi=7dae0bdaefa7156e56db1d013e7fdab237b33943

Dickson-Deane, C., Chen, H.-L.: Understanding user experience. In: Encyclopedia of Information Science and Technology, 4th edn., pp. 7599–7608. IGI Global (2018)

Fidan, M., Gencel, N.: Supporting the instructional videos with chatbot and peer feedback mechanisms in online learning: the effects on learning performance and intrinsic motivation. J. Educ. Comput. Res. **60**(7), 1716–1741 (2022). https://doi.org/10.1177/07356331221077901

Hobert, S., Følstad, A., Law, E.L.-C.: Chatbots for active learning: a case of phishing email identification. Int. J. Hum Comput Stud. **179**, 103108 (2023)

Hwang, G.-J., Chang, C.-Y.: A review of opportunities and challenges of chatbots in education. Interact. Learn. Environ. **31**(7), 4099–4112 (2023). https://doi.org/10.1080/10494820.2021.1952615

Iniesto, F., et al.: Creating 'a simple conversation': designing a conversational user interface to improve the experience of accessing support for study. ACM Trans. Accessible Comput. **16**(1), 1–29 (2023). https://doi.org/10.1145/3568166

Jamil, M.B.A., Shahzadi, D.: A systematic review a conversational interface agent for the export business acceleration. Lahore Garrison Univ. Res. J. Comput. Sci. Inform. Technol. **7**(2), 37–49 (2023)

Kuhail, M.A., Alturki, N., Alramlawi, S., Alhejori, K.: Interacting with educational chatbots: a systematic review. Educ. Inf. Technol. **28**(1), 973–1018 (2023). https://doi.org/10.1007/s10639-022-11177-3

LeMahieu, P.G., Nordstrum, L.E., Potvin, A.S.: Design-based implementation research. Qual. Assur. Educ. **25**(1), 26–42 (2017)

Moore, J.L., Dickson-Deane, C., Galyen, K.: E-learning, online learning, and distance learning environments: are they the same? Internet Higher Educ. **14**(2), 129–135 (2011). https://doi.org/10.1016/j.iheduc.2010.10.001

Moore, S., Hodges, C.:. So You Want to Temporarily Teach Online. Inside Higher Ed. (2020). https://www.insidehighered.com/advice/2020/03/11/practical-advice-instructors-faced-abrupt-move-online-teaching-opinion

Okonkwo, C.W., Ade-Ibijola, A.: Chatbots applications in education: a systematic review. Comput. Educ. Artif. Intell. **2**, 100033 (2021)

Plantak Vukovac, D., Horvat, A., Čižmešija, A.: Usability and user experience of a chat application with integrated educational chatbot functionalities. In: Zaphiris, P., Ioannou, A. (eds.) HCII 2021. LNCS, vol. 12785, pp. 216–229. Springer, Cham (2021). https://doi.org/10.1007/978-3-030-77943-6_14

Senevirathne, G., Manathunga, K.: Impact of E-Learning system user interface design on user satisfaction. In: 2021 IEEE 9th Region 10 Humanitarian Technology Conference (R10-HTC), 01–06 (2021). https://ieeexplore.ieee.org/abstract/document/9641570/

Tsivitanidou, O., Ioannou, A.: Envisioned pedagogical uses of chatbots in higher education and perceived benefits and challenges. In: Zaphiris, P., Ioannou, A. (eds.) HCII 2021. LNCS, vol. 12785, pp. 230–250. Springer, Cham (2021). https://doi.org/10.1007/978-3-030-77943-6_15

Tools to Support the Design of Network-Structured Courses Assisted by AI

Juan-Luis López-Javaloyes[1] , Alberto Real-Fernández[1] ,
Javier García-Sigüenza[1,2] , Faraón Llorens-Largo[1] ,
and Rafael Molina-Carmona[1(✉)]

[1] Grupo de investigación Smart Learning, University of Alicante,
San Vicente del Raspeig, Spain
{juanluis.lopez,alberto.real,javierg.siguenza,Faraon.Llorens,
rmolina}@ua.es
[2] ValgrAI - Valencian Graduate School and Research Network for Artificial
Intelligence, Valencia, Spain

Abstract. The integration of Information Technologies into education
has lately focused on implementing learning systems to enhance the
educational experience through innovative teaching methodologies. The
rise of Artificial Intelligence has enabled the development of advanced
strategies and algorithms, catering to individual learning styles. However,
implementing these innovative approaches requires teachers to learn during the design and structuring of course content. As an example of this
we have Khipulearn, a learning platform based on Customised Adaptive Learning Model (CALM), that offers a personalized educational
experience. It allows the teachers to structure knowledge into interconnected competences, forming a competence graph for learners to navigate. The platform also employs an AI algorithm to select activities based
on learners' characteristics and needs. We propose two tools for teachers to optimize course design on Khipulearn. The first tool, a shortest
path viewer, helps identify critical competences, providing control over
essential knowledge of the course. The second tool visualizes the number
of activities required for each competence, aiding in improving the efficiency on an adaptive activity selection. These tools aim to streamline
the design process, ensuring teachers can leverage CALM's adaptability and personalization principles without hindrance on the Khipulearn
platform.

Keywords: learning design · AI tools · graph structure

Khipulearn platform that supports this research is funded by the AdaptLearn project of
the University of Alicante, within the UniDigital action of the Recovery, Transformation
and Resilience Plan of the Government of Spain. The work of Javier García-Sigüenza
has been supported by ValgrAI - Valencian Graduate School and Research Network
for Artificial Intelligence and the Generalitat Valenciana.

1   Introduction

In recent years, the progress of Information Technologies and their application in education has led to the emergence of new teaching methodologies and models that enhance the learning experience of learners [1,2]. The power of Artificial Intelligence has facilitated the use of advanced strategies and algorithms that seek to adapt the learning process to each learner and their unique way of acquiring knowledge [3].

However, one aspect often overlooked in the use of technology in education is the course design phase performed by the teacher. The novel nature of these innovative methodologies implies the need for a learning process in the part of the teachers who will use them for designing and structuring course content. Making proper use of the system during this stage should be independent of the teacher's knowledge of the subject, so it is essential to provide tools that offer unequivocal indicators of the state of their design and provide appropriate advice on how to optimize the use of the system in the process.

The Khipulearn learning platform employs one of these innovative models, called CALM (Customised Adaptive Learning Model), to provide learners with a personalised and adaptive educational experience [12]. The objective of this paper is to propose two review and validation tools that facilitate the proper design of courses by teachers on this platform without requiring them to be familiar with the theory behind the employed model.

With this goal in mind, we first review the current state of the platform and identify the features of the model that may require assistance for teachers to harness its full potential. We then proceed to describe the functioning of the two implemented tools that are intended to assist in the design process. Finally, we analyse the results obtained and present the main conclusions.

2   Learning Platform Concepts

2.1   Personalized and Adaptive Learning Platform

Khipulearn platform began its development in 2019 under the name Adaptive Learning, and shortly afterwards it was used in the teaching of two courses that served as pilot tests. At this point, the platform had very limited functionalities but was based on the CALM model to offer the learner a certain degree of autonomy in the choice of their learning path [9]. However, it is in 2022, with the granting of the subsidy for the digitization of education from the Ministry of Universities to the University of Alicante within the so-called UniDigital Plan, when the implementation of the complete model begins, aiming to achieve an open, collaborative, flexible and easily scalable system. In this context, the University of Alicante started the development of this project along with the collaboration of four other Spanish universities: the Polytechnic University of Valencia (UPV), the University of Valencia (UV), the Universitat Jaume I (UJI) and the National University of Distance Education (UNED).

As a pilot experience to validate the platform and the model, two courses directly linked to official subjects at the University of Alicante have been launched in this academic year 2023/2024, offering an adaptive and personalised educational experience to over 200 learners. The platform provides them with an automated selection of activities to do at a given time based on their own characteristics, needs and their history on the platform [11,13,15]. It also gives them autonomy when it comes to personalize their learning, offering them a non-linear structuring of the teaching content through which they can navigate according to their preferences, with the aim of improving their motivation [2,8]. All this under the control of the teacher who has designed the course and who decides the strategy to be applied.

2.2   Learner's Autonomy

One of the most significant characteristics of CALM, the model implemented in the Khipulearn platform, is the autonomy it offers to learners, allowing them to select the path to follow in their learning process [14]. This is due to the way the educational content is structured, in the form of a directed graph called competence map. This graph is composed of nodes representing the competences that learners must acquire, and the edges between them, which indicate the dependency between those competences.

Each competence have a value associated, called strength, that represents the score achieved by the learner. Then, there are two thresholds associated with it, indicating the minimum and maximum levels of strength that learners can achieve in them. The minimum threshold indicates the minimum strength that the learner must achieve in the competence for it to be considered passed. The maximum threshold, on the other hand, indicates the maximum strength the learner can achieve in the competence, even if they continue the practise of the competence after having achieved it. The dependencies between competences have also a threshold that indicates what strength the learner must achieve in the source competence in order to unlock the target. These dependencies can be related to each other to obtain logical OR or AND connections between competences, so that in some cases it will be sufficient to pass any of the previous competences and in others it will be necessary to pass all of them. We can see an example of this in Fig. 1.

At any time, the learner can select any of the competences that are currently unlocked and the system will offer them activities to complete from those available in the competence [10,16]. As they complete activities, the strength of the competence increases, what may unlock one of the competences that depend on it, and also the learner will continue to complete activities until their strength exceeds the minimum threshold. At this point the competence will be considered passed. Since a map can have several initial competences and several final competences, a course is considered overcome once all competences between an initial and a final competence have been passed.

It is up to the teacher to create the competence map of the desired complexity for their course. It could follow a linear structure to obtain a more traditional

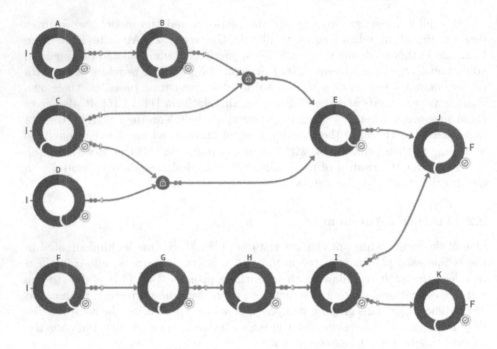

Fig. 1. Competence map, showing the competences as nodes and the dependencies as edges between them.

model, or form a more complex structure with different learning paths from which the learner could choose to progress. In order to provide an adequate sense of autonomy and personalisation of learning, the map should be as far away from a rigid linear structure as possible.

2.3 Adaptive Learning Concept

Another of the main characteristics of the model is the adaptive learning, concept that can be described as the capacity of the system to adjust, evolve and modify the learning process according to the learner at any time, which has been shown to improve engagement [5,7].

To this end, an artificial intelligence engine has been implemented, capable of choosing the most appropriate activity for each learner at a given time [6]. When the learner chooses a competence, the engine selects from all the available activities the most appropriate one depending on the individual characteristics of the learner and their state in the learning process [11,15].

To carry out this task, the engine requires that both the learners and the activities are parameterised in characteristic vectors that can be processed and interpreted [13]. The vector of an activity is static and established by its own designer, who defines its values in terms of learning style, cognitive level and type of knowledge, among others. On the other hand, the vector of a learner changes as the learner makes use of the system, as their ease or difficulty in performing certain types of activities is known, etc. These two vectors allow the algorithm of the selection engine to make a decision based on their values and choose the appropriate activity at each moment, and thus be able to adapt to the learner in question.

The adaptability of the system depends not only on the correct characterization of the activities, but also on the number and variety of activities available for each competence in a course. A competence with few activities will be more likely to offer the same activities to all learners who wish to practise it, and if all activities are similar to each other the engine will not be able to adapt its choice to the needs of each learner. Therefore, a teacher who wants to take advantage of the adaptive features of the platform will have to relate the competences to a wide range of activities and the activities will have to be significantly different from each other.

3   Design Revision Tools

3.1   Shortest Paths

If the tenets of the model are properly followed, a graph-like structuring of the competence map will be achieved, leading to the emergence of different paths or itineraries for completing the course. However, the more intricate the map, the more challenging it becomes for its designers to determine which competences are the most critical and which ones are more optional when a learner completes the course, aiming for an efficient use of their time.

This is why a tool is needed to indicate teachers which competences are part of the shortest path, i.e. which competences at least the learner has to pass in order to finish the course. Moreover, since a course may have several final competences, the tool must be able to provide both the overall shortest path of the course and the shortest path leading to each of those final competences.

With this objective in mind, an algorithm has been developed that is capable of working with the competence map to obtain the shortest paths. If the map were a standard graph, it would be possible to apply Dijkstra's algorithm [4] to find the shortest paths between one of the final nodes and each of the initial nodes. By taking the shorter of those, we would obtain the fastest path to reach that final node. However, the model applied has the peculiarity of allowing the use of one competence for the creation of several joint dependencies (AND type logic gates) towards the same competence, which makes possible the existence of several different edges between the same two nodes. This cannot be expressed using standard graph theory. For example, with a standard dependency graph, it is not possible to represent that D can be reached by fulfilling the joint dependency of A and B or by fulfilling the joint dependency of B and C. Therefore, in our algorithm, in addition to implementing the resolution of the dependency graph, we have added an initial phase for creating auxiliary nodes that allow representing this set of dependencies, as well as a final phase that allows removing the auxiliary nodes and expressing the shortest path using only the original nodes.

The implemented algorithm receives the complete graph of the map, as well as the initial and final nodes, and returns the shortest path for each final node. The first thing it does is to go through the edges of the graph looking for those that are part of a joint dependency, and if it finds one, it makes an auxiliary copy of the source node (with a new identifier formed by the original identifier and the joint dependency's identifier) and its edge with the target node, and then deletes the original edge. This modification to the graph ensures that if a node had multiple dependencies leading to another node, there is now a different copy of the node for each of those edges, and each copy has a single edge to the target node, as shown in Fig. 2.

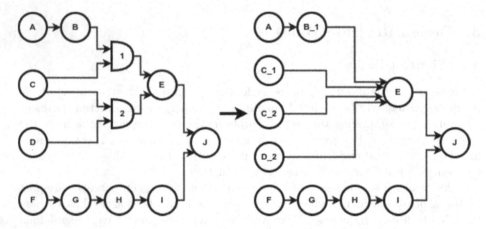

Fig. 2. Creation of auxiliary nodes for the representation of multiple dependencies between two nodes. C changes from being a node with two edges to E (through two joint dependencies) to becoming two nodes, each with an edge to E.

Next, the algorithm calculates the shortest path for each of the final nodes. This calculation is done differently depending on whether or not it has detected any joint dependencies in the graph.

If no joint dependency has been detected, Dijkstra's algorithm is used to find all the shortest paths between the initial nodes and the observed final node, and the one with the shortest length is selected. This process is repeated for each final node to obtain the respective shortest path for each of them.

If a joint dependency has been detected, the use of an algorithm adapted to the characteristics of the graph is required. Before determining the shortest paths, the algorithm must first calculate all expanded paths. An expanded path is a way of representing a path with joint dependencies as if it were a simple path with all the nodes that need to be passed through.

To perform this expansion, the first step is to obtain all the simple paths to the final node from each initial node, as shown in the first diagram of Fig. 3. For each of them, their expanded version is found by traversing the path backwards from the final node. Every time a node that is part of a joint dependency is found, the algorithm finds all the shortest paths from the initial nodes to the other nodes involved in that dependency. It then adds the shortest paths for each of them to the expanded path. This process is carried out recursively to ensure that the path expands whenever a new node that is part of a joint dependency is encountered, until a set of linear paths leading to the final node is obtained. An example of expanded paths is show in the second diagram of Fig. 3. Then the original identifier is restored for the nodes, eliminating any duplicates that may exist due to multiple dependencies using the same node. The only remaining task is to choose the shortest of all simple path obtained, as shown in Fig. 4. After performing these steps for each final node, the algorithm successfully obtains the shortest path for each of them.

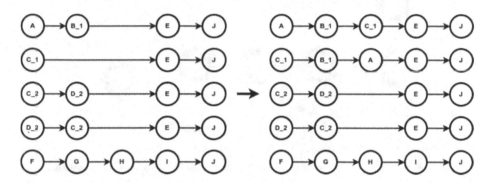

Fig. 3. Obtaining of the expanded paths between all the initial nodes and a final node by processing the simple paths.

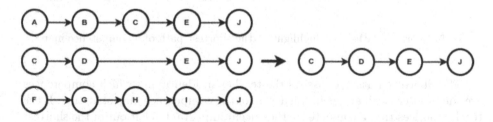

Fig. 4. Obtaining the shortest path of a final node, after restoring the nodes identifiers and eliminating duplicates on the expanded paths.

Following the determination of the minimum paths for each final node, the platform selects the shortest path among them and highlights it on the competence map, as seen in Fig. 5. The tool allows the teacher to choose another final competence to highlight the shortest path leading to it.

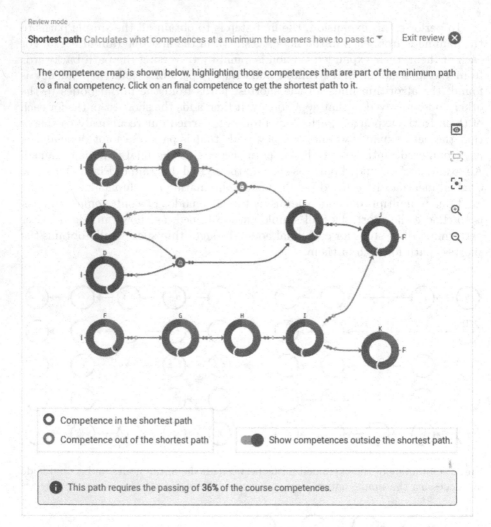

Fig. 5. Shortest Paths tool, highlighting the shortest path of a competence map.

The Shortest Path tool assists the teacher in identifying which competences are the most critical, aiding in the design of the competence map structure. If the teacher notices that a competence they deem important is left out of the shortest paths, they might consider reformulating the map so that the Competence is part of the shortest paths and the learner is more likely to practise it. Conversely, if they consider a competence to be quite secondary but realizes it is included in the shortest paths, they might want to alter the structure to exclude it, allowing it to have a more optional nature for the learners.

3.2 Number of Activities

As previously mentioned, the adaptability of the system depends to a large extent on the number of activities available to the learners in each competence of the course. The selection engine is unable to perform its job effectively if the number of activities to choose from is limited, as the probability of offering the same activity to two different learners increases.

In addition, the strength that a learner can gain in a competence by doing activities must be sufficient for them to progress through the map and to reach and pass one of the final competences. If the activities are scarce and provide less strength than the minimum threshold of the competence, it can never be exceeded. Similarly, if the strength they contribute to a competence is less than one of its outgoing dependency thresholds, the dependency can never be unlocked and the learner may be stuck at a point in the itinerary without being able to advance.

As a result, the teacher needs a tool that easily shows how many activities each competence on the map should have in order to be completed. Not only that, but it should also indicate when competences do not have enough activities for adaptability to be carried out effectively.

To achieve this goal, a tool has been developed that sets warnings for competences based on the number of activities related to them and their thresholds, and calculates how many activities need to be added to each competence for the system to function properly, as shown in Fig. 6.

The warnings that are set for each competition may be as follows:

- Red warning. The competence needs more activities because the strength that learners can obtain in it at most is:
  - Either insufficient to reach its minimum threshold.
  - Or insufficient to reach any of the dependency thresholds of its outgoing dependencies.
- Yellow warning. It is recommended to add more activities to the competence because:
  - Either the strength that learners can obtain in it is insufficient to reach its maximum threshold.
  - Or the number of activities related to it is not high enough to provide adequate variety to ensure the adaptability of the system.
- Green warning. The quantity of activities related to the competence is sufficient to ensure the progress of the learner on the map and for the engine to work adaptively.

The calculation of the number of activities to be added is made on the assumption that the difficulty of the missing activities will be the minimum level, and that therefore each one will contribute at most a strength of 1 to the competence when the learner completes it correctly. Additionally, the calculation is performed based on the warning level of the competence:

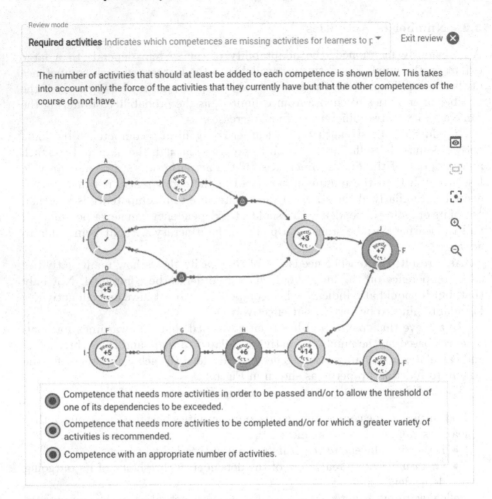

Fig. 6. Required Activities tool, showing the number of activities that should be added to each competence.

– Red warning: the number of required activities is equal to the highest value among the minimum threshold of the competence and all the dependency thresholds of its outgoing dependencies. With this value, the strength contributed by the currently added activities is subtracted, and the result is rounded up. This provides the number of activities the competence is missing to exit the red warning.
– Yellow warning: to obtain the recommended number of activities, it is necessary to have previously calculated the number of required activities as described above. The recommended number of activities is calculated using the highest value among the maximum threshold of the competence and this required number of activities. This value is multiplied by a factor to propose a sufficiently high number of activities to ensure variety. With this value, the

strength contributed by the currently added activities is subtracted, and the result is rounded up. This provides the number of activities the competence is missing to exit the yellow warning.

Using this tool, the teacher is able to easily distinguish which competences need more reinforcement in terms of activities. At a glance, they can identify which competences require additional activities and even determine the number of activities they should add.

4   Conclusions

Khipulearn provides learners with an adaptive and autonomous experience in their knowledge acquisition process by implementing algorithms capable of learning from their platform usage, and by applying a model that enables learners to make decisions in their journey through the course. However, the design process by teachers should also be facilitated, as the proper functioning of the system depends on a well-structured content.

In order to enhance the unique features of CALM, we propose two tools to assist educators during the design process. The first tool highlights on the competence map those competences that are part of the shortest path, making it easy to distinguish which competences are more crucial for completing a course and which are more secondary. The second tool indicates how many activities should be added to each competence to ensure learners' progress within the map and to facilitate system adaptability with a sufficient number of activities.

These tools provide unequivocal information about the state of the course design. Teachers can access them to determine if they are using the system appropriately during the design process and make decisions regarding restructuring the content in order to achieve the desired learning experience for the learners.

In the future, we propose to continue developing new tools that bring the model closer to the teachers involved in the design process, allowing them to carry out a course efficiently without needing an in-depth understanding of the system's intricacies.

References

1. Area-Moreira, M., Adell-Segura, J.: Tecnologías digitales y cambio educativo. una aproximación crítica. In: REICE. Revista Iberoamericana sobre Calidad, Eficacia y Cambio en Educación, pp. 83–96 (2021). https://doi.org/10.15366/reice2021.19. 4.005
2. Bedenlier, S., Bond, M., Buntins, K., Zawacki-Richter, O., Kerres, M.: Facilitating student engagement through educational technology in higher education: a systematic review in the field of arts and humanities. Australasian J. Educ. Technol. **36**(4), 126–150 (2020). https://doi.org/10.14742/ajet.5477, https://ajet.org. au/index.php/AJET/article/view/5477

3. Chiu, T.K., Xia, Q., Zhou, X., Chai, C.S., Cheng, M.: Systematic literature review on opportunities, challenges, and future research recommendations of artificial intelligence in education. vol. 4, p. 100118 (2023). https://doi.org/10.1016/j.caeai.2022.100118, https://www.sciencedirect.com/science/article/pii/S2666920X2200073X
4. Dijkstra, E.W.: A note on two problems in connexion with graphs. In: Edsger Wybe Dijkstra: His Life,Work, and Legacy, New York, NY, USA, pp. 287–290. Association for Computing Machinery (2022). https://doi.org/10.1145/3544585.3544600
5. El-Sabagh, H.A.: Adaptive e-learning environment based on learning styles and its impact on development students' engagement. Int. J. Educ. Technol. High. Educ. **18**(1), 53 (2021)
6. García-Sigüenza, J., Real-Fernández, A., Molina-Carmona, R., Llorens-Largo, F.: Two-phases AI model for a smart learning system. In: Zaphiris, P., Ioannou, A. (eds) HCII 2023. LNCS, vol. 42–53. Springer, Cham (2023). https://doi.org/10.1007/978-3-031-34411-4_4
7. Iglesias, A., Martínez, P., Aler, R., Fernández, F.: Learning teaching strategies in an adaptive and intelligent educational system through reinforcement learning. Appl. Intell. **31**(1), 89–106 (2009)
8. Molina-Carmona, R., Llorens-Largo, F.: Gamification and advanced technology to enhance motivation in education. Informatics **7**(2) (2020). https://doi.org/10.3390/informatics7020020, https://www.mdpi.com/2227-9709/7/2/20
9. Molina-Carmona, R., et al.: Prototipo de plataforma de aprendizaje adaptativo (2023)
10. Real-Fernandez, A., Llorens-Largo, F., Molina-Carmona, R.: Smart learning model based on competences and activities. In: Innovative Trends in Flipped Teaching and Adaptive Learning, Hershey, PA, USA, pp. 228–251. IGI Global (2019). https://doi.org/10.4018/978-1-5225-8142-0.ch011, https://services.igi-global.com/resolvedoi/resolve.aspx?doi=10.4018/978-1-5225-8142-0.ch011
11. Real-Fernández, A., Molina-Carmona, R., Llorens Largo, F.: Characterization of learners from their learning activities on a smart learning platform. In: Zaphiris, P., Ioannou, A. (eds.) HCII 2020. LNCS, vol. 12205, pp. 279–291. Springer, Cham (2020). https://doi.org/10.1007/978-3-030-50513-4_21
12. Real-Fernández, A.: CALM: un modelo de aprendizaje adaptativo y personalizado. phdthesis, Universidad de Alicante (2022)
13. Real-Fernández, A., Molina-Carmona, R., Llorens-Largo, F.: Computational characterization of activities and learners in a learning system, vol. 10 (2020). https://doi.org/10.3390/app10072208. https://www.mdpi.com/2076-3417/10/7/2208
14. Real-Fernández, A., Molina-Carmona, R., Llorens-Largo, F.: How suitable is for learners an autonomous, interactive and dynamic learning model? In: 2021 World Engineering Education Forum/Global Engineering Deans Council (WEEF/GEDC), pp. 617–623 (2021). https://doi.org/10.1109/WEEF/GEDC53299.2021.9657378
15. Real-Fernández, A., et al.: Caracterización de los Aprendices por su Estilo de Aprendizaje a Través de un Sistema de Smart Learning, pp. 466–478. Dykinson, S.L., 1, 12/31/21 edn. (2021). http://www.jstor.org/stable/j.ctv2gz3s4b.40
16. Real-Fernández, A., Molina-Carmona, R., Llorens-Largo, F.: Aprendizaje adaptativo basado en competencias y actividades [Adaptive learning based on competences and activities]. La innovación docente como misión del profesorado: Congreso Internacional Sobre Aprendizaje, Innovación y Competitividad, pp. 98–103 (2017)

The Co-design Process of an Instructor Dashboard for Remote Labs in Higher Education

Kamila Misiejuk and Mohammad Khalil[✉]

Centre for the Science of Learning and Technology (SLATE), Faculty of Psychology,
University of Bergen, Bergen, Norway
{kamila.misiejuk,mohammad.khalil}@uib.no

Abstract. Laboratory experimentation is one of key elements of higher scientific education. Remote Intelligent Access to Labs in Higher Education (RIALHE) is an ambitious project involving three European partners aimed at promoting online access to state-of-the-art laboratory simulations and their environments. As part of the initiative to facilitate remote lab access, researchers and instructors require insights into the students attending these labs. This paper presents the co-design process for developing a low-fidelity instructor dashboard for remote labs in higher education, aiming to support the pedagogical design of labs and enhance student engagement and understanding in higher education laboratory experimentation. Our design journey is documented within the LATUX framework for co-designs from the field of learning analytics. Challenges encountered throughout the co-design principles are discussed, along with considerations for future directions.

Keywords: Co-design · Remote labs · Instructor dashboards · Learning Analytics

1 Introduction

Lab work is popular at the higher education level in applied disciplines, such as engineering, science or STEM. Lab work exposes students to practical work in a respective field that complements the theory that they are learning and helps them develop problem-solving skills important for their future workplace [1]. However, many higher education institutions do not have capacities to accommodate all students to do lab work due to financial costs or logistical challenges. In addition, the challenges of the COVID-19 pandemic, when face-to-face teaching and learning, including lab work, was not possible, strengthened the interest in online alternatives [3].

Remote labs are types of online labs that are "based on remote experimentation on real lab equipment" [17, p. 530]. Depending on the approach, remote labs can enable students to either observe an experiment being performed in a lab in real-time using streaming platforms or even influence how an experiment is conducted either by interacting with the researcher or by, for example, connecting remotely to the lab equipment. Remote labs enable sharing of expensive equipment with multiple institutions and were implemented

© The Author(s), under exclusive license to Springer Nature Switzerland AG 2024
P. Zaphiris and A. Ioannou (Eds.): HCII 2024, LNCS 14722, pp. 65–76, 2024.
https://doi.org/10.1007/978-3-031-61672-3_5

successfully in disciplines, such as engineering and biology [2]. Bhute and colleagues [3] proposed a categorization of lab experiments based on the objective: 1) hands-on skills, where the focus is on exposing students to procedures and equipment handling; 2) data acquisition, where the procedure and equipment per se are not central, rather how to use specific equipment to successfully collect data; 3) simulation, where exposing students to specific phenomena in real-live is the focus. Overall, remote labs should support the development of students' conceptual knowledge and inquiry skills [10]. A recent literature review by Post et al. (2019) reported positive effects of remote labs on students' learning, engagement and learning satisfaction.

In this paper, we report on the co-design process of a low-fidelity instructor dashboard in an interconnected RIALHE (Remote Intelligent Access to Labs in Higher Education) European project that facilitates providing students with remote access to state-of-the-art real lab experiments and scientist expertise in the context of higher education systems. RIALHE promotes student active learning and student collaboration by giving the possibility to relive the experimentation and participate in a learning community to support the development of a deeper understanding of the experiments. This project is based on an international collaboration between three European institutes, University of Bergen from Norway, University of Technology of Compiegne from France and a Centre for Advanced Studies, Research and Development (CRS4) from Italy.

2 Background

2.1 Collaborative Learning in Remote Labs

Collaborative learning is defined as: "a situation in which two or more people learn or attempt to learn something together" [7, p. 1]. A successful student collaboration requires the learning task to be complex enough to require collaboration, and that both every member of a group and the group as a whole has the skills to tackle the task. Collaborative learning opens an opportunity to share complementary knowledge in a group and enable error-correction by different group members. In addition, group dynamics can hinder the effectiveness of collaboration by diffusion of responsibility or by some individuals in a group feeling intimidated [19].

Although the details of lab work may vary depending on the discipline and context, there are three main phases common for most lab activities: 1) preparation for the experiment, 2) lab experiment, and 3) experiment analysis and writing of a report. Lab work is typically performed as a collaborative learning activity, where students work together in different degrees at every phase [3]. There are many ways that a student may need help during a lab when collaborating with other students. Help requests may focus on conceptual misunderstandings, issues regarding time management and task planning, social activities or regulation of the collaborative process, and, finally, technical problems [10].

2.2 Supporting Orchestration of Collaborative Learning with Learning Analytics

Orchestration is the process of structuring and real-time management of learning activities by the instructor to increase student learning [9]. Orchestration systems can support instructors in different activities, such as design/planning of learning activities, regulation/management of learning activities, adaptation/intervention of learning activities during the execution of learning activities, awareness/assessment of students, or changing the role of the instructor or other stakeholders to manage the orchestration load [24]. A recent meta-analysis reported that orchestration systems have a medium effect on learning and instruction, and mostly focus on supporting instructor's awareness [9].

One of the ways to support the orchestration of collaborative work is the use of learning analytics [18]. Learning analytics is a field focused on analysing student data to better understand and optimise learning, while its subfield uses "methods for automated data capture from group settings (often considering multiple data sources), and their automated analysis, to inform actionable insights for improving collaboration and group learning" is called *collaboration analytics* (CA) [13, p. 126]. CA can be implemented in a variety of settings: online, face-to-face or blended. There is a growing body of research focusing specifically on using multimodal data from sensors to explore collaboration (e.g., [6, 16, 21]). CA can provide instructors with insights and awareness about students' learning and collaboration patterns, thus, supporting orchestration. To aid the instructor's sense-making of the collaboration data, the insights are typically displayed in the form of a dashboard or a report. For example, [25] generated monitoring reports for instructors based on learning analytics data to support the learning design of courses. Another approach is to develop dashboards that inform instructors about student learning and collaboration [4, 13]. Analytics presented to the instructor can be *descriptive* (provide an overview of past or current student activities), *predictive* (include information about the student's potential future performance), or *prescriptive* (include an actionable recommendation) [23]. As identified by a recent systematic review [26], the most common data sources for instructor dashboards are learning management systems, social media tools and collaborative writing tools. The most popular indicators identified were student forum participation, a network of student interaction in a forum, or student communication using live chats. Rarely, the indicators are based on data extracted from multiple data sources.

In the RIALHE project, we aim to develop a descriptive instructor dashboard that will combine data from two main sources. The Timeline tool which is developed by the Italian partner, Center for Advanced Studies, Research and Development in Sardinia [27], is used to facilitate both live stream sessions and record of remote labs and subsequent sequencing and enriching of their recordings (see Fig. 1).

The second tool is Ubikey, developed by the University of Technology of Compiègne, that provides an interface to collaborate by, for example, writing post-it notes, adding images and accessing the web browser (see Fig. 2). Ubikey was developed to support the Halle Numérique platform that enables collaboration on a variety of devices, mainly interactive tabletops and interactive screens, as well as personal computers or even mobile phones [5].

Previous research to develop instructor dashboards to support the orchestration of collaborative activities using tabletops is limited. Do-Lenh [8] designed a tabletop learning environment, TinkerLamp 2.0, that was used to support classroom orchestration using specific cards to get student attention during collaborative work. In addition, instructors could get more insights into students' activities using TinkerBoard, a visualisation tool

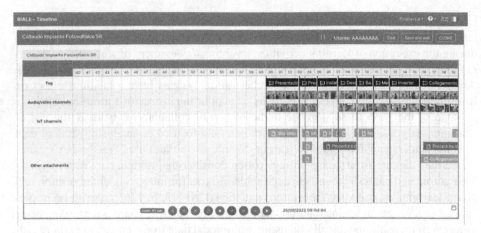

Fig. 1. Screenshot of the TimeLine interface

Fig. 2. Screenshot of the Ubikey interface

showing which activity a group is involved in and how intensively they work, and the history of their work during the activity. This study showed that the use of the TinkerBoard increased students' understanding and problem-solving scores in comparison to the condition of no TinkerBoard or paper/pencil conditions. Another example is MTClassroom and MTDashboard developed by [15] to support teacher orchestration of a collaborative multi-tabletop activity. MTClassroom refers to a tool logging student activities on interconnected multi-touch interactive tabletops, while MTDashboard is a dashboard that not only shows each group's activities, such as the number of touches on the tabletop per student and equality of the number of touches among the group members or the size distance between teacher's map visualisation and each group's map visualisation but also enables the instructor to send messages to students, or block or unblock their tabletops to get their attention.

3 RIALHE Project

The global learning scenario in the RIALHE project includes four main phases:

1. *Experimentation preparation*, where students design an experiment protocol in a collaborative activity using the Ubikey platform.
2. *Experimentation execution*, where a remote laboratory experiment is streamed. During the experiment, students can interact with the researchers and ask questions.
3. *Timeline preparation*, where a video sequencing tool, Timeline, is used to enhance the recorded remote lab session with additional materials.
4. *Experimentation analysis*, where students work collaboratively using the Ubikey platform to develop an experiment report. During the activity, students can refer to the sequenced recording of the remote lab session enhanced with additional materials in Timeline.

These phases are adopted by each instructor depending on the logistics of the course, the target group and discipline requirements. In every activity phase, different data is generated and collected:

In the *experimentation preparation phase*, students collaboratively write their experiment protocols (student artefacts), which are used later during the experimentation execution to guide the experiment, as well as during the experimentation analysis, when students can refer to it while writing the experiment report. Some introductory material about the experiment equipment will be available for students in the Timeline tool (Timeline digital traces). In addition, students will use the Ubikey platform to facilitate collaboration (Ubikey digital traces). Data captured from both platforms will contribute to an instructor dashboard.

In the *experimentation execution phase*, the video, audio and student interactions in the chat from a remote lab session will be recorded (video, audio, text). Both video and audio will be used to develop the time scale of the experiment in the Timeline preparation phase. Students will explore the data generated from the experiment to write the experiment report in the experimentation analysis phase (experiment data).

In the *Timeline preparation phase*, instructors and/or researchers collaborate to develop and enhance the timeline of the remote lab session for students (Ubikey digital traces) in the Timeline tool.

During the *experimentation analysis phase*, students write an experiment report (student artefacts). Student navigation of the recorded lab session (Timeline digital traces) and their collaborative process (Ubikey digital traces) will contribute to the instructor dashboard and the analysis of their learning using learning analytics.

The biggest challenge in this design process is to account for the heterogeneity of scenarios, where a remote lab and collaborative work are integrated into the learning activity (see Table 1).

Table 1. Mapping of different learning scenarios in the RIALHE project

	Instructor 1 (NO)	Instructor 2 (FR)
Discipline	Deep sea biology	Fluid biomechanics
Class size / Group size	10–18 students (2–4 students per group)	2 students
Learning context	Part of a course	Part of a research project
Lab researcher	Instructor	Students
Student influence on the lab experiment	No influence (simulation)	Full influence (experiments can be repeated)
Lab experiment type	simulation, data acquisition	data acquisition
Remote lab(s)	1. Sample collection and analysis on the cruise ship 2. Microbiology experiments in a lab	1. Development of microcapsules
Role of the recorded lab	– To be re-used in future courses – Resource for writing the group report	To help detect what did and what did not work during the experiment
Possible Timeline enhancement	– Presentation of equipment to collect samples – Presentation of the lab equipment	None
Collaborative activities	– Collaborative tabletop activity to develop the experiment hypothesis – Collaborative tabletop activity to discuss to summarise the results from different groups	Collaborative tabletop activity to develop the experiment protocol(s)
Instructor involvement	– Possible monitoring during the collaborative activity to intervene	– No monitoring during the labs and collaborative activity – Regular check-in face-to-face meeting
Assessment	Group work + reports + oral presentation	Individual and collaborative work + reports + oral presentation

4   Co-design of the Instructor Dashboard

Co-design approach includes the opinions and needs of the relevant stakeholders in all or most stages of the design process [20]. Instructors are the target group of a dashboard aiming at supporting student orchestration and collaboration. Thus, they were involved at all stages of the co-design process. The development of the instructor's dashboard was guided by the LATUX workflow, a set of guidelines to design, evaluate and deploy learning analytics tools [14]. This five-stage workflow is planned to be adapted to the RIALHE project as follows:

1. *Problem identification*
2. , where the requirements and possibilities of an LA platform are mapped. We started with mapping the data generated by two tools, Timeline and Ubikey. Next, we interviewed instructors in 1-h semi-structured interviews about their pedagogy and teaching context. In particular, we inquired about the role of remote labs and the Timeline tool in their teaching and their plans for orchestrating student collaboration using Ubikey. Finally, we considered the ethical and privacy challenges that may emerge, and possible evaluation methods to examine the dashboard's effectiveness.
3. *Low-fidelity prototyping*, where an early prototype of a system is developed. The analysis of instructor interviews provided context information about learning activities, goals of the learning activity, and a list of challenges when orchestrating collaborative activities. The comparison of the instructor's needs and available data was the basis of the development of dashboard indicators and potential visualisations.
4. *Higher-fidelity prototyping*, where a functioning prototype of a system is aimed to be developed.
5. *Pilot studies: Classroom use*, where the prototype is subjected to user experience testing during pilot studies.
6. *Validation in-the-wild: Classroom use*, where the prototype is tested on a larger scale and for a longer time than during the pilot studies.

In the ongoing phase of the dashboard development, considerable time has been allocated to comprehend the intricacies associated with integrating the learning analytics dashboard with both the Timeline and the Ubikey systems. During this phase, large efforts were directed towards mapping data types and assessing the data availability from both systems, which has laid the groundwork for the preliminary design of the dashboard. Following this, we recruited instructors to interviews to ascertain their preferences and inquiries regarding dashboards and to gather insights into their requirements for remote labs.

5 Results and Discussion

Instructor interviews at the *problem identification* stage were the starting point for the development of dashboard indicators (see Table 2). It is noteworthy that the pedagogical needs varied among the instructors depending on the pedagogical design of their course and disciplinary constraints. Also, there were some considerations regarding sharing of the data with the students or the wider public, as the results of some experiments may be subject to patenting or later research publication. In addition, the target group in all courses were advanced Master's students interested in research. Hence, a high level of independent work and development of problem-solving skills was expected, and the instructor's role was conceptualised as guiding rather than intervening.

Table 2. Summary of instructor's needs for a dashboard identified in interviews

Needs	Instructor 1	Instructor 2
Contact the instructors during the collaborative session to intervene	Yes	No
Collaboration statistics important	Yes	No
Collaboration statistics as a report	Yes	Yes
Statistics on the use of resources and tools	Yes	Yes

Some ethical and privacy considerations emerged during the interviews. Instructors worried about students not feeling judged through constant monitoring, as it could negatively influence their work. Instructors did not feel comfortable with tracking all details about students' work, as it would be a sign of a lack of trust. Finally, the issues of student consent were emphasised.

In light of the interviews, the dashboard could be evaluated based on its usefulness to the instructor. Although the instructors did not express the need for live monitoring of student activities, they were interested in reports regarding the quality of the engagement and collaboration, as well as information about the use of the Timeline tools. Since the learning context involves small courses, where students are in close contact with the instructor and many pedagogical challenges can be detected in class, the dashboard should provide information that complements the instructor's knowledge of student collaboration.

Low-fidelity prototyping stage resulted in a list of indicators and possible visualisations that will be evaluated by the instructors. The needs reported by instructors (see Table 2) were compared with the types of data captured by Ubikey and Timeline tools.

Both Ubikey and Timeline tools capture student clicks data with timestamps. Ubikey stores information about student actions, such as deleting, creating or updating items, such as post-its, PDFs, images, drawings. In addition, information about the changes in formatting or aesthetics of the items is collected. Finally, the x and y coordinates, rotation, scaling or adding text to every item is stored. If students are working on a combination of an interactive tabletop and an interactive screen, it is not possible to track the clicks of every individual student in a group, rather the data is stored on a group-level. However, working in Ubikey via individual devices (e.g., computers) would result in more granular data, as every user has assigned an ID. In comparison, the Timeline tool stores click data about student navigation on the experiment timeline (position in the timeline), stopping and starting of the experiment video, clicking on attachments, volume changes, zooming, or activating the full screen mode. The data reveals a session snapshot of what was visible on the interface during each action or every 30 s, when the timeline window is active. This gives information about, for example, if a pop-up window with attachments and videos or the list of contents are visible. Timeline is not a collaborative tool. Each user has a separate account and their individual actions are tracked. Based on the data available and instructor's needs expressed in the interview, we mapped digital traces to learning constructs as depicted in Fig. 3 [13, 28].

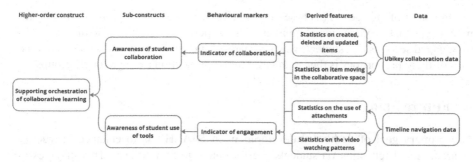

Fig. 3. Mapping from Ubikey and Timeline data to supporting orchestration of collaborative learning

As instructors requested a simple report on student activities, we designed a simple dashboard mock-up (see Fig. 4). Dashboard consists of four main elements: 1) indicator of collaboration, 2) indicator of engagement, 3) indicator of tool integration, and 4) the use of resources. Two first indicators are visualised in a form of a simple bar that indicates group performance in comparison to the average of all groups. More details about student collaboration are provided by hovering or clicking on the information icon. The third binary indicator shows an ample (green/red) sign, if students used Timeline during their collaborative session. The fourth indicator divides the Timeline attachments into three categories: 1) attachments not used by any of the group, 2) attachments used by every group, and 3) statistics about other attachments. The number of attachments in each category is shown, and detailed information about each attachment is available in a table that pops up, when the info icon is clicked.

Indicator of collaboration is calculated based on the sum of all items created, deleted, updated, moved and rated, and the number of words added to the items. If groups were working only using an interactive tabletop, this number would be compared to the average number of all groups. If all groups worked using individual devices, then this sum would be normalised by the total of each member group.

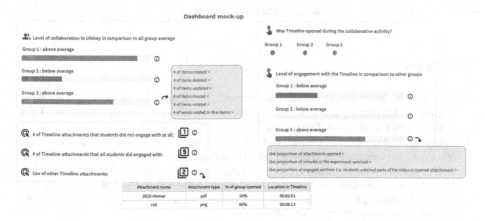

Fig. 4. The overview of the dashboard mock-up

Indicator of engagement is based upon three proportions: the proportion of attachments opened, the proportion of minutes of the experiment watched, and the proportion of engaged sections (i.e. students watched parts of the video or opened attachment). The sum of these proportions is then compared to the proportion average for all groups.

6   Future Plans

The primary goal of dashboard development in RIALHE is to enhance instructors' awareness and reflection on students' performance in remote labs. This involves the dashboard serving as a catalyst for prompting subsequent modifications in the design of laboratory activities, ultimately empowering teachers to identify learning weaknesses during specific sessions and segments of the laboratory activities.

Currently, the process of problem identification has been a time-consuming endeavour, encompassing both technical and non-technical aspects. Non-technically, this involves understanding the nature of remote labs included in the RIALHE project, such as enrolment capacity, pedagogical goals, and the planning of live and recorded sessions by instructors and researchers. Concurrently, we considered the instructors' workload, aiming not to burden them with additional responsibilities.

On the technical front, problem identification revolves around understanding the Timeline and Ubikey systems, assessing data availability, accessibility, and structure. This involves creating a channel to extract data for the dashboard development without overwhelming the users.

Our future plan involves evaluating the mock-ups designed based on semi-structured interviews with lab professors. We intend to conduct brief follow-up interviews, sharing the designs beforehand to gather their opinions. Subsequently, we aim to delve into the development of a higher-fidelity prototype, estimating a 12-month timeframe. Adhering to LATUX guidelines [14], we will prioritise Human-Computer Interaction (HCI) standards to ensure usability and efficiency in delivering the intended functionality [11, 12].

Acknowledgements. Both authors are partially funded by the European Commission Erasmus+ project RIALHE (2022-1-NO01-KA220-HED-000087273).

References

1. Achuthan, K., Raghavan, D., Shankar, B., Francis, S.P., Kolil, V.K.: Impact of remote experimentation, interactivity and platform effectiveness on laboratory learning outcomes. Int. J. Educ. Technol. High. Educ. **18**(1), 1–24 (2021)
2. Alkhaldi, T., Pranata, I., Athauda, R.I.: A review of contemporary virtual and remote laboratory implementations: observations and findings. J. Comput. Educ. **3**, 329–351 (2016)
3. Bhute, V.J., Inguva, P., Shah, U., Brechtelsbauer, C.: Transforming traditional teaching laboratories for effective remote delivery—a review. Educ. Chem. Eng. **35**, 96–104 (2021)
4. Broisin, J., Venant, R., Vidal, P.: Lab4CE: a remote laboratory for computer education. Int. J. Artif. Intell. Educ. **27**, 154–180 (2017)

5. Chartres, I., Gidel, T., Moulin, C.: The importance of individual work in collaborative design meeting: impact on design tools and methodologies. Proc. Des. Soc. **3**, 3405–3414 (2023)
6. Chejara, P., et al.: Exploring indicators for collaboration quality and its dimensions in classroom settings using multimodal learning analytics. In: European Conference on Technology Enhanced Learning, pp. 60–74. Springer, Cham (2023). https://doi.org/10.1007/978-3-031-42682-7_5
7. Dillenbourg, P.: What do you mean by collaborative learning? In: Collaborative-Learning: Cognitive & Computational Approaches, pp. 1–19. Elsevier (1999)
8. Do-Lenh, S., Jermann, P., Legge, A., Zufferey, G., Dillenbourg, P.: TinkerLamp 2.0: designing and evaluating orchestration technologies for the classroom. In: Proceedings of the 7th European Conference of Technology Enhanced Learning, pp. 65–78 (2012)
9. Feng, S., Zhang, L., Wang, S., Cai, Z.: Effectiveness of the functions of classroom orchestration systems: a systematic review and meta-analysis. Comput. Educ. **203**, 104864 (2023)
10. Furberg, A.: Teacher support in computer-supported lab work: bridging the gap between lab experiments and students' conceptual understanding. Int. J. Comput.-Support. Collab. Learn. **11**, 89–113 (2016)
11. Hartson, R., Pyla, P.S.: The UX Book: Process and Guidelines for Ensuring a Quality User Experience. Elsevier (2012)
12. Helms, J.W., Arthur, J.D., Hix, D., Hartson, H.R.: A field study of the Wheel—a usability engineering process model. J. Syst. Softw. **79**(6), 841–858 (2006)
13. Martinez-Maldonado, R., Gašević, D., Echeverria, V., Fernandez Nieto, G., Swiecki, Z., Buckingham Shum, S.: What do you mean by collaboration analytics? A conceptual model. J. Learn. Anal. **8**, 126–153 (2021)
14. Martinez-Maldonado, R., Pardo, A., Mirriahi, N., Yacef, K., Kay, J., Clayphan, A.: LATUX: an iterative workflow for designing, validating, and deploying learning analytics visualizations. J. Learn. Anal. **2**(3), 9–39 (2015)
15. Martinez-Maldonado, R., Kay, J., Yacef, K., Edbauer, M.T., Dimitriadis, Y.: MTClassroom and MTDashboard: supporting analysis of teacher attention in an orchestrated multi-tabletop classroom. In: Proceedings of the Conference on the Computer-Supported Learning, pp. 320–327 (2013)
16. Martinez-Maldonado, R., Kay, J., Buckingham Shum, S., Yacef, K.: Collocated collaboration analytics: principles and dilemmas for mining multimodal interaction data. Hum.-Comput. Interact. **34**(1), 1–50 (2019)
17. Mikroyannidis, A., et al.: Forge: an elearning framework for remote laboratory experimentation on fire testbed infrastructure. In: Building the Future Internet Through FIRE, pp. 521–559. River Publishers (2022)
18. Khalil, M.: Learning analytics in massive open online courses. arXiv preprint arXiv:1802.09344 (2018)
19. Nokes-Malach, T.J., Richey, J.E., Gadgil, S.: When is it better to learn together? Insights from research on collaborative learning. Educ. Psychol. Rev. **27**, 645–656 (2015)
20. Ouatiq, A., Riyami, B., Mansouri, K., Qbadou, M., Aoula, E.S.: Towards the co-design of a teachers' dashboards in a hybrid learning environment. In: Proceedings of the 2nd International Conference on Innovative Research in Applied Science, Engineering and Technology, pp. 1–6 (2022)
21. Pijeira-Díaz, H.J., Drachsler, H., Järvelä, S., Kirschner, P.A.: Investigating collaborative learning success with physiological coupling indices based on electrodermal activity. In: Proceedings of the 6th International Conference on Learning Analytics & Knowledge, pp. 64–73 (2016)
22. Post, L.S., Guo, P., Saab, N., Admiraal, W.: Effects of remote labs on cognitive, behavioral, and affective learning outcomes in higher education. Comput. Educ. **140**, 103596 (2019)

23. Pozdniakov, S., Martinez-Maldonado, R., Singh, S., Khosravi, H., Gašević, D.: 15. Using learning analytics to support teachers. In: Handbook of Artificial Intelligence in Education, 322 (2023)

24. Prieto, L.P., Holenko Dlab, M., Gutiérrez, I., Abdulwahed, M., Balid, W.: Orchestrating technology enhanced learning: a literature review and a conceptual framework. Int. Jo. Technol. Enhanced Learn. **3**(6), 583–598 (2011)

25. Rodríguez-Triana, M.J., Martínez-Monés, A., Asensio-Pérez, J.I., Dimitriadis, Y.: Scripting and monitoring meet each other: aligning learning analytics and learning design to support teachers in orchestrating CSCL situations. Br. J. Edu. Technol. **46**(2), 330–343 (2015)

26. Romão, T., Pestana, P., Morgado, L.: A systematic review of teacher-facing dashboards for collaborative learning activities and tools in online higher education. In: 4th International Computer Programming Education Conference. Schloss Dagstuhl-Leibniz-Zentrum fur Informatik GmbH, Dagstuhl Publishing (2023)

27. Salis, C., et al.: Multimodal access to scientific experiments through the RIALE platform - main steps of bioinformatics analysis. In: Auer, M.E., Centea, D. (eds.) ICBL 2020. AISC, vol. 1314, pp. 77–85. Springer, Cham (2021). https://doi.org/10.1007/978-3-030-67209-6_9

28. Wise, A.F., Knight, S., Shum, S.B.: Collaborative learning analytics. In: Cress, U., Rosé, C., Wise, A.F., Oshima, J. (eds.) International Handbook of Computer-Supported Collaborative Learning. CCLS, vol. 19, pp. 425–443. Springer, Cham (2021). https://doi.org/10.1007/978-3-030-65291-3_23

Using Self-determination Theory to Design User Interfaces for Instructor Dashboards

Anasilvia Salazar Morales$^{(\boxtimes)}$ (ID) and Evrim Baran (ID)

Iowa State University, Ames, IA 50011, USA
{kareen,ebaran}@iastate.edu

Abstract. Automated classroom analytics is promising to become one of the most potent tools for instructors to analyze, reflect and change their teaching strategies in the classroom. One of the challenges encountered when implementing automated classroom analytics systems is how to display the data to the instructors in a way that promotes changes in their teaching. A common way to display this data is through an instructor dashboard; however, suitable design heuristics for instructor dashboards are challenging to find in the literature. Hence, a study was conducted using the self-determination theory (SDT) to design an instructor dashboard user interface (UI) to support instructors' motivation and dashboard usability.

This research explores the intersection between instructor dashboard UI design and SDT to discover the practical application of this theory. A set of design heuristics rooted in the SDT was created to guide the design of an instructor dashboard UI. The resulting UI prototype was tested through a usability study at a higher education institution. Results showed that the participants perceived the usability of the instructor dashboard prototype UI as good or excellent. All participants exhibited high intrinsic motivation to use the dashboard. A strong positive relationship between perceived usability and intrinsic motivation was found. An emotion and sentiment analysis revealed that all participants trusted, anticipated, and enjoyed the experience of navigating the instructor dashboard. Consequently, this study shows that using the SDT theoretical constructs in designing instructor dashboards impacts perceived usability and user motivation positively.

Keywords: Instructor Dashboards · Self-Determination Theory · User Interface Design Heuristics

1 Introduction

The recent incursion of automated classroom analytics in educational settings is essential to the teaching-learning reflection process. The data gathered from the classroom analytics and presented through the instructor dashboard enables instructors to analyze the leading indicators of their classroom dynamics and reflect on them, supporting their decisions and strategies in their teaching (Alzoubi et al., 2021; Sedrakyan et al., 2019; Verbert et al., 2014).

While instructor dashboard design is a promising research area in HCI and interdisciplinary studies, the need for uniformity and the underdeveloped user-centered approach

© The Author(s), under exclusive license to Springer Nature Switzerland AG 2024
P. Zaphiris and A. Ioannou (Eds.): HCII 2024, LNCS 14722, pp. 77–90, 2024.
https://doi.org/10.1007/978-3-031-61672-3_6

in the literature negatively affect their design (Ezzaouia, 2020). The wide range of user-centered methods in the HCI field that can guide the design need a grounded theory that informs the design from a broader perspective. Hence, in this study, a look at how instructor dashboard design can be informed by Self-Determination Theory (SDT) is presented, aiming to maximize the motivation and engagement of instructors while using dashboards in their daily activities, exposing the benefits of SDT in instructor dashboard design.

This research presents a set of design heuristics developed based on the SDT and used to design an instructor dashboard UI prototype. The dashboard's usability and user motivation were evaluated through a series of usability tests, System Usability Scale questionnaires, User Motivation Inventory questionnaires, and semi-structured interviews.

While researchers have focused on learning analytics dashboards examination (e.g., Verbert et al., 2014) and the use and impacts of instructor dashboards (e.g., Molenaar & Knoop-van Campen, 2017), an approach to designing instructor dashboards informed by a motivational theory is missing from the literature; which lead to little evidence about the benefits from a theory-informed design.

This study aimed to design user interfaces for instructor dashboards using the SDT to inform usability and promote user motivation. The main research question for this study was: **How can user interfaces (UI) of instructor dashboards be designed using the SDT to support usability and user motivation?** The sub-questions to support the main research question are: (1) what is the usability of the instructor dashboard UI, and how do users perceive it? (2) how do the users' sentiments and emotions take part in the user experience of the instructor dashboard UI? and (3) how does the UI of the instructor dashboard promote user motivation?

2 Background and Previous Work

2.1 Dashboards

Executive Information Systems (EISs) developed in the 80s, and the Balanced Scorecard emerged in the early 90s, giving rise to what nowadays we know as dashboards. Both tools displayed key performance indicators and financial information (Few, 2006). Stephen Few defined the term as "a visual display of the most important information needed to achieve one or more objectives; consolidated and arranged on a single screen so the information can be monitored at a glance" (Few, 2004, p. 3). In 2017, Wexler et al. added to this definition that the purpose of the data displayed in the graphics is to "monitor conditions and/or facilitate understanding" (Wexler et al., 2017, p. xiv). Besides the graphs, dashboards usually have specific characteristics that differentiate them from other information and visualization tools. One of the most important characteristics is that the dashboard fits the screen size without scrolling.

Dashboard Design. The first consideration in dashboard design is that data must be displayed on only one page to view it at a glance (Few, 2006; Maldonado & Méndez, 2014; Pappas & Whitman, 2011). Another consideration is choosing the appropriate graphs and visualizations for displaying the information in an easy-to-understand and meaningful way for the user. Filters play an important role in interactive dashboards. Color coding is beneficial when keeping the user's attention to specific data or actions (Pappas & Whitman, 2011). Efficient graphs for data visualization include bullet bars, sparklines, line charts, tables, scatter charts, funnels, combo charts, and icons. Less efficient graphs for data visualization include pie charts, speedometers, bubbles, radar graphs, 3-D graphs, and round-shaped graphs (Few, 2006; Maldonado & Méndez, 2014; Pappas & Whitman, 2011).

The dashboards' look and feel are equally important as their functionality and accuracy of the data. The usability of dashboards is critical to overcoming the challenges tied to the visualization of various components on a single screen without transmitting confusion and mess (Few, 2006). A properly designed dashboard must promote ease and intuitive use, good look and feel, and effectiveness.

Instructor Dashboards. The recent technology for classroom observation has arisen new ways of getting feedback from face-to-face sessions. This feedback can be displayed in dashboards specially designed for teachers or instructors. These types of dashboards can facilitate data accessibility and promote reflection and awareness among instructors (AlZoubi et al., 2021); can provide instructors with advanced data to inform their decisions and practices; and can facilitate better communication between instructors and their colleagues (Ezzaouia, 2020). Although vast research has been conducted on dashboard design, it is challenging to determine how to design dashboards for instructors that are helpful and easy to understand (Martinez Maldonado et al., 2012) due to the need for guidelines and principles to drive the design. Dashboards for teachers (instructor dashboards) can include information about students' and instructors' activities, participation, and speech, assist instructors in the classroom, and promote instructors' awareness and reflections (Ezzaouia, 2020; Kelley et al., 2021).

2.2 Self-determination Theory

The SDT proposed by Ryan and Deci in 1985 (Deci & Ryan, 1985) is a motivation theory. The SDT highlights the various types of motivation responsible for changing behavior and the basic psychological needs (BPNs) to be fulfilled to achieve it. Three basic BPNs of autonomy, competence, and relatedness are specified by SDT and rooted in a broad spectrum of the human being that encompasses needs, goals pursuit, intrinsic motivation, and regulatory processes (Deci & Ryan, 2000). Focusing on these BPNs, instructors can enhance effectiveness and learning when the context conditions are changing, social integration that drives a better channel for transmitting knowledge between groups, and vitality to adapt their behaviors following their perceived needs and capabilities (Deci & Ryan, 2000). The BPN of autonomy implies one's government and refers to the power of choosing and acting following one's holistic self-concept (Deci & Ryan, 2000). The BPN of competence appears when one feels effective in social interactions (Ryan & Deci, 2017). The third BPN is relatedness. Ryan and Deci (2017) define relatedness as connection, involvement, and feeling part of a group. Regarding technology, Peters et al. (2018) suggest that design should be directed to stand for empathy mediated by satisfying these BPNs.

Self-determination Theory in HCI. The SDT is currently one of the most widely used theories within HCI and motivation research, such as motivation and well-being (Peters et al., 2018; Villalobos-Zúñiga & Cherubini, 2020), motivation and videogames (Ryan et al., 2006; Tyack & Mekler, 2020), education (Chiu, 2021; Huang et al., 2019; van Minkelen et al., 2020), virtual assistants and chatbots (Nguyen & Sidorova, 2018; Yang & Aurisicchio, 2021), and artificial intelligence (Chiu & Chai, 2020; De Vreede et al., 2021; Xia et al., 2022). SDT has had a significant influence on HCI research on the user experience. Likewise, SDT has contributed to designing positive user experiences, user interfaces from a motivational perspective, and design applications oriented toward health and well-being (Ballou et al., 2022). The SDT has also contributed to evaluating interactions, usability, and user experience through motivation. SDT-based assessment tools, such as the User Motivation Inventory (UMI), have been developed within the HCI evaluation sub-field (Brühlmann et al., 2018). Similarly, the SDT has been applied in evaluating the user experience from emotions and the satisfaction of basic psychological needs (Partala & Kallinen, 2011).

3   Method

This study was conducted in the context of a research project funded by the National Science Foundation (NSF) and implemented at a U.S. Midwestern University. The project deployed a computer vision-based classroom sensing system in instructors' classrooms that gathered behavioral indicators for each class session. The purpose was to improve instructors' use of active learning strategies in their classrooms through analytics-based reflections and decision making.

A mixed-method approach was followed in this study because of the necessity to simultaneously measure the quantitative and qualitative aspects of the instructor dashboard UI. This method approaches the study's internal validity through triangulation, specifically by applying multiple methods (Merriam & Tisdell, 2016), and offers a comprehensive approach through a deeper contextualized understanding of quantitative data by combining and analyzing the participants' insights from the qualitative data. Quantitative research techniques and strategies followed in the research process included (1) questionnaires, (2) sentiment and emotion analysis, and (3) quantitative usability test. The qualitative research techniques and strategies applied included (1) literature and theoretical review, (2) design heuristics writing, (3) instructor dashboard prototyping, (4) think aloud for usability testing, and (4) semi-structured interviews and survey.

3.1   Design Heuristics Rooted in the SDT

A set of design heuristics was shaped as a result of a theoretical review of the SDT and a literature review on dashboard design principles (Few, 2006), teacher-centered dashboard design process (Ezzaouia, 2020), app taxonomies based on SDT (Villalobos-Zúñiga & Cherubini, 2020), multidimensional measures of motivation rooted in SDT (Brühlmann et al., 2018), and a need-satisfaction-based model for motivation, engagement and user experience (Peters et al., 2018). In the case of instructor dashboards, the users' main goal is to improve their teaching strategies and techniques (Alzoubi et al., 2021). Instructors need information that can be used to identify problems in the classroom, make decisions, and implement changes. Reflections on what happens in the classroom help identify problems regarding teaching strategies; by identifying these problems through frequent reflections, instructors can improve their practices and keep track of their goals (Alzoubi et al., 2021). The design heuristics below were developed to support higher education instructors' BPNs and help them accomplish their teaching goals.

Design heuristics to support autonomy are presented in three categories that include: (1) voluntary experiences, (2) freedom and control over the UI, and (3) promotion of behaviors (Table 1).

Table 1. Design heuristics to support autonomy.

Design Heuristic	Taxonomy	Feature
Experiences must be voluntary	Welcome page	Ask what the instructor wants to see
	Metrics page	The share button is slightly visible
	Reflections page	Reflections are optional and only guided, not required questions
		After submitting the reflections, show a confirmation message and ask the instructor what is next
	Goals page	Goals setting is optional
		After goal setting, show a confirmation message and ask the instructor what is next
Give instructors access and control always	Metrics page	Personalized layout (adding, deleting, and sorting metrics)
		Metrics appear visible in all the modules
	Profile page	Option to add, modify and delete profile picture and information
	Reflections page	The instructor can navigate over the reflection topics before submitting them
	Progress page	Option to select filters and graph types
Give instructors some direction, but do not push the desired behaviors	Goals page	Show relevant indicators (avg, min, max) of the goal
		Give the instructor freedom to move the goals lower or higher than the actual ones
	Reflections page	Show progress in the reflection form

Design heuristics to support competence are presented in three categories that include: (1) facilitate user effectiveness, (2) achievements recognition, and (3) positive feedback (Table 2).

Design heuristics to support relatedness are presented in three categories that include: (1) look after the user, (2) connect with the user, and (3) facilitate human connections (Table 3).

Table 2. Design heuristics to support competence.

Design Heuristic	Taxonomy	Feature
Recognize the instructors' success in developing a competency	Metrics page	Display big check icons when goals are achieved and progress icons for those not
Give instructors tools to be more effective	Metrics page	Metrics baseline self-set and adjusted through reflections
		Option to display qualitative, quantitative, or both forms of indicators
		Option to reorder metrics by relevance
	Progress page	Option to display and save the most relevant graphs and filters
Give instructors real-time and positive feedback during the key processes	Reflections page	Congratulation message when submitting reflections
	Goals page	Congratulation message when finishing goal settings
	Progress page	Confirmation message when saving graphs and filters

Table 3. Design heuristics to support relatedness.

Design Heuristic	Taxonomy	Feature
Instructors' needs must be taken care of	All pages	The help button is visible and easily accessible
	Metrics page	"More info" and help buttons in each metric
	Reflections page	Assistance with the chosen learning strategy
		Tips for goals achieving
Give instructors a sense of belonging and relationship with the system	Welcome page	A personalized welcome message with the instructor's name
Provide instructors the option to connect outside the system	Metrics page	Option to share and export metrics with other instructors and students
Provide instructors the ability to situate themselves among others	Progress page	Comparisons among peers, classes, and overall learning indicators

3.2 Design of the Instructor Dashboard UI

The design of the instructor dashboard UI followed an agile and iterative process. Design heuristics driven by the SDT were developed to guide the design of a UI prototype for an instructor dashboard. Three versions of the prototype were designed on Figma. Recommendations and changes to the UI arose based on the design heuristics on each prototyping iteration, resulting in more refined and theory-driven heuristics. The design heuristics below were developed to support instructors' BPNs and help them accomplish their goals. These heuristics were classified based on their support for one of the three components of the SDT (Fig. 1).

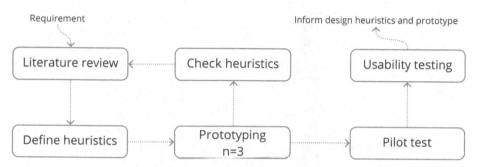

Fig. 1. Design process of the instructor dashboard UI.

Utilizing an agile methodology facilitated the design of new features and redesigning of the existing ones upon the same version of the prototype. The design heuristics guided the design of the architecture of the instructor dashboard prototype. The four main modules of the prototype were designed based on the taxonomies proposed in the design heuristics. Following are the modules' names and their respective taxonomy from the design heuristics:

- Module name: MyDashboard
      Taxonomy: Metrics page
- Module name: MyReflections
      Taxonomy: Reflections page
- Module name: MyGoals
      Taxonomy: Goals page
- Module name: MyProgress
      Taxonomy: Progress page

Adding the prefix "my" to the module's name was intended to support the BPN of relatedness and give the user a sense of belongingness with the instructor dashboard. The design heuristics established features included in each module. For some of the features, the design heuristics also included basic guidelines for the look and feel of the feature in the UI (e.g., display big check icons when goals are achieved and progress icons for those not) and their interaction flow (e.g., the instructor can navigate over the reflection topics before submitting them). Table 4 shows the final prototype of the instructor dashboard.

Table 4. Instructor dashboard prototype.

Taxonomy	UI design
Home Page	
Metrics Page	
Reflections Page	
Goals Page	
Progress Page	

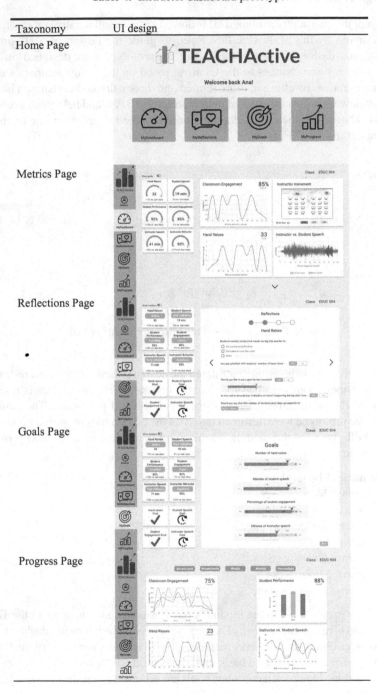

3.3   Evaluation of the Instructor Dashboard UI

The evaluation of the UI was conducted with seven users (teaching assistants and professors), and it included a demographics survey, remote moderated usability testing using scenarios, the think aloud protocol, and the System Usability Scale (Brooke, 1995), motivation measurement using the User Motivation Inventory (Brühlmann et al., 2018), and semi-structured interviews. The think-aloud protocol used for the usability testing sessions collected user emotions and sentiments, which were analyzed using the NRC Word-Emotion Association Lexicon (Mohammad & Turney, 2010) (Fig. 2).

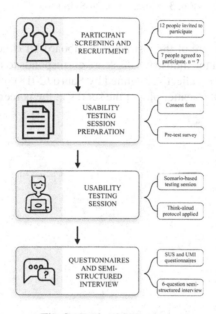

Fig. 2. Evaluation Process.

4   Results

The scores from the SUS questionnaires were calculated using the questionnaire formula. The overall SUS for the usability study was 79.64. Although it is a quantitative measure of the user's perceived usability, the calculated score lacks meaning when interpreted as raw data. The SUS score makes sense when compared with a population or similar groups (Lewis, 2018).

SUS scores and the overall SUS of this study can be compared with the average SUS score of 68. A SUS score higher than 68 means better usability than the average population of systems tested (Klug, 2017). The following figure compares individual SUS scores obtained in this usability study, the average SUS for industry, and the overall SUS score obtained (Fig. 3).

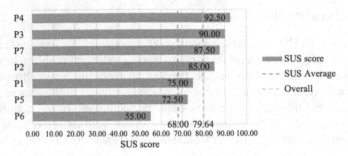

Fig. 3. Comparison of SUS scores.

The obtained SUS score of the instructor dashboard UI is better than the usability of 82% of the systems in the industry. This score corresponds to an adjective from good to excellent on the scale of adjectives defined by Sauro (2018) for raw SUS scores. The following figure shows the scatter plot of the scores in the percentile ranks (Fig. 4).

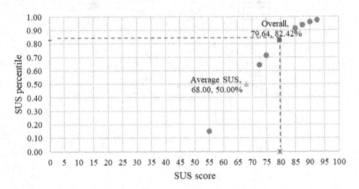

Fig. 4. SUS scores vs. percentiles.

Data from the UMI were analyzed following the guidelines recommended by Brühlmann et al. (2018). Results from this questionnaire show that self-determined behavior is prevalent over non or less self-determined behavior. These results revealed that the usability perceived by the participants with high motivation levels is higher than that perceived by the participants with low motivation levels (Fig. 5).

Finally, the emotions and sentiment analysis results revealed that all participants trusted the instructor dashboard prototype and anticipated the interactions. The participants experimented with positive emotions of trust, anticipation, joy, and surprise, while negative emotions such as disgust, anger, fear, and sadness were present at low levels. The following figure shows that the most expressed emotions by the participants were trust (32%) and anticipation (27%). In comparison, joy (16%) and surprise (10%) show moderated levels, and sadness (5%), fear (5%), anger (3%) and disgust (2%) were expressed in shallow frequency (Fig. 6).

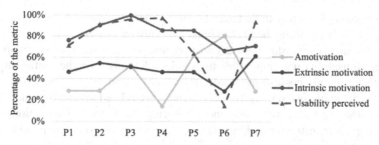

Fig. 5. Types of motivation vs. usability perceived.

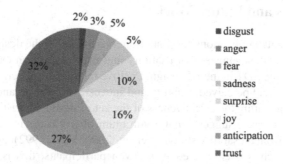

Fig. 6. Summary of participants' emotions.

5 Discussion

Specific design heuristics rooted in SDT were implemented and reviewed through the usability testing of an instructor dashboard UI prototype to satisfy the three BPNs of autonomy, competence, and relatedness. Results show that participants who found support for the BPNs in the instructor dashboard UI went forward with self-determined behaviors in the task completions and experienced the usability of the instructor dashboard as good or excellent. This finding is aligned with the literature and shows consistency with other field-related studies (e.g., Brühlmann et al., 2018; Villalobos-Zúñiga & Cherubini, 2020). However, one of the participants found the UI of the instructor dashboard prototype unhelpful in satisfying the BPNs. This participant demonstrated high levels of amotivation and less self-determined behaviors; consequently, the perceived usability of the prototype was rated low. This finding aligns with the SDT, which states that the satisfaction of the BPNs is the key to developing intrinsic motivation, leading to self-determined actions. When the BPNs are unsatisfied, developing intrinsic motivation and self-determined actions is very improbable (Ryan & Deci, 2017).

The results show a robust positive relationship between usability perceived and intrinsic motivation. In contrast, external motivation is expected to have a positive relationship with usability perceived, this statement could not be confirmed by the results of this study. However, the study shows a negative relationship between perceived usability and amotivation.

Overall results from this study have shown that user interfaces for instructor dashboards can be designed using the SDT to impact usability and user motivation positively. However, a strong relationship between positive and negative sentiments, amotivation, and perceived usability was impossible to establish. Results from the sentiment analysis show that a mainly positive user experience (constituted by positive sentiments) is related to intrinsic motivation. Positive experiences are related to positive emotions and sentiments. These positive user experiences can trigger self-determined actions toward the pursued goals in instructor dashboards (such as goal setting, reflections, and changes in teaching strategies).

6 Conclusions and Future Work

This research presents implications for practitioners involved in the design of instructor dashboards. The findings suggest that usability and user motivation can be positively impacted by using the SDT in the UI design. Positive relationships were found between intrinsic motivation and perceived usability and intrinsic motivation and more positive user experience, indicating the effectiveness of the set of design heuristics generated.

Although the literature suggests that a minimum of five users is enough to obtain significant results from a usability study (Nielsen, 2000; Virzi, 1992), and the usability study in this research was conducted with seven participants, this is not enough to conclude the statistical significance of the sample and make inferences about the context of use in a wide range of target users (Barnum, 2011; Spool & Schroeder, 2001).

Future research can help to determine the causes of low perceived usability and amotivation. The design heuristics proposed are intended to create the environment in which the user's BPNs can be satisfied, aiming to develop intrinsic motivation. It is not the intention to imply that the instructor dashboard UI design should be only grounded in SDT; in contrast, it is proposed that SDT can combined with design principles (e.g., principles for dashboard design) to generate guidelines for instructor dashboard design. Looking forward, the design heuristics rooted in the SDT presented in this study can guide and promote future research on instructor dashboards.

Acknowledgments. This research was supported in part by NSF award #2021118. The opinions, findings, and conclusions or recommendations expressed are those of the author(s) and do not necessarily reflect the views of the National Science Foundation.

References

Alzoubi, D., et al.: TeachActive feedback dashboard: using automated classroom analytics to visualize pedagogical strategies at a glance. In: Extended Abstracts of the 2021 CHI Conference on Human Factors in Computing Systems, pp. 1–6 (2021). https://doi.org/10.1145/3411763.3451709

Ballou, N., et al.: Self-determination theory in HCI: shaping a research agenda. In: CHI Conference on Human Factors in Computing Systems Extended Abstracts (2022). https://doi.org/10.1145/3491101.3503702

Barnum, C.M.: Usability Testing Essentials: Ready, Set-- Test. Morgan Kaufmann Publishers (2011)

Brooke, J.: SUS - A quick and dirty usability scale. 8(1995)

Brühlmann, F., Vollenwyder, B., Opwis, K., Mekler, E.D.: Measuring the "Why" of Interaction: Development and Validation of the User Motivation Inventory (UMI) [Preprint]. PsyArXiv. https://doi.org/10.31234/osf.io/mkw57 (2018)

Chiu, T.K.F.: Digital support for student engagement in blended learning based on self-determination theory. Comput. Hum. Behav. **124**, 106909 (2021). https://doi.org/10.1016/j.chb.2021.106909

Chiu, T.K.F., Chai, C.: Sustainable curriculum planning for artificial intelligence education: a self-determination theory perspective. Sustainability **12**(14), 5568 (2020). https://doi.org/10.3390/su12145568

De Vreede, T., Raghavan, M., De Vreede, G.-J.: Design foundations for AI assisted decision making: a self determination theory approach. In: Hawaii International Conference on System Sciences (2021). https://doi.org/10.24251/HICSS.2021.019

Deci, E.L., Ryan, R.M.: Intrinsic Motivation and Self-Determination in Human Behavior. Springer, Cham (1985). https://doi.org/10.1007/978-1-4899-2271-7

Deci, E.L., Ryan, R.M.: The "What" and "Why" of goal pursuits: human needs and the self-determination of behavior. Psychol. Inq. **11**(4), 227–268 (2000). https://doi.org/10.1207/S15327965PLI1104_01

Ezzaouia, M.: Teacher-Centered Dashboards Design Process [Preprint]. EdArXiv (2020). https://doi.org/10.35542/osf.io/p7cdv

Few, S.: Dashboard Confusion. Perceptual Edge, 4 (2004)

Few, S.: Information Dashboard Design: The Effective Visual Communication of Data, 1st ed. O'Reilly (2006)

Huang, Y.-C., Backman, S.J., Backman, K.F., McGuire, F.A., Moore, D.: An investigation of motivation and experience in virtual learning environments: a self-determination theory. Educ. Inf. Technol. **24**(1), 591–611 (2019). https://doi.org/10.1007/s10639-018-9784-5

Kelley, J., AlZoubi, D., Gilbert, S.B., Baran, E., Karabulut-Ilgu, A., Jiang, S.: University implementation of TEACHActive – an automated classroom feedback system and dashboard. In: Proceedings of the Human Factors and Ergonomics Society Annual Meeting, vol. 65, no. 1, pp. 375–379 (2021). https://doi.org/10.1177/1071181321651186

Klug, B.: An overview of the system usability scale in library website and system usability testing. Weave: J. Lib. User Exper. **1**(6) (2017). https://doi.org/10.3998/weave.12535642.0001.602

Lewis, J.R.: The system usability scale: past, present, and future. Int. J. Hum.-Comput. Int. **34**(7), 577–590 (2018). https://doi.org/10.1080/10447318.2018.1455307

Maldonado, S., Méndez, A.: The Red Book of Dashboard Design, p. 34. Sweetspot Intelligence Inc., New York (2014)

Martinez Maldonado, R., Kay, J., Yacef, K., Schwendimann, B.: An interactive teacher's dashboard for monitoring groups in a multi-tabletop learning environment. In: Cerri, S.A., Clancey, W.J., Papadourakis, G., Panourgia, K. (eds.) Intelligent Tutoring Systems, pp. 482–492. Springer, Heidelberg (2012)

Merriam, S.B., Tisdell, E.J.: Qualitative research: a guide to design and implementation, 4th edn. Jossey Bass (2016)

Mohammad, S.M., Turney, P.D.: Emotions evoked by common words and phrases: using mechanical Turk to create an emotion lexicon. In: Proceedings of the NAACL-HLT 2010 Workshop on Computational Approaches to Analysis and Generation of Emotion in Text, 9 (2010)

Molenaar, I., Knoop-van Campen, C.: Teacher dashboards in practice: usage and impact. In: Lavoué, É., Drachsler, H., Verbert, K., Broisin, J., Pérez-Sanagustín, M. (eds.) Data Driven Approaches in Digital Education, pp. 125–138. Springer, Cham (2017). https://doi.org/10.1007/978-3-319-66610-5_10

Nguyen, Q.N., Sidorova, A.: Understanding user interactions with a chatbot: a self-determination theory approach. In: AMCIS 2018 Proceedings, 3, 5 (2018)

Nielsen, J.: Why You Only Need to Test with 5 Users. Nielsen Norman Group (2000). https://www.nngroup.com/articles/why-you-only-need-to-test-with-5-users/

Pappas, L., Whitman, L.: Riding the technology wave: effective dashboard data visualization. In: Smith, M.J., Salvendy, G. (eds.) Human Interface 2011. LNCS, vol. 6771, pp. 249–258. Springer, Heidelberg (2011). https://doi.org/10.1007/978-3-642-21793-7_29

Partala, T., Kallinen, A.: Understanding the most satisfying and unsatisfying user experiences: emotions, psychological needs, and context. Interact. Comput. **24**(1), 25–34 (2011). https://doi.org/10.1016/j.intcom.2011.10.001

Peters, D., Calvo, R.A., Ryan, R.M.: Designing for motivation, engagement and wellbeing in digital experience. Front. Psychol. **9**, 797 (2018). https://doi.org/10.3389/fpsyg.2018.00797

Ryan, R.M., Deci, E. L.: Self-determination theory: Basic psychological needs in motivation, development, and wellness, pp. xii, 756. The Guilford Press (2017). https://doi.org/10.1521/978.14625/28806

Ryan, R.M., Rigby, C.S., Przybylski, A.: The motivational pull of video games: a self-determination theory approach. Motiv. Emot. **30**(4), 344–360 (2006). https://doi.org/10.1007/s11031-006-9051-8

Sauro, J.: 5 Ways to Interpret a SUS Score – MeasuringU (2018). https://measuringu.com/interpret-sus-score/

Sedrakyan, G., Mannens, E., Verbert, K.: Guiding the choice of learning dashboard visualizations: linking dashboard design and data visualization concepts. J. Comput. Lang. **50**, 19–38 (2019). https://doi.org/10.1016/j.jvlc.2018.11.002

Spool, J., Schroeder, W.: Testing web sites: Five users is nowhere near enough. In: CHI '01 Extended Abstracts on Human Factors in Computing Systems - CHI 2001, 285 (2001). https://doi.org/10.1145/634067.634236

Tyack, A., Mekler, E.D.: Self-determination theory in HCI games research: current uses and open questions. In: Proceedings of the 2020 CHI Conference on Human Factors in Computing Systems, pp. 1–22 (2020). https://doi.org/10.1145/3313831.3376723

van Minkelen, P., et al.: Using Self-determination theory in social robots to increase motivation in L2 word learning. In: Proceedings of the 2020 ACM/IEEE International Conference on Human-Robot Interaction, pp. 369–377(2020). https://doi.org/10.1145/3319502.3374828

Verbert, K., et al.: Learning dashboards: an overview and future research opportunities. Pers. Ubiquit. Comput. **18**(6), 1499–1514 (2014). https://doi.org/10.1007/s00779-013-0751-2

Villalobos-Zúñiga, G., Cherubini, M.: Apps that motivate: a taxonomy of app features based on self-determination theory. Int. J. Hum Comput Stud. **140**, 102449 (2020). https://doi.org/10.1016/j.ijhcs.2020.102449

Virzi, R.A.: Refining the test phase of usability evaluation: how many subjects is enough? Hum. Fact. J. Hum. Fact. Ergon. Soc. **34**(4), 457–468 (1992). https://doi.org/10.1177/001872089203400407

Wexler, S., Shaffer, J., Cotgreave, A.: The Big Book of Dashboards: Visualizing Your Data Using Real-World Business Scenarios. Wiley (2017)

Xia, Q., Chiu, T.K.F., Lee, M., Sanusi, I.T., Dai, Y., Chai, C.S.: A self-determination theory (SDT) design approach for inclusive and diverse artificial intelligence (AI) education. Comput. Educ. 104582 (2022). https://doi.org/10.1016/j.compedu.2022.104582

Yang, X., Aurisicchio, M.: Designing conversational agents: a self-determination theory approach. In: Proceedings of the 2021 CHI Conference on Human Factors in Computing Systems, pp. 1–16 (2021). https://doi.org/10.1145/3411764.3445445

Digital Pedagogies for Higher Education: The Design of an Online Training Programme for Academic Staff

María Victoria Soulé and Elis Kakoulli Constantinou⁽⊠⁾

Cyprus University of Technology, Limassol, Cyprus
{mariavictoria.soule,elis.constantinou}@cut.ac.cy

Abstract. This paper explores the design of an online training programme within the Transformative Digital Pedagogies for Higher Education (TDP4HE) Erasmus+ KA2 project, aiming to empower academic staff with competences for transformative digital pedagogies. The programme addresses three core priorities: fortifying academic readiness for digital education, fostering innovation in learning and teaching, and recognising excellence in education. Grounded in the UN's 2030 Sustainable Development Goals and responding to challenges highlighted by the COVID-19 pandemic, the TDP4HE project integrates transformative pedagogies, primarily learner-centric approaches, with digital technologies. The online training programme, developed with a needs analysis from the European University of Technology (EUt+), includes a self-assessment framework, learner-centred curriculum design, and a delivery mode involving webinars for wider academic consumption. The TDP4HE project envisions a digitally adept, student-centred, resilient, and innovative higher education landscape, aligned with global aspirations for quality education.

Keywords: Digital Pedagogies · Online Training Programme · Digital Competence · Higher Education

1 Introduction

1.1 Background

Within the framework of the United Nations 2030 agenda, quality education emerges as a pivotal element among the 17 Sustainable Development Goals, serving as a fundamental pillar in the global endeavour to reshape our societal landscape [1]. Over the preceding decade, substantial efforts have been made to endow educators and institutions with transferable proficiencies essential for adequately preparing students to navigate the complexities of the 21st century [2]. Integral to this evolution has been the process of digitization in education, playing a decisive role in shaping the educational landscape [3]. Aligned with the Digital Agenda, the European Commission has advocated not only for the integration of digital technologies into the curricula of schools and universities but also for investments in the training of educators to proficiently employ

P. Zaphiris and A. Ioannou (Eds.): HCII 2024, LNCS 14722, pp. 91–102, 2024.
https://doi.org/10.1007/978-3-031-61672-3_7

digital technologies in teaching and to facilitate student learning [4]. During this period, various frameworks, self-assessment tools, and training programmes were developed to delineate the dimensions of digital competence for educators. Among these, the European framework for the digital competence of educators (DigCompEdu) emerged as a notable initiative [5]. Nevertheless, despite the heightened emphasis on digital technologies in teaching and learning over the past decade, substantial evidence of widespread transformation remains limited [6].

Furthermore, the Education and Training Monitor report by the European Commission [7] underscores persistent technological challenges faced by educators and educational institutions. These challenges encompass equipment-related issues (e.g., insufficient number of computers, tablets, inadequate internet access), attitude-related impediments (e.g., teachers' lack of interest in utilising digital technologies), and pedagogy-related challenges (e.g., inadequate skills of teachers, insufficient technical and pedagogical support, difficulty in integrating digital technologies into the curriculum, and a dearth of pedagogical models for utilising digital technologies in learning). In an effort to surmount these challenges and contribute to the development of digital readiness, resilience, and capacity in the higher education context, the Transformative Digital Pedagogy for Higher Education (TDP4HE) project [8] proffers a transformative pedagogical model that comprehensively incorporates digital technologies. This innovative approach, grounded in transformative pedagogical strategies, seeks to advance quality education for sustainable development. This methodology encompasses lifelong learning, social collaborative learning, problem-based learning, project-based learning, case-based learning, inquiry-based approaches, active and experiential learning, and student empowerment [9]. Transformative strategies, in this context, aspire to instigate change in both the learner and the organisation, responding dynamically to shifts in the external environment. They are characterised by a learner-centric orientation, in stark contrast to transmissive (teacher-centred) approaches. This paper elucidates the design of an online training programme tailored for academic staff, representing a key objective of the TDP4HE project. This initiative aims to address the aforementioned challenges and pave the way for a distinctive pedagogical model that transcends disciplinary boundaries.

1.2 Pedagogical Competences

There have been various attempts to define pedagogical competences in the literature through the years, the majority of which agree that pedagogical competences relate to multiple variables [10, 11]. According to Suciu and Mâță [12], "pedagogical competences have been regarded either as an ensemble of potential behaviours/ capacities allowing for efficient manifestation of an activity, or as a minimum professional standard, often specified by law, which professionals should reach". Pedagogical competences should be regarded as the cognitive and metacognitive skills pertaining to learning how to become an educator [13]. In their systematic literature review of teachers' pedagogical competences in higher education, Moreira et al. [13] state that the main teaching competences in Higher Education involve personal skills and traits, curriculum and instruction competence (didactic competence, communicative competence, and ICT/ digital competence), interpersonal competence and cultural and ethical competence.

The enhancement of pedagogical competences and motivation in the education profession is listed amongst the strategic priorities of European Union's Council Resolution on a strategic framework for European cooperation in education and training towards the European Education Area and beyond (2021–2030) [14]. Educators need to be pedagogically competent in order to support innovative, inclusive, quality education. To this end, Higher Education institutions must provide opportunities for professional learning and development. Nevertheless, despite the importance of pedagogical competence in Higher Education, the majority of academic staff do not receive any formal training on pedagogy; this applies mostly to members of academic staff with no educational background [15]. Moreover, opportunities for the development of pedagogical competences in Higher Education are not offered widely. Therefore, realising the significance of the provision of opportunities for professional development in relation to pedagogical competence, Higher Education institutions need to embrace academic staff needs towards this direction and work for the provision of such opportunities to ensure quality, equity and inclusive education. This need becomes more intense with the integration of new and emerging technologies in education.

1.3 Digital Competence in Higher Education

The rapid technological advances and constantly changing needs of 21st century citizens have shifted the requirements for being a competent educator in the Higher Education context. Pedagogical competence nowadays involves digital competence amongst other kinds of competences; the ability of academic staff to apply appropriate digital technologies in their teaching as well as to enhance students' digital competences are considered to be of utmost importance [16]. As Amhag et al. [17] support, "digital competence consists of managing and keeping abreast of different digital devices and their software in order to use the Internet and digital technology in an educational and critical approach".

Going through the era of the fourth industrial revolution, where developments in technology have changed the way people communicate and have allowed the integration of extended reality (XR) and artificial intelligence (AI) in various aspects of life, the ability to incorporate technology in the education process is necessary. Additionally, the importance of the use of digital technologies in education, also lies in the fact that they can promote inclusion since they can make learning environments and learning material adaptable to suit diverse learners' needs. Therefore, drawing on the significance of pedagogical competences, as discussed in the previous section, and based on the fact that digital competence is one of the most important aspects of pedagogical competence, Higher Education institutions need to employ strategies and create opportunities for members of the academic staff to develop these competences.

1.4 Transdisciplinarity

Globalisation has given rise to intricate, interconnected, and interdependent challenges in human society that defy linear understanding. These issues transcend specific sectors or disciplines and elude easy prediction. In the capacity of sanctioned societal entities, Higher Education institutions bear a significant responsibility in cultivating a well-educated, critical, knowledgeable, and adaptable workforce essential for navigating the complexities of the contemporary and future global human society—spanning economic, social, transnational, and transcultural dimensions. The imperative for transformation in Higher Education curricula is evident, moving beyond the confines of single or monodisciplinary approaches, transcending disciplinary boundaries, and progressing towards transdisciplinarity. Transdisciplinarity, as a guiding principle, advocates for the unity of knowledge beyond disciplinary confines. Its approach entails comprehensive interaction among, between, and beyond disciplines, adopting a real-life problem-based perspective [18].

According to Nicolescu [19], within Higher Education institutions, there is no necessity to establish novel departments or introduce new chairs, as such actions would run counter to the essence of transdisciplinarity. Transdisciplinarity does not represent a novel discipline, and a researcher adhering to this approach is not a distinct type of specialist. A more suitable resolution involves establishing workshops dedicated to transdisciplinary research within each educational institution. These workshops would serve as focal points for assembling a cohort of educators and students from a specific institution, fostering their autonomy in organising and overseeing activities, all guided by the transdisciplinary mindset. In the same line, Steiner and Posch [20] highlight the importance of recognising that within the transdisciplinary paradigm students, teachers and researchers have to abandon the idea of the teacher as provider of information and the students as "consumers" of the provided information. Knowledge and competences imparted in university classes need to be applied simultaneously within the real-world case to allow a demand-driven process of mutual learning in which students are self-responsible and decide which tools to apply in the process of attaining sustainable development.

The TDP4HE online training programme aims to incorporate these recommendations. The following sections describe how the programme was designed.

2 The Training Programme

The underlying principle of TDP4HE online training programme is to equip educators with more than just technological competence; it emphasises the importance of integrating content, pedagogy, and technology cohesively in an innovative and transformative manner. For this purpose, an iterative and participative methodology was adopted.

2.1 Methodology

Design-based research (DBR) was chosen to develop the TDP4HE online training programme. DBR is "a systematic but flexible methodology aimed to improve educational practices through iterative analysis, design, development, and implementation" [21]. DBR is an iterative methodology that typically involves several phases including: (1) problem identification and definition, (2) context analysis, (3) design and development, (4) implementation, (5) evaluation, (6) reflection and redesign, and (7) communication and dissemination [22]. This paper reports on phases (1) to (4). In particular, we focus on the description of the design of new educational materials such as learning activities, or a professional development programme, which, according to Bakker [23], are a crucial part of design research in education.

2.2 Problem Identification

In recent years, there has been a growing demand for digital transformation, emphasising the development of digital readiness [1, 5]. This need is particularly pronounced in Higher Education institutions, where many educators still lack the essential skills and competences to effectively utilise technology for enhancing and transforming classroom practices [7]. Additionally, there is a scarcity of academic teaching staff possessing expertise in both digital literacy and innovative pedagogies [6, 9]. This dual knowledge is crucial for educators to effectively support learning in a digitally enriched world. Moreover, within educational contexts such as those of the TDP4HE consortium (composed of technical universities), there is an absence of continuous training programmes addressing pedagogical and digital competences for academic staff.

In a recent study conducted in the context of the EUt+ Alliance, the purpose of which was to define the teaching profiles of the academic staff all across the eight Universities of this Alliance, amongst the most important insights yielded was the fact that the majority of teachers surveyed taught mostly in a traditional way before the COVID-19 pandemic, i.e. face-to-face using mostly teacher-centred methods such as lectures and tutorials with little use of technology [24]. Furthermore, despite the fact that the pandemic "imposed" in a way the use of technology, a lot still remained to be done to reach digital transformation in pedagogy. All of the aforementioned highlight a gap between technical fields and pedagogical skills, often accompanied by varying degrees of digital illiteracy.

2.3 Context and Target Audience

The TDP4HE training programme is primarily designed for academic teaching staff in Higher Education institutions, encompassing individuals within and beyond the TDP4HE consortium and EUt+ Alliance. Furthermore, the programme is also designed to appeal to researchers, scholars, and administrative staff involved in the exploration and implementation of innovative learning and teaching practices. Moreover, the programme targets European, national, and regional associations that specialise in didactics and pedagogies within Higher Education.

2.4 Programme Design

The programme is designed according to the results obtained in a needs analysis about the pedagogical practices implemented in the eight universities that form The European University of Technology (EUt+). The needs analysis was conducted by members of the EUt+ European Laboratory For Pedagogical Action, Research And Student-Centred Learning (ELaRA) in the form of a SWOT analysis (Strengths, Weaknesses, Opportunities, Threats) [25] of the eight institutions forming ELaRA in Fall 2021. More specifically, the analysis was conducted using a SWOT matrix which included sections targeting the eight universities assets and resource strengths (material, financial, expertise, human capital, etc.), the identified needs and resource weaknesses (material, financial, expertise, human capital, etc.), the potential concerns and threats; and prospective opportunities for ideas and objectives. The data collection process involved ELaRA representatives conducting document analysis [26], supplemented by consultations with personnel knowledgeable about the targeted topics, such as Human Resources personnel and Heads of Departments, who provided relevant responses. Data was analysed following qualitative content analysis [27]. The results indicated that all the institutions possess suitable spaces, resources, and infrastructure for pedagogical experiments in many of the partner premises, as well as previous experience in pedagogical research. However, the results also indicated the need to train the academic teaching staff in advanced pedagogical methodologies. Furthermore, this staff has no institutional support to analyse their own teaching and there is a lack of understanding and appreciation of pedagogical training as well as lack of internal support to put into practice innovative approaches: the academic teaching staff of these eight institutions feel that they do not have enough institutional support to implement innovative approaches that usually require a lot of effort.

The design of the programme is based on a backward approach to curriculum design [28], according to which the curriculum derives from what the academic staff should be able to do after receiving the training or the learning outcomes or goals. In other words, the desired results of the training programme have been identified, and the content of the programme along with materials and tasks have been decided on.

The programme is also designed based on contemporary learning theories, more specifically those of social constructivism and connectivism. As regards social constructivism, this is founded on Vygotsky's [29] view of the construction of knowledge as a rather social process. For social constructivism people learn when they are involved in social interaction, collaboration and problem-solving activities. Connectivism [30] has similarities with social constructivism in the sense that social interaction is emphasised again. For connectivism, however, learning can reside outside of ourselves (within an organisation or a database), is focused on connecting specialised information sets, and networking is very important.

2.5 Aims and Learning Outcomes

The main aim of the programme is to empower academic teaching staff with competences for the implementation of transformative digital pedagogies in their teaching practices. Based on this, the learning outcomes of the programme are outlined as follows; by the end of the training programme the participants should:

1. Recognise what effective teaching and learning in Higher Education involve;
2. Point the role of technology in pedagogy in today's Higher Education context;
3. Develop learning objectives, course content and learning outcomes;
4. Apply and evaluate different teaching methods (learner-centred approaches, inquiry-based approaches, problem-based learning and problem solution skills, project-based learning, case-based learning, critical thinking, social-collaborative learning);
5. Integrate new/ emerging technologies in the pedagogical process;
6. Apply different assessment methods;
7. Use digital resources to facilitate the learning process;
8. Identify ways in which they can develop their pedagogical practices in a rapidly developing world.

2.6 Content

Based on the aims and learning outcomes, the content of the programme focuses on enabling academic staff to acquire competences needed for the implementation of transformative digital pedagogies in the education process. For this reason, a comprehensive approach was adopted in relation to the selection of the topics and themes, that would touch upon all aspects of the educational process.

The TDP4HE Online Training programme consists of six modules. Table 1 offers a summary of these modules. The main topics covered during the training can be summarised as: learner-centred approaches, inquiry-based approaches, problem-based learning and problem solution skills, project-based learning, case-based learning, critical thinking, social-collaborative learning, inter- and transdisciplinary thinking skills, and lifelong learning.

Table 1. Overview of the TDP4HE online training programme modules

Module 0. Introduction to the programme	Aims of the programme Facilitators Module description Responsibilities, tasks, actions, or behaviours anticipated or required from the participants
Module 1. Introduction to Teaching and Learning in Higher Education in the digital era	1.1 What teaching and learning in Higher Education involves 1.2 How developments in technology have affected Higher Education pedagogy
Module 2. Didactic Foundation of Learning/Teaching through the use of new/ emerging technologies	2.1. Learning objectives, course content and learning outcomes (interdisciplinarity, the development of transversal competences) 2.2. Effective teaching methods, models, strategies, learning dynamics (learner-centred approaches, inquiry-based approaches, problem-based learning and problem solution skills, project-based learning, case-based learning, critical thinking, social-collaborative learning) 2.3 New/ emerging technologies in pedagogy 2.4. Assessment, feedback and reflection (self-assessment, students' assessment, peer observation)
Module 3. Didactic Principles of Study Process	3.1. Effective study environment, resources and materials (including online/face-to-face) 3.2. Effective use and management of digital resources (selection, use, modification to improve the study process)

(*continued*)

Table 1. (*continued*)

Module 4. Introduction to Psychology and Inclusive Education	4.1. Individual differences of students, personalization (student-centred approach) 4.2. Guidelines of inclusive education and how new/emerging technologies can contribute 4.3. Psychological aspect of effective interaction in the digital era
Module 5. Professional Development of Academic Staff	5.1. Continuous self/professional development in the digital era 5.2. Communication and pedagogical competence of academic staff 5.3. Implementation of innovative teaching/learning 5.4. Lifelong learning 5.5. Effective professional practice (including peer observation/supervision) and commercialization insights

Each module is structured in pre-tasks, a synchronous session, and post-task/assessment. Pre-tasks and readings include diverse resources such as papers, videos, websites, pre-quizzes, and forum discussions on Moodle. Each module of the programme emphasises clear learning outcomes and offers a comprehensive webinar content package, featuring slides, video recordings, relevant links, and worksheets. For post-tasks and assessments, methods like quizzes on Moodle with feedback or structured reflections in checklist format (using Google Forms/links) are employed. The modules also integrate various tools such as Padlet, Google Docs, or Mentimeter, among others, to enhance the overall learning experience.

Following the principles of social constructivism, the programme encourages active participation of learners in student-centred and problem-based activities, which involve collaboration and co-construction of knowledge. Similarly, the fact that the course is delivered online favours connectivist approaches to learning, which are further enhanced through the formulation of an Open Community of Practice that will allow networking, communication and exchange of ideas on good practices.

2.7 Mode of Implementation

The TDP4HE programme is designed for delivery in a fully online mode, incorporating synchronous online sessions presented as webinars that include both theoretical discussions and hands-on participation. Each session is structured with pre-tasks lasting 60–120 min, a synchronous session of 90 min, and a post-task/assessment segment lasting 30 min. The synchronous sessions take place with the use of teleconferencing platforms, such as ZOOM or Teams. Moodle serves as the primary platform for hosting all materials in this training programme.

The implementation of the programme comprises two sequential phases. The first phase, designated as the Pilot Phase, involves the participation of academic teaching staff affiliated with The European University of Technology (EUt+). Within this stage, a meticulous examination of the content transpires through testing with a pilot group. Employing the Design-Based Research (DBR) methodology, this phase serves the dual purpose of eliciting feedback and refining both the design and content components. To gather feedback, participants receive questionnaires, and focus group interviews with a limited number of participants are also conducted. Additionally, feedback and analysis of the training programme's implementation are undertaken to facilitate continuous improvement. The subsequent phase, referred to as the Second Phase, broadens its scope to encompass academic teaching staff from both the European Union (EU) and international Higher Education institutions.

3 Discussion

The design of the online training programme described in this study represents a response to the evolving landscape of Higher Education, characterised by the increasing integration of digital technologies. Over the past decades, significant efforts have been made to equip educators with the necessary skills to prepare students for the complexities of the 21st century [2]. The process of digitalization in education has played a crucial role in shaping this transformation [3], with initiatives such as the Digital Agenda by the European Commission advocating for the integration of digital technologies into educational curricula [4].

The TDP4HE online training programme has responded to Novianti and Nurlaelawati's [15] advocacy for supporting academic staff through the provision of pedagogical training. By equipping academics with these skills, the programme enables them to engage in professional development initiatives, thereby enhancing the quality of education for all stakeholders, particularly the students. This aligns with the prioritisation of competence enhancement in EU education strategy as well [14]. Moreover, the significance of digital competence in higher education, as underscored by Basilotta-Gómez-Pablos et al. [16], is duly acknowledged in the programmer's design through the incorporation of specific modules (see Table 1). These modules not only encompass the management and familiarity with diverse digital devices and their software for effective utilisation of the Internet and digital technology within educational settings, as elucidated by Amhag et al. [17], but also aim to cultivate a critical approach among participants towards their use.

Another strength of the training programme lies in its adoption of a transdisciplinary approach. This approach transcends traditional disciplinary boundaries, moving towards a more integrated and holistic perspective. Transdisciplinarity advocates for the synthesis of knowledge beyond disciplinary confines, emphasising comprehensive interaction both within and beyond disciplines, and adopting a problem-based perspective rooted in real-world contexts [18]. More importantly, our training programme transcends Nicolescu's [19] call for designing workshops dedicated to transdisciplinary research within each educational institution. Instead, we have developed a programme that extends beyond any single institution, bringing together trainers and educators from both the TDP4HE consortium and the EUt+ Alliance, fostering collaboration and exchange across disciplines and diverse educational contexts.

The training programme not only addresses gaps identified in the literature but also stems from the findings of two studies conducted within the EUt+ Alliance. Firstly, in its design, consideration was given to the results of the SWOT analysis conducted by ELaRA. Specifically, despite the technological infrastructure available at these institutions, there was a notable need for advanced pedagogical training among academic teaching staff. Moreover, the results indicate that staff perceive a lack of institutional support for self-analysis of teaching methods, as well as a deficiency in understanding and appreciation of pedagogical training. Additionally, they also perceive that there is insufficient internal support for implementing innovative approaches. Module 5 of the programmeme acknowledges these results by including specific components such as Continuous self/professional development in the digital era, Communication and pedagogical competence of academic staff, Implementation of innovative teaching/learning, Lifelong learning, and Effective professional practice. Secondly, insights into the prevailing teaching practices across the EUt+ eight universities were taken into account. These revealed a predominant use of traditional, teacher-centred methods such as lectures and tutorials, with limited integration of technology [24]. Modules 2 and 3 of the TDP4HE training programme recognise the significance of these findings by including sections dedicated to effective teaching methods, models, strategies, learning dynamics (learner-centred approaches, inquiry-based approaches, problem-based learning and problem solution skills, project-based learning, case-based learning, critical thinking, social-collaborative learning), as well as new/ emerging technologies in pedagogy, and effective use and management of digital resources (selection, use, modification to improve the study process), among others.

4   Limitations

This paper reports on a study which is still in progress. Despite the fact that the programme has been designed, it still remains to be piloted, in other words be implemented and evaluated. As stated in the methodology section, DBR involves an iterative process of improvement, therefore, a pilot phase is necessary for the identification of the effectiveness of the programme and potential improvements that will need to be made.

Acknowledgments. The work presented in this publication has been partially funded by the European Union's Erasmus Plus programme, grant agreement 2022-1-LV01-KA220-HED-000085277. This publication reflects the views only of the authors, and the European Commission cannot be held responsible for any use which may be made of the information contained therein.

References

1. United Nations: Transforming our World: The 2030 Agenda for Sustainable Development (2015). https://sdgs.un.org/publications/transforming-our-world-2030-agenda-sustainable-development-17981
2. Partnership for21st Century Skills: P21's Framework for 21st Century Learning (2009). http://www.p21.org/about-us/p21-framework

3. Matveeva, S., Akatova, N., Shcherbakov, Y., & Filinova, N.: Digitalization of Higher Education and Professional Development of Educators: Technologies and New Opportunties. Amazonia Investiga, 9(29), 77–86 (2020). https://doi.org/10.34069/AI/2020.29.05.10
4. European Commission: Communication from the Commission – A Digital Agenda for Europe (2010). https://eur-lex.europa.eu/LexUriServ/LexUriServ.do?uri=COM:2010:0245: FIN:EN:PDF
5. European Commission, Joint Research Centre, Redecker, C.: European framework for the digital competence of educators: DigCompEdu, Publications Office, 2017 (2017). https:// data.europa.eu/doi/10.2760/178382
6. Blundell, C., Lee, K.T., Nykvist, S.: Moving beyond enhancing pedagogies with digital technologies: frames of reference, habits of mind and transformative learning. J. Res. Technol. Educ. 52(2), 178–196 (2020). https://doi.org/10.1080/15391523.2020.1726235
7. European Commission, Directorate-General for Education, Youth, Sport and Culture: Education and training monitor 2021: executive summary (2021). https://data.europa.eu/doi/10. 2766/480191
8. Transformative Digital Pedagogies for Higher Education. Transformative Digital Pedagogies for Higher Education - TDP4HE (n.d.). https://transformative-pedagogies.univ-tech.eu/
9. Bourn, D., Soysal, N.: Transformative learning and pedagogical approaches in education for sustainable development: are initial teacher education programmemes in England and Turkey ready for creating agents of change for sustainability? Sustainability 13, 8973 (2021). https:// doi.org/10.3390/su13168973
10. Gliga, L. (coord.): Standarde profesionale pentru profesia didactică. Bucureşti: M.E.C. (2002)
11. Madhavaram, S., Laverie, D.A.: Developing pedagogical competence: issues and implications for marketing education. J. Market. Educ. XX(X), 2–10 (2010)
12. Suciu, A.I., Mâță, L.: Pedagogical competences-the key to efficient education. Int. Online J. Educ. Sci. 3(2), 411–423 (2011)
13. Moreira, M. A., et al.: Teachers' pedagogical competences in higher education: A systematic literature review. J. Univ. Teach. Learn. Pract. 20(1), 90–123 (2023). https://doi.org/10.53761/ 1.20.01.07
14. Council of the European Union.: Council Resolution on a strategic framework for European cooperation in education and training towards the European Education Area and beyond (2021–2030) (2021). https://op.europa.eu/en/publication-detail/-/publication/b00 4d247-77d4-11eb-9ac9-01aa75ed71a1
15. Novianti, N., Nurlaelawati, I.: Pedagogical competence development of university teachers with non-education background: the case of a large University of Education in Indonesia. Int. J. Educ. 11(2), 172 (2019). https://doi.org/10.17509/ije.v11i2.15711
16. Basilotta-Gómez-Pablos, V., Matarranz, M., Casado-Aranda, L.A., Otto, A.: Teachers' digital competencies in higher education: a systematic literature review. Int. J. Educ. Technol. Higher Educ. 19(8) (2022). https://doi.org/10.1186/s41239-021-00312-8
17. Amhag, L., Hellström, L., Stigmar, M.: Teacher educators' use of digital tools and needs for digital competence in higher education. J. Digital Learn. Teacher Educ. 35(4), 203–220 (2019). https://doi.org/10.1080/21532974.2019.1646169
18. Hyun, E.: Transdisciplinary higher education curriculum: a complicated cultural artefact. Res. Higher Educ. J. 11, 1 (2011)
19. Nicolescu, B.: The need for transdisciplinarity in higher education in a globalized world. Transdisciplinary J. Eng. Sci. 3 (2012). https://doi.org/10.22545/2012/00031
20. Steiner, G., Posch, A.: Higher education for sustainability by means of transdisciplinary case studies: an innovative approach for solving complex, real-world problems. J. Clean. Prod. 14(9–11), 877–890 (2006). https://doi.org/10.1016/j.jclepro.2005.11.054
21. Wang, F., Hannafin, M.J.: Design-based research and technology-enhanced learning environments. Educ. Tech. Res. Dev. 53, 5–23 (2005)

22. McKenney, S., Reeves, T.: Conducting Educational Design Research. Routledge, London (2012)

23. Bakker, A.: Design Research in Education: A Practical Guide for Early Career Researchers. Routledge, London (2018)

24. Kakoulli Constantinou, E., Verchier, Y., Flynn, P.: Defining the teaching profiles of academic staff across a European Universities Alliance: Lessons learned after the pandemic and the way into the future. [Manuscript submitted for publication] (n.d.)

25. Benzaghta, M.A., Elwalda, A., Mousa, M.M., Erkan, I., Rahman, M.: SWOT analysis applications: an integrative literature review. J. Global Bus. Insights 6(1), 54–72 (2021)

26. Salminen, A., Kauppinen, K., Lehtovaara, M.: Towards a methodology for document analysis. J. Am. Soc. Inf. Sci. **48**, 644–655 (1997). https://doi.org/10.1002/(SICI)1097-4571(199707)48:7%3c644:AID-ASI12%3e3.0.CO;2-V

27. Selvi, A.F.: Qualitative content analysis. In: McKinley, J., Rose, H. (eds.) The Routledge Handbook of Research Methods in Applied Linguistics, pp. 440–453. Routledge (2019)

28. Wiggins, G., McTighe, J.: Understanding by Design (2nd edn). Association for Supervision and Curriculum Development (2005)

29. Vygotsky, L. S.: Mind in Society: The Development of Higher Mental Processes. Harvard University Press (1978)

30. Siemens, G.: Connectivism: a learning theory for the digital age. Int. J. Instruct. Technol. Dist. Learn. **1**, 1–8 (2005)

User-Centered Design of Adaptive Support in a Continuing Education Online Course: Findings from a Design-Based Research Process

Katharina Teich[1,2]([✉]) [iD], Vanessa Loock[1] [iD], and Nikol Rummel[1,2]

[1] Ruhr University Bochum, Bochum, Germany
{katharina.teich,vanessa.loock,nikol.rummel}@rub.de
[2] Center for Advanced Internet Studies (CAIS) gGmbH Bochum, Bochum, Germany

Abstract. Online courses in continuing education often entail a self-paced format, resulting in high levels of autonomy for adult learners. This autonomy, however, requires learners to self-regulate their learning process. Research has shown that self-regulated learning (SRL) in online courses can be challenging, and support might therefore be needed. While there is evidence that adaptive support systems can improve students' SRL in formal school and higher education settings, little is known about adaptive SRL support in continuing education online courses. The present paper addresses this research gap applying a design-based research approach. First, we re-analyzed an existing dataset that comprises survey data of 60 adult learners from four course iterations and matched survey measures on learning processes with learners' perceptions of their SRL strategy use. The analyses revealed that adult learners especially struggled with structuring their learning environment and managing learning time. Based on these findings, adaptive support features were iteratively designed to address the identified challenges. We developed a course overview, an adaptive learning-time display, and adaptive highlighting of recommended content. Second, we investigated learners' perceptions of the design and functionality of these features by means of interactive co-design sessions. Finally, initial usability testing with students was conducted.

Keywords: continuing education · online learning · self-regulated learning · design-based research

1 Introduction

Online courses can be distinguished from traditional face-to-face learning environments by providing learners with significant autonomy regarding the timing, content, and method of learning. This flexibility is particularly advantageous for adult learners, who often take continuing education and training (CET) courses in addition to their regular employment. However, this autonomy also presents challenges, including the lack of direct support and reduced opportunities for interaction. Accordingly, learners need to be able to self-regulate and take full responsibility for their learning journey [1, 2]. Self-regulated learning (SRL), which involves making strategic decisions about what to learn

P. Zaphiris and A. Ioannou (Eds.): HCII 2024, LNCS 14722, pp. 103–123, 2024.
https://doi.org/10.1007/978-3-031-61672-3_8

and how to allocate resources to a task, is therefore a crucial aspect of online learning [3, 4]. Research suggests that self-regulation in online courses is challenging [e.g. 1, 2]. It seems plausible that such challenges especially affect adult learners, as an efficient use of time is essential to meet course requirements while balancing multiple commitments [5]. Given that adult learners may lack recent experience in SRL [6], they may require assistance to fully take advantage of the benefits of online courses. Adaptive SRL support appears to be a promising approach in this regard. The overall goal of adaptive support is to optimize learning by tailoring the educational experience to individual strengths while addressing weaknesses [7]. Studies have demonstrated positive effects of adaptive SRL support in various educational settings, including schools [e.g. 8], higher education [e.g., 9], and massive open online courses (MOOCs) [e.g., 10]. However, research on adaptive SRL support specifically tailored to adult learners is scarce, and findings from other learning environments cannot simply be generalized. While MOOCs also commonly target adult learners, the present study focuses on work-related, on-the-job CETs, which come with notable differences: In the majority of cases, such courses are mandated by employers and must be completed within specific time frames, requiring effective time management. Moreover, most adult learners in this context are in full-time employment, a characteristic shared with some but not all MOOC learners. In sum, shifting the focus to SRL in on-the-job CET online courses underlines two important research gaps: First, research on SRL in the context of adult learning is largely limited to informal work-place learning [e.g., 11], with little focus on work-related CET online learning. Second, research on adaptive SRL support for adult learners is limited to research on SRL support in MOOCs, which cannot be directly transferred to on-the-job CET online courses.

To address these research gaps, we applied a three-step design cycle following a design-based research (DBR) approach with the aim to design and develop an adaptive support intervention that addresses the main challenges faced by adult learners in self-regulated online on-the-job learning.

2   Theoretical Background

2.1   Self-regulated Learning in Continuing Online Education

Effective SRL entails actively employing and adapting cognitive, metacognitive, and motivational strategies to establish learning objectives and monitor progress [3, 4, 12]. Zimmerman's socio-cognitive SRL model [3, 12] emphasizes motivational factors and learning strategies, particularly in settings characterized by a high degree of autonomy. The model describes SRL activities as cyclical, comprising three phases, each involving the use of SRL strategies: The *forethought phase* involves setting learning goals and activating prior knowledge, the *performance phase* involves cognitive and metacognitive strategies, and the *self-reflection phase* involves self-evaluation and adjustment. Most SRL models are based on formal school and higher education contexts, while research exploring how adult learners self-regulate their learning is scarce [13–17]. Drawing on Zimmerman's model and the corresponding strategies, Sitzman and Ely [11] developed a framework that highlights which SRL strategies are relevant for learning success in workplace learning. We refer to these strategies throughout this paper.

Although success in online learning depends on the effective use of SRL strategies [18], adult learners face several key challenges [19–21], including managing conflicting responsibilities [19], which creates difficulties in applying *time management* strategies. Such strategies are particularly important for adult learners, who also have work-related commitments, and include creating schedules that fit into daily routines to help them learn within time constraints [11]. Online learning predominantly takes place at home, where its integration with other responsibilities can have a negative impact on attention regulation and environmental structuring. SRL strategies for *environmental structuring* and *attention regulation* help learners to establish a dedicated study space, minimize distractions, and remain focused. A further challenge for adult learners lies in balancing effort across multiple work and personal commitments, highlighting the need for effective *effort regulation* strategies to allocate energy efficiently. As adult learners may have gaps in prerequisite knowledge and essential skills, *goal setting* is critical [19], as learning goals need to be clear and achievable.

In view of the lack of research on SRL in work-related CET online courses, an in-depth exploration of adult learners' SRL experiences in this specific context is needed. In particular, the following question is critical: What are the specific challenges that adult learners face when attempting to apply SRL strategies within the unique landscape of online CETs? The present investigation not only highlights the existing research gap, but also seeks to pave the way for practical solutions to enhance SRL experiences in this specific educational setting.

2.2 Adaptive SRL Support

Given that many adult learners struggle to apply SRL strategies successfully, support might be needed. To relate to the SRL experiences of learners, the use of adaptive learning designs is a promising approach. Adaptive support refers to educational interventions that are designed to adapt and personalize the learning experience based on learners' needs, preferences, and performance. These systems use data-driven insights and technologies to tailor instructional content, pace, and assessments to promote a more personalized and effective learning journey for each learner [7].

In the context of CET online courses, adaptive support is needed for several reasons: First, adult learners often lack recent experience of formal learning and thus SRL [6], and therefore face difficulties in managing CET courses alongside their work commitments. Second, there is large heterogeneity in adult learners' SRL abilities, with research highlighting the importance of designing SRL support features with individual learner prerequisites in mind, such as prior knowledge and experience [1, 2, 22, 23]. Studies have demonstrated the effectiveness of adaptive support in different educational contexts, including schools [24] and higher education [25]. For instance, learner dashboards [8, 26] and adaptive scaffolding [25] have been found to be beneficial for applying cognitive and metacognitive SRL strategies. In addition, in MOOCs, adaptive support, including personalized scaffolding of planning activities [27], improved engagement and the management of learning time. In view of these positive findings, the following question arises: How can adaptive support be best designed to foster SRL? In the context of MOOCs, five design requirements have been identified [28], which can help to design adaptive support for CET online courses: First, the design should integrate seamlessly with different platforms to *complement existing platforms*. Second, the design should include features that *support effective SRL strategies* that are relevant in the given context. Third, the design needs to extend support beyond the learning platform to *provide comprehensive support for learners*. External resources such as note-taking should be seamlessly integrated. Fourth, recognizing SRL as an active process, the design should facilitate the analysis of the learning journey to provide *different perspectives for information analysis*. Visualizations that provide feedback should allow for interaction, enabling learners to monitor their progress. Finally, a robust self-regulation process requires the *inclusion of targets, standards, or comparison criteria* to help learners assess the need for adjustments in their learning process.

While adaptive SRL support has shown positive effects in different educational settings, and design requirements are provided for MOOCs, the following questions remain to be addressed with regard to the unique landscape of CET online courses for adult learners: (a) How can adaptive SRL support be designed to address the SRL challenges faced by adult learners in online CETs, and (b) how do adult learners evaluate the design of such adaptive support?

3 Methodological Approach

In this research, we applied a DBR approach [29–31] to address the research questions identified above and to develop adaptive support features to foster SRL in a CET online course. Specifically, we adopted the integrative learning design (ILD) framework [32], which refines the DBR process into four main phases: *informed exploration*, *enactment*, *local evaluation*, and *broader evaluation*. The enactment phase is further structured into three steps: initial intervention design, prototype articulation, and the development of a more fully detailed intervention.

Cycle 1 of this research addresses an *informed exploration* [30–32], which involves exploring the learning context, recognizing challenges, and determining areas requiring support. Cycle 2 addresses the *design or enactment phase* [30–32], which centers on the collaborative involvement of learners to generate insights and feedback on the design of support. Following the ILD framework, this cycle is divided into three steps and is the central component of our DBR approach. Cycle 3, the *local evaluation* [30–32], involves assessing the support's effectiveness and usability, with usability referring to the extent to which a product can be used to achieve specified goals effectively, efficiently, and with satisfaction [33]. By using standardized metrics, such as the System Usability Scale (SUS, [33]) or the Technology Acceptance Model (TAM, [34]), users' perceptions of the system can be quantitatively assessed.

4 Context

This research was conducted within the Six Sigma GreenBelt program, which addresses Lean Management. In the context of this research, four course iterations of the CET program were conducted each lasting three months, with new participants recruited for each iteration. The course followed a hybrid model, divided into two online self-study phases, which took up the majority of the program, and two in-person phases. Here, we focus on the online self-study phases, in which participants had to study the learning materials independently. These phases were supported by the learning management system (LMS) Moodle. The Moodle course was organized by topics (i.e., modules) encompassing seven modules and two quiz sections. The learning materials of the modules were characterized by different formats (videos, texts, quizzes, etc.).

5   Cycle 1: Informed Exploration

The goal of this cycle was to identify challenges adult learners face when self-regulating their online learning. We performed a secondary analysis of survey data collected from adult learners attending four iterations of a CET online course. The survey examined adult learners' needs for SRL support in this specific course.

5.1   Participants

We re-analyzed survey data of $N = 60$ adult learners from four iterations of the CET course introduced above. All learners participated in one of the four course iterations. During each course, participants were asked to complete a survey multiple times. An overview of the number of participants and survey iterations is provided in Table 1.

Table 1. Number of participants and survey iterations in the courses.

	Time	Participants	Survey Iterations
Course #1	Nov 2020 - Feb 2021	$N = 15$ (20% female, 80% male)	19
Course #2	Mar 2021 - May 2021	$N = 14$ (14% female, 86% male)	11
Course #3	Oct 2021 - Dec 2021	$N = 14$ (64% female, 36% male)	11
Course #4	Apr 2022 - June 2022	$N = 17$ (35% female, 65% male)	9
		$N = 60$	50

5.2   Dataset

The dataset comprised survey data collected multiple times during each course iteration. Participants completed at least one survey in each module. The number of surveys to be completed by each participant was reduced between the course iterations based on feedback from participants. As not all participants completed all surveys, 621 completed surveys were available for our analyses. Within each course, the multiple survey iterations included the same questions, allowing for an overview of how the course attendees self-regulated their learning over a three-month duration. The composition of measures in the surveys was slightly adapted within each course. Table 2 provides an overview of the measures comprised in the four course iterations. The question formats included ratings on Likert scales as well as open questions.

Table 2. Measures from the dataset corresponding with the SRL strategies described in [11].

SRL Strategy	Definition [11]	Measures from the dataset	Course[1]
Self-Efficacy	Learners' confidence in their own competence and trust in successfully completing tasks	Subjective Comprehension	1–4
		Recollection	2–4
		Reproduction	3
		Comprehension	3
		$KIM^2_{pressure/tension}$ ([35]; 1 item)	3
		$KIM_{perceived\ competence}$ ([35]; 3 items)	2–4
Metacognitive Strategies	Including self-determination and self-control over individual, task-related, and environmental influences	$KIM_{perceived\ choice}$ ([35]; 3 items)	3
Attention	Extent to which learners are able to direct their attention to a task and concentrate on monitoring their learning	Cognitive Load ([36]; 1 item)	2–4
		Distractions: Loudness, Smartphone	1–3
Time Management	Scheduling study sessions, dedicating adequate time to learning, and monitoring one's own progress to meet deadlines or appointments	*See previous analysis* [37]	
Environmental Structuring	Choosing a learning location that is free from distractions. This strategy is especially important in contexts where the learning location can be chosen autonomously	Location of learning	1
		Distractions	1–3
Motivation	Actively committing to the learning content. Learners' motivation is influenced by their interest in the content	Learning-Related Enjoyment ([38]; 5 items)	1–4
		$KIM_{interest/enjoyment}$ ([35]; 3 items)	3
Effort	Amount of time and resources learners invest in learning	Cognitive Load ([36]; 1 item)	2–4
		Learning time per module	1–4

---

[1] Due to the distribution of measures in the dataset, not all participants answered all questions.

[2] KIM (*"Kurzskala instrinsische Motivation"*) refers to a short scale for assessing intrinsic motivation.

5.3 Data Analysis

To analyze adult learners' SRL strategy application according to Sitzman and Ely's framework [11], we identified measures as follows: *Environmental structuring* refers to choosing a learning location that is free from distractions [11]. Based on this definition, we selected measures from the dataset that asked participants about their learning location and distractions. *Self-efficacy* was assessed using measures of learners' confidence in their competence, performance, and worry about completing the task. *Metacognitive strategies*, such as self-directed planning, were assessed according to how learners structured their learning. *Attention* was measured by mental effort and distractions. *Motivation* was measured by participants' enjoyment, its impact on work intensity, and interest of learning. *Effort* analysis included cognitive load items and learning time per unit compared to estimated time. The measures described in Table 2 were quantitatively analyzed, with scores for each strategy determined by calculating the averages of the corresponding measures. Before computing the averages, we checked for homogeneity of variance in the data, given that data were gathered over four course iterations. Our analysis revealed variance homogeneity for all measures.

5.4 Results

The analyses provided insights into which SRL strategies learners applied and where they experienced challenges. Table 3 provides an overview and a more detailed description of the different scales and the descriptive statistics of the measures.

Table 3. SRL Strategies and Descriptive Statistics of the Measures Extracted from the Dataset.

SRL Strategy	Measures from the dataset	Scale	M (SD)
Self-Efficacy	Subjective Comprehension	7-point Likert scale	5.68 (0.62)
	Recollection	1–100%	77.59 (11.61)
	Reproduction	1–100%	77.74 (12.60)
	Comprehension	1–100%	76.95 (13.93)
	$KIM_{pressure/tension}$	5-point Likert scale	2.48 (0.80)
	$KIM_{perceived\ competence}$	5-point Likert scale	3.48 (0.52)
Metacognitive Strategies	$KIM_{perceived\ choice}$	5-point Likert scale	4.32 (0.45)
Attention	Cognitive Load	7-point Likert scale	4.16 (0.86)
	Distractions: Loudness, Smartphone, TV	yes/no	–
Time Management	*See previous analysis* [37]		
Environmental Structuring	Location of learning	Workplace, at home	–
	Distractions: other adults	Frequency	9.50 (8.41)
	Distractions: family/work-related commitments	1 (never) – 7 (always)	2.50 (1.27)/2.57 (1.60)

(continued)

Table 3. (*continued*)

SRL Strategy	Measures from the dataset	Scale	M (SD)
Motivation	Learning-Related Enjoyment	7-point Likert scale	4.7 (0.99)
	$KIM_{interest/enjoyment}$	5-point Likert scale	3.81 (0.53)
Effort	Cognitive Load	7-point Likert scale	4.16 (0.86)
	Duration of learning time per module	in minutes	164.96 (126.97)

All three measures of *self-efficacy* indicate that learners trusted their recollection ($M = 77.59\%$), comprehension ($M = 76.95\%$), and reproduction ($M = 77.74\%$) of the learning content. Overall, learners were confident that they understood the content ($M = 5.68$), perceived themselves as competent ($M = 3.48$), and tended not to worry about their performance during the course ($M_{pressure/tension3} = 2.48$). These results indicate a high level of self-efficacy of learners during their learning process.

The self-paced format of the course required participants to self-direct their learning process by applying *metacognitive strategies*. The results show that participants worked on the units following their own plans and procedure ($M_{perceived\ choice} = 4.32$).

Responses to the cognitive load item demonstrate a high perceived cognitive load ($M = 4.16$), implying that participants were guiding their *attention* to the learning content. Nevertheless, 60% of the participants were distracted by their smartphones.

Participants mainly studied in the evenings (59%) and in their free time (98%). This points to challenges of integrating learning into working hours, as had been intended, and of applying *time management* strategies [37].

Regarding *environmental structuring*, the participants mainly learned at home. Measures of distractions reveal that learners were often distracted by other adults ($M = 9.50$ times). Furthermore, participants were "sometimes" distracted by family/work-related commitments ($M = 2.50/2.57$). In summary, adult learners had difficulties in structuring their learning environment to allow for focused learning.

The results suggest that participants enjoyed learning the units ($M = 4.7$). We further investigated the factors of fun, interest, and entertainment of the course. All three scales indicated that participants enjoyed learning and were interested in learning more ($M = 3.81$). In general, the data revealed a high *motivation* when learning the units.

The reported mental *effort* was high, with an average of $M = 4.16$. As participants' average learning time per unit matched the learning time that was predefined by the course coordinators, participants' investment in engaging with the learning content can be considered adequate.

5.5 Conclusion from Cycle 1

In conclusion, Cycle 1 of our research highlights the critical importance of effective *time management* for adult learners engaged in CET online courses. As learners often devote their evenings and scarce free time to learning, taking time away from personal relaxation and family, it is crucial to support learners to use their time as effectively and wisely as possible. It was further evident that learners struggled to integrate their learning with their multiple other work- and life-related responsibilities, highlighting the need for effective *effort regulation* and resource management. The challenges in creating a dedicated study space and managing distractions highlight the importance of *environmental structuring* and *attention regulation* strategies. Lastly, although not reflected in the dataset, existing research has highlighted the importance for adult learners of *setting* specific *learning goals*, particularly in relation to overcoming gaps in prerequisite knowledge. Our findings emphasize the need for adaptive support to help learners manage their learning process better, enabling them to maximize their learning outcomes without significant disruption to their personal lives. The findings provide a basis for addressing the specific challenges faced by adult learners in self-paced online learning environments and lay the groundwork for the design and implementation of adaptive support features.

6 Cycle 2: Enactment

Taking up the challenges identified in Cycle 1 and following the ILD framework, in Cycle 2, we conducted two design iterations with a design study in between. In the first design iteration (*initial intervention design*), we designed the support based on the findings from Cycle 1 and existing research. The second step of this cycle (*prototype articulation*) focused on piloting the design and functionality of the adaptive support intervention. This phase involved a small-scale survey and co-design sessions with participants of a CET online course. Building on the findings of this study, the second design iteration (*development of a revised design*) involved modifying the design and conducting a follow-up survey to validate our adjustments.

6.1 Step 1: Initial Intervention Design

To address the challenges identified in Cycle 1, we developed an adaptive SRL support intervention (Fig. 1) including the following three components:

1. A course overview to facilitate *environmental structuring* and *attention regulation*.
2. An adaptive learning-time display to facilitate *time management* and *effort regulation*.
3. An adaptive highlighting of recommended content to facilitate *setting learning goals*[3] and *attention regulation*.

The support intervention was designed in accordance with the design requirements [28] and with existing adaptive SRL support features documented in the literature described in Sect. 2.2. Based on insights concerning individualized visualizations [8], the first feature, (1) the course overview (Fig. 1), presents all course content in a table view. The table is structured into thematically grouped modules and subdivided into separate columns by the pictorial display of the media format of the content. The overview aims to promote *environmental structuring* by providing an organized overview of the course content. By means of visually highlighted modules and progress bars, learners

---

[3] Although our analysis did not reveal evidence for *goal setting*, it is important to note that research on the challenges faced by adult online learners identifies goal setting as a significant barrier. To address this, we incorporated goal setting support into our adaptive intervention.

	Individual Learning-Time	Overall Learning Goals	Quiz	Videos	Exercises & Solutions	Fact & Info Sheets	Quiz	Learning Diaries
Introduction	10 Min.	Learning Goals Introduction	SRL Pre-Survey	Introduction video				
Module 1	1h 10 Min.	Learning Goals Module 1	Pre-Quiz 1	Video 1 (~3min.) Video 2 (~10min.)	Task 1 Solution Task 1	Fact & Info Sheet 1	Quiz 1	Learning Diary 1
Module 2	1h 50 Min.	Learning Goals Module 2	Pre-Quiz 2	Video 3 (~15min.) Video 4 (~18min.)	Task 2 Solution Task 2	Fact & Info Sheet 2	Quiz 2	Learning Diary 2
Module 3	3h 30 Min.	Learning Goals Module 3	Pre-Quiz 3	★Video 5 (~8min.) Video 6 (~15min.) ★Video 7 (~10min.) Video 8 (~5min.)	★Task 3 ★Solution Task 3 Task 4 Solution Task 4	Fact & Info Sheet 3 Fact & Info Sheet 4	Quiz 3	Learning Diary 3
Module 4	7h	Learning Goals Module 4	Pre-Quiz 4	Video 9 (~5min.) ★Video 10 (~8min.) ★Video 11 (15min.) ★Video 12 (~10min.) Video 13 (~15min.)	Task 5 Solution Task 5 Task 6 Solution Task 6 ★Task 7 ★Solution Task 7	Fact & Info Sheet 5 Fact & Info Sheet 6 Fact & Info Sheet 7	★Quiz 4	Learning Diary 4
Quiz Module 1	40 Min.						Check Quiz 1 Check Quiz 2 ★Check Quiz 3	

(left annotation: Adaptive learning-time display; callout in table: Adaptive highlighting of recommended content)

Fig. 1. Initial design of the adaptive support intervention.

can monitor and structure their learning progress. In addition, the overview helps learners to manage their *attention* more effectively by providing a clear outline of the learning material, allowing them to navigate and focus on specific modules or topics.

Based on the insights from personalized scaffolding through planning tools [27], the second feature, (2) the adaptive learning-time display (see second column of the overview in Fig. 1), aims to support learners' *time management* by providing an indication of the time required for each module, allowing them to plan and allocate their study time more effectively, and thus also supporting *effort regulation*.

Third, based on research on adaptive scaffolding for learning goals [25], we developed (3) a highlighting of recommended content (see star highlights in Fig. 1) to support learners' *goal setting*, by drawing attention to specific learning material that is considered as individually relevant. This further supports *attention regulation* by directing learners' focus to relevant material and increasing focus on goals.

Features (2) and (3) were adapted to learners' individual prerequisites. We embedded both features in the overview (1), as seen in Fig. 1. The adaptability of features (2) and (3) was achieved through a scoring system that categorized learners into risk groups based on data collected from previous course iterations. The variable of learning time per module revealed a range from approximately 20% less to 20% more time than the average learning time defined by the course organizers. Longer learning time was associated with limited prior knowledge and less familiarity with online learning, while faster learners tended to have more prior knowledge and online learning experience. Based on the learners' results on a pre-questionnaire assessing these variables (i.e., prior knowledge, online learning experience, professional background, project management experience, and self-directed learning experience), we divided learners into three risk groups: a high-risk group (i.e., limited prior experience of online and self-directed learning, jobs unrelated to the course topics, and minimal prior knowledge), an average group (i.e., average scores on the above variables), and a low-risk group (i.e., high scores, indicating substantial prior experience and knowledge). This initial design of the adaptive support provided a robust platform from which to refine and evaluate actual users' perception of the adaptive support intervention in further iterations.

6.2 Step 2: Prototype Articulation

Participants. Learners' perception of the initial design of the adaptive support was explored with 14 adult learners of the third iteration of the CET program. All participants completed a survey and 12 participants additionally joined co-design sessions.

Procedure. The participatory design study encompassed five Zoom sessions, each lasting between 90 and 120 min. First, participants were asked to complete an online survey that included closed-ended questions in which they rated the design drafts of the adaptive elements (e.g. Figs. 2 and 3).

Fig. 2. Design drafts of the adaptive learning-time display.

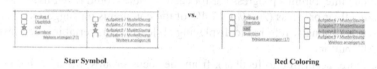

Fig. 3. Design drafts of the adaptive highlighting of recommended content.

Additionally, participants were asked about their need for further explanation of the features, choosing between an explanatory pop-up, an explanatory box that needs to be actively opened, or the option "no explanation necessary". While completing the survey, participants did not receive detailed information about the support features, as we aimed to determine which presentation of the adaptive features was clearer to participants without any further explanation of the elements.

After completing the survey, during co-design sessions, participants were asked to comment on and annotate different design options through notes on an interactive whiteboard. The whiteboard displayed different design drafts, and participants placed cards to make annotations about what they liked and disliked about the designs. They were encouraged to make notes on elements for which they suggested changes, followed by a facilitated focus group discussion that began by reviewing the notes. If elements were criticized, participants were asked how they could be changed. After reviewing the designs, we evaluated the functionality of the support features with the participants. The focus group sessions were documented by note-taking.

Data Analysis. The survey data were analyzed quantitatively, and the focus group were analyzed using qualitative content analysis through inductive category development [39]. We structured the data according to the questions asked during the discussions, i.e., comments on the overall design appearance and the assistance necessary to understand the support. Two raters coded the data independently, discussed their ratings, and clarified any disagreements.[4] The coding was performed using MAXQDA[5].

Results. The survey and co-design session data revealed that all participants preferred the learning time to be displayed in a separate column (see first option in Fig. 2). Concerning the adaptive highlighting of recommended content, most participants preferred the star symbol (see first option in Fig. 3). Regarding the form of assistance, participants showed a positive attitude toward the explanatory box, while the pop-up explanation was frequently criticized (37.6%). For instance, one focus group participant criticized that "the explanation is not available permanently".

Additionally, the qualitative analysis yielded implications regarding the functionality of the adaptive support: Participants rated the overview as helpful for organizing the material (21.3%) and simplifying the navigation (11.5%), but criticized its complexity (19.7%) and suggested, for instance, differentiating the modules by colors. Furthermore, they noted that integrating a progress bar for each module would foster their motivation by visualizing their progress (26.1%). 17.4% of the comments on suggested changes to the overview additionally referred to displaying all learning material in a cell instead of a "Show All" button.

Furthermore, according to feedback from the focus groups, the adaptive learning-time display might increase pressure (14.6%), with one participant mentioning: "It is demotivating when you need three times as long (as indicated)". However, participants noted that they would use the recommendation for planning their study time (37.5%), with one participant stating that "the learning time for each module definitely helps with time management". Participants additionally suggested adding a total score for each online self-study phase to plan the learning more efficiently (30%). Participants appreciated the adaptive highlighting of recommended content, although the focus groups indicated that there is a risk of only looking at highlighted content (24%). For instance, one participant stated: "It could happen that–if there's time pressure–you only look at the highlighted stuff".

6.3 Step 3: Development of a Revised Design

Based on the results of Step 2, we modified the design as presented in Fig. 4:

---

[4] The intercoder reliability Kappa indicated an almost perfect agreement for all five groups (1: $K = 0.87$; 2: $K = 0.89$, 3: $K = 0.84$, 4: $K = 0.95$, 5: $K = 0.95$).

[5] https://www.maxqda.com/de/.

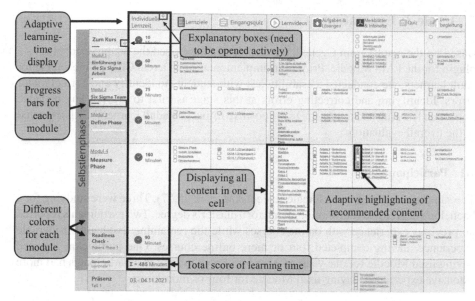

Fig. 4. New design of the adaptive support intervention.

We changed the overview by differentiating the modules by colors to reduce complexity, added a progress bar to visualize the learning progress for each module, and displayed all learning materials in the cells instead of a "Show All" button, thus revealing at a glance that some modules are more extensive than others. Concerning the learning time, we integrated a total score. Finally, we implemented (a) the adaptive learning-time display in a separate column, (b) the adaptive highlighting of recommended content with a star symbol, and (c) explained the elements through explanatory boxes.

Subsequently, we conducted a follow-up survey to evaluate our changes, comparing the old design version (Fig. 1) with the new design (Fig. 4). Six of the 14 participants completed the follow-up survey, of whom five rated the new design as an improvement.

6.4 Conclusion from Cycle 2

In summary, the participatory design study provided insights into graphical interface preferences, suggesting potential refinements to reduce complexity, and revealed positive feedback on the adaptive learning-time display and highlighting of recommended content. However, the need for additional explanation underlined the importance of a user-friendly design. It is important to address this need because adaptive support features are intended to facilitate SRL without requiring additional effort to understand them. Based on these findings, we refined the adaptive support, ensuring alignment with learners' perceptions and needs. Overall, in Cycle 2, we developed adaptive support tailored to the needs and challenges of CET online courses for adult learners. The iterative nature of this cycle allowed for continuous improvement based on user feedback, ensuring that the intervention was closely aligned with learners' perceptions.

7 Cycle 3: Evaluation

Based on the results from Cycle 2, we technically developed the adaptive support as a plugin for the LMS Moodle. Prior to its implementation in a real CET online course for adult learners, we conducted a usability test with students to identify and correct major errors. Identifying and correcting errors at this stage is vital to prevent any negative impact on learning and to maximize the positive impact on adult learners' SRL expected in the overall evaluation.

7.1 Participants

The sample comprised seven female students ($M_{age} = 25.57$). Three were studying for a bachelor's degree and four were studying for a master's degree. Two participants reported no previous experience with online courses while the remaining five had considerable experience, having completed four or more online courses. One participant reported having used Moodle for one year, another for two years, and five participants had more extensive experience, having used Moodle for four or more years.

7.2 Procedure

To evaluate the technical functionality of the support, we provided the students with comprehensive scripts containing detailed instructions for assessing specific features, such as verifying the correct display of progress bars in the interface, confirming the correct ticking of checkboxes upon completion, and validating the accuracy of the adaptive learning-time display and the adaptive content highlighting. The scripts also included a link to a questionnaire to assess participants' feedback on the usability of the support intervention across a range of scales, which are discussed in the next section.

7.3 Dataset and Data Analysis

The dataset encompassed demographic variables, including age, educational background, and prior experience with online learning and Moodle. Technical variables such as the device, screen size, browser, and the technical functionality of the features were also assessed. Participants responded to items (Table 4) adapted from the SUS [33] and the TAM [34, 40–42]. The TAM measures the *perceived ease of use, perceived usefulness*, and *intention to use* a technology. *Perceived ease of use* refers to users' belief that interacting with the technology will be effortless, while *perceived usefulness* refers to users' belief that the technology will improve their performance.

Quantitative data analysis was conducted using descriptive statistics to provide an overview of participants' demographics, technical setup, and responses to the Likert scales. Additionally, we calculated the SUS score [33], which was used to interpret the overall usability of the system, with higher scores indicating better usability.

Table 4. Scales employed in the usability testing.

Scale	Example Item
System Usability Scale	"I think that I would need the support of a technical person to be able to use this system." [33]
Ease of Use (5 items)	"I think using the course overview is easy" [40]
Usefulness (5 items)	"Using the course overview would improve my performance in the online course" [40]
Behavioral Intention to use (1 item)	"Assuming I had a course with such a course overview, I would intend to use it" [40]

Table 5. Means and standard deviations for the scales from the usability testing.

Scale	α	M	SD
System Usability Scale (Likert scale 1–5; 1–100%)	.73	4.2/80	0.39/9.68
Ease of Use (Likert scale 1–7)	.94	5.83	0.93
Usefulness (Likert scale 1–7)	.66	6.03	0.63
Behavioral Intention to use (Likert scale 1–7)	–	6.57	0.54

7.4 Results

The usability testing revealed high ratings for all measures, as summarized in Table 5.

The *SUS* indicated a favorable perception of the usability based on the Likert scale mean and an average usability rating of 80%. Participants rated the *ease of use* at $M = 5.83$, indicating a high level of perceived ease of use. Similarly, participants' rating of *usefulness* ($M = 6.03$) suggested that they perceived the intervention to be highly useful. Furthermore, participants expressed a strong *behavioral intention to use* the system.

7.5 Conclusion from Cycle 3

The positive findings of the usability testing suggest a favorable perception and high acceptance of the support among student participants, underlining its potential effectiveness and usability in supporting SRL in CET online courses. Although the survey scales indicated a favorable usability of the support, specific questions about basic functions and the look and feel of the interface indicated factors requiring adjustment for a seamless integration into the Moodle interface. The usability testing in Cycle 3 led to the integration of the following design (Fig. 5).

Further testing of the usability with actual adult learners is needed to ensure the generalizability of the positive results observed with students. We plan to conduct a study to explore the impact of the support on adult learners' use of SRL strategies, and ultimately provide insights into the field of adaptive SRL support in adult online education.

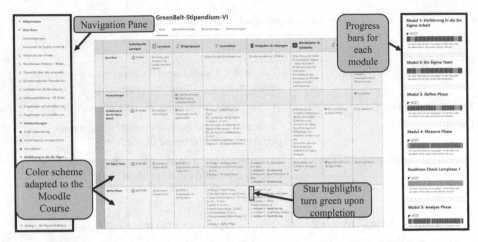

Fig. 5. Current design of the adaptive support intervention integrated into the Moodle course.

8 Overall Discussion and Conclusion

Following a DBR process comprising three cycles, we developed a design for adaptive features to support adult learners' application of particular SRL strategies in online courses. In Cycle 1, we focused on investigating adult learners' main challenges, revealing significant difficulties in structuring their learning environment and managing learning time. The focus of our work addresses a noticeable gap in understanding how adult learners, with their diverse and complex responsibilities, navigate SRL in online courses and how they might be supported [13–17]. Our contribution to the research in this area is twofold. First, our findings confirm the proposition that managing conflicting responsibilities, particularly in balancing work and learning commitments, is a significant challenge in this group of learners [19], underlining the importance of time management, as already pointed out by Jo et al. [5]. Additionally, our study identified challenges in applying strategies to help organize the learning environment and manage attention. By identifying such challenges, our findings not only reflect the difficulties outlined in the literature, but also point at a need for specific support to help learners manage their learning time efficiently, among other responsibilities and distractions.

Second, our work addresses the lack of research on the design of SRL support for CET online courses. By introducing a design for adaptive support tailored to the specific needs of adult learners in this specific context, we advance the discourse on adaptive SRL support. This adaptive support, iteratively designed in Cycle 2 Enactment, aimed at enhancing SRL strategies that we had identified as critical for adult learners in Cycle 1, including: time management, effort, attention, environmental structuring, and goal setting [11]. The developed support includes a course overview for better environmental structuring, an adaptive learning-time display for improved time management and effort regulation, and adaptive highlighting of recommended content to promote goal setting and attention regulation. Table 6 summarizes the features of the support tool.

In designing the support features outlined in the table above, we adopted a two-step approach: First, our support features were designed based on design requirements [28]

Table 6. Features of the adaptive support intervention under development

	Course overview	Adaptive learning-time display	Adaptive highlighting of recommended content
Purpose	Provides a comprehensive overview of the entire course structure and all course content	To help learners manage their study time effectively	Facilitates prioritization of relevant content by scaffolding individual learning goals
SRL strategies	Environmental structuring, Attention regulation	Time management, Effort regulation	Goal setting, Attention regulation
Functionality	Integrates pictorial displays of the media format as well as two adaptive features	Integrates individualized study time information for each module within the course	Highlights specific content deemed essential for learners based on adaptive criteria
Potential benefits	Improves organization and navigation, providing a holistic view of modules and highlighting content	Aids in planning study sessions, allowing learners to allocate time efficiently	Guides learners to focus on essential material, supporting their self-directed learning
Feedback mechanism	Visual elements, such as progress bars and color-coded modules, help learners understand their learning journey	Provides insight into the time required for each module, enabling learners to measure their progress and manage their time	Provides visual cues to draw attention to specific content, helping learners to identify and engage with key learning material

derived from the literature and insights into adaptive designs [8, 25–27], as described in Sect. 2.2. We designed our tool as a Moodle plugin to ensure compatibility across different courses within the Moodle LMS, effectively addressing the need for cross-course support. Our approach emphasizes support for specific SRL strategies relevant to adult learners, extending beyond course boundaries to include planning activities such as scheduling study activities in external calendars. The system's visual feedback mechanism, such as marking completed content, facilitates a basic form of self-monitoring, although it is not highly interactive. In addition, despite the lack of comprehensive comparison criteria, the tool supports goal setting through individual content highlighting and progress tracking.

Second, we integrated adult learners' feedback from a user study into the design process. Together with the underlying research and design requirements, this ensured that our adaptive support is both theoretically grounded and closely aligned with the real-world needs and preferences of the target group. This participatory approach underlines our commitment to developing interventions that are both research-based and learner-centered, providing valuable insights into how such support is perceived by adult learners and confirming its potential to enhance their learning experience. Finally, usability testing conducted in Cycle 3 Evaluation showed positive results regarding the support's ease of use, usefulness, and overall usability, confirming the potential effectiveness of our intervention. To conclude, our findings provide new perspectives on the design of adaptive support in CET settings, thereby enriching the understanding of how such support can be effectively tailored to meet the specific needs of this learner population.

However, certain limitations of the present research need to be acknowledged. First, although the ability to analyze a large dataset in Cycle 1 was advantageous, not all participants completed every survey iteration, which may have biased the data, although our findings are consistent with existing research on adult SRL [5, 19]. Moreover, our analyses were limited to an existing dataset. The process of matching the measures from the dataset to SRL strategies does not guarantee that our measures fully represent every aspect of the respective strategy. Future research should therefore investigate whether our results can be further consolidated when implementing pre-established SRL instruments. Second, as the study in Cycle 2 was conducted with a specific sample of adult learners attending a specific CET course, we may have overlooked the diverse learning preferences and needs of a broader population. Further research on this topic should consider other courses and different samples of adult learners. Finally, in Cycle 3, we assumed that learners had high technological literacy, as we conducted the usability testing with students. Differences in adult learners' familiarity with online learning platforms may affect how they perceive the system's usability.

In conclusion, our research brings new insights for the design of adaptive SRL support tools specifically designed for adult learners in CET online courses. Our study contributes to the research gaps outlined above by providing empirical evidence on the unique SRL challenges faced in this context. Moreover, our study presents an approach to designing adaptive SRL support tailored to the specific needs of adult learners. This contribution enriches the current understanding of SRL and adaptive support by providing a practical framework for designing support systems that specifically address the learning needs of adult learners, and demonstrates how adaptive mechanisms can be effectively integrated into educational platforms to enhance adult learners' SRL. Furthermore, by focusing on the customization of learning based on individual learner profiles, our research sheds light on the potential of personalized education to significantly improve the overall learning experience. This not only broadens the theoretical basis of SRL and adaptive learning, but also provides actionable insights for educators seeking to implement such support in educational contexts. Our work provides a basis for future research to assess the impact of such interventions on learners' SRL skills and to examine their lasting effects on academic achievement. Future studies should continue working closely with educators and learners to ensure that tools remain relevant and effective in the ever-changing educational environment, fostering a learner-centered approach that supports the complex journey of adult learners in self-regulating their learning.

Acknowledgments. This work was funded by the Federal Ministry of Education and Research (BMBF) under Grant Number 01JD1907A. We would like to express our special thanks to the team of lean2sigma GmbH and the Academy of the Ruhr University, especially Dr. Markus Maier and Dr. Yves Gensterblum, for their valued support in organizing the CET program. Lastly, we would like to acknowledge the significant contribution of Dr. Anna Keune in the initial idea and design of the adaptive support intervention.

References

1. Kizilcec, R.F., Pérez-Sanagustín, M., Maldonado, J.J.: Self-regulated learning strategies predict learner behavior and goal attainment in massive open online courses. Comput. Educ. **104**, 18–33 (2017). https://doi.org/10.1016/j.compedu.2016.10.001
2. Littlejohn, A., Hood, N., Milligan, C., Mustain, P.: Learning in MOOCs: motivations and self-regulated learning in MOOCs. Internet High. Educ. **29**, 40–48 (2016)
3. Zimmerman, B.J.: A social cognitive view of self-regulated academic learning. J. Educ. Psychol. **81**(3), 329–339 (1989). https://doi.org/10.1037/0022-0663.81.3.329
4. Panadero, E.: A review of self-regulated learning: Six models and four directions for research. Front. Psychol. **8**, 422 (2017). https://doi.org/10.3389/fpsyg.2017.00422
5. Jo, I.H., Kim, D., Yoon, M.: Constructing proxy variables to measure adult learners' time management strategies in LMS. J. Educ. Technol. Soc. **18**(3), 214–225 (2015). https://www.jstor.org/stable/jeductechsoci.18.3.214
6. BMBF - Bundesministerium für Bildung und Forschung: Weiterbildungsverhalten in Deutschland 2020. Ergebnisse des Adult Education Survey - AES-Trendbericht. Berlin: BMBF (2022)
7. Aleven, V., McLaughlin, E.A., Glenn, R.A., Koedinger, K.R.: Instruction based on adaptive learning technologies. Handb. Res. Learn. Instr. **2**, 522–560 (2016)
8. Molenaar, I., Horvers, A., Dijkstra, R., Baker, R.S.: Personalized visualizations to promote young learners' SRL: the learning path app. In: Proceedings of the Tenth International Conference on Learning Analytics & Knowledge, pp. 330–339 (2020). https://doi.org/10.1145/3375462.3375465
9. Azevedo, R., Cromley, J.G., Winters, F.I., Moos, D.C., Greene, J.A.: Adaptive human scaffolding facilitates adolescents' self-regulated learning with hypermedia. Instr. Sci. **33**, 381–412 (2005)
10. Wong, J., Baars, M., Davis, D., Van Der Zee, T., Houben, G.J., Paas, F.: Supporting self-regulated learning in online learning environments and MOOCs: a systematic review. Int. J. Hum. Comput. Interact. **35**(4–5), 356–373 (2019)
11. Sitzmann, T., Ely, K.: A meta-analysis of self-regulated learning in work-related training and educational attainment: what we know and where we need to go. Psychol. Bull. **137**(3), 421–442 (2011). https://doi.org/10.1037/a0022777
12. Zimmerman, B.J.: Self-regulated learning and academic achievement: an overview. Educ. Psychol. **25**(1), 3–17 (1990). https://doi.org/10.1207/s15326985ep2501_2
13. Jossberger, H., Brand-Gruwel, S., van de Wiel, M.W., Boshuizen, H.: Exploring students' self-regulated learning in vocational education and training. Vocat. Learn. **13**(1), 131–158 (2020)
14. Schulz, M., Roßnagel, C.S.: Informal workplace learning: an exploration of age differences in learning competence. Learn. Instr. **20**(5), 383–399 (2010). https://doi.org/10.1016/j.learnstruc.2009.03.003
15. Fontana, R.P., Milligan, C., Littlejohn, A., Margaryan, A.: Measuring self-regulated learning in the workplace. Int. J. Train. Dev. **19**(1), 32–52 (2015). https://doi.org/10.1111/ijtd.12046

16. Cuyvers, K., Van den Bossche, P., Donche, V.: Self-regulation of professional learning in the workplace: a state of the art and future perspectives. Vocat. Learn. **13**, 281–312 (2020). https://doi.org/10.1007/s12186-019-09236-x

17. Tsai, C.W., Shen, P.D., Fan, Y.T.: Research trends in self-regulated learning research in online learning environments: a review of studies published in selected journals from 2003 to 2012. Br. J. Edu. Technol. **44**(5), 107–110 (2013). https://doi.org/10.1111/bjet.12017

18. Broadbent, J., Poon, W.L.: Self-regulated learning strategies & academic achievement in online higher education learning environments: a systematic review. Internet High. Educ. **27**, 1–13 (2015)

19. Kara, M., Erdogdu, F., Kokoç, M., Cagiltay, K.: Challenges faced by adult learners in online distance education: a literature review. Open Praxis **11**(1), 5–22 (2019). https://doi.org/10.5944/openpraxis.11.1.929

20. Frey, B.A., Alman, S.W.: Applying adult learning theory to the online classroom. New Horiz. Adult Educ. Hum. Resour. Dev. **17**(1), 4–12 (2003). https://doi.org/10.1002/nha3.10155

21. Loock, V.S., Fleischer, J., Scheunemann, A., Froese, L., Teich, K., Wirth, J.: Narrowing down dimensions of e-learning readiness in continuing vocational education—perspectives from the adult learner. Front. Psychol. **13**, 1033524 (2022). https://doi.org/10.3389/fpsyg.2022.1033524

22. Pedrotti, M., Nistor, N.: How students fail to self-regulate their online learning experience. In: Scheffel, M., Broisin, J., Pammer-Schindler, V., Ioannou, A., Schneider, J. (eds.) Transforming Learning with Meaningful Technologies: 14th European Conference on Technology Enhanced Learning, EC-TEL 2019, Delft, The Netherlands, September 16–19, 2019, Proceedings, pp. 377–385. Springer International Publishing, Cham (2019). https://doi.org/10.1007/978-3-030-29736-7_28

23. Milligan, C., Fontana, R.P., Littlejohn, A., Margaryan, A.: Self-regulated learning behaviour in the finance industry. J. Work. Learn. **27**(5), 387–402 (2015)

24. Dignath, C., Buettner, G., Langfeldt, H.P.: How can primary school students learn self-regulated learning strategies most effectively?: a meta-analysis on self-regulation training programmes. Educ. Res. Rev. **3**(2), 101–129 (2008)

25. Azevedo, R., Cromley, J.G., Moos, D.C., Greene, J.A., Winters, F.I.: Adaptive content and process scaffolding: a key to facilitating students' self-regulated learning with hypermedia. Psychol. Test Assess. Model. **53**(1), 106 (2011)

26. Molenaar, I., Horvers, A., Dijkstra, R.: Young learners' regulation of practice behavior in adaptive learning technologies. Front. Psychol. **10**, 2792 (2019)

27. Davis, D., Triglianos, V., Hauff, C., Houben, G.J.: SRLx: a personalized learner interface for MOOCs. In: Pammer-Schindler, V., Pérez-Sanagustín, M., Drachsler, H., Elferink, R., Scheffel, M. (eds.) EC-TEL 2018. LNCS, vol. 11082, pp. 122–135. Springer, Cham (2018). https://doi.org/10.1007/978-3-319-98572-5_10

28. Pérez-Álvarez, R., Maldonado-Mahauad, J., Pérez-Sanagustín, M.: Design of a tool to support self-regulated learning strategies in MOOCs. J. Univ. Comput. Sci. **24**(8), 1090–1109 (2018)

29. Collins, A., Joseph, D., Bielaczyc, K.: Design research: theoretical and methodological issues. J. Learn. Sci. **13**(1), 15–42 (2004). https://doi.org/10.1207/s15327809jls1301_2

30. McKenney, S., Reeves, T.C.: Conducting Educational Design Research. Routledge, New York: Routledge (2018). https://doi.org/10.4324/9781315105642

31. Sandoval, W.A.: Educational design research in the 21st century. In: Luckin, R., Puntambekar, S., Goodyear, P., Grabowski, B.L., Underwood, J., Winters, N. (eds.) Handbook of Design in Educational Technology, pp. 388–396. Routledge (2013).

32. Bannan-Ritland, B.: The role of design in research: the integrative learning design framework. Educ. Res. **32**(1), 21–24 (2003). https://doi.org/10.3102/0013189X032001021

33. Brooke, J.: SUS: a "quick and dirty" usability scale. Usability Eval. Ind. **189**, 4–7 (1996)

34. Davis, F.D.: Perceived usefulness, perceived ease of use, and user acceptance of information technology. MIS Q. **13**(3), 319–340 (1989). https://doi.org/10.2307/249008

35. Wilde, M., Bätz, K., Kovaleva, A., Urhahne, D.: Überprüfung einer Kurzskala intrinsischer Motivation (KIM) [Review of a short scale of intrinsic motivation (KIM)]. Zeitschrift für Didaktik der Naturwissenschaften **15**, 31–45 (2009)

36. Klepsch, M., Schmitz, F., Seufert, T.: Development and validation of two instruments measuring intrinsic, extraneous, and germane cognitive load. Front. Psychol. **8**, 1997 (2017)

37. Teich, K., Froese, L., Loock, V., Rummel, N.: Self-regulated learning in online continuing education: managing learning time is a key challenge. In: Proceedings of the 17th International Conference of the Learning Sciences-ICLS 2023, pp. 1863–1864 (2023)

38. Pekrun, R., Goetz, T., Perry, R.P.: Academic Emotions Questionnaire (AEQ)—User's Manual. Department of Psychology, University of Munich, Munich, Germany (2005)

39. Mayring, P.: Qualitative content analysis: theoretical foundation, basic procedures and software solution. Klagenfurt (2014). https://nbn-resolving.org/urn:nbn:de:0168-ssoar-395173

40. Wu, J.H., Wang, S.C.: What drives mobile commerce?: an empirical evaluation of the revised technology acceptance model. Inf. Manage. **42**(5), 719–729 (2005)

41. Park, S.Y.: An analysis of the technology acceptance model in understanding university students' behavioral intention to use e-learning. Educ. Technol. Soc. **12**(3), 150–162 (2009)

42. van der Heijden, H.: User acceptance of hedonic information systems. MIS Q. **28**(4), 695–704 (2004). https://doi.org/10.2307/25148660

How to Design Features for Promoting Social and Emotional Interactions During Computer Supported Collaborative Learning

Mariano Velamazán[(✉)] [iD], Patricia Santos [iD], and Davinia Hernández Leo [iD]

Pompeu Fabra University, 08544 Barcelona, NJ, Spain
mariano.velamazan01@estudiant.upf.edu

Abstract. Promoting social presence, social interactions and group regulation is one of the most recent and active research lines in Computer Supported Collaborative Learning (CSCL). Students who engage in CSCL tasks often encounter socio-emotional challenges that are not well addressed. These challenges are more likely to arise when teachers are not monitoring the process. The goal of our study is to develop, implement and evaluate a prototype of a communication tool (called *me&co*) that provides UX/UI features to help teenage students deal with these challenges and maintain a productive atmosphere in their groups. Specifically, this paper addresses two gaps that are underexplored in the literature: 1) The regulation of learning in CSCL has mostly been examined in specific, research-defined moments: i.e., before, during or after collaboration. Therefore, we provide insights on how our prototype is used throughout the whole process of collaboration respecting its natural flow. 2) The regulation of learning has been investigated only in formal settings but we tested the prototype in situations where the teacher is not supervising the activity.

We adopt a Design Based Research (DBR) approach and, after examining previous CSCL tools that aimed at enhancing social and emotional awareness, we describe our design choices and the features implemented in our prototype. Then, we report the outcomes of two iterations of testing and redesigning. To assess the prototype, students ($> = 15$ years old, n1 = 42, n2 = 64) completed a survey about their experience with the features, doing real tasks for homework in small groups.

The results show that students think the most useful features are the anonymous messages, the avatar selection and the visual messages composer. Students claim that when they already know each other quite well from class these features are not really necessary. In contrast, they report the features and affordances provided are useful and should be maintained for other users (who do not know each other previously). We propose several further research options to contribute with knowledge about how to design tools to support the emotional side of CSCL that inspires students to change their learning behavior.

Keywords: Socio-emotional regulation · group chat · social affordances

P. Zaphiris and A. Ioannou (Eds.): HCII 2024, LNCS 14722, pp. 124–144, 2024.
https://doi.org/10.1007/978-3-031-61672-3_9

1 Introduction

As previous research has shown, the challenges that students may face during collaboration can be mainly categorized as: cognitive, motivational and socio-emotional [1, 2]. Most of the studies within the realm of Computer Supported Collaborative Learning (CSCL) primarily center on the examination of cognitive challenges inherent in collaborative endeavors. However, it is imperative to underscore the notable gap in research that delves into the nuanced dynamics of how emotional, social, and motivational factors contribute to and shape specific challenges encountered during collaborative learning activities. Such challenges during collaboration appear more easily when teachers are not supervising the process and, in order to face them, students first need to be aware (and secondly learn) how to deal with these kinds of issues. Gilbert and Moore [3] and Isohätala et al. and Kreijns [2, 4] use the term social interaction for the socio-emotional and affective exchanges between learners in the task context.

The theory of the Social Regulation of Learning [5] has described three modes and three phases of regulation in collaborative learning [5, 6]. The modes are self-regulation, co-regulation (a student helps another student) and socially-shared regulation (that refers to the regulation of the group as such). The phases are planning, monitoring and reflection. In this paper we focus on the co- and socially-shared regulation modes and on the least studied monitoring phase. This theory tries to describe the interactions between the cognitive, the motivational and the social and emotional. In this paper we are focusing on the motivational and socio-emotional which are the least studied [7]. Pintrich [8] pointed out that some teachers expect students to learn regulation skills by just putting them to work together but regulation is difficult and must be learned [9]. Without the successful regulation of emotions, the cognitive side of learning can be ineffective [10, 11]. But in many cases students do not neither recognize nor activate any kind of control or regulation over these affective aspects since being aware of them requires learning and experience [12, 13]. Thus, a primary need is to be aware of them and this is the first goal of the tool that we have designed, tested and presented in this paper.

In this paper our goal is to design and prototype features with social and hedonic affordances. Then, collect data about what features are positively rated by students, their use and experience of it and if they find those features useful filling up the gaps found in existing tools concerning social interactions of group conversations and collaboration. We believe that these features would improve if their design was approached from a DBR perspective [14].

2 Theoretical Background

In this section we present the different theories and research that we have used to design the *me&co* prototype.

Socio-Emotional Challenges. Refer to differences in participation (i.e. free riders), personalities and identities (i.e. low self-esteem, low esteem of someone else in the group), different interest in the topic [15] or communication [9, 16]. Motivational challenges can occur when members have different goals, different self-efficacy perceptions and different interests. These challenges should trigger the need to regulate socio-emotional aspects of collaboration [17, 18]. Researchers have found that if challenges are to be recognized, members need to be aware of their own and others socio-emotional states [6].

Social Presence. Theory [19] explains communication media according to their potential to make "the other" present through socio-emotional cues. Social cohesion refers to the nature and quality of the emotional bonds of friendship such as liking, caring, and closeness among group members [20]. Shared identity may act as a stimulus to instigate the action of contributing information to an online chat. People may more readily contribute information under conditions where shared group identification is salient [21]. Avatars' representation liberates users from feeling exposed. It has been studied how it affects the behavior of users in video games and social media [22]. The effect of avatars in classroom contexts has been also studied [23, 24] but not in informal and outside school settings as a collaboration facilitator [25].

Sharing Emotions. Is one of the possibilities of face-to-face communication that technology mediated conversations lack and previous research has reported to improve regulation [26, 27]. Emojis appeared as a way to overcome this disadvantage. But there are no emojis for emotions during collaborative learning: researchers have described three categories of emotions during learning: social, epistemic and achievement emotions [28]. Emotion regulation is important for reducing negative responses and atmosphere in the group. Emotional valence is a measure of the positive or negative value that members perceive from the emotion. Low envy is perceived as good but low enjoyment is perceived as bad [29, 30].

Finally, Zschocke and colleagues [31] researched **appraisals and motivation** in group work context; the conclusion was that positive appraisals of the cognitive side is a significant factor for the activation of positive emotions. Positive socio-emotional interactions foster positive emotions [32]. In turn, negative socio-emotional interactions can provoke negative emotions [15] and this can lead to off-task behavior and disengagement of joint learning collaboration [33].

2.1 CSCL and the Socio-Emotional Side of Learning

Kreijns and colleagues [2] took social presence theory as a starting point in order to identify the pitfalls for social interactions in CSCL and offered a model that included cognitive and socio-emotional processes. Later, they provided a framework for designing CSCL environments based upon technological, educational and social affordances [34]. A CSCL environment has certain features that enable and support social interaction among learners. These features are called social affordances, and they are related to the social and contextual aspects of the learning situation.

Technology has changed and improved since then and their model was updated [35, 36] to include concepts like educability and hedonicity. Hedonicity, the concept we use in this paper, expresses the degree of enjoyment and positive experience that (online) collaborative learning tools provide. With this concept, they posit that the influence of the games and putting a fun spin on interaction will result in learning that is not only effective but also something to be enjoyed.

2.2 Existing CSCL Tools for the Socio-Emotional Side of Learning

The concepts and models previously discussed have been widely utilized by numerous researchers since their publication. To begin with, Kirschner et al. implemented a widget for group awareness [34]. Miller and Hadwin [37] introduced an important distinction between scripting and awareness tools. Awareness tools are supposed to be less invasive and can help students detect the challenges they face. Our work focuses on group awareness tools because there are less existing tools of this kind. Other scholars, following the theory of regulation of learning, have also got inspiration from the findings presented above [4, 38, 39]. We have already reviewed most of these tools in a previous study [40]. As indicated, these tools tested socio-emotional aspects of collaboration in specific moments (before, after or in the middle of collaboration) or modes (self-, co- or socially-shared), not during the natural flow of collaboration. Moreover, since they did not apply a DBR methodology they did not integrate students in the process of design and did not find it necessary to get the opinion of students or to test if they found them useful. Now, we will offer here a brief overview of the main limitations of each tool (Table 1).

Table 1. Overview of tested theoretical constructs by previous research tools

Tool	Phase	Self-regulation	Co-regulation	Socially-shared regulation	Social identity/ presence	Self (re-) presentation
SEST	Evaluation	yes	no	no	no	no
Radar	Planning, evaluation	yes	no	yes	no	no
S-Reg	Monitoring (but interrupting collaboration)	no	yes	yes	no	no
EMA Tool	Planning, evaluation	yes	no	no	no	no
Collabucate	Monitoring	yes*	yes*	yes*	no	no
DREW + EAT	Monitoring	yes	yes	no	no	no

* No specific features were provided: Collabucate focuses on providing scripts for strategies to overcome challenges

Since we want to test our features in real contexts with complex teacher supervision during collaboration, we decided to follow Hoadley and Campos [14] suggestion; that the testing has to integrate a good design of the tool. This implies not only a good theoretical background to inspire the features but also a good graphic and interaction design so that students feel it is a sound alternative to their usual communication software. We had found out that previous authors [12] had reported that learners did not find the tools as useful as they could be [9]. Our primary goal was to create a tool with an intuitive graphical user interface and simple interaction. This tool integrates new social and emotional awareness features, along with cognitive and educational functionalities, into comprehensive communication software. It is designed to be effective in environments where teachers supervise teenagers with limited experience in asynchronous online collaboration for school tasks.

2.3 Research Questions

Thus, our main research question for this study is:

Which features and affordances, according to students' opinions and experience, are adequate to facilitate students' participation and social, emotional and motivational awareness during online collaboration and support self-, co- and socially shared regulation?

This RQ has the following objectives that guided each of the iterations presented after the methodology:

- Determine how a digital tool can support learners to be aware and face the potential socio-emotional issues during their collaboration
- Following the conclusions of the previous point, how to implement and evaluate our fully functional prototype (*me&co*)?
- Do students find those features/affordances useful? Which are their favorite ones? Determine how learners perceive, use and experience the support provided.

3   Methods, Participants and Instruments

3.1   Methods

Design based research (DBR) is the main methodology followed in this research. As described by McKenney and Reeves [41] it consists of three iterative phases (analysis, design and evaluation). The reason for this choice was that although this methodology is still under continuous revision and improvement, there is enough consensus about its benefits for the learning sciences [14, 42].

Combined with DBR, we use the User Centered Design methodology (UCD). UCD is defined in an ISO norm (International Organization for Standardization [ISO], 2019) that states that human-centered design is a methodology in the development of interactive systems that prioritizes the users, their needs, and requirements. It applies knowledge and techniques from human factors/ergonomics and usability to create systems that are not only usable but also useful. This approach boosts efficiency and effectiveness, enhances user satisfaction, promotes accessibility and sustainability, and improves human well-being. Moreover, it mitigates potential negative impacts on human health, safety, and performance that may arise from system usage. UCD consists of four general phases, which are: (1) specifying the context of use, (2) specifying user requirements, (3) designing solutions, and (4) evaluating the design [12]. Other authors like Sharp, Preece, and Rogers (Sharp et al., 2019) defined the UCD as a "user-centered approach" which has five basic principles. Furthermore, they outlined four basic phases of interaction design in which such principles could be applied. The phases consist of: (1) requirements discovery, (2) solution design, (3) prototyping, and (4) evaluation.

It is an iterative process in which final users are part of some or all the steps, and designers and tool developers obtain insights from their participation.

Different evidence-based strategies are typically used for UCD processes such as focus groups, co-creation sessions, associative object-based techniques or surveying (Dopp et al., 2019). We apply different techniques from UCD, like questionnaires, interviews and paper prototyping to identify the final functionalities needed and how to organize them in a graphical interface (Design stage).

We explain our specific method in each of the following sections. But in general, we followed these steps for our DBR process. The main objective of the first iteration was to create a first prototype based on previous research trying to fill the gaps found and get students' opinions in order to improve it. In the second iteration, the objective was to present a refined version of the features and get new students' opinions and experiences for comparison with the first iteration.

3.2 Participants

Iteration 1. The first version of the prototype (more detail and images below) was tested with 42 students from two classes from a public high school in a town close to Seville (Valencina de la Concepción). The students were 16 years old from the first year of the Baccalaureate in Spanish Education System. IES Las Encinas, the name of their high school, is placed in a rural area from medium-low income level.

The researcher and the teacher created a collaborative activity for the students who were enrolled in a compulsory subject about Technology. The topic was basic computer networks and security. The goal of the task was to prepare a presentation about the different types of networks, the protocols and the devices. The task was assigned as homework and they used the tool for 5 days (outside school without teacher supervision) to organize and prepare the presentation.

The students were informed that they were expected to discuss and agree the content through the prototype of the collaborative tool. The groups (of 4) were also made by the teacher with students who did not usually work together in order to provoke more moments of socio-emotional challenges.

Iteration 2. This new version of the prototype (below more detail and images) was tested with 64 students from three classes from a public high school in a town close to Cádiz (Conil). The students were 16 years old from the first year of the Baccalaureate in Spanish Education System, IES Atalaya. It is a high school placed in a rural area during winter but touristic beach during summer from medium income level.

The researcher and the teacher created a collaborative activity for the students who were enrolled in a compulsory subject about philosophy. This time, trying to make the task more collaboration-focused and avoid dividing the task among members, the topic was preparing a debate about one of the themes proposed in the activity. The students were used to preparing debates since the teacher uses that type of task to make them practice and study philosophy. The theme selected had to be agreed upon by the members but from a list of topics provided by the teacher. After choosing one topic of discussion, they had to come up with arguments pro or against it. The groups were also made by students who did not usually work together in order to provoke more moments of socio-emotional challenges. They had to deliver a document with all the best arguments agreed upon for the debate. The task was assigned as homework and they used the tool for five days (outside school without teacher supervision) to share and select their arguments for the debate.

All students signed the consent form about data privacy and ethics in research. Again, all students tested the same version of *me&co* and a brief introduction of the socio-emotional awareness features integrated in the app was provided by the main author.

3.3 Instruments

This article presents research that embodies two iterations. Both iterations imply the redesign of a first prototype that we present below. The objective of the iterations was to obtain a refined version of the prototype to be considered for implementation. Both iterations are interrelated.

The main instruments used were:

- The prototype to test (students had to solve a task for a real class)
- A post-task questionnaire asking about the experience of use of the features provided in the prototype
- Analysis of the chat conversations logs

For each iteration, after evaluating the collected data from the questionnaire, we obtained a version of the prototype that would be used for the analysis of the next iteration. In the following sections we present the two instruments.

The Me&co Prototype. To design and implement the first prototype, we started by ideating the features and tools that could improve the previous research tools reviewed in the theoretical background. We wanted to give support for social presence, participation, regulation and motivation in order to facilitate addressing those socio-emotional challenges.

In Table 2 we show the features designed and implemented in the *me&co* prototype with the research constructs that we try to facilitate.

We then started to define the UX/UI and implement the features. In the following sections we present the features of the prototype and how they evolved across the two iterations.

Feature 1: *Social Presence and Hedonicity: The Representation of Group Members*

Iteration 1: With the theory of social presence introduced in the background section in mind, we have tried to reinforce social presence, group cohesion and a sense of community through the design of a set of avatars (different but with common characteristics) that the users could choose as a profile picture (Fig. 1).

Students could choose their favorite avatar when they signed in *me&co*, our communication tool prototype. To promote social presence and group cohesion, these avatars were always visible during the whole collaboration. Their position in columns during

Table 2. Features integrated in the prototype related to the theoretical background that supports them and the provided functionality description

Feature	Theory support	Functionality description
Anonymous messages	Socially-shared and co-regulation. Promoting social interactions and participation	We hypothesized that including the possibility of sending on-demand anonymous messages to the chat could facilitate and increase the participation of shy members and support facing socio-emotional challenges
Avatar selection	Representation of the self, identity. SIDE model. Hedonic affordances and social affordances	When students create their account in the prototype, they can choose an avatar from some predefined options
Profile page	Self- and co- regulation. Social presence	We designed a personal profile panel. The goal of this panel was to let users describe/present themselves to the rest of the group as collaborator students. The profile panel included a survey based on EMSR-Q to let members present to each other how they see themselves as collaborators
My emotions panel	Self- and co-regulation and awareness of emotions	We designed a panel for each member with a list of emotions during collaborative learning. Students could select how much of the emotion they felt in a likert scale and the other members of the group could see how the rest of the members felt. We hypothesized that students could benefit from being more aware of emotions because that would help them self-regulate and co-regulate
Visual messages composer	Socially-shared and co-regulation. Promoting motivation and hedonicity	Students can visually create fun, motivational messages using the members' avatars together with other texts and graphics. Our aim was to provide some kind of hedonic support, a fun way of motivating the group and facilitating the socially-shared regulation of learning

the conversations was used to know who was writing each message (thanks also to the position of the icon of the type of message, see Figs. 4 and 5). That way, we hypothesized, the interface would also be seen as something more specifically designed for groups. In other similar communication tools, group conversations are presented with the same UI than those for a one-to-one conversation.

Fig. 1. The avatars for members.

We used the analysis of the conversations and the answers to the questionnaire of this iteration 1 (see Table 2 in the Results section for more information) to refine the design of the features and include new ones.

Iteration 2: In the second iteration, to improve the social presence and create a stronger emotional connection with the users we decided to show the name of the group and the avatars of all members (instead of just the user like in Fig. 2) of the selected group on the home page. The goal was to give more group cohesion and social presence to the group and the members from the start (Fig. 3).

The icon indicating the sender of the message was not understood by many students (Fig. 4) so we changed the graphic representation of the message bubble. In this iteration, it had a triangle pointing to the avatar which indicated what member had sent the message (Fig. 5). We placed the avatars at the bottom of the chat page so that the chat bubble pointed to them in a more hedonic, personal and emotional way (as if it was conversation between the avatars).

Fig. 2. Iteration 1, only the avatar of the current student is shown in the tasks panel.

Fig. 3. Iteration 2, the tasks panel shows the avatars of all the members of the group.

Feature 2: *Facilitating Participation and Social Interactions: The Anonymous Messages*

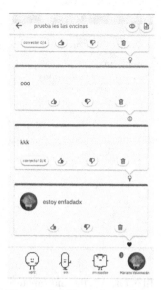

Fig. 4. In iteration 1, the members were on top and the icon under the user avatar indicated the person sending the message.

Fig. 5. The chat bubbles point to the avatars at the bottom to show who is sending the message.

Iteration 1: We hypothesized that including the possibility of eventually sending anonymous messages to the chat could facilitate and increase the participation of shy members and support facing socio-emotional challenges.

This is the feature that we designed and implemented in the prototype to test if it had the expected positive effects (Figs. 6 and 7) over students. In such messages, the other users could not see who sent those anonymous messages.

Iteration 2: To facilitate and promote anonymous participation to address socio-emotional challenges and regulation we included 6 ready made messages from common socio-emotional challenges during collaboration. The ready-made messages were taken from Alonso Tapia and colleagues' questionnaire EMSR-Q [43].

Feature 3: *Facilitating Social and Self Awareness of Emotions*

Iteration 1. We designed a panel for each member with a list of emotions during collaborative learning. Students could select how much of the emotion they felt in a likert scale (Fig. 8) and the other members of the group could see how the rest of the members felt simply clicking on that user's avatar (Fig. 14).

Iteration 2. In Fig. 9 we show the second iteration of this panel simplifying the likert scale: only one slider that was enabled when an emotion was selected instead of having one slider per emotion which made the panel overloaded with UI components). We hypothesized that students could benefit from being more aware of emotions such as relief, enjoyment, curiosity and admiration to name a few because that would help them self-regulate and co-regulate their emotional mood during collaborative learning. The

Fig. 6. In iteration 1, the anonymous message feature just included an explanation of that type of message.

Fig. 7. In iteration 2, the anonymous messages feature included ready-made sentences and an open-ended textfield.

interface components work choosing one emotion and grading its value in a single scale component at the bottom of the panel.

The emotional valence [28] was expressed in our UI with a green or red thumbs up/down (Fig. 14) by the emotion value [44].

We also created a background color for the emotion selection. So, when a user shares an emotion, the avatar of the user is sent with the background color for the emotion in order to make it clearer and more emotional (Fig. 9).

Feature 4: *Promoting Motivation and Hedonicity During Collaborative Learning*

Iteration 1: We tried to support a positive group atmosphere through appraisals and motivation of members provided by a tool that also incorporated a creative and hedonic user experience. There were 4 ready made messages (Figs. 10 and 11) but we included the possibility of creating customized messages by clicking on the "pen" icon at the bottom of the panel (Fig. 10). Using the socio-emotional and motivational messages composer students can visually create fun messages using the members' avatars together with other texts and graphics (Figs. 12 and 13).

Iteration 2: In iteration 2 we placed the button for the "Motivational messages composer" in a more visible position (top-right, Fig. 11) because it was a feature really enjoyed (but not seen in iteration 1 by some students). In the Visual Messages Composer feature we provided a larger canvas for more complex custom messages (Fig. 13).

With this feature, our aim was to provide some kind of hedonic support [36], a fun way of motivating the group and facilitating the socially-shared regulation of learning (because the default messages included all the members of the group, Fig. 11).

Feature 5: Improving social presence and regulation: the personal profile panel.

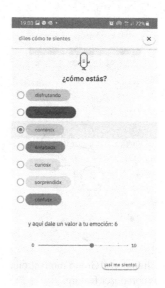

Fig. 8. In the first iteration there was a list of emotions, a description of it and a likert scale per emotion to select their intensity.

Fig. 9. In iteration 2 the likert scale was only one and linked to the selected emotion. We also included a background color to make identifying emotions easier.

Fig. 10. Iteration 1. Ready-made motivational messages feature.

Fig. 11. In iteration2, the button "Motivational messages composer" in a more visible position (top-right).

Iteration 1: We also designed a personal profile panel. The goal of this panel was to let users describe/present themselves to the rest of the group as collaborator students.

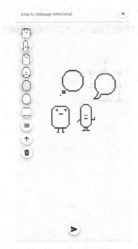

Fig. 12. Iteration 1 Group motivational messages composer feature.

Fig. 13. In iteration 2 we provided a larger canvas to allow more complex messages.

The profile panel included a survey based on EMSR-Q to let members present to each other how they see themselves as collaborators [43].

Iteration 2: To further promote participation with hedonic affordances, in the second iteration we improved the member's page layout to show the 'likes' of the messages (Fig. 15). We included a "thumbs up/down button" in every chat bubble to afford this functionality. This is a feature that a user requested in the previous version. We also allowed to show/hide the rest of the information about a member's profile to make it more usable and easy to read (Figs. 14 and 15) thanks to an "accordion" component.

The Questionnaires. Since the tools were new designs and different from previous research we could not find previous research questionnaires to use as a reference or a starting point. Thus, in both iterations, the questionnaire was designed by the authors. We created questions for each feature to:

- Students ratings of the features offered through a likert scale between 1 (not useful at all) and 5 (very useful)
- Their opinion (yes/no) if they would keep that feature in future iterations
- Suggestions to improve the features or possible new features to include in the me&co tool. These were open questions.
- A final open-ended question to know their general impression about the *me&co* tool through a likert scale (between 1, not useful and 5, very useful)

We also analyzed the chat conversations looking for possible socio-emotional challenges to see their reactions.

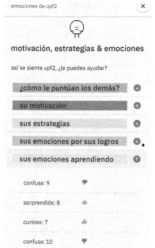

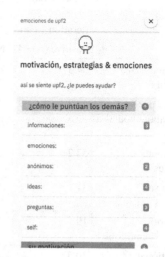

Fig. 14. Iteration 2: how other members see one member's emotions.

Fig. 15. Iteration 2: profile page with new information counting the "liked" messages.

4 Results

In this section we present the evaluation and results of the use of the tools (post task questionnaire). The following Table 3 summarizes the results of the questionnaires of each iteration.

Since the first iteration was used mainly to improve the UX/UI of the prototype, we present now a brief overview of the results of the second iteration (sometimes in comparison to the results of the first iteration).

Personal Avatar Selection. Students are very positive (74.4% > =4) about the possibility of choosing an avatar to represent themselves. Better results than in the first iteration (64.3%).

Personal Public Profile About You as a Student. Learners are quite positive (65.6% > = 4) about presenting themselves with the questions about how they think they study and collaborate. This is a much better result than in our first iteration (45.2%), so the changes included had a positive effect.

Anonymous Messages. Very positive opinions about the anonymous messages feature: 79.7% over four points (and much better than in the first iteration 57.2%).

Sharing Self-Emotions Feature. Being able to value/grade their own emotions is considered just slightly positive (60.9%) but much better than in the first iteration (31%).

Other Members' Emotions. But being able to see other members' emotions does not seem to be so useful for them since only 46% of students rated the feature over four. Moreover, 31.3% of students rated it below three.

Table 3. Feature and ratings of students per iteration

Feature	Iteration 1 (%)		Iteration 2 (%)	
	Positive (>= 4)	Negative (<= 2)	Positive (>= 4)	Negative (<= 2)
Personal avatar selection	64.3	23.8	74.4	4.7
Personal public profile about you as a student	45.2	18.6	65.2	9.4
Anonymous messages	57.2	28.6	79.7	1.6
Sharing self emotions	31	40.4	60.9	17.2
Seeing other members' emotions	19	50	46	31.3
Motivational messages composer	30.5	42.8	64.1	12.5
General awareness of the socio-emotional challenges of the group	21.4	45.2	54.7	9.4

Motivational Messages Composer: Students are quite positive (64.1%) about the feature that lets them send motivational, ready-made messages to the rest of the group. Again a much more positive result than in our first iteration (30.5%). A more positive result (67.2% > = 4) for the possibility to create custom motivational messages themselves.

Awareness of the Socio-Emotional Challenges of the Group. To the general question about the app having made them be more aware of the socio-emotional challenges during collaboration they are much more positive than in our first iteration (54.7% vs. 21.4%).

Unfortunately, they reported that the specific features and affordances to facilitate socio-emotional awareness were not very used during collaboration. This was, according to their explanations, because they knew each other quite well from previous similar tasks and most of the groups concentrated on getting the task done.

5 Discussion

Through two DBR iterations, we have ideated, designed, refined and tested five features to promote social interactions and support social presence, hedonicity and self-, co- and socially shared regulation. Using this methodology, and the integration of a human centered approach through gathering students' opinions and experience using the app and integrating them in its design allowed us to show new results never studied before. Compared to the previous research tools we contribute with new knowledge from our tool because it integrates several features for several socio-emotional purposes into one tool that could be used during the natural flow of collaboration.

In general, students have reported that they understood the purpose and how to interact with the UI. Asked about their general experience they answered that they (58 out of 64 students) found the features useful and that they would keep them as part of *me&co*.

Best Rated Features. From the interaction with the interface, the anonymous messages composer (co- and socially shared regulation), the avatars (social presence) and the visual messages composer (hedonicity and socially-shared regulation) were the best rated by students (according to the students' answers to the questionnaire).

The Anonymous Messages. Surprisingly, even if they rated it high, the anonymous message tool does not seem to be very used; most students used their real names or the nicknames by which they are known in class. On one occasion, one student tried to start facing a challenge using the anonymous message feature and another answered asking why s/he was using the anonymous messages (instead of just saying it without hiding behind anonymity). Students explain that since they know each other, they do not need it.

The Avatars. Choosing their avatars was really appreciated. In general, everything that involved avatars was enjoyed. Anyway, the purpose of this feature was mainly to establish a more emotional connection with students. Avatars were more a support to other features that could be used to address the socio-emotional challenges (like the anonymous messages or the sharing emotions panel).

The Personal Profile Page. Most students took the time to fill up the data of this section and they said they would keep this feature in the *me&co* tool.

The Visual Messages Composer. The ready made messages were used but with little explicit effect over the rest of the members, students created their own messages, some of them really original, but they did it for fun.

The Self-Emotions Panel. This panel was hardly used. This can be explained because students said they prefer to work on their own, admit that in general they do not share their emotions easily with others and report they are aware of the emotions of the other members without any help. Adding that their main motivation when they work together is 1) to get a good grade and 2) to have fun together can also help to understand why students think that the feature for being aware of their emotions was the lowest rated.

This contradiction between rating the features high but not using them can be explained because students reported that they simply didn't need them. They claimed that they do not need the features because they know each other and they are already aware of their emotions and the challenges of collaboration.

It seems that the features that allow them to have fun (like the visual messages composer or the anonymous message feature) are preferred over those that are more 'introspective' (like the self-emotions tool). From their answers to the questionnaire, their second most important goal when collaborating is 'having fun' (right after 'getting a good grade'). For the self-emotions tool we think it was a good idea from students to include "stress" and "upset by the lack of work of others" in the list of available emotions.

Regarding the avatars, many students asked for more characters, others wanted to have a tool to create them or to create avatars with gestures of the emotions or with personality traits. These can be ideas for future designers.

Another proposal we find interesting is their personal profile page as students and collaborators. Even though it was a long questionnaire, many students rated it quite high. It is again a feature connected to 'identity' (like the avatars) and it seems that students appreciate this type of information that makes them reflect about how they are.

6 Limitations

Gathering valuable insights from students is crucial, when applying a human-centered design approach, to comprehensively understand their needs and opinions before deploying an application in a genuine collaborative environment. While our study successfully obtained feedback on students' experiences with the tool's features, it is important to note that our experimental design was limited to a single task. Consequently, the data collected may not provide a thorough understanding of the tool's broader impact on collaboration. Particularly in the initial iteration, students engaged with the tool, yet some features were utilized primarily for testing and enjoyment rather than fostering genuine collaborative interactions. This highlights the necessity of a more extensive exploration of student perspectives and utilization patterns before implementing the application in real collaborative settings.

7 Conclusion

This research is, to the best of our knowledge, the first to design and test a tool specifically tailored to facilitate socio-emotional aspects during the whole process of online collaboration. Moreover, in a real task, done during homework and thus, with very little teacher supervision. This is important because the existing tools have tested only specific moments of collaboration or specific modes or phases of socio-emotional interactions. In our opinion and other authors [14], using DBR in order to study the whole potential of the affordances developed, it was essential to involve students in the design process and to have a good design available anytime, anywhere so that students could use the features when needed.

In general, as we have also introduced before, when the members of the group know each other from class, the vast majority of students claim they do not need such features. They hardly used the tools for practical purposes or real challenges. We have seen challenges in our analysis (that students also reported in the interviews) that were not addressed with the tool. Many students reported having members not working as much as the others but everyone accepted that situation. Research has described these challenges [12, 13], we have seen them and students admit they find them as well but, noticeably, when offered specific features to face them in a dedicated tool they do not even try to solve those issues (as we saw before when talking about the anonymous message tool, even though they claim they find the features useful -for other groups-). We hypothesize that if they use the features provided they may feel they are less 'mature' or a kind of 'hiding' or cowardly person in front of classmates they know. They have problems and challenges collaborating (like differences in commitment and effort put forth) but they do not face them; they do not want to 'complicate' things, they want to get the task done, get a good grade and have fun.

We also conjecture that, knowing that there was no teacher supervision, may have had a negative impact on the use of the app because they mostly used it for fun. In our analysis of the chats we learned that me&co did facilitate and promote social interactions but these were not supporting or improving their cognitive collaboration. At least in our experiments, most of these interactions were just about testing the tool in a fun way, not really as part of the collaboration to solve the task. From the Kreijns and Kirschner model [36], we hypothesized that social presence and learning outcomes affect each other but in our test, if this happened, it was not evident. Testing other conditions of anonymity, like anonymous to peers but not to the teacher, or testing the tool with students that do not know each other could also clarify if students would make a more productive use of the features provided.

On the positive side, as we presented, the average rate of the tool was high. They also explained that in other groups they have previously worked with, the features would have been useful (because they did not know each other so well). It seems that for these students, *me&co* was good to make them more aware of that side of collaboration.

8 Future Research

As a future research line we propose to explore whether the features would be more useful in tests where students are unfamiliar with each other.

The design of the avatars could have potential benefits because students really enjoyed them. For example, it would be a good idea to link personality traits to the avatars so that they could define an avatar not only with an image but also with some kind of identity. The same goes for the anonymous messages and for new versions of the existing avatars adapted to graphically express emotions. The ambiguous results presented above encourage us to believe that these features could also be improved and tested in a different context: with students that do not know each other at all.

Finally, there were limitations that could also make the testing of *me&co* more contextually rich and realistic like the lack of notifications which made working on the tasks asynchronously quite difficult. As we also comment in the limitations section, longer experiments with more tasks and in depth interviews would be needed in order to get better data about the effect of our features during collaboration.

We have learned that future features or tools shouldn't just support awareness or script potential actions. Instead, they should also be focused on supporting discussions about challenges and conflicts in a more enjoyable and fun manner. This could include using chatbots or automatic agents to add an entertaining element to conversations.

Acknowledgments. Thanks to Erica Ho, Gustavo Zurita and all the teachers involved in *Matemagymkhana* de Sevilla, especially Modesto Ruiz, Manuel Morente and Pilar Flores. Thanks also to Laura Ortega, Raquel Vázquez, Isabel Santos, Luisa Huertas, Pablo Álvarez, Margarita Nicolás and Lola Benedicto for her generous help with the students and the interviews.

Funding. This work was supported in part by PID2020-112584RB-C33 funded by MCIN/ AEI /https://doi.org/10.13039/501100011033, the Ramón y Cajal programme (P. Santos), ICREA under the ICREA Academia programme (D. Hernández-Leo, Serra Hunter), and the Department of Research and Universities of the Government of Catalonia (SGR00930).

Disclosure of Interests. None.

References

1. Isohätälä, J., Näykki, P., Järvelä, S.: Cognitive and socio-emotional interaction in collaborative learning: exploring fluctuations in students' participation. Scand. J. Educ. Res. **64**(6), 831–851 (2019). https://doi.org/10.1080/00313831.2019.1623310
2. Kreijns, K., Kirschner, P.A., Jochems, W.: Identifying the pitfalls for social interaction in computer-supported collaborative learning environments: a review of the research. Comput. Hum. Behav. **19**(3), 335–353 (2003). https://doi.org/10.1016/S0747-5632(02)00057-2
3. Gilbert, L., Moore, D.R.: Building interactivity into Web courses: tools for social and instructional interactions. Educ. Technol. **38**(3), 29–35 (1998)
4. Isohätälä, J., Näykki, P., Järvelä, S.: Convergences of joint, positive interactions and regulation in collaborative learning. Small Group Res. **51**(2), 229–264 (2020). https://doi.org/10.1177/1046496419867760
5. Hadwin, A., Järvelä, S., Miller, M.: Self-regulation, co-regulation, and shared regulation in collaborative learning environments. In: Schunk, D.H., Greene, J.A. (eds.) Handbook of Self-Regulation of Learning and Performance, pp. 83–106. Routledge (2017). https://doi.org/10.4324/9781315697048-6
6. Järvelä, S., Hadwin, A.F.: New frontiers: regulating learning in CSCL. Educ. Psychol. **48**(1), 25–39 (2013). https://doi.org/10.1080/00461520.2012.748006
7. Järvenoja, H., Näykki, P., Törmänen, T.: Emotional regulation in collaborative learning: when do higher education students activate group level regulation in the face of challenges? Stud. High. Educ. **44**(10), 1747–1757 (2019). https://doi.org/10.1080/03075079.2019.1665318
8. Pintrich, P.R.: The role of goal orientation in self-regulated learning. In: Handbook of Self-Regulation, pp. 451–502. Elsevier (2000). https://doi.org/10.1016/B978-012109890-2/50043-3
9. Lyons, K.M., Lobczowski, N.G., Greene, J.A., Whitley, J., McLaughlin, J.E.: Using a design-based research approach to develop and study a web-based tool to support collaborative learning. Comput. Educ. **161**, 104064 (2021). https://doi.org/10.1016/j.compedu.2020.104064
10. Boekaerts, M.: Emotions, emotion regulation, and self-regulation of learning. Handb. Self-Regul. Learn. Perform. **5**, 408–425 (2011)
11. Järvelä, S., et al.: Enhancing socially shared regulation in collaborative learning groups: designing for CSCL regulation tools. Educ. Technol. Res. Dev. **63**(1), 125–142 (2015). https://doi.org/10.1007/s11423-014-9358-1
12. Järvelä, S., et al.: Socially shared regulation of learning in CSCL: understanding and prompting individual- and group-level shared regulatory activities. Int. J. Comput. Support. Collab. Learn. **11**(3), 263–280 (2016). https://doi.org/10.1007/s11412-016-9238-2
13. Järvelä, S., Gašević, D., Seppänen, T., Pechenizkiy, M., Kirschner, P.A.: Bridging learning sciences, machine learning and affective computing for understanding cognition and affect in collaborative learning. Br. J. Educ. Technol. (2020). https://doi.org/10.1111/bjet.12917

14. Hoadley, C., Campos, F.C.: Design-based research: what it is and why it matters to studying online learning. Educ. Psychol. **57**(3), 207–220 (2022). https://doi.org/10.1080/00461520.2022.2079128

15. Mänty, K., Järvenoja, H., Törmänen, T.: The sequential composition of collaborative groups' emotion regulation in negative socio-emotional interactions. Eur. J. Psychol. Educ. (2022). https://doi.org/10.1007/s10212-021-00589-3

16. Khosa, D.K., Volet, S.E.: Productive group engagement in cognitive activity and metacognitive regulation during collaborative learning: can it explain differences in students' conceptual understanding? Metacognition Learn. **9**(3), 287–307 (2014). https://doi.org/10.1007/s11409-014-9117-z

17. Bakhtiar, A., Webster, E.A., Hadwin, A.F.: Regulation and socio-emotional interactions in a positive and a negative group climate. Metacognition Learn. **13**(1), 57–90 (2018). https://doi.org/10.1007/s11409-017-9178-x

18. Sobocinski, M., Malmberg, J., Järvelä, S.: Exploring temporal sequences of regulatory phases and associated interactions in low- and high-challenge collaborative learning sessions. Metacognition Learn. **12**(2), 275–294 (2017). https://doi.org/10.1007/s11409-016-9167-5

19. Gunawardena, C.N.: Social presence theory and implications for interaction and collaborative learning in computer conferences. Int. J. Educ. Telecommun. **1**(2), 147–166 (1995)

20. Van den Bossche, P., Gijselaers, W.H., Segers, M., Kirschner, P.A.: Social and cognitive factors driving teamwork in collaborative learning environments: team learning beliefs and behaviors. Small Group Res. **37**(5), 490–521 (2006). https://doi.org/10.1177/1046496406292938

21. Flanagin, A.J., Hocevar, K.P., Samahito, S.N.: Connecting with the user-generated Web: how group identification impacts online information sharing and evaluation. Inf. Commun. Soc. **17**(6), 683–694 (2014). https://doi.org/10.1080/1369118X.2013.808361

22. Beyea, D., Van der Heide, B., Ewoldsen, D., Eden, A., Meng, J.: Avatar-based self-influence in a traditional CMC environment. J. Media Psychol. Theor. Methods Appl. (2021)

23. Guegan, J., Buisine, S., Mantelet, F., Maranzana, N., Segonds, F.: Avatar-mediated creativity: when embodying inventors makes engineers more creative. Comput. Hum. Behav. **61**, 165–175 (2016)

24. Ratan, R.A., Dawson, M.: When Mii is me: a psychophysiological examination of avatar self-relevance. Commun. Res. **43**(8), 1065–1093 (2016)

25. Ho, E.: Tuvatar: an avatar-mediated small group learning environment. In: Proceedings of the 15th International Conference on Computer-Supported Collaborative Learning-CSCL 2022, pp. 581–582, International Society of the Learning Sciences (2022)

26. Avry, S., Molinari, G., Bétrancourt, M., Chanel, G.: Sharing emotions contributes to regulating collaborative intentions in group problem-solving. Front. Psychol. **11**, 1160 (2020). https://doi.org/10.3389/fpsyg.2020.01160

27. Lavoué, E., Kazemitabar, M., Doleck, T., Lajoie, S.P., Carrillo, R., Molinari, G.: Towards emotion awareness tools to support emotion and appraisal regulation in academic contexts. Educ. Technol. Res. Develop. **68**(1), 269–292 (2019). https://doi.org/10.1007/s11423-019-09688-x

28. Pekrun, R., Vogl, E., Muis, K.R., Sinatra, G.M.: Measuring emotions during epistemic activities: the epistemically-related emotion scales. Cogn. Emot. **31**(6), 1268–1276 (2017). https://doi.org/10.1080/02699931.2016.1204989

29. Pekrun, R.: The control-value theory of achievement emotions: assumptions, corollaries, and implications for educational research and practice. Educ. Psychol. Rev. **18**(4), 315–341 (2006)

30. Vogl, E., Pekrun, R., Murayama, K., Loderer, K.: Surprised–curious–confused: epistemic emotions and knowledge exploration. Emotion **20**(4), 625–641 (2020). https://doi.org/10.1037/emo0000578

31. Zschocke, K., Wosnitza, M., Bürger, K.: Emotions in group work: insights from an appraisal-oriented perspective. Eur. J. Psychol. Educ. **31**, 359–384 (2016)
32. Linnenbrink-Garcia, L., Rogat, T.K., Koskey, K.L.K.: Affect and engagement during small group instruction. Contemp. Educ. Psychol. **36**(1), 13–24 (2011). https://doi.org/10.1016/j.cedpsych.2010.09.001
33. Näykki, P., Järvelä, S., Kirschner, P.A., Järvenoja, H.: Socio-emotional conflict in collaborative learning—a process-oriented case study in a higher education context. Int. J. Educ. Res. **68**, 1–14 (2014). https://doi.org/10.1016/j.ijer.2014.07.001
34. Kirschner, P., Strijbos, J.-W., Kreijns, K., Beers, P.J.: Designing electronic collaborative learning environments. Educ. Technol. Res. Dev. **52**(3), 47–66 (2004). https://doi.org/10.1007/BF02504675
35. Kreijns, K., Kirschner, P.A., Vermeulen, M.: Social aspects of CSCL environments: a research framework. Educ. Psychol. **48**(4), 229–242 (2013). https://doi.org/10.1080/00461520.2012.750225
36. Kreijns, K., Kirschner, P.A.: Extending the SIPS-model: a research framework for online collaborative learning. In: Pammer-Schindler, V., Pérez-Sanagustín, M., Drachsler, H., Elferink, R., Scheffel, M. (eds.) Lifelong Technology-Enhanced Learning: 13th European Conference on Technology Enhanced Learning, EC-TEL 2018, Leeds, UK, September 3-5, 2018, Proceedings, pp. 277–290. Springer International Publishing, Cham (2018). https://doi.org/10.1007/978-3-319-98572-5_21
37. Miller, M., Hadwin, A.: Scripting and awareness tools for regulating collaborative learning: changing the landscape of support in CSCL. Comput. Hum. Behav. **52**, 573–588 (2015). https://doi.org/10.1016/j.chb.2015.01.050
38. Hadwin, A.F., Bakhtiar, A., Miller, M.: Challenges in online collaboration: effects of scripting shared task perceptions. Int. J. Comput.-Support. Collab. Learn. **13**(3), 301–329 (2018). https://doi.org/10.1007/s11412-018-9279-9
39. Malmberg, J., Järvelä, S., Järvenoja, H., Panadero, E.: Promoting socially shared regulation of learning in CSCL: progress of socially shared regulation among high- and low-performing groups. Comput. Hum. Behav. **52**, 562–572 (2015). https://doi.org/10.1016/j.chb.2015.03.082
40. Velamazán, M., Santos, P., Hernández-Leo, D.: Socio-emotional regulation in collaborative hybrid learning spaces of formal–informal learning. In: Gil, E., Mor, Y., Dimitriadis, Y., Köppe, C. (eds.) Hybrid Learning Spaces, pp. 95–111. Springer International Publishing, Cham (2022). https://doi.org/10.1007/978-3-030-88520-5_7
41. McKenney, S., Reeves, T.C.: Educational design research. In: Michael Spector, J., David Merrill, M., Jan Elen, M.J., Bishop, (eds.) Handbook of Research on Educational Communications and Technology, pp. 131–140. Springer New York, New York, NY (2014). https://doi.org/10.1007/978-1-4614-3185-5_11
42. Kali, Y., Hoadley, C.: Design-based research methods in CSCL: calibrating our epistemologies and ontologies. In: Cress, U., Rosé, C., Wise, A.F., Oshima, J. (eds.) International Handbook of Computer-Supported Collaborative Learning, pp. 479–496. Springer International Publishing, Cham (2021). https://doi.org/10.1007/978-3-030-65291-3_26
43. Alonso-Tapia, J., Calderón, E.P., Díaz Ruiz, M.A.: Development and validity of the emotion and motivation self-regulation questionnaire (EMSR-Q). Span. J. Psychol. **17**, E55 (2014). https://doi.org/10.1017/sjp.2014.41
44. Järvenoja, H., Malmberg, J., Järvelä, S., Näykki, P., Kontturi, H.: Investigating students' situation-specific emotional state and motivational goals during a learning project within one primary school classroom. Learn. Res. Pract. **5**(1), 4–23 (2018). https://doi.org/10.1080/23735082.2018.1554821

Innovative Design of Interactive Shadow Puppets for Children Based on STEAM Education Concept

Chen Wang[1](✉), Jianan Liu[1], Lingyan Zhang[2], Xinyi Chen[2], and Yichen Wu[1]

[1] School of Industrial Design, China Academy of Art, Hangzhou, China
wangchen6171@sina.com, 2221351252@caa.edu.cn
[2] Design Innovation Centre, China Academy of Art, Hangzhou, China

Abstract. STEAM education has attracted much attention as a comprehensive education method. This educational concept not only promotes interdisciplinary learning and stimulates children's creativity, but also guides the design of many children's interactive products. This research focuses on children's STEAM education, takes traditional Chinese mythology as the theme, and puts forward an innovative proposal for shadow puppet products based on screen interaction technology. Chinese shadow puppet is not only a treasure of Chinese culture, but also recognized as World Intangible Cultural Heritage by UNESCO. This is a wonderful combination of STEAM and traditional culture, empowering the vibrant future development of technology and education through innovative means. In order to verify the feasibility of the product details, this study used experiments, questionnaires, observations, etc., inviting 20 children aged 7–12 and multiple design workers to conduct user experiments, and record their usage processes and results. The results obtained are as follows: (1) In terms of the toughness, weight, light transmittance and dyeing effect of the material, cowhide is still the most suitable material for shadow puppet production; (2) The structural complexity has a certain impact on the user control experience, but not the most important factor; (3) In terms of robot vertical movement, 15mm*15mm*1mm square neodymium iron boron magnets are considered the best choice; (4) Projection is currently the most stable, feasible and effective display method. This research provides references and ideas for the design of STEAM educational interactive products, and also provides methods and paths for the activation of Chinese shadow puppet culture and other traditional arts.

Keywords: STEAM Education · Shadow Puppets · Multimodal Interaction Design · Children · Traditional Culture · Robot · Creativity

1 Introduction

Chinese shadow puppet has important connections with social organizations, seasonal festivals, and folk beliefs. It carries numerous cultural information such as cultural history, social humanities, folk literature, people's livelihood and folk customs, contains

P. Zaphiris and A. Ioannou (Eds.): HCII 2024, LNCS 14722, pp. 145–161, 2024.
https://doi.org/10.1007/978-3-031-61672-3_10

the unique spiritual values, ways of thinking, and culture consciousness of the Chinese nation, and directly reflects the people's spiritual pursuits, thoughts and feelings. Chinese shadow puppet is not only a treasure of Chinese culture, but also recognized as World Intangible Cultural Heritage by UNESCO. Through the art form of shadow puppets, people can experience and understand these cultural elements, expand their understanding of traditional culture, and then promote their knowledge accumulation and understanding in history, morality and culture. However, as video games, pop culture and other forms of modern entertainment have become a staple of people's daily lives, many traditional cultures, such as shadow puppets, are gradually fading out of public view. At the same time, in the face of huge employment pressure, engaging in intangible cultural heritage work is difficult to become a survival advantage for the young generation. In this situation, individual survival rationality has replaced traditional cultural identity. The inheritance of intangible cultural heritage, such as shadow puppets, will naturally encounter difficulties concerning insufficient endogenous motivation [1]. The existence of these problems makes the inheritance and development of these techniques face severe challenges.

At present, a new round of scientific and technological revolution with information technology as the core is gestating and emerging, which allows the organic integration of traditional art and modern technology, and also brings new possibilities for the performance form and gameplay of shadow puppets. STEAM (Science, Technology, Engineering, Arts, Mathematics) education emphasizes multi-field and interdisciplinary concepts, aiming to improve students' innovative thinking and application abilities, which to a certain extent makes up for the shortcomings of the traditional teaching model. It can effectively promote teachers' teaching level and develop students' core competencies. According to statistics, about 40% of teenagers in China have participated in STEAM education and training courses, and this proportion is increasing year by year [2]. Therefore, how to integrate STEAM education and empower shadow puppet skills through digital intelligence technology to help them regenerate has become an important research direction of this paper.

This paper aims to explore the innovation of children's interactive shadow puppet products based on the STEAM education concept. The full text will be divided into six parts. In the part 2, we briefly review the related concepts of STEAM education and shadow puppet art. In the part 3, we introduce the basic overview, research methods and experimental process of the research in detail; and in the part 4 we analyze the experimental results and data. Based on the above results, we elaborate on the design concept and specific corresponding design details in Sect. 5. Finally, we highlight the study conclusions, implications, and limitations.

2 Literature Review

2.1 Digital and Intelligent Upgrade of STEAM Education Concept

STEAM education originally originated from the "Undergraduate Science, Mathematics, and Engineering Education" report of the U.S. National Science Council in 1986, covering four aspects: Science (S), Technology (T), Engineering (E), and Mathematics (M). Later, some scholars began to reflect on the limitations of science and engineering education and proposed incorporating art into STEM, thereby making this educational concept more comprehensive and possessing aesthetic value [3]. With the rapid development of science and technology and the popularization of digital intelligence technology, the concept of STEAM education is constantly evolving. Its digital intelligence upgrade aims to integrate digital intelligence technology into STEAM education to improve students' learning effects and comprehensive literacy. Among them, intelligent robots have been widely explored and applied as an effective carrier of STEAM education. It has two application methods: one is as a learning object, and the other is as a learning method for recognizing other subjects. Both are closely related to the STEAM education concept.

Currently, there are various STEAM educational robot platforms on the market, most of which focus on teaching computer, programming or engineering knowledge. For example: Mindstorms EV3, NAO, mBot, etc. [4]. "toio", as a typical representative of STEAM education, is a multi-functional modular robot developed by Sony Interactive Entertainment. It is mainly aimed at multiple fields such as programming enlightenment, creative bionics, music creation, strategy development and rule development. It not only educates and entertains, but also stimulates children's potential and helps children develop in an all-round way. Although many STEAM education applications have emerged on the market, there are still many challenges in integrating contemporary technology with traditional Chinese culture to meet modern needs, especially in the localization of STEAM education.

2.2 Modern Innovation of Shadow Puppet Art

Shadow Puppets originated in Asian countries and was gradually introduced to Europe and the United States. Now it has evolved into an entertaining dramatic art form. Shadow puppet art is life-like, aesthetic, comprehensive and practical, which provides good support for children's mental enlightenment and ability development [5]. At the same time, the entertainment value of shadow puppets is similar to the entertainment nature of children's interactive products, and its national attributes are complementary to the elements missing in the children's interactive product market.

Nowadays, influenced by modern technologies such as artificial intelligence, cloud computing, and virtual reality, digital research on shadow puppet art has become increasingly common. The inheritance of shadow puppets has gradually separated from the common recognition of skills. On the one hand, it can be used as a means of understanding the external world. For example, Gray et al. used shadow puppets to present the life stories of minority scientists to motivate children and set an example for them [6], Masunah et al. tried to cultivate students' entrepreneurial motivation through the artistic performance of shadow puppets [7]; on the other hand, it can also be used as learning content to creatively transform it [1, 5]. For example: introducing digital technologies such as AR and VR to enhance users' perception of shadow puppet culture [8], applying it to daily life products, and giving it entertainment or educational attributes while retaining the traditional form [9].

At present, the modern application innovation of shadow puppets mainly focuses on two aspects—lifestyle products and interactive devices (Table 1). The former has certain differences compared with traditional shadow puppets: firstly, the reduction in size makes it easier to display shadow puppet performances on the desktop; secondly, in terms of operation, it reduces the difficulty for users to get started by reducing or abandoning the joystick and sacrificing character flexibility; In terms of themes, fairy tales or popular IPs are added to attract children's interest and expand the audience; in terms of materials, modern industrial materials such as colored cardboard and PP plastic paper that can be mass-produced are mostly used instead of cowhide. This type of product transforms theater-style shadow puppet performances into a family-style entertainment activity or daily product [8–10]. The latter integrates software and hardware technologies such as motion capture, wearable devices, and screen interaction. For example, users can control shadow puppet characters through body interaction, thereby reducing learning costs, enhancing user participation and sense of substitution, and maximizing the flexibility of shadow puppet characters. This type of device is mainly used for offline exhibition interactive experience, and its forms of expression are mostly related to image animation, interactive media and technical expression, so its playability is greatly limited [11–13].

Table 1. Modern innovative features of shadow puppets

Category	Features	References
Lifestyle products	1.Small size, convenient for desktop display 2.Simple operation, consistent with common interaction methods 3.Themes closely follow popular culture 4.Materials are more environmentally friendly and durable	Wang, 2020; Zhao, 2024; Yang, 2018
Interactive installation	1.Integrating cutting-edge digital and intelligent technologies 2.Operation is natural and intuitive 3.Focus on enhancing user experience 4.Non-practical purpose	Talib et al. 2012; Ozcan, 2002; Ozcan et al. 2007

2.3 STEAM Education Concept and Shadow Puppet Innovation

Within the scope of STEAM education concept, the innovative design of shadow puppet products has become an educational method that has attracted much attention. Traditional shadow puppets themselves have characteristics that are consistent with the STEAM education. For example: S (Science): The product can tell knowledge about astronomy, geography, animals, ecology, etc. through shadow puppet stories, stimulating children's interest in science and desire to explore; T (Technology): Children can use modern technology, such as touch screens, virtual reality, voice recognition and other technologies, participate in the shadow puppet story, experience the fun and surprises brought by technology, and understand its principles at the same time; E (Engineering): Emphasizing the process of production, it is also the core of STEAM education. The process of decomposing each shadow puppet character from joints to construction corresponds to the process of assembling modules or parts into a complete body in engineering [14]; A (art): Shadow puppet, as a traditional art form, itself incorporates character creation, scene construction, music soundtrack and other artistic elements; M (mathematics) is defined as three important abilities: operations and coordination, spatial imagination, and logic. In traditional shadow puppet art, mathematical attributes are mainly reflected in the latter two aspects. For example: the distance between the shadow puppet and the curtain determines the size and degree of virtuality of the figure, which gives the shadow puppet performance a three-dimensional sense of space and helps cultivate children's spatial imagination [15]. Therefore, under the context of today's prevailing STEAM education concept, the design direction of shadow puppet art and children's interactive products has certain development potential.

As an important part of World Intangible Cultural Heritage and Chinese culture, shadow puppet has a long history and rich cultural connotation. Integrating shadow play with modern technology and STEAM education concepts will help to better inherit and carry forward its excellent tradition, while providing children with a rich and interesting educational experience with profound cultural heritage.

3   Methodology

3.1   Research Objects and Methods

Sony's toio is a STEAM education solution suitable for multiple ages. Therefore, this research selected this modular robot (referred to as "toio") as the carrier (as shown in Fig. 1) to develop children's interactive shadow puppet products. In order to verify the compatibility of "toio" and the peripheral shadow puppet device, this study mainly adopts experimental methods, and cooperates with observation, measurement, questionnaire and interview methods to conduct investigations. The survey targets include children and design workers, aiming to understand their attitudes towards four aspects: interactive shadow puppet materials, number of joints, movement methods, and presentation carriers. A total of 20 children aged between 7 and 12 years old (all of whom had participated in STEAM education courses) and a number of design workers aged between 25 and 40 participated in the study. The data collected from all experiments will provide a reference for further case studies in this field.

Fig. 1. Experimental materials—"toio" and control loop

3.2   Research Process and Experiments

This study is divided into four parts, as shown in Table 2. The first is material testing. Considering that the shadow puppet characters may be repeatedly pulled by robots, the shadow puppet materials need to have a certain degree of solidity and toughness. In the early stages of the research, we have eliminated common materials such as thinner sulfuric acid paper and cardboard on the market, and finally selected 1mm-thick acrylic sheets, PP (polypropylene) imitation leather paper and cowhide for material experiments.

Table 2. Research steps

No.	Experimental method	Experimental content	Target users
1	Experiments, Measurement	Material testing	Designers
2	Experiments, Questionnaires	Joint test	Children
3	Experiments, Interviews	Exercise test	Children
4	Experiments, Observation	Display carrier test	Children

The second part is joint testing. In this game setting, we designed the shadow puppet characters to attack, defend, obtain props and other actions. Therefore, the shape characteristics and joint number of shadow puppets are particularly important. These factors determine whether the shadow puppets can show widely different, personal and vivid movements. After preliminary testing, it was found that when the joint number is more than 5, the shadow puppet image can show more vivid movements, so in this step of testing, we identified several shadow puppet characters with different joint number. Then, let the children perform the restoration according to the set actions, and let them rate the control situation after the operation, as shown in Table 3.

Table 3. Joint test score sheet

Set action	Joint number	Manipulating satisfaction
	6	1 2 3 4 5 6 7 8 9 10
	7	1 2 3 4 5 6 7 8 9 10
	8	1 2 3 4 5 6 7 8 9 10

The third part is to study the influence of magnets on "toio" motion. The main difficulty lies in how "toio" can be attached to the wall and move freely and smoothly. This part of the investigation used a combination of experimental methods and interviews to specifically explore whether the vertical movement of "toio" under the action of different magnets on the same route will affect the game control experience.

The focus of the fourth part is to conduct carrier testing to determine how the virtual screen is combined with the physical shadow puppet robot, and how to ensure the beauty of the product. In this part, we will try different carrier forms, including but not limited to projection screens, transparent screens, and other possible presentation methods to ensure good visual effects and viewing experience.

4 Experimental Results and Analysis

4.1 Material Testing

In the material test, we mainly explored two aspects: (1) Comparing the impact of different materials on the "toio" movement; (2) Comparing the laser engraving effects of different materials to determine which material is more suitable for the production of shadow puppets. During the process, we also interviewed many designers to obtain relevant experience and suggestions.

We carved the shadow puppet character "Chenghuang" of three different material types and pasted them on the top of the two robots (official data shows that the maximum load of a single robot is 200 g), compared the linear movement distance of the robots in the same time period, and obtained user subjective feedback. In order to display the experimental results more intuitively, this experiment also set up a group of robots without characters as a control group. The experimental results show (Table 4) that under no load-bearing condition, the robot moved 1023 mm in 10 s, while the module carrying the acrylic shadow puppet character only moved 245 mm, although the total load did not exceed the sum of the maximum load of the two robots (400 g), but according to operator feedback, there is a serious sense of interaction delay. Modules carrying imitation leather paper and cowhide materials performed better, with less difference in movement distance compared to those without load-bearing.

The 1mm acrylic sheet material is transparent, and stacking multiple sheets will produce a sense of overlap and have a better visual effect. However, in actual operation, problems such as loose joints, excessive weight, poor durability, and inability to perform fine carvings were found. During the laser engraving process, the edges of PP imitation leather paper will melt and release a pungent smell; in addition, the material is opaque and the visual effect is poor, far from achieving the expected effect. Cowhide is tough enough, suitable for laser cutting, and has good light transmission properties. After processing and dyeing, the cowhide can present a unique visual effect, making the shadow puppet characters clearer, brighter and easier to watch during performances. Although the processing cost of cowhide is high and the requirements for laser cutting parameters are strict (it is easy to burn), it is still the most suitable production material at present, and it also meets the needs of shadow puppet cultural inheritance and performance (Fig. 2).

Table 4. Effects of different materials on robot movement distance

Experiment type	Material	Loading capacity/g	Movement distance/mm	Control feedback
Control group	None	0	1023	Smooth control, no lag
Test group	Acrylic	366 g	245	There is severe lag, almost no movement, and interactive feedback is delayed
	Imitation leather paper	258 g	986	The control is relatively smooth and there is no obvious lag
	Cowhide	212 g	992	The control is relatively smooth and there is no obvious lag

Fig. 2. The engraving effect of PP imitation leather paper (left) and cowhide (right)

4.2 Joint Testing

In the joint test stage, we used a 10-point Likert scale, taking the shadow puppet character "Chenghuang" as an example, to explore the impact of different joint numbers on children's control experience. We collected feedback from 20 children on their satisfaction scores with different joint numbers. The overall data is shown in Table 5.

The analysis results show that when the number of joints is 6, children's control satisfaction is the lowest (6.7); while the number of joints of 7 (8.6) and 8 (8.25) has less impact on children's use experience. Through frequency analysis (shown in Fig. 3),

Table 5. Overall situation of joint test scores

Joint number	Maximum	Minimum	Average	Median
6	9	4	6.7	7
7	10	6	8.6	9
8	10	7	8.25	8

we can learn more about children's satisfaction with different joint numbers. When the number of joints is 6, the highest satisfaction score reaches 7 points, accounting for 55%. When the number of joints increased to 7, the satisfaction level reached a maximum of 9 points, accounting for 60%. In addition, when the number of joints is 8, 40% have a satisfaction score of 8, and 35% have a satisfaction score of 7. The two are equivalent. It can be seen that the increase in the number of joints does not significantly improve the control experience, but may increase the production cost of the product. To sum up, considering the children's control experience and production cost, 7 joints is currently the best choice. In addition, in order to enhance the layering and richness of the shadow puppet characters, we also layered some decorative elements, such as cloud patterns and flames. We attach these elements to the shadow puppets by pasting or fixing them to enhance the visual effect.

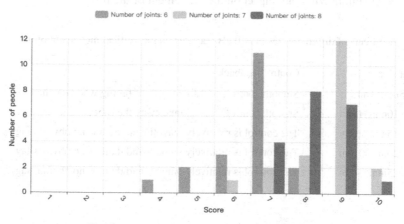

Fig. 3. Frequency analysis chart of joint testing

4.3 Exercise Testing

First, we tried magnets made of three different materials, namely ferrite magnets, neodymium (NdFeB) magnets and alnico magnets. We glued these magnets of the same size (about 10 mm * 10 mm * 1 mm) to the bottom of the "toio" and let them stick to the magnetic whiteboard. Subsequently, we invited 20 children to conduct tests along the preset route to obtain their control feelings and opinions (shown in Table 6). Experimental results show that the adsorption force of robots equipped with ferrite magnets and alnico magnets on vertical walls is weak. In view of the stability of the game, we finally chose NdFeB magnet as the preferred material.

Table 6. Effects of different types of magnets on the vertical movement of the robot

Magnet type	Control feedback
Ferrite magnet	Smooth control, occasional risk of falling when touched
NdFeB magnet	The control is relatively smooth and there is no obvious lag
Alnico magnet	Smooth control, easy to take away the robot

Second, we need to determine the effect of magnet size on motion. We tried five different sizes of magnets (Table 7). In view of the limited space at the bottom of "toio", we found that when the magnet thickness reaches 2mm, the robot will float in the air, so we set the magnet thickness to 1mm. The results show that when the size of the NdFeB magnet is 15mm*15mm*1mm, the user's control experience is the best, and the increase in the magnet area does not have a significant impact on game control. In summary, we finally determined a 15mm*15mm*1mm square NdFeB magnet to ensure adsorption strength while minimizing the impact on the movement of the robot.

Table 7. Effects of different sizes of NdFeB magnets on the vertical movement of the robot

Magnet size	Control feedback
5mm*5mm*1mm	Smooth control, occasional risk of falling when touched
10mm*10mm*1mm	Smooth control, easy to take away the robot
15mm*15mm*1mm	The control is relatively smooth and there is no obvious lag
20mm*20mm*1mm	The control is relatively smooth and there is no obvious lag
25mm*25mm*1mm	The control is relatively smooth and there is no obvious lag

4.4 Display Carrier Testing

We considered two virtual screen carrier solutions: transparent screens and projectors. Although the transparent screen is more expensive, its effect is remarkable. It can realize the movement of shadow puppets behind the screen, creating a spatial effect of characters traveling through the scene. In comparison, projectors are lower in cost, but have poorer effects in terms of color rendering and sense of space. At the same time, they have higher requirements for the darkness of the environment, which is detrimental to the final display effect. Considering the feasibility and completion of the solution in the short term, we finally chose a projector as the preferred display carrier.

5   Design Practice

5.1   Design Concept

This product is a children's STEAM education collector's edition kit based on the "toio" programming robot, with new interpretations of traditional stories and new games from the Classic of Mountains and Seas as its theme, and combining shadow puppets with

Fig. 4. Product renderings and scene diagrams

AI and smart hardware (Fig. 4). The kit includes a console, two game controllers, four "toio" robots, game mats, DIY character materials, etc., as well as an additional OLED screen or projector if required. Through the application of smart devices, innovative interactive gameplay and shadow puppet art style expression, it aims to achieve inter-disciplinary education and enlightenment in STEAM education, exercise social skills, decision-making, hand-eye coordination and other abilities, and subtly impart geography, culture, biology and other knowledge, as well as cooperation, kindness, gratitude and other good qualities.

5.2 Product Details

Storyline and Gameplay Description. The game is set in the background of "The Classic of Mountains and Seas". Various rare and exotic beasts are stationed in the valleys and rivers on the continent. They have independent territories and ethnic groups. In some areas, there are also skill fruits that can increase the attack power of mythical beasts. The mythical beast needs to occupy more territory and enhance its skills by obtaining skill fruits to defeat other monsters on the way.

The game is divided into single and multiplayer modes. The single-player mode focuses on character development. Players use their bracelets to control the movement of their characters, and follow the prompts to complete the storyline and complete the main mission. Multiplayer modes include competitive mode and cooperative mode. The competitive mode has a high degree of freedom in gameplay, requiring players to choose a character and use skills to repel monsters on the way. The first party to reach the opponent's initial position wins. The cooperative mode requires both parties to cooperate to complete the task and pass the set level, otherwise both parties will fail.

Visual Image Description. The game scene is based on the map of "The Classic of Mountains and Seas" and is divided into three scenes: land, water and sky according to the difficulty of the game (shown in Fig. 5). The land scene in the first level features rocks. The character cannot pass directly through the rocks and must take a detour. Cracked stones can be broken using skills to create new roads. The overall difficulty of this level is low, with fewer obstacles and a wider route to help players adapt to the game operations. The underwater scene in the second level contains elements such as aquatic plants, coral reefs, and monsters. The difficulty is slightly increased and the route is more complex. The character cannot pass directly through the water-weed area and needs to use skills to clear the water-weed. The sky scene design of the third level includes elements such as suspended islands, flying birds, and floating clouds. It also adds a mechanism to automatically return to the initial starting point when encountering large monsters. The difficulty is once again increased compared to the first two levels.

In the design of shadow puppet characters, taking "Chenghuang" in "The Classic of Mountains and Seas" as an example, we extracted the shapes of clouds, tails, animal claws, flames and other elements from traditional shadow puppets, as well as specific hollow patterns to continue the traditional appearance of shadow puppets and achieve the purpose of spreading traditional shadow puppet culture and aesthetic value. In terms of material selection, we still use strong and tough cowhide to prevent damage to the shadow puppets during frequent play. Structurally, we have divided the shadow puppet

Fig. 5. Overview of game scene map

characters into joints. For example, "Chenghuang" is divided into seven parts: head, upper body, lower body, limbs, tail, cloud patterns, and other decorative patterns. Among them, the head, limbs, cloud patterns, etc. are pasted on the upper and lower bodies to create a sense of layering, while the upper and lower bodies are articulated to ensure the flexibility of the character (Fig. 6). In addition, we have also designed a variety of characters with different shapes, which can show different actions and use various skills (shown in Fig. 7).

Structural Details. This product includes two parts: shadow puppet character and stage. The shadow puppet is fixed on the top surface of the "toio" (as shown in Fig. 8). Two robots (referred to as A and B respectively) control the upper and lower bodies of the shadow puppet so that it can make some large movements. The user controls the robot to move and make corresponding actions by controlling the joysticks and buttons of the bracelet. Compared with traditional stick control, it greatly reduces the difficulty of getting started. Take the gameplay of the "Huayu" character as an example (Fig. 9). Its body has multiple joints and its movement is characterized by twisting (the two robots move in a curve). Its attack skill is to swing its tail (robot B rotates 180° left and right), and its protection skill is to curl up into a ball with its head and tail connected (robot A rotates 160° counterclockwise, and robot B rotates 160° clockwise).

The stage consists of three parts: a transparent screen, a "toio" operating pad, and a magnetic board (Fig. 10). The stage hung on the wall corresponds to the traditional vertical shadow puppet stage, which is convenient for viewing and display, and enhances children's sense of participation and desire for expression. At the same time, this design helps protect the child's cervical spine and develop hand-eye coordination. The introduction of smart screens makes traditional shadow puppet backgrounds more flexible, allowing content to be changed at will and dynamic feedback added.

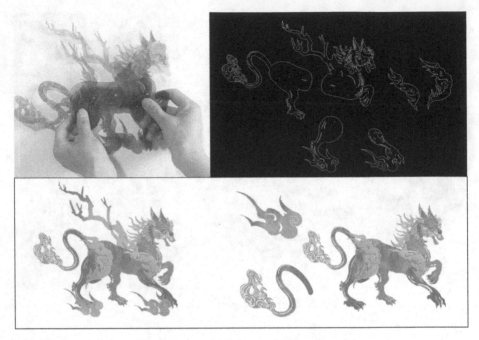

Fig. 6. Structural diagram of "Chenghuang"

Fig. 7. Other shadow puppet characters

Functional Details. This product mainly contains three functions. (1) The image is displayed in real time. The game's graphic content, such as game maps, characters, and animated special effects, can be displayed on the screen in real time. In addition, game images can also be projected onto TVs, monitors, tablets or projectors at home; (2) Game and shadow puppet control. The user can control the movements of the shadow puppet through the bracelet, and at the same time trigger corresponding image changes; (3) Picture and sound feedback. The toio robot has a built-in camera and a variety of sensors. When it moves to a specific location, it can identify the program code of that

Fig. 8. Shadow puppet control diagram

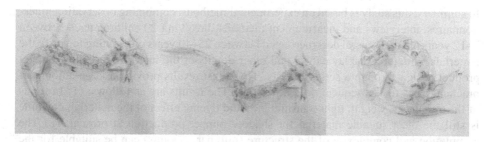

Fig. 9. How to play the role of "Huayu"

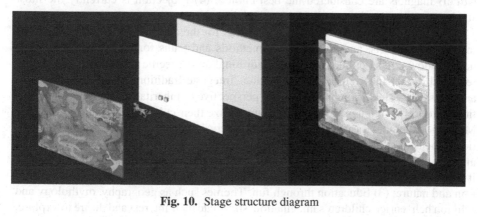

Fig. 10. Stage structure diagram

location, or drive the robot to make corresponding actions or make sounds by identifying the coordinates on the map pad.

Interaction Details. This product establishes three types of interaction methods: user and physical hardware, user and virtual interface, and user-to-user. (1) User interaction with physical hardware. Users can use the bracelet to control the free movement of the "toio" robot, including forward, backward, steering, twisting, shaking and other actions. This control method helps improve children's fine operation and spatial perception abilities, and enhances hand-eye coordination; (2) User interaction with virtual interface. In the single-player plot mode, the user transforms into an alien beast and shuttles through the virtual scene by controlling the physical shadow robot, triggering animations, dialogues, sounds, and completing plot tasks according to prompts; (3) User-to-user interaction. This part of the interaction is mainly reflected in the multiplayer mode, and a shadow puppet character can be jointly controlled by one or two players. This can exercise children's cooperation, coordination and social skills, while enhancing feelings, promoting physical and mental health and personality perfection.

6 Conclusion

In summary, this study is based on experimental methods, combining observation, questionnaires, interviews and measurement methods, involving 20 children aged between 7–12 years old and several designers aged between 25–40 years old, aiming to verify the materials, structure, display carrier and other details of the interactive shadow puppet product design through a series of tests. These test results provide a large amount of practical basis for subsequent design practice. The results are as follows: (1) In terms of the toughness, weight, light transmittance and dyeing effect of the material, cowhide is still the most suitable material for shadow puppet production at present; (2) The completion and complexity of the structure (number of joints) can be suitable for the required functions; (3) In terms of robot vertical movement, 15mm*15mm*1mm square NdFeB magnets are considered the best choice; (4) Projection is currently the most stable, feasible and effective display method.

This research provides references and ideas for the design of STEAM educational interactive products, and also provides methods and paths for the activation of Chinese shadow puppet culture and other traditional arts. Specific innovations are mainly reflected in: (1) Inheritance and innovation. Integrate traditional Chinese stories and ancient skills—shadow puppets from the perspective of inheritance, and interpret traditional stories from a new perspective to maximize their cultural and market value; (2) Multi-modal mode. Based on toio core technology, it breaks through the spatial interaction dimension, uses the combination of virtual and real to enhance sensory experience, and achieves multi-modal interaction with a higher degree of freedom; at the same time, it exercises children's hand-eye-brain trinity ability and releases their creative inspiration and nature; (3) Education through fun. Themes such as geography, mythology and religion help enrich children's imagination, stimulate their interest and desire to explore, and then cultivate their multi-faceted thinking, interests and personality traits.

At the same time, this study also has certain limitations, mainly manifested in: due to time constraints, the number of questionnaire samples is relatively small, which may affect the comprehensiveness of the results. In addition, due to cost and short-term implementation considerations, a transparent display with better effect was not selected for presentation. The above deficiencies need to be continuously improved in future research.

Acknowledgments. This study was supported by the General Scientific Research Project of the Zhejiang Provincial Department of Education (Y202354040).

References

1. Ma, Z.Y., Chang, G.Y.: On the expansion of the problem domain of intangible inheritance. Journal of South Central University for Nationalities (Humanities and Social Sciences Edition), 1–12 (2024)
2. iResearch Industry Research Part 14: Turning the tables and returning to purity. Market Demand Insight Report on China's Education Industry—Adolescents and Children (eds.) Proceedings of the 2023 iResearch March Research Report Conference, pp. 774–828 (2023)
3. Basogain, X., Gurba, K., Hug, T., Morze, N., Noskova, T., Smyrnova-Trybulska, E.: STEM and STEAM in contemporary education: challenges, contemporary trends and transformation: a discussion paper (2020)
4. Kalaitzidou, M., Pachidis, T.P.: Recent robots in STEAM education. Educ. Sci. **13**(3), 272 (2023)
5. Xiao, S.Z., Chen, Z., Chen, F., Ma, L.: The educational value of excellent Chinese traditional arts and its application in kindergarten. Preschool Educ. Res. **07**, 91–94 (2023)
6. Gray, P., Rule, A.C., Gentzsch, A., Tallakson, D.: Shadow puppet plays in elementary science methods class help preservice teachers learn about minority scientists. J. STEM Arts Crafts Constructions **1**(1), 4 (2016)
7. Masunah, J., Dyani, P.L., Gaffar, V., Sari, M.: Production of shadow puppet performances in building artistic entrepreneurship. J. Sustain. Tourism Entrepreneurship **3**(2), 89–100 (2021)
8. Wang, Y.P.: Master's degree thesis on practical research on junior high school STEAM curriculum based on traditional culture. Shenyang University (2020)
9. Zhao, H.: Shadow puppet story machine based on STEAM programming. Media (01), 105 (2024)
10. Yang, L.: Research on product design of intangible cultural heritage from an emotional viewpoint: a case study based on Chinese shadow puppet. In 2018 11th International Symposium on Computational Intelligence and Design, vol. 1, pp. 275–279. IEEE (2018)
11. Talib, A.Z., Osman, M.A., Tan, K.L., Piman, S.: Design and development of an interactive virtual shadow puppet play. In: Brooks, A.L. (ed.) ArtsIT 2011. LNICSSITE, vol. 101, pp. 118–126. Springer, Heidelberg (2012). https://doi.org/10.1007/978-3-642-33329-3_14
12. Ozcan, O.: Cultures, the traditional shadow play, and interactive media design. Des. Issues **18**(3), 18–26 (2002)
13. Ozcan, O., Thomassen, A., Baumann, K., Holmgren, M., Lindell, R., Graz, F.J.: The role of traditional shadow play on creativity in interaction design. In: Media in Transition 5: creativity, ownership, and collaboration in the digital age, Massachusetts Institute of Technology (2007)
14. Chen, J., Zhu, L.C., Wang, J., Fan, Q.W., Wu, J.B., Ren, H.B.: Exploration and practice of ideological and political teaching in engineering training courses. J. Higher Educ. **S2**, 5–8 (2023)
15. Hu, J.R.: Focusing on shadow puppet elements to enrich mathematical practice—taking the "Position and Movement of Figures" comprehensive practice activity as an example. Hubei Educ. **09**, 14–15 (2023)

Investigating Learning Experiences

Uses of Robotics to Improve the Instrumental Skills of Students with Autism Spectrum Disorder Through the Development of New Inclusive Contexts (Divintech)

David Fonseca Escudero[1]($\boxtimes$) ID, Selene Caro-Via[1] ID, Javier Herrero-Martin[2] ID,
Xavi Canaleta[1] ID, Rosario Valdivieso[2] ID, Daniel Amo-Filvà[1] ID, Meritxell Nieto[3],
Neus Ramos[3], and Claudia Bardia[3]

[1] La Salle, Ramon Llull University, Barcelona, Spain
{david.fonseca,selene.caro,xavier.canaleta,
daniel.amo}@salle.url.edu
[2] Department of Preprimary and Primary Education, Education Faculty of La Salle University Center, Universidad Autónoma de Madrid, Madrid, Spain
{j.herrero,r.valdivieso}@lasallecampus.es
[3] La Salle La Seu d'Urgell, La Seu d'Urgell, Lleida, Spain
{mnieto,nramos,cbardia}@lasalle.cat

Abstract. The DivInTech (from Diversity, Inclusion, and Technology) project originates from the specific orientation of addressing a concrete issue linked to the thematic priority of "Culture, Creativity, and Inclusive Society," as defined in the programming of the Spanish State Plan for Scientific, Technical, and Innovation Research 2021–2023. From a multidisciplinary perspective intersecting the thematic areas of Education Sciences (the main domain), Psychology, and ICTs (as defined by the State Research Agency), the aim is to enhance social inclusion, particularly in the educational and family domains, for students affected by autism spectrum disorder (ASD). This is achieved through the design, implementation, evaluation, and scalability of STEAM (Science, Technology, Engineering, Arts, and Mathematics) activities in specifically designed spaces. The current proposal conceptualizes the project's need, its participants, phases, and methodology to foster new collaborations that enable a broader impact with the scalability of its activities.

Keywords: Educational robotics · social robotics · educational innovation · STEAM · inclusion · diversity · Autism Spectrum Disorder

1 Introduction

There is a growing issue in Spain, which could primarily be extrapolated to other countries in the European Economic Community, where an increasing number of children are identified with some form of diversity gap [45]. When we talk about diversity, one of the main focuses of study and research in recent years has been centered on gender issues,

P. Zaphiris and A. Ioannou (Eds.): HCII 2024, LNCS 14722, pp. 165–180, 2024.
https://doi.org/10.1007/978-3-031-61672-3_11

followed by racial and disabilities. However, we cannot overlook other socio-economic, cultural, religious, and, of course, those associated with disabilities [3]. In this regard, there are various disabilities, both physical, resulting from trauma, and a broad range of mental disabilities that can affect both physical and psychological levels, leading to disabilities as such, or disorders, deficits, or dysfunctions with a historical bias in terms of study and educational adaptations [34]. DivInTech is a project focused on students identified and certified with Autism Spectrum Disorder (ASD), a type of mental disorder defined in the DSM-5 [40, 46].

Given the selected profile, it is important to note that the identification of cases with ASD in non-university education has increased by 8.07% (4,497 individuals) in the last school year with verified data (2020–21), resulting in a total of 60,198 students (50,372 boys and 9,826 girls) identified in some of its dimensions [47]. This increase is not isolated, as confirmed by Autism Spain, based on the analysis of data from the 2020–2021 academic year published by the Ministry of Education and Vocational Training. This upward trend has continued for the tenth consecutive year.

Considering that individuals with ASD have been recognized as a group with special vulnerability in the new Employment Law [20] and that specific repetitive work with these profiles improves the integration of the student in many aspects [21], the DivInTech project adapted to the call for Knowledge Generation Projects, 2023 call, from the Ministry of Science and Innovation of Spain. In this sense, the project secured funding for the period 2023–2026 as applied research, as it addresses the resolution of specific problems related to challenges and priorities defined at both the national and international levels.

In the following sections, we will detail the project's description, its components, methodologies, and phases, as well as the expected results. The goal is to reach more institutions, both universities and earlier stages of education so that the proposals can be replicated and scaled.

2 Project Description

The DivInTech project is committed to addressing the rising issue described in the Introduction to enhance the skills and social inclusion of students with ASD. The methodology is based on STEAM action research, using educational robotics as a tool tailored to the diverse profiles of students.

By identifying the behavioral profiles of students affected by ASD, the project aims to design, implement, analyze, and scale interaction models with robots, where robots serve as facilitating support for learning and everyday tasks. These activities will take place in designated spaces to improve their academic assessment alongside social integration.

As an additional objective, a territorial diversity map will be created for each operating center. This serves two purposes: to externalize and scale the methodological proposals and work interventions carried out with students from other centers with similar characteristics, and to establish an open forum for the exchange of best practices and support among educational centers and nearby social entities, ensuring effective and satisfactory long-term social integration.

The approach can be defined as innovative due to its mixed approach and technological uses. The project operates at both macro and micro social levels, focused on improving the social inclusion of students with ASD in their immediate environment, given the increasing magnitude of this group. At the micro level, the interactions of children will be monitored qualitatively by tutors and teachers, and quantitatively using biometric bracelets to synchronize activity with physiological responses. This allows the identification of significant moments in the process concerning the physiological response of the student during specific interactions with the robot.

At the macro level, one objective is to create a map of ASD diversity in the environments and territories of the study centers. This map can be scaled at three levels: within the network of La Salle Spain-Portugal (ARLEP), to other national schools outside the ARLEP network or national schools in countries with which a consortium collaboration can be established through projects like Erasmus +, and finally, to any other educational center in the territory.

In summary, the project arises from the real and current needs faced by schools. The first pilot case of the three designed to be developed in the project is La Salle La Seu d'Urgell school, which has strong integration in the territory. The school covers pre-university formal education as well as vocational training cycles that stimulate job opportunities for young people within the regional industrial fabric. Adapting the training of students with behavioral disorders or different disabilities at any educational stage improves their school and family inclusion and, in turn, allows educational centers to have innovative spaces to address the needs of these students and others in various aspects—social, psychological, technological, or creative.

3 Justification and Main Contributions. Initial Hypothesis

As introduced, the proposal aligns with the thematic priority of "Culture, Creativity, and Inclusive Society." In this regard, a national and European priority is to promote STEAM approaches and vocations with special consideration for users affected by any diversity gap: gender, social, economic, immigration, religious, or disability-related factors. This involves creating unique spaces that enhance creativity and multidisciplinary activities [18, 22]. The main objective of the project is to improve the inclusion of students affected by autism spectrum disorder (ASD). Specifically, the aim is to enhance their skills in their sociocultural environment. To achieve these objectives, personalized educational activities mediated by robots will be created.

Previous work in the field of Human-Robot Interaction has revealed that, like most children, those affected by ASD enjoy playing with robots because they behave predictably, repeating actions in the same way, reinforcing knowledge [30]. This repetitive behavior, along with consistent and structured instructions, is crucial in aiding the learning process of students with ASD. Ultimately, robotic behavior and the mentioned aspects are just some of the reasons why students with ASD often perceive a robot as less intimidating than a human and why robots seem more advantageous in facilitating learning for this student profile [4, 10, 12, 25, 26].

Students with ASD face challenges in interacting with everyday activities, both at home and in class, as well as in their surrounding environment. Given the project's significance, initial contacts have been established between schools, families, and robotics development teams to explore specific issues and define the approach of each instruction to ensure that the contribution aligns with the needs of each stakeholder at the appropriate time. In this regard, it has been observed that students with ASD have a strong obsession with time, its control, and monitoring, and a high difficulty in paying attention to any activity they are doing, no matter how small.

Other identified aspects include difficulty in describing a specific situation or a lack of behavioral guidelines for certain activities as common as entering a classroom or a store. Previous work in the field of robotics with social uses demonstrates how motivation, empathy, cognitive stimulation, and even certain skills and competencies of students affected by gaps such as age or neurodevelopmental disorders like ASD can be improved through programmed interaction with specific types of robots [32, 35].

Based on the previous exploration in both scientific literature and the field of action, we define the following initial hypotheses:

- H1: Personalized STEAM interventions for each student with ASD are more effective in improving social processes and behavioral conduct.
- H2: The use of biometric bracelets in the classroom allows distinguishing those STEAM practices with a greater impact on the learning of social processes and behavioral conduct.

One of the most used STEAM approaches in classrooms is educational and/or social robotics. By using simple programs with Arduino, Scratch, Micro:bit, or simple robots (such as BeeBot), it becomes possible to explain complex content in a different way, often reducing resistance. The creativity inherent in these approaches tends to improve student responses on emotional, motivational, and ultimately, curricular levels [1, 6, 7, 19, 24, 36, 41]. In addition to the previously mentioned project contributions to solving problems in the thematic area, the goal is also to characterize unique spaces to meet the specific needs of students with ASD. Previous studies [3, 14] demonstrate how the creation of comfortable multidisciplinary spaces, blending technological and traditional pedagogical elements, allows for better monitoring of students, enabling them to focus on instructional designs without distractions.

A variant of STEAMLabs is the SIEI (Intensive Support for Inclusive Education, from the Spanish "*Soporte Inclusivo a la Educación Inclusiva*"), multidisciplinary spaces where the focus is on helping students with certain disabilities, usually mental and/or intellectual. Adapting SIEI for children with ASD to interact with robot-created proposals, while characterizing the interaction with data collection by the facilitator through biometric bracelet monitoring without making them feel like subjects of study, is fundamental and a relevant contribution of the proposal. Based on the identification of behavioral or social situations to improve for each case, as mentioned earlier, various instructions and practices will be programmed to allow students to interact with the robot and improve in their shortcomings. The sought-after improvement intended by the project will directly impact the integration of the child with their environment, both in the classroom and in leisure moments, and their relationships with the social actors around them: family, neighbors, classmates, teachers, etc.

To personalize interventions based on students with ASD, profiles will be created for each student to identify the recognized degree of disability, any other pre-existing dysfunction, as well as the typology of behaviors and responses to common social situations and those to be improved. In this way, and to intervene in social communication processes, variables related to expression level, non-verbal communication, stereotyped sentences, and expressions will be identified, among others. In terms of social inter-action, the variables to be studied will cover manifestations of affection or expression of emotions, interest in social activities and participation in shared games, theory of mind, or positive/negative emotional expression, among others. Finally, to assess param-eters related to restricted and repetitive behaviors, aspects such as fixation on specific objects, the typology of imagination in games and tasks, cognitive inflexibility, possible self-injuries, etc., will be analyzed.

The study and weighting of all these variables that make up the initial student profile are, in themselves, one of the project's highlighted contributions, as it will allow for exportation and application to any other educational institution and level, allowing for a much better parameterization of the support that students with ASD can and should receive.

The second relevant contribution of the project will be instructional designs through interaction with robots, given their customization based on the student's profile. The intervention guidelines where the robot assists the student will focus on specific aspects tailored to their needs, reducing generalization, and potentially increasing their impact and success. Thus, research on the programming possibilities, gestures, and interac-tion that the robot can offer, and what and how can be changed semi-automatically to adapt the interaction interface to small variations in new students (for example, changing interaction volume, the background color of a game, a favorite music, a reaction to a positive or negative action, or being able to change the student's name, etc.), is another relevant and differential aspect of the proposal [6]. The personalization of teaching activ-ities must address diversity. From a user-centered design approach [2, 27], usability and accessibility of interactive dynamics will be optimized, considering the user's needs in coordination with all surrounding actors, from family to educators, an approach relevant from a scientific methodology perspective for educational improvement, as previous studies in other educational fields have demonstrated [3, 11, 15, 38].

The third relevant contribution is the mixed approach of variables [13, 17, 39] col-lected in the learning and interaction monitoring process with the robot. From the instruc-tional point of view of each instructional design, a form will be created to assess the degree of achievement/success/failure of each action, and this information will be col-lected by the facilitator accompanying the student. Additionally, the session will be recorded on video to synchronize the student's activity with the robot and a biometric sensor (bracelet) that quantitatively collects data throughout each practice. This way, the activity of the data collected by the bracelet can be synchronized with the actions and reactions of the student under study, allowing for the focus, adaptation, enhancement, or softening of the robot's programming based on the student's response. In this sense, the subjective component of previous studies based on qualitative data is reduced, and those qualitatively collected by the facilitator will be related to biometric responses.

The fourth major contribution of the proposal will focus on objective 2, which we will describe later. In this case, the creation of a territorial ASD diversity map as an open learning resource that allows for sharing experiences, identifying best practices, locating centers specialized in certain disabilities or approaches, and generating syner-gies between centers, seems to be a result of exponential impact. As good practices can be shared and the mapping of centers, initiatives, projects, and practices increases, a service will be provided to the educational community that allows for greater inclusion of students with ASD, a process still lacking in many centers due to a lack of knowledge of how to address personalized learning, a lack of a suitable support space, or simply a lack of identification of these profiles, aspects that are resolved by the present proposal in the other relevant contributions identified.

4 Objectives, Methodology, and Work-Plan

Two main objectives have been identified for development in the project, along with a series of specific objectives that define the concrete results or outputs of the project:

- Objective 1: Develop robotized intervention sequences.

- O1.1: Identify profiles of students with ASD. Through collaboration with teachers, the SIEI team, and families, profiles characterizing the emotional, behavioral, relational, and academic variables of students with ASD will be generated. The profile of each student will be used to characterize and establish the objectives of intervention sequences in the SIEI. Robots will serve as a means for their execution.

1. Result 1 (R1): ASD student profile.

- O1.2: Design robotized instructional sequence. After identifying different profiles, instructional designs for each learning activity related to social processes and behavioral behaviors will be developed (based on research into the capabilities of the robotic platform). All designs will integrate the use of a robot, an electronic device (tablet, computer…), and determined interaction elements. Collaboration will occur between application developers familiar with the robot's potential, SIEI teachers, and psychologists specializing in ASD.

2. Result 2 (R2): Set of instructional designs.

- O1.3: Implement and evaluate instructional sequence. Sequences will be implemented in a familiar space adapted to the needs of students, ensuring comfort. The size and layout of the space, furniture, and any other evaluation elements must be integrated not to disrupt the sequence.

3. Result 3 (R3): Characterization of ASD attention spaces.
4. Result 4 (R4): Multilayer recording of the intervention (multimedia, biometric data, observations).

- Multimedia: Video recording of the interaction, aiming to synchronize any moment of success or failure in the sequences with the physiological response of the student:

  - Biometric data: The student with ASD will wear a biosensing data bracelet, capturing various physiological parameters in real-time: heart rate, temperature, skin moisture level (sweat), arm acceleration, and orientation.

– Observations: Support personnel will fill out an observation form, documenting indicators of success/failure and interaction. This subjective evaluation will assess the user experience (UX) from the observer's standpoint.
– O1.4: Scale instructional sequences. Using data from O1.3, sequences will be modified based on identified usability and accessibility issues. A second round of intervention will be conducted with the selected student and others susceptible to study.

5. Result 5 (R5): Analysis, evaluation, and improvement of R2.
6. Result 6 (R6): Open dissemination of R5 through an Educational Open Resource (OER), scaling to other centers with similar student profiles.

• Objective 2: Create a Social Diversity Observatory. The second general objective of the project seeks to represent diversity in its social and cultural context, interconnecting the ASD educational community. Throughout the three years of the project, a clear, contextual, and local representation of real diversity, specifically for students with ASD, will be constructed. This representation will relate to the social and cultural environment of each educational center. In parallel with the proposed initial development, suitable instruments for utilizing robotics to develop and enhance skills will be developed. The aim is to analyze, using an inductive mechanism, the unique reality of each environment. The proposed work design establishes the specific objectives outlined above:

– O2.1: Identify institutions hosting individuals with ASD. A field study will be conducted to identify practices, resources, or institutions with users affected by ASD and/or resources to enhance the social integration of any user affected by diversity gaps, especially in autism spectrum disorders.

7. Result 7 (R7): Field study.

– O2.2: Connect ASD realities. Mapping centers, user types, resources, and systems aim to design and implement a platform acting as a mediator between educational entities and other social agents to promote the inclusion of these users.

8. Result 8 (R8): Platform design and development.
9. Result 9 (R9): ASD diversity mapping on an open platform.

– O2.3: Generate a learning community. In the platform, besides identifying and mapping initiatives, centers, and user typologies, a learning community will be created. This open community will allow the sharing, replicating, and publishing of results, improving processes affecting users with ASD in their daily interactions.

10. Result 10 (R10): Open access to Educational Resources.

From a methodological standpoint, the proposed research follows a course of convergent approach, resulting from the disposition of layers of quantitative and qualitative analysis, as will be seen below. From a general perspective, the design presents a strategy of analysis based on the case study, so that the integration of it into its context allows for a scalable and valid intervention of the information to be collected [37]. In this way, the analysis and observation of selected and controlled cases of children with ASD in their school context are proposed.

In terms of modality, the case study has an instrumental character, as the investigative axis is situated on a transcendent level regarding the subject, constituting the object of the inquiry related to the understanding of the instrumental elements that ensure the educational and social inclusion of students with cognitive-functional diversity and ASD. Based on the two main objectives planned for the project, we can break down the methodology as follows:

- O1: The work proposal aims to ultimately generate a defined set of robotic resources for social intervention that facilitates the development of inclusive environments for children with autism spectrum disorders. To achieve this, this objective is defined in terms of the degree of instrumental facilitation for the development of skills and competencies, using the social robot, to enable effective adaptation to the conditions of daily life. This level of the project consists, in turn, of several integral steps associated with specific objectives:

  - O1.1: Case selection and study. Following [31], the following steps are considered in the methodological discourse: 1) Selection and definition of the case; 2) Elaboration of an argument; 3) Location of data sources; 4) Analysis and interpretation; 5) Preparation of results reports. In turn, the proposed study has an explanatory character or inductive approach, as it considers the need to explain in depth the development of communicative, cognitive, and social competencies as a phenomenon to be addressed, substantiating the treatment from the data to build an appropriate theoretical framework [23].
  - O1.2 and O1.3: Methodological design of intervention. Once the cases are selected, the regulatory principle, in terms of design, follows a circular approach, through a multichannel methodological discourse, based on the principle of action research. As a basic process of analysis, each case is contextualized in a pre-post process, of a quasi-experimental nature, which has been previously used in designs related to the use of robotics in intervention with ASD [44], as well as in general education [8]. For the configuration of data collection, a system of convergent analysis layers has been defined in this previous intervention context, following the following sequence: 1) Definition of the didactic intervention sequence; 2) Robotic programming; 3) Observation recording of behaviors; 4) Videotaping of the intervention session; 5) Collection and analysis of psychophysiological data: "biosensing" measures; 6) Collection of communicative-linguistic segments for transcription and analysis. Overall, the general intervention design per case is presented in Fig. 1:
  - O1.4: Transfer and scaling. Finally, the analysis and interpretation of the results will be developed following the established multichannel pattern, interpretative convergence, and circularity based on the action research principle. For this, the computational analytics of the data collected in the biosensor channels, the analysis of the keys and integrated stimulus patterns in the intervention sequences, observational analysis and interpretation, and the processing of linguistic and communicative segments throughout the observation window are contemplated. Overall, the

result aims towards the operational definition of objective and subjective change keys as a result of the intervention process, in a clear mixed approach to the project.

- O2: This objective is based on an inductive mechanism methodology that allows identifying the local realities of schools and social environments. The generation of a map of diversity contextualized in the territories of schools with students with ASD has a methodological component of application development based on a user-centered approach, where, based on the standard ISO-92411 [48], the user experience will be evaluated to obtain a usable and accessible platform that is effective, efficient, and satisfactory in its use. In this sense, the approach of the objective is eminently quantitative, and it can be complemented with qualitative evaluations (such as Bipolar Laddering Assessment, [5, 11, 16, 29, 33, 42]) and/or focused on evaluations with expert groups [28], defining a generally mixed approach.

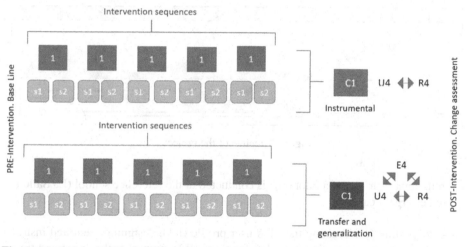

Fig. 1. Methodological design of intervention sequences. Conditions, events, and contexts. Note: U4: case study; R4, social robot; E4: support educator.

In summary, from a methodological and general perspective of the project, it is clear that it seeks to generate a systemic inclusion environment, facilitating the integration of perspectives, both at a micro-analytical level, considering the benefit of incorporating robotics into the social, dialogical, and cultural context of the person with ASD, and at a macro-analytical level, by building the representation of diversity itself by pointing out those markers and dimensions that constitute it. The combination of both levels of analysis enhances the possibilities of change [43], by facilitating inclusive processes for human development based on the understanding of various ASD patterns [9]. The proposed work design establishes the following general annual processes (Fig. 2):

The project timeline adheres to the following schedule, see Fig. 3:

From the schedule and methodology explained, it is evident that we are dealing with a project comprising three distinct phases over the years:

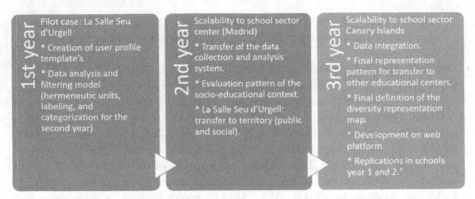

Fig. 2. Deployment process of the research line related to the construction of the representation of diversity.

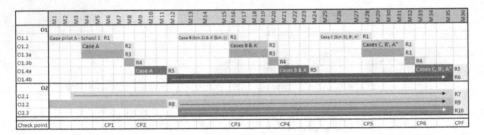

Fig. 3. Timeline of the project.

- In the first year/phase, a pilot case is conducted at the reference school (La Salle La Seu d'Urgell, case A):

    - Regarding O1: Creating the TEA user profile (R1), designing identified instructions, and programming the robot for them (R2), preparing the space and training the user and facilitators to establish an optimal implementation environment (R3), conducting the experience with the TEA user (R4), and finally analyzing interaction data to improve the created instructions (R5).
    - Simultaneously, the collection of TEA initiatives begins (R7), a process spanning all three years dynamically and in collaboration with all supporting project stakeholders (including entities endorsing Support EPO letters, mentioned later). Also, the development and functional testing of the interactive platform takes place (R8), aiming to have a functional system by the end of the first year.

- In the second year/phase, and concerning the two main objectives of the project:

    - The study continues with new case studies and/or monitoring of the previous year's case study at the pilot school (Case B, consolidation phase), while scaling the methodology to a second center (Case A', pilot phase). Processes related to R2, R3, R4, and R5 from the first year are replicated. With the completion of Case

A, it is scaled and disseminated to other centers, both within the ARLEP Network and external ones (R6), a process that continues until the end of the project and beyond.
- Regarding Objective 2, the identification of initiatives (R7) continues, now with new study areas that include the region of the school in Case B, and the mapping of all initiatives found on the finished platform begins (R9), with initial functional tests conducted with end-users so they can contribute information to the platform (R10). This process also extends until the completion of the project and beyond.

- In the third year/phase:

  - A new center is added as scalability of the initial work (pilot case A"), and the methodology is consolidated in the previous centers (initial with case C, and the second-year case B'). The procedure for profile identification (R1), instructional adaptation (R2), training and preparation (R3), implementation (R4), and analysis and improvement (R5) are consolidated in the three working centers and any others not initially identified but resulting from the external scalability of the project (R6).
  - Objective 2 is consolidated with new data at all levels, both identified in the territorial areas of the centers (including the new center C, for R7), its digital mapping (R9), and the synchronization of best practices and documentation support among centers (R10).

In addition, a project monitoring system is established to track its progress, identify critical points, and generate a contingency plan for any issues. As seen in the schedule, checkpoints are set annually (in each phase) at two moments:

- Identification of TEA work profiles (CP 1, 3, and 5): It is crucial that the coordinated process of obtaining information from families, schools, and the weighing of variables takes place with sufficient time to adapt the robot's instructions, considering the skills and interactions to be improved in each case. These three checkpoints occur at the time of profile selection and identification of developmental needs, allowing support for programming through the resources available to the research team.
- Implementation of instructions with TEA students (CP 2, 5, 6): Once implementations with selected students are done (O1), it is vital to review that all documentation from the experimentation is collected in an organized manner for evaluation, study, and improvement. This ensures that it can be included in the documentation to be exported in O2.
- Finally, in the last month, and preparation for the project justification, the status of implementations in all project centers, both the three working ones and the external ones, is compiled to standardize this information (CPFinal).

5 Impact

What happens when a family detects a case of ASD? Families with children with ASD initially experience a strong impact, especially considering how they will ensure their child's social integration, how it will affect their education, how to improve certain behaviors, how to ensure their well-being and future, what economic impact it will have on the family, etc. From a local social perspective, the project aims to strengthen family-school communication and improve certain behaviors or situations identified by both actors in the daily life of students with ASD.

Understanding the behavior of a student with ASD and their everyday needs for social interaction will help create an environment that does not exclude them for not knowing how to behave with them but rather reacts by providing clear and inclusive instructions. Therefore, both the parameterization of best practices to improve personal interactions and the reflection of centers, activities, good practices, initiatives, etc., provided by objective 2, creating a diversity map focused on the nearby territory of each area of action, are aspects aimed at having a high social impact of the project.

This project has a clear scalability vocation. As reflected in 3.3, the intention is to internationalize the approach and scale it initially in a national network with a high educational and social impact (ARLEP), to subsequently open it to other centers and educational networks (as demonstrated by some of the letters of support for the project from external agents to the network). The ARLEP network of La Salle currently has 95 schools spread across 6 sectors, 15 socio-educational works, and 2 universities. In total, we are facing a community of more than 80,000 students and 65,000 families, supported by a network of about 6,100 teachers. Throughout the network, the New Learning Context (NCA from the Spanish: *"Nuevo Contexto de Aprendizaje"*) is being implemented, which since 2018 promotes new educational methodologies in all areas and educational levels based on an intensification of competencies such as spatial, mathematical, STEAM, all with special attention to diversity.

Returning to the family approach, the possibility of identifying resources, initiatives, and ways of acting that demonstrate their effectiveness (diversity map), as well as society's integrative initiatives, directly supports their economy by focusing efforts and allowing them to identify those centers, actions, institutions, or companies that can help them with the education and inclusion of their child with ASD. The economic impact also affects the school level. Schools with a program for diversity in ASD will position themselves locally against a growing problem, and resource optimization through the collaborative ASD collaboration network to be mapped will not only generate this positioning but at a lower economic cost than doing it individually with singular, private, and isolated initiatives.

In conclusion, the social and economic impact derived from the anticipated results has a very high functional value at the school level, and there is a possibility of scalability at the research level as more profiles, best practices, and centers are added, leading to an improvement in quantitative data and consolidation of the approach undertaken.

6 Conclusions

This research project proposes an innovative approach to address the educational needs of children with ASD. Through the integration of social robots in school environments, the aim is to develop personalized intervention sequences that enhance the communicative, cognitive, and social skills of this group of students.

The project's methodology combines quantitative and qualitative approaches, employing a case study design to thoroughly analyze the educational and social inclusion of students with ASD. The research is structured around two main objectives: the first focuses on the development of robotized intervention sequences, while the second aims to create a Social Observatory on Diversity.

In the current academic year 2023–24, different user profiles have already been identified through the design and implementation of user profiles. This process allows us to categorize and subsequently customize robotic instruction sequences. In this regard, the reception by students and families has been very positive, establishing empathic relationships with robotic interactions and showing some improvement in the skills of these students. This demonstrates the potential and impact of the project.

Acknowledgements. This research was supported by the Spanish National Program of Projects of Knowledge Generation 2022. The publication is part of the project PID2022-140284OB-I00, funded by MCIN/AEI/https://doi.org/10.13039/501100011033/FEDER, UE titled "Uses of robotics to improve the instrumental skills of students with autism spectrum disorder through the development of new inclusive contexts. (DivInTech)".

References

1. Alonso De Castro, M.G., García-Peñalvo, F.J.: Overview of European educational projects on eLearning and related methodologies: data from erasmus+ project results platform. In: ACM International Conference Proceeding Series. IGI Global, pp 291–298 (2020)
2. Altay, B.: User-centered design through learner-centered instruction. Teach. High. Educ. **19**, 138–155 (2014). https://doi.org/10.1080/13562517.2013.827646
3. Amo, D., et al.: CreaSTEAM. Towards the improvement of diversity gaps through the compilation of projects, best practices and STEAM-Lab spaces. In: ACM International Conference Proceeding Series. Association for Computing Machinery, New York, NY, USA, pp 92–97 (2021)
4. Begum, M., Serna, R.W., Yanco, H.A.: Are robots ready to deliver autism interventions? A comprehensive review. Int. J. Soc. Robot. **8**, 157–181 (2016). https://doi.org/10.1007/s12369-016-0346-y
5. Campanyà, C., Fonseca, D., Amo, D., Martí, N., Peña, E.: Mixed analysis of the flipped classroom in the concrete and steel structures subject in the context of COVID-19 crisis outbreak. Pilot Study. Sustain. **13**, 5826 (2021). https://doi.org/10.3390/su13115826
6. Caro-Via, S., Espuña, M., Ros, R.: Expanding the use of robotics in ASD programs in a real educational setting. In: Cavallo, F., et al. (eds) Social Robotics, pp 171–182. Springer Nature Switzerland, Cham (2022). https://doi.org/10.1007/978-3-031-24670-8_16
7. Caro-Via, S., Garangou-Culebras, A., Falcó-Olmo, A., Parés-Morlans, C., Ros, R.: An educational, semi-autonomous telepresence robot called sally. In: Zaphiris, P., Ioannou, A. (eds.) Learning and Collaboration Technologies, pp. 142–157. Springer International Publishing, Cham, Novel Technological Environments (2022). https://doi.org/10.1007/978-3-031-05675-8_12
8. Casado Fernández, R., Checa Romero, M.: Robótica y Proyectos STEAM: Desarrollo de la creatividad en las aulas de Educación Primaria. Pixel-Bit (2020)
9. Crespi, B.: Pattern unifies autism. Front Psychiatry **12**, 621659 (2021)

10. Diehl, J.J., Schmitt, L.M., Villano, M., Crowell, C.R.: The clinical use of robots for individuals with autism spectrum disorders: a critical review. Res. Autism Spectr. Disord. **6**, 249–262 (2012). https://doi.org/10.1016/j.rasd.2011.05.006

11. Escudero, D.F., Domínguez, E.R., Valls, F.: Motivación y mejora académica utilizando realidad aumentada para el estudio de modelos tridimensionales arquitectónicos. Educ Knowl Soc EKS **17**, 45–64 (2016). https://doi.org/10.14201/eks20161714564

12. Feil-Seifer, D., Matarić, M.J.: Toward socially assistive robotics for augmenting interventions for children with autism spectrum disorders. In: Khatib, O., Kumar, V., Pappas, G.J. (eds.) Experimental Robotics, pp. 201–210. Springer, Berlin, Heidelberg (2009). https://doi.org/10.1007/978-3-642-00196-3_24

13. Fonseca, D., et al.: Mixed assessment of virtual serious games applied in architectural and urban design education. Sensors **21**, 3102 (2021). https://doi.org/10.3390/s21093102

14. Fonseca, D., et al.: CreaSTEAM. Hacia la mejora de brechas en diversidad mediante la recopilación de proyectos, buenas prácticas y espacios STEAM - [CreaSTEAM. Towards the improvement of diversity gaps through the compilation of projects, best practices and STEAM spaces]. In: Maria Luisa Sein-Echaluce, Ángel Fidalgo Blanco FJG-Peñalvo (ed) In: Sein-Echaluce Lacleta, M.L., Fidalgo-Blanco, Á., García-Peñalvo, F.J. (eds.) Innovaciones docentes en tiempos de pandemia. Actas del VI Congreso In-ternacional sobre Aprendizaje, Innovación y Coope-ración, CINAIC 2021 (20–22 de Octubre de 2021, Madrid. Servicio de Publicaciones. Universidad de Zaragoza, Madrid, pp. 38–43 (2021)

15. Fonseca, D., García-Peñalvo, F.J.: Interactive and collaborative technological ecosystems for improving academic motivation and engagement. Univers Access Inf Soc **18**, 423–430 (2019). https://doi.org/10.1007/s10209-019-00669-8

16. Fonseca, D., Pifarre, M., Redondo, E., Alitany, A., Sanchez, A.: Combination of qualitative and quantitative techniques in the analysis of new technologies implementation in education: Using augmented reality in the visualization of architectural projects | Combinaci?n de t?cnicas cuantitativas y cualitivas en el an?li. In: Iberian Conference on Information Systems and Technologies, CISTI (2013)

17. Fonseca, D., Redondo, E., Villagrasa, S.: Mixed-methods research: a new approach to evaluating the motivation and satisfaction of university students using advanced visual technologies. Univers Access Inf Soc **14**, 311–332 (2015). https://doi.org/10.1007/s10209-014-0361-4

18. Fonseca, D., et al.: Characterization of spaces and didactic units for the improvement of diversity gaps. In: Zaphiris, P., Ioannou, A. (eds.) Learning and Collaboration Technologies, pp. 335–346. Springer International Publishing, Cham, Designing the Learner and Teacher Experience (2022). https://doi.org/10.1007/978-3-031-05657-4_24

19. García-Corretjer, M., Ros, R., Mallol, R., Miralles, D.: Empathy as an engaging strategy in social robotics: a pilot study. User Model User-Adapt Interact **33**, 221–259 (2023). https://doi.org/10.1007/s11257-022-09322-1

20. Gestión: Autismo colectivo de especial vulnerabilidad en Ley de Empleo. In: Autismo Esp (2022). https://autismo.org.es/autismo_nuevaleyempleo/. Accessed 9 Nov 2023

21. Gestión: Testimonio madre de niño autista - Mejora en C.A.I.T y colegio. In: Autismo Esp (2022). https://autismo.org.es/talcomosomos_atenciontemprana/. Accessed 9 Nov 2023

22. Hasti, H., Amo-Filva, D., Fonseca, D., Verdugo-Castro, S., García-Holgado, A., García-Peñalvo, F.J.: Towards closing STEAM diversity gaps: a grey review of existing initiatives. Appl. Sci. **12**, 12666 (2022). https://doi.org/10.3390/app122412666

23. Jiménez Chaves, V.E.: El estudio de caso y su implementación en la investigación. Rev Int Investig En Cienc Soc **8**, 141–150 (2012)

24. Jurado, E., Fonseca, D., Coderch, J., Canaleta, X.: Social steam learning at an early age with robotic platforms: a case study in four schools in Spain. Sens Switz **20**, 1–23 (2020). https://doi.org/10.3390/s20133698

25. Kozima, H., Nakagawa, C., Yasuda, Y.: Children–robot interaction: a pilot study in autism therapy. In: von Hofsten, C., Rosander, K. (eds.) Progress in Brain Research, pp. 385–400. Elsevier (2007)
26. Kumazaki, H., et al.: Optimal robot for intervention for individuals with autism spectrum disorders. Psychiatry Clin. Neurosci. **74**, 581–586 (2020). https://doi.org/10.1111/pcn.13132
27. Laux, L.F., McNally, P.R., Paciello, M.G., Vanderheiden, G.C.: Designing the World Wide Web for people with disabilities: a user centered design approach. In: Proceedings of the Second Annual ACM Conference on Assistive technologies. Association for Computing Machinery, New York, NY, USA, pp 94–101 (1996)
28. Linstone, H.A.: The delphi technique. In: Covello, V.T., Mumpower, J.L., Stallen, P.J.M., Uppuluri, V.R.R. (eds.) Environmental Impact Assessment, Technology Assessment, and Risk Analysis, pp. 621–649. Springer, Berlin, Heidelberg (1985)
29. Llorca, J., Zapata, H., Redondo, E., Alba, J., Fonseca, D.: Bipolar laddering assessments applied to urban acoustics education. In: Rocha, Á., Adeli, H., Reis, L.P., Costanzo, S. (eds.) WorldCIST'18 2018. AISC, vol. 747, pp. 287–297. Springer, Cham (2018). https://doi.org/10.1007/978-3-319-77700-9_29
30. marketing.admin: Why do children with autism learn better from robots? In: LuxAI SA (2021). https://luxai.com/blog/why-children-with-autism-learn-better-from-robots/. Accessed 9 Nov 2023
31. Montero, I., León, O.G.: Clasificación y descripción de las metodologías de investigación en Psicología. Int. J. Clin. Health Psychol. **2**, 503–508 (2002)
32. Pennisi, P., et al.: Autism and social robotics: a systematic review. Autism Res. **9**, 165–183 (2016). https://doi.org/10.1002/aur.1527
33. Pifarré, M., Tomico, O.: Bipolar laddering (BLA): a participatory subjective exploration method on user experience. In: Proceedings of the 2007 Conference on Designing for User Experiences, DUX 2007 (2007)
34. Polo Sánchez, M.T., Chacón-López, H., Caurcel Cara, M.J., Valenzuela Zambrano, B.: Attitudes towards persons with disabilities by educational science students: importance of contact, its frequency and the type of disability. Int. J. Disabil. Dev. Educ. **68**, 617–626 (2021). https://doi.org/10.1080/1034912X.2020.1716960
35. Rabbitt, S.M., Kazdin, A.E., Scassellati, B.: Integrating socially assistive robotics into mental healthcare interventions: applications and recommendations for expanded use. Clin. Psychol. Rev. **35**, 35–46 (2015). https://doi.org/10.1016/j.cpr.2014.07.001
36. Ros, R., Espona, M.: Exploration of a robot-based adaptive cognitive stimulation system for the elderly. In: Companion of the 2020 ACM/IEEE International Conference on Human-Robot Interaction. Association for Computing Machinery, New York, NY, USA, pp. 406–408 (2020)
37. Sabariego, M., Bisquerra, R.: Fundamentos metodológicos de la investigación educativa. Metodol. Investig. Educ. **1130**, 20–49 (2004)
38. Sánchez Riera, A., Redondo, E., Fonseca, D.: Geo-located teaching using handheld augmented reality: good practices to improve the motivation and qualifications of architecture students. Univers Access Inf Soc **14**, 363–374 (2015). https://doi.org/10.1007/s10209-014-0362-3
39. Sanchez-Sepulveda, M., Fonseca, D., Franquesa, J., Redondo, E.: Virtual interactive innovations applied for digital urban transformations mixed approach. Future Gener. Comput. Syst. **91**, 371–381 (2019). https://doi.org/10.1016/j.future.2018.08.016
40. Silk, J.S., Nath, S.R., Siegel, L.R., Kendall, P.C.: Conceptualizing mental disorders in children: where have we been and where are we going? Dev. Psychopathol. **12**, 713–735 (2000). https://doi.org/10.1017/S0954579400004090
41. Valls Pou, A., Canaleta, X., Fonseca, D.: Computational thinking and educational robotics integrated into project-based learning. Sensors **22**, 3746 (2022). https://doi.org/10.3390/s22103746

42. Villagrasa, S., Fonseca, D., Durán, J.: Teaching case: applying gamification techniques and virtual reality for learning building engineering 3D arts. In: ACM International Conference Proceeding Series, pp. 171–177 (2014)
43. Woodman, A.C., Smith, L.E., Greenberg, J.S., Mailick, M.R.: Contextual factors predict patterns of change in functioning over 10 years among adolescents and adults with autism spectrum disorders. J. Autism Dev. Disord. **46**, 176–189 (2016). https://doi.org/10.1007/s10 803-015-2561-z
44. Yáñez, C., et al.: Uso terapéutico de robótica en niños con Trastorno del Espectro Autista. Andes Pediatr **92**, 747–753 (2021). https://doi.org/10.32641/andespediatr.v92i5.2500
45. Milner, H.R.: Start where you are, but don't stay there: understanding diversity, opportunity gaps, and teaching in today's classrooms. Choice Rev. Online **48**, 48–7061 (2011). https://doi.org/10.5860/choice.48-7061
46. Guha, M.: Diagnostic and statistical manual of mental disorders: DSM-5 (5th edition). Ref. Rev. **28**(3), 36–37 (2014). https://doi.org/10.1108/RR-10-2013-0256
47. El alumnado con autismo aumentó un 8% en el último curso escolar respecto al curso anterior – SID. https://sid-inico.usal.es/noticias/el-alumnado-con-autismo-aumento-un-8-en-el-ultimo-curso-escolar-respecto-al-curso-anterior/. Accessed 9 Nov 2023
48. UNE-EN ISO 9241–11:2018 (Ratificada) Ergonomía de la interacci. https://www.une.org/encuentra-tu-norma/busca-tu-norma/norma?c=N0060329. Accessed 9 Nov 2023

In the Footsteps of Learning: A Comparison of Robotic and Human Instructor Movement in the Classroom

Glen Hordemann$^{(\boxtimes)}$ ⓘ, Francis Quek, and Gabriela Gomez ⓘ

Texas A&M University, College Station, TX 77843, USA
{hordemann,quek,geg2297}@tamu.edu

Abstract. The movement of instructors in the classroom is more than simply walking about; it is a carefully choreographed ballet that includes or excludes students, shifts the focus of the entire classroom, and manipulates student behavior. Our work explores the impact of using a telepresence robot as an instructor avatar on the instructor's movement and resting position patterns in a real-world classroom. We use heatmaps to identify high and low usage traffic patterns and to analyze the resting positions instructors use to monitor or engage with the class.

The movement and resting positions of the instructor have a profound impact on student engagement, discipline, and on-task behavior. Seating arrangements have an inevitable impact on how an instructor can move through the classroom. We examine how, in a group work scenario in a local high school, a horse shoe arrangement of desks is navigated by both co-situated human instructors and by those same instructors when they are remote and using a telepresence robot for instruction. We use the lens of spatial pedagogy and embodied pedagogy to evaluate how an telepresence embodiment differs from a co-located one.

Our results show that the telepresence embodiment has a significant impact on both movement and resting position. It promotes use of the periphery of the classroom and the Supervisory Space, reduces dependence on the Authoritative Space, and shifts resting positions from the Authoritative space to the Surveillance space. We also share some insights on designing a classroom for more effective telepresence use.

Keywords: Embodied Pedagogy · Instructional Proxemics · Spatial Pedagogy · Human-centered computing · Human computer interaction (HCI) · Interaction paradigms

1 Introduction

The movement of instructors in the classroom is more than simply walking about; it is a carefully choreographed ballet that includes or excludes students, shifts the focus of the entire classroom, and manipulates student behavior. Classroom proxemics and spatial pedagogy investigate how a teacher uses movement through

© The Author(s), under exclusive license to Springer Nature Switzerland AG 2024
P. Zaphiris and A. Ioannou (Eds.): HCII 2024, LNCS 14722, pp. 181–195, 2024.
https://doi.org/10.1007/978-3-031-61672-3_12

the classroom and spatial positioning in the classroom to direct student behavior and influence student mindset. Embodied pedagogy explores how the embodied presence of the teacher influences both their choices on how to interact with the student and the students' interaction with the teacher.

The spatial and embodied factors of teaching are not limited to a co-present teacher. As technology increasingly becomes incorporated into the classroom, even the teacher themself can become a technological element. Telepresence robots are being used for instruction [29], which leads to the inevitable questions of how the telepresent teacher's embodiment differs from that of the co-present teacher and how this will influence the teacher's use of the classroom space.

The movement and resting positions of the instructor have a profound impact on student engagement, discipline, and on-task behavior. Classroom arrangements have an inevitable impact on how an instructor can move through the classroom. We examine how, in a group work scenario in a local high school, a horse shoe arrangement of desks is navigated by both co-situated human instructors and by those same instructors when they are remote and using a telepresence robot for instruction.

Our work explores the impact of using a telepresence robot as an avatar on instructor movement and resting position patterns in a real-world classroom. We use heatmaps to identify high and low usage traffic patterns and to analyze the resting positions instructors use to monitor or engage with the class. We analyze this movement and positioning data through the lens of spatial pedagogy to examine how the use of telepresence differs from co-located presence.

2   Background

There are several aspects of the spatial classroom that inform our study. The static arrangement of students and their work areas is the most easily modified aspect of the classroom ecology. Within that arranged space, the instructional proxemics of teacher movement patterns and the changing places the teacher chooses to loiter can be framed within the context of spatial pedagogy to describe and evaluate both the locales the teacher moves through and those they rest in, as well as how they use the space. Finally, we can examine how the embodied pedagogy of the teacher shapes and influences their choices about how to use the space, and how their changing embodiment from human self to robot self alters their patterns of spatial usage.

2.1   Classroom Arrangement

Wheldall et al. [36] demonstrate that, for individual tasks, on-task behavior is highest when students are arranged in rows instead of grouped at tables, and the least successful and attentive students are most impacted by the switch from tables to rows. Bonus and Riordan [3] extend this idea by showing that different seating configurations result in better on-task behavior for different lessons, indicating that the seating arrangement must be matched to the goal of the lesson. Rosenfield et al. [30] showed that, for group tasks, circle or cluster formations were more effective than row layouts. The students in our research are arranged in a semi-circle of tables, grouping students who are working together at a table.

2.2 Proxemics and Spatial Pedagogy

Hall's [12] seminal work on proxemics proposed a set of interpersonal distance categories, Public, Social-Consultative, Causal-Personal and Intimate. Lim et al. [21] developed the concepts of spatial pedagogy from Hall's work. Lim et al. states, "four different types of space in the classroom which are situated within Hall's Social-Consultative Space are proposed. They are namely (1) Authoritative Space, (2) Personal Space, (3) Supervisory Space and (4) Interactional Space."

The Authoritative Space is the front-center of the classroom, from which lecture-based instruction tends to originate. The Supervisory Space occurs where the teacher moves between students, pacing up and down rows or otherwise performing non-interactive movement. This is a space of motion. Within the Supervisory Space is the subspace of the Surveillance Space, "where extreme control and power are exerted implicitly through a sense of 'invisible' monitoring." The Interactional Space, while still within Hall's Social-Consultative Space, edges towards the Causal-Personal. It includes those spaces where the teacher stands next to a student or their desk to converse with the student. The Personal Space is the spaces used by the teacher for non-interactive purposes, such as the area behind their desk where the teacher prepares for a lesson.

The use of the Supervisory Space of teacher movement in the classroom can reduce disruptive behavior [31] and increase engagement [6,11]. Despite the advantages of teacher mobility, teachers often spend a large portion of their time immobile [7], often loitering in the Authoritative Space. Thus, any mechanism we can use to increase teacher mobility is likely to be beneficial.

How a teacher should move around the classroom is often prescribed by teaching guides [1]. Marx et al. [23] discuss "action zones" that occur in classrooms with physically present teachers, first described by Sommer [33]: regions of interaction that occur in the front and in the middle of the classroom, finding them in a T-shape for traditional row arrangements and in a triangular shape for circular or horseshoe arrangements such as our classroom exhibited. Moore [25] suggests this "action zone" originates with the teacher rather than the students. These action zones reflect the Authoritative Space of spatial pedagogy.

In his book, "Teach like a champion: 49 techniques that put students on the path to college (K-12)", Doug Lemov discusses the importance of breaking the plane of the front of the classroom and moving past the first five feet of the room. An instructor must "be able to simply and naturally stand next to a student", engage with the students while circulating, and must move systematically while remaining facing as much of the class as possible [17]. This requires moving out of Lim et al's Authoritative Space.

However, McArthur [24] reports that academic research on teachers' use of space is limited and lacking in empirically-based research. Cheong et al. [6] found that, "the patterns of teachers' instructional proxemics in teaching are shaped by the existing classroom layout, students' seating arrangement, and the instructional activity of the day." This suggests that the teachers' use of space is intuitive and ad hoc, rather than based on empirical academic research.

2.3   Embodied Pegagogy

Although the emergent field of embodied pedagogy "appears fragmented and loosely structured" [13], we can find useful sources for the role of the body in both placement and motion in the learning space. Burbeles and Bruce [4] describe traditional models of teaching that promote certain bodily positions for teachers. Estola and Elbaz-Luwisch [9] expand on these concepts, "Teachers should maintaining eye contact, should move around the classroom, should or should not touch students. In some circumstances, however, teachers can break with these expected positions and form new combinations of positions. This is possible because people orient themselves through their bodies: if the learned positions do not work, the body develops new positions and ways of acting." Dixon and Senior [8], in their paper on embodied pedagogy, discuss how the position and stance of an instructor can influence students towards positive behavioral modes and inspire feelings of inclusion. They emphasize the importance of where in the learning space the teacher positions themself.

The role of the specific embodiment of the teacher, actual-self or telerobotic avatar, may play a role in how the teacher incorporates spatial movement and spatial positioning into their teaching. If motion and body position is an emergent property of the teacher's embodied experience as Estola and Elbaz-Luwisch report, then any emergent patterns from use of a telepresence robot will be better suited to telepresence use. We can compare how these patterns change to deduce the impact of the change in embodiment modes.

In our research, we seek to determine how well the learned positions of the teacher's body are reflected in the telepresence embodiment of the teacher, as well as how the teachers learn new positions and ways of acting that better suit their telepresence experience. We explore how the resting positions of the teacher changes between in-person and telepresence, as well as how their movement is influenced by one mode versus the other.

2.4   Telepresence Robots as Teachers

Despite the growing role of technology in education, there is a relative dearth of research on the use of telepresence robots by teachers. There is research on using telepresence robots in the classroom by students [5,10,19,26,27,32], but significantly less concerning the role of a teacher as a telerobotic presence.

Leoste at al [18] used a telepresence robot as a vehicle for a supportive instructor to work with a classroom with a physically present instructor. Their research question was, "What are the aspects of a telepresence robot attending a hands-on higher education STEAM workshop, as perceived by [telepresence robot], [physically present students] and a physically present teacher?" They found that most students were comfortable with the robot but roughly half had difficulty contacting or being contacted by the robot, but did no research into the movement of the robot through the instructional space

Wernbacher et al. [35] performed a case study where a lecturer presented a PowerPoint lecture via Zoom to a class while also using an Ohmnilabs robot. The lecture was presented to a hybrid class of both physically present and Zoom-situated students. The authors reported that the lecturer felt "it was extremely exhausting in terms of concentration and attention" from having to monitor his own workspace, the robot's embodied environment, and the Zoom environment all at the same time. Despite this robot being a vehicle for full embodiment of the lecturer, this study focuses on the mental demands of robot usage rather than any spatial or interactional usage of the robot.

Fig. 1. RobotAR [34], a desktop robot tutor.

Villanueva et al. [34] created RobotAR, a desktop robot that an instructor can drive on the student's desktop. The robot utilizes a smartphone to allow the remote instructor to view the student's workspace and, using augmented reality, draw or write on a view of that workspace that will be shown on the phone's screen (See Fig. 1). This system was evaluated for student preference and learning outcomes in one-on-one tutoring scenarios, but, as a small desktop robot, does not allow for any classroom mobility or full-scale embodiment of the teacher.

It should be mentioned that while there is a reasonable body of work using social robots to tutor children [2,16,20], these are not telepresence robots and thus fall far outside the scope of our research.

3   Methodology

Our study took place over the course of a month at a local high school, teaching
a course on Making [14] and micro-manufacture. Twelve students took part, and
two STEM instructors taught the course. The regular classroom teacher was co-
present in the classroom at all times, but typically did not assist in instruction
or classroom regulation.

The students were twelve high school students who attend the local high
school. These students signed up for a month-long course on Making and micro-
manufacture, and the majority of the students planned to take part in the high
school's robotics program in the following semester.

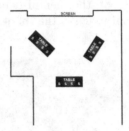

Fig. 2. Classroom layout

Based on the works discussed in Sect. 2 the study classroom was arranged
in a semi-circle of tables to maximize group engagement and interaction. This
configuration was selected to provide the maximum number of free movement
pathways around the room, within the constraints of the classroom topology,
while still maintaining a seating arrangement most conducive to group work.

The classroom, as shown in Fig. 2, has a screen at the front of the room and
three tables arranged in a horseshoe shape. Four students sat at each table (each
marked by an 'S' in the figure). All students sat either on the same side of the
table or the same side plus one student on the end. This allowed all students
to see the screen at the front of the classroom without turning around. The
classroom continues to the left to a small entryway and the door, and to the
bottom to the regular teacher's desk and work area, but none of those areas
were used for instruction.

The course was primarily centered around group work on physically pred-
icated tasks, such as soldering, wiring circuits, assembling electronic components, and programming micro-controllers such as the Arduino. In addition to
the hands-on work, there were also elements of lecture-based material to explain
theory or teach new concepts. During remote instruction, an Ohmnilabs [28]
telepresence robot (See Fig. 3) was used by one STEM instructor and a Zoom
session projected on a screen at the front of the classroom was used by the other

Fig. 3. Ohmnilabs Telepresence robot. This robot has a supplemental Augmented Reality subsystem that uses a second screen.

instructor to provide any lecture-based content. The same screen was used for slides or other materials as needed during co-present instruction.

The instructors were given some initial instruction in driving the telepresence robot and were given familiarization time driving the robot. However, no guidance was given on how they should navigate through the classroom or otherwise make use of the robot. An equal number of days of remote instruction using the telepresence robot and Zoom and of in-person instruction were evaluated for this paper.

Movement data for the classroom was recorded by two cameras, one at the front of the classroom and one at the rear, both having a full field of view of the classroom. Video from the telepresence robot was also captured for analysis. These video streams were synchronized and composited together, and then an analysis of instructor position and navigation was performed on the composited video. For movement data, the information was broken into a grid of one by one foot squares. For resting position data, the locations were divided into two by two foot squares. The higher grid resolution for movement was chosen to highlight any potential awkwardness or lack of smoothness in robot navigation.

4   Results

4.1   Instructor Movement

In Fig. 4, the left image shows the heatmap for the movement of the co-located instructors moving through the classroom in person. The heatmap shows that, as noted by Lemov [17], there is a significant amount of movement in the plane of the front of the classroom. Matching the existing research on active zones, the co-present instructors have a significant amount of movement in the front and center of the classroom.

The right image of Fig. 4 shows the movement of instructor when using the telepresence robot. The robot is much more diverse in its movement and the instructor breaks free of the typical "active zone" of this seating configuration. Of particular note is the preference of the instructor for the rear of the classroom in this mode.

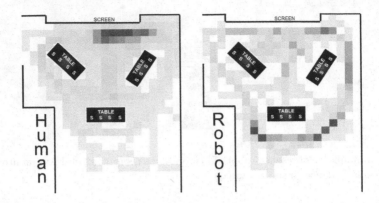

Fig. 4. Heatmap of Combined Movement of Human Instructors (left) and Telepresence Robot Instructor (right).

Table 1. Percent of total moving time spent in the Supervisory Space.

Embodiment	Supervisory Space
Humans Combined	33%
Human 1	20%
Human 2	44%
Robot	62%

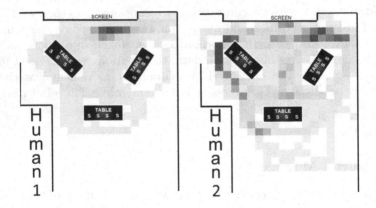

Fig. 5. Heatmap of the Individual Movement of the two Human Instructors

How much time each embodied presence spends in Lim's different types of classroom spaces (See Subsect. 2.2) is particularly interesting. As shown in Table 1, when embodied as a robot the instructor spends almost twice as much time moving through the Supervisory Space as when they are co-present. There is a notable difference in how much time each instructor spends in the supervisory space, but even the more supervisory instructor spends much less time in the Supervisory Space than the robot does.

Figure 5 breaks the movement of the two instructors apart, showing the movement of each instructor. The two instructors generally did not address the same student or issue, which is reflected in the heat maps that show them moving through different areas of the classroom. Despite this, there is a strong predilection towards being positioned in the front of the classroom for both instructors.

4.2   Instructor Resting Positions

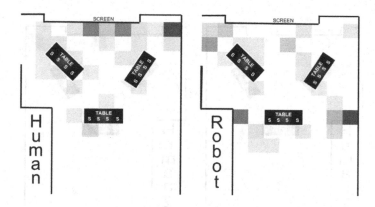

Fig. 6. Heatmap of the Combined Resting Positions of Human Instructors (left) and the Telepresence Robot Instructor (right).

The resting positions of the instructor are significantly different (See Fig. 6) between the in-person and the telepresence embodiments. In person, the instructors almost uniformly stand at the front of the class. When embodied in the robot the instructor typically avoids the front and center of the classroom. Instead, the telepresence instructor stops in a variety of positions around the classroom to observe or interact with the class.

Table 2 shows how the instructors, whether embodied in person or as a telepresence robot, spend time in different instructional spaces. When co-located, the instructors spend the plurality of their time in the Authoritative Space, while when embodied as a telepresence robot they spend the least time in the Authoritative Space.

While when embodied in-person the instructor does spend a higher percentage of their resting time in the classroom in the Interactional Space compared to

Table 2. Percent of total resting time spent in the Authoritative, Interactional, and Surveillance Spaces by the Human and Robot embodiments.

Space	Human	Robot
Authoritative	49%	10%
Interactional	27%	19%
Surveillance	24%	69%

the telepresence embodiment, this result does not rise to the level of statistical significance (p > .05). When co-located, the instructors spent considerably less time in the Surveillance Space than when using the telepresence robot.

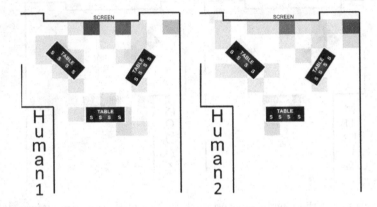

Fig. 7. Heatmap of the Individual Resting Positions of the two Human Instructors.

Figure 7 shows the individual resting positions of the two human instructors. Both instructors tended to gravitate to the front of the classroom when not moving to interact with a student.

Table 3. Percent of total resting time spent in the Authoritative, Interactional, and Surveillance Spaces by individual Human embodiments and the Robot embodiment.

Space	Human 1	Human 2	Robot
Authoritative	53%	44%	10%
Interactional	33%	19%	19%
Surveillance	14%	37%	69%

Table 3 shows the resting times of the two co-located instructors broken out individually. While the Authoritative Space and the Surveillance Space percentages remain statistically significantly different, the use of the Interactive Space is notably different between the two instructors. The first instructor has a significantly different rate of Interactional Space usage when co-located compared to the robot embodiment, while the second instructor almost exactly matched the robot embodiment.

5   Discussion

5.1   Instructor Movement

The motion of the co-present instructors is strongly focused on the front of the classroom. The co-present instructors tend to travel to the rear of the classroom by crossing to the left side of the classroom, while the robotic embodiment has a more even route selection and tends to favor the right side of the classroom. Even when looked at individually, this dichotomy remains. The heatmaps (Figs. 4 and 5) also show that robot movements tend to be more precise, while the co-located movements are more varied in exactly how they move along a particular route.

This route selection and precision of route usage is likely due to the fact that the right side of the classroom provides a more easily navigated straightaway, while the left requires a dog-leg. When embodied in-person, moving through such a crooked path is natural and automatic, while navigating a robot through is more difficult than driving through a straightaway. This suggests that classrooms designed for telepresence use can use the placement of turns and of straight routes to help shape teacher movement through the Supervisory Space. It also suggests that a telepresent teacher will be more likely to choose a "path of least resistance" compared to an in-person teacher due to the nature of their embodiment.

The telepresence embodiment also typically avoided moving through the center of the classroom. This may be due to reduced situational awareness, as it is extremely difficult to determine what is happening behind the robot. As a co-located presence a teacher can glance behind themselves, which the telepresence embodiment can not do. Classroom layouts without significant interior spaces are likely to be better suited to telepresence embodiment.

The fact that the telepresence robot embodiment of the instructors spent significantly more time moving through the supervisory space can be partially explained by the presence of another instructor connected through Zoom on the screen at the front of the class. It is possible that this virtual presence in the Authoritative Space encouraged the telepresence instructor to shift out of this space. However, when we examine the individual resting positions of the co-present instructors we see that they typically rest in the Authoritative Space. It may be that the Zoom virtual presence has an out-sized effect on claiming the Authoritative Space.

Another interesting artifact of the telepresence embodiment's movement is that it tends to move well clear of both desks and walls. The narrower viewing angle of the robot's camera may account for this discrepancy. The remote instructor is encouraged to move more often and thoroughly through the classroom so that they can supervise all students, rather than believing they can adequately supervise all students from one area. There may also be a lack of confidence in immediate, close-proximity spatial awareness, due to the inability to "glance" in a direction by turning the head or neck, which the robot does not currently possess.

5.2   Instructor Resting Positions

The resting positions of the instructors varied significantly depending on whether they were embodied in-person or embodied as a telepresence robot. When co-located, the instructors gravitated very strongly to the Authoritative Space and the front of the room. While the far right of the front of classroom can be considered the Surveillance Space, when only the front four feet of the room is considered, the co-located instructors spent 66% of their time in this area. This is the "first five feet" that Lemov [17] says it is important to move past.

When the instructors were embodied as telepresence robots they spent almost no time in the same spaces they typically inhabited in person. The telepresence embodiment does not merely leave the Authoritative Space claimed by the virtual presence of the Zoom instructor by moving to the side, but moves fully to the rear of the classroom. The telepresence embodiment seemed to drive them to the Surveillance Space in the corners of the classroom. This suggests that the use of a telepresence robot may be even better for student supervision and surveillance than an in-person instructor, at least in terms of use of space.

These corners gave clear lines of sight to all of the students. The need for clear lines of sight may explain why, even when staking out positions in the Surveillance Space, the telepresence instructors never moved to the rear of the classroom. At 4'8", the robot is significantly shorter than either instructor and may be unable to clearly see past sitting students.

One potentially concerning statistic is the amount of time spent in the Interactional Space. While the overall difference is not statistically significant, when broken out by individual instructor there is a case where an co-located instructor embodiment spent significantly more time in the Interactional Space than the telepresence instructor embodiment. This is likely due to one of the technological limitations of this telepresence embodiment: reduced communication. The telepresence embodiment strips away body language, especially gesture and gaze expressions. This makes communication less efficient, which may serve as a barrier to initiate or request interactions, both for the instructor and for the students.

6   Conclusion

In this paper we examine the impact of telepresence robotic embodiment on spatial pedagogy and embodied pedagogy, compared to a co-located presence in the classroom. We show that the telepresence embodiment is a viable alternative to a co-located embodiment and has a significant impact on the use of space and teacher motion in the classroom. The telepresence embodiment is more likely to roam the classroom, but may also focus on straighter and more navigable paths than a co-located embodiment of the teacher would.

A telepresence embodiment is more mobile than a co-located embodiment, but has reduced situational awareness. This leads to a movement approach that focuses more on the periphery of the classroom than the interior and lends itself to the telepresence embodiment spending significantly more time in the Supervisory Space. Thus the telepresence embodiment is well suited to a supervisory role.

One area where a telepresence embodiment may be lacking is in direct interaction. Extra effort should be made to promote and facilitate teacher-student interactions.

7 Future Work

The impact of telepresence embodiment on embodied pedagogy can be more fully explored in future work. The impact of robot use on student perceptions and comfort is something we plan to explore in future work. Martinec's [22] extension of Hall's [12] work, by including body angles to measure engagement, is another potential expansion of this research. Additionally, while this paper looks at movement amounts, future work can examine direction and flow of movement to compare how a telepresence embodiment alters them.

Finally, there are technological improvements to the base telepresence robot that may heavily influence the embodiment of the teacher. Shared gestural spaces for the telepresence teacher and the student [15], greater head and neck mobility, and other improvements in interaction ability may profoundly shape the nature of the telepresent teacher's embodiment.

Acknowledgment. This research has been supported by NSF #1917950 and #1949439.

Disclosure of Interests.. The authors have no competing interests in this research.

References

1. Arends, R.: Learning to Teach. McGraw-Hill Higher Education (2014)
2. Van den Berghe, R., Verhagen, J., Oudgenoeg-Paz, O., Van der Ven, S., Leseman, P.: Social robots for language learning: a review. Rev. Educ. Res. **89**(2), 259–295 (2019)
3. Bonus, M., Riordan, L.: Increasing student on-task behavior through the use of specific seating arrangements. Dissertations/Theses Reports (1998)
4. Burbules, N.C., Bruce, B.C.: Theory and research on teaching as dialogue (2001)
5. Capello, S.A., Gyimah-Concepcion, M., Buckley-Hughes, B.: Using telepresence robots for doctoral education: student and faculty experiences. Am. J. Distance Educ. 1–15 (2022)
6. Cheong Yin Mei, C., Buai Chin, H., Taib, F.: Instructional proxemics and its impact on classroom teaching and learning. Int. J. Mod. Lang. Appl. Linguist. **1**(1), 69–85 (2017)

7. Denny, R.K., Epstein, M.H., Rose, E.: Direct observation of adolescents with serious emotional disturbance and their nonhandicapped peers in mainstream vocational education classrooms. Behav. Disord. **18**(1), 33–41 (1992)
8. Dixon, M., Senior, K.: Appearing pedagogy: from embodied learning and teaching to embodied pedagogy. Pedagogy Cult. Soc. **19**(3), 473–484 (2011)
9. Estola, E., Elbaz-Luwisch, F.: Teaching bodies at work. J. Curriculum Stud. **35**(6), 697–719 (2003)
10. Gleason, B., Greenhow, C.: Hybrid education: the potential of teaching and learning with robot-mediated communication. Online Learn. J. **21**(4), 159–176 (2017)
11. Gunter, P.L., Shores, R.E., Jack, S.L., Rasmussen, S.K., Flowers, J.: On the move using teacher/student proximity to improve students' behavior. Teach. Except. Child. **28**(1), 12–14 (1995)
12. Hall, E.T.: The Hidden Dimension, vol. 609. Anchor (1966)
13. Hegna, H.M., Ørbæk, T.: Traces of embodied teaching and learning: a review of empirical studies in higher education. Teach. High. Educ. **29**, 420–421 (2021)
14. Hordemann, G., Natarajarathinam, M., Chu, S.L., Kuttolamadom, M., Quek, F., Okundaye, O.J.: Everybody needs somebody to teach: Embodiment, telecommunication, and telepresence in stem learning. In: 2020 ASEE Virtual Annual Conference Content Access (2020)
15. Hordemann, G., Quek, F., Powell, L.: Reaching across the communication gap: evaluating how augmented reality shared gestural spaces impact gesture and language usage. In: 2023 IEEE Frontiers in Education Conference (FIE), pp. 1–6. IEEE (2023)
16. Kennedy, J., Baxter, P., Senft, E., Belpaeme, T.: Social robot tutoring for child second language learning. In: 2016 11th ACM/IEEE international conference on human-robot interaction (HRI), pp. 231–238. IEEE (2016)
17. Lemov, D.: Teach like a Champion: 49 Techniques that Put Students on the Path to College (K-12). Wiley (2010)
18. Leoste, J., Virkus, S., Kasuk, T., Talisainen, A., Kangur, K., Tolmos, P.: Aspects of using telepresence robot in a higher education STEAM workshop. In: Pardede, E., Delir Haghighi, P., Khalil, I., Kotsis, G. (eds.) International Conference on Information Integration and Web, pp. 18–28. Springer (2022). https://doi.org/10.1007/978-3-031-21047-1_2
19. Leoste, J., Virkus, S., Talisainen, A., Tammemäe, K., Kangur, K., Petriashvili, I.: Higher education personnel's perceptions about telepresence robots. Front. Robot. AI **9**, 976836 (2022)
20. Leyzberg, D., Spaulding, S., Toneva, M., Scassellati, B.: The physical presence of a robot tutor increases cognitive learning gains. In: Proceedings of the Annual Meeting of the Cognitive Science Society, vol. 34 (2012)
21. Lim, F.V., O'Halloran, K.L., Podlasov, A.: Spatial pedagogy: mapping meanings in the use of classroom space. Camb. J. Educ. **42**(2), 235–251 (2012)
22. Martinec, R.: Interpersonal resources in action. Semiotica **2001**(135), 117–145 (2001)
23. Marx, A., Fuhrer, U., Hartig, T.: Effects of classroom seating arrangements on children's question-asking. Learning Environ. Res. **2**, 249–263 (1999)
24. McArthur, J.A.: Matching instructors and spaces of learning: the impact of space on behavioral, affective and cognitive learning. J. Learn. Spaces **4**(1), 1–16 (2015)
25. Moore, D.W.: Variation in question rate as a function of position in the classroom. Educ. Psychol. **4**(3), 233–248 (1984)

26. Newhart, V.A., Olson, J.S.: My student is a robot: how schools manage telepresence experiences for students. In: Proceedings of the 2017 CHI Conference on Human Factors in Computing Systems, pp. 342–347 (2017)
27. Newhart, V.A., Warschauer, M., Sender, L.: Virtual inclusion via telepresence robots in the classroom: an exploratory case study. Int. J. Technol. Learn. **23**(4), 9–25 (2016)
28. OhmniLabs, I.: Ohmnilabs (2023). https://ohmnilabs.com/
29. Okundaye, O., et al.: Telepresence robotics for hands-on distance instruction. In: Proceedings of the 11th Nordic Conference on Human-Computer Interaction: Shaping Experiences, Shaping Society, pp. 1–11 (2020)
30. Rosenfield, P., Lambert, N.M., Black, A.: Desk arrangement effects on pupil classroom behavior. J. Educ. Psychol. **77**(1), 101 (1985)
31. Shores, R.E., Gunter, P.L., Jack, S.L.: Classroom management strategies: are they setting events for coercion? Behav. Disord. **18**(2), 92–102 (1993)
32. Soares, N., Kay, J.C., Craven, G.: Mobile robotic telepresence solutions for the education of hospitalized children. Perspect. Health Inf. Manage. **14**(Fall), 1e (2017)
33. Sommer, R.: Classroom ecology. J. Appl. Behav. Sci. **3**(4), 489–503 (1967)
34. Villanueva, A.M., et al.: RobotAR: an augmented reality compatible teleconsulting robotics toolkit for augmented makerspace experiences. In: Proceedings of the 2021 CHI Conference on Human Factors in Computing Systems, pp. 1–13 (2021)
35. Wernbacher, T., et al.: TRinE: telepresence robots in education (2022)
36. Wheldall, K., Morris, M., Vaughan, P., Ng, Y.Y.: Rows versus tables: an example of the use of behavioural ecology in two classes of eleven-year-old children. Educ. Psychol. **1**(2), 171–184 (1981)

Discovering Improvement Opportunities and Challenges for Pharmaceutical Companies Adopting Digital Training Technologies: A Case Study

Lasse Nielsen Langendorf[1,2] and Md. Saifuddin Khalid[1](✉)

[1] COMPUTE - Department of Applied Mathematics and Computer Science,
Technical University of Denmark, Kongens Lyngby, Denmark
skhalid@dtu.dk
[2] Novo Nordisk A/S, Copenhagen, Denmark

Abstract. The adoption of learning technology in industry has outpaced its effective implementation, leading to a gap between adoption and evaluation. The current scientific literature lacks sufficient job-specific training studies in pharmaceutical production settings. To address the gap, a case study was conducted in a Danish pharmaceutical company to explore challenges associated with digital training technology adoption and evaluation effectiveness. Data was collected through depth interviews and observations. Analysis was conducted using affinity diagrams, PACT analysis, and Rich Picture. The study identified challenges in technology, organization, attitude, competence, regulation, demand, and data access. Challenges regarding the training process include a lack of standardization, and limited resources. Adoption of digital training technologies faces challenges such as lack of documented effect and usability issues. Evaluating of training faces challenges such as a lack of established protocols, and variance in processes, contexts, and user groups. Future work should establish measurable indicators for learning linked to production metrics, conducting small-scale experiments, creating a general evaluation procedure, and expanding evaluation to additional sites.

Keywords: digital training technology · job-specific training · evaluation · adoption · pharmaceutical industry

1 Introduction

The rapid advancement of learning technology has outpaced companies' ability to effectively implement these innovations, resulting in a widening disparity between the adoption of learning technology and the evaluation of its effectiveness. While adoption of new technologies is often associated with improvements in productivity, industry is often reluctant to make changes to their processes without evidence of their effectiveness [44]. This is especially true for the pharmaceutical industry and other GxP (Good Manufacturing/Clinical/Laboratory

© The Author(s), under exclusive license to Springer Nature Switzerland AG 2024
P. Zaphiris and A. Ioannou (Eds.): HCII 2024, LNCS 14722, pp. 196–213, 2024.
https://doi.org/10.1007/978-3-031-61672-3_13

Practice) [13] regulated industries, which must comply regulations and where any changes could potentially compromise performance and compliance. GxP-regulated training ensures that employees comply with these regulations, covering topics like process steps, documentation, quality control, risk management, and record-keeping [13]. In these industries, much factory work requires job-specific training for practical processes. A growing interest have been shown in utilizing digital training technologies in industry [39] for job-specific training. Reported in the paper is the case of a pharmaceutical company's challenges with the adoption of job-specific training technologies & concepts, which include: E-Learning, Digital Instructions, Virtual Reality (VR) and Augmented Reality/Mixed Reality (AR/MR). As of yet however, the case company and pharmaceutical industry at large, still relies on more traditional training methods such as structured Peer-Training, the most typical form of On-The-Job training [1], and Reading and Understanding of SOP (Standard Operating Procedure) manuals.

1.1 Objectives

The scientific literature currently lacks sufficient studies conducted in GxP regulated factory settings to explore the adoption, utilization, evaluation and impact of digital learning technologies, as far as the authors are aware. To address the lack of empirical research, a case study was conducted in an international pharmaceutical company headquartered in Denmark, with production sites spread globally. The study aimed to answer the following research questions:

- *What are the challenges of conducting job-specific training in the regulated context of a pharmaceutical company?*
- *What are the challenges associated with the adoption of digital training technologies?*
- *What evaluation methods are applied as part of the evaluation process of job-specific training and what improvement opportunities and challenges exist associated with the process?*

To answer the research questions, a variety of empirical data was gathered, mainly through conducting depth interviews and observations. Rich Picture, PACT analysis, and Affinity Diagrams were utilized to synthesize the data using different approaches.

2 Background and Related Work

2.1 Case Context

Founded in 1923, the case company, Novo Nordisk is a pharmaceutical company that initially specialized in diabetes medication but has since broadened its focus to drug development for other conditions. The company has over the last 10 years made a concerted effort to enhance and standardize training programs across production lines to ensure the competence of their line workers, in response to increased regulatory requirements. Due to the introduction of GLP-1-receptor agonists followed by a significant rise in public demand, Novo has had to expand existing production lines and establish new ones. The establishing of new production lines and expansion of existing production lines leading to a greater training need have motivated Novo to explore digital training technologies. The company intend to device a process to assess the effectiveness of their GxP-regulated job-specific training, internally called *Functional Training*, in general and to identify if and where these digital training technologies can be utilized effectively.

2.2   Evaluating Training

Regulated industries employ various frameworks to evaluate the effectiveness and impact of training, used interchangeably with the term learning. Commonly used frameworks for evaluating learning in the industry include Kirkpatrick's levels of evaluation [19], the Phillips ROI Model [33], Kaufman's Evaluation Method [18], Brinkerhoff's Success Case Method [8], and several others. To allow for comparison of different types of training, standard evaluation measures in addition to task-specific and training-specific measures and metrics are often necessary for evaluation [11]. The most widespread form of evaluation, **Surveys** [40], represent a cost-effective way to collect information about specific training outcomes as they can be easily administered to a large group of respondents [38]. Learning analytics have been applied to evaluate performance on digital training platforms. However, while learning analytics have shown promise in improving performance in some educational settings, large-scale evidence supporting their effectiveness in promoting study success is still lacking [16]. For job-specific training in an industrial setting, a survey alone may not yield adequate data regarding the impact of a training method or technology on performance. On the other hand, evaluating all aspects of job-specific training for performance impact can be both time-consuming and expensive [40]. Organizations however, often need to address broader evaluation issues, such as investigating the factors that contribute to successful training transfer, including technological and cultural aspects to improve future training programs [4].

2.3   Evaluating Digital Training Technologies

While research is limited in an industrial setting, studies exploring the subject mostly focus on evaluating technology, experience or impact through usability (ISO 9241-11) on the different parameters of Effectiveness, Efficiency, Satisfaction [5] and user experience (ISO 9241-210). While other standards for training exist, they generally incorporate the three categories of technology, experience, and impact within their definitions. The metrics used to evaluate these parameters are typically task-specific such as **Error Rate** (Effectiveness) [23,27], **Task Completion Time** (Efficiency) [21,41]. For satisfaction metrics and evaluation of the system, instruments such as **System Usability Scale (SUS)** [24], **Single Easy Question (SEQ)** [26], **Net Promoter Score (NPS** [37],**Interviews**

[42], and **Task Load Index (NASA-TLX)** [10] have been utilized. While many studies focus on either technology or experience, only a limited number have assessed the potential impacts of integrating digital training technologies. For instance, a tractor production facility in Turkey implemented a VR system for process training which was estimated to reduce training time per individual by 25% and resulted in a 27.9% improvement in complex industrial assembly task performance [17]. In another instance, a study at a factory in Malta estimated that implementing a tablet-based AR system for maintenance could increase Overall Equipment Efficiency (OEE) by up to 11% [6]. Furthermore, various studies conducted in Europe and North America have indicated significant productivity gains by incorporating Extended Reality (XR, includes AR & VR) systems in both training and live production environments [22,32,36]. Although there are various instruments available to evaluate digital technologies, there is a lack of standardized and thoroughly validated evaluation protocols for emerging training technologies such as augmented reality (AR) and virtual reality (VR) in the pharmaceutical industry, as far as the authors are aware.

3   Methodology

This paper reports the outcomes of the discover and define activities of a **Case Study** [9] as part of a larger research project, focused on developing tools to evaluate training in a pharmaceutical production context, applying the ,**Double Diamond Framework** [20]. Figure 1 shows the Study Design and included methods, followed by a description of population, data collection methods & data analysis methods.

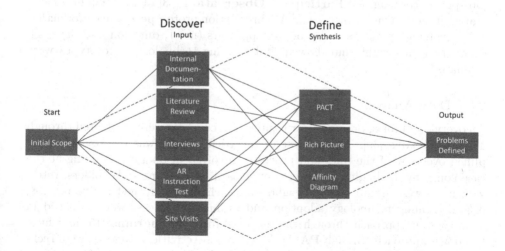

Fig. 1. Study Design, Overlayed on the Double Diamond Framework

3.1   Study Participants

The study involved employees who were related to the training of individuals engaged in GxP activities. The selection of these participants was based on their role, knowledge, and extensive experience in interacting with and receiving feedback from operators and other relevant personnel. The specific participants include: production line managers/operator team leaders (n = 3), local process supporters (n = 4), digital training developers (n = 4), global training managers (n = 3) & global training standard owners (n = 3).

3.2   Data Collection

The data collection methods employed include: (1) semi structured **Depth Interviews** [34] (n = 17, 15–30 min) with individuals throughout the company working in roles associated with job-specific training. Interviews were conducted in danish and directly translated into English during note-taking. Quotes presented in the report were proofread after final analysis. The goal of these interviews were to gain qualitative insights on the three research questions formulated into the following two topics: a) *the key challenges concerning the training process & utilization of digital training technology at the company* & b) *the key challenges which exist in regards to carrying out evaluation of training at the company.* (2) **Observations** [14] (n = 3, duration= 1–5 h) of production sites and lines to understand the different types of processes involved in the pharmaceutical production, and the different training processes. (3) **Participant Observation** [43] of courses focused on training operators, process supporters and AR developers (n = 4, duration = 4–8 h), to gain insights into what knowledge trainers possess and what training is provided to individuals delivering job-specific training. (4) **Participant Observation** [43] observation of a moderated, in-person, assessment of an AR-instruction prototype at a live production line, involving operators and process supporters (n = 1, duration = 2 days, 4 h each), to gain insights into how digital training technologies prototypes were evaluated.

3.3   Data Analysis

An overview of roles, processes, structures, and concerns were illustrated through a **Rich Picture** [30]. The purpose of the Rich Picture was to provide a simplified overview of the roles and processes involved in operator training at the case company, highlighting concerns expressed by relevant stakeholders. Interview notes were organized and insights on the challenges in the training process, digital training technology adoption and evaluation process were analyzed in a bottom-up approach through the use of **Affinity Diagrams** [15] and by a top-down approach through **PACT** [5] (People, Activities, Context, and Technologies). The purpose of utilizing an affinity diagram was to identify patterns among the perceived challenges of the different stakeholders, by grouping related statements. The purpose of a PACT analysis was to examine the factors that influence performance, including the individual's knowledge and skills, the activity being performed, the environmental context, and the available technology.

3.4 Ethical Issues and Trustworthiness of Data

Before publishing, sensitive information related to the subjects has been anonymized in compliance with the EU General Data Protection Regulation (GDPR) [35]. Additionally, the roles of the subjects have been generalized to maintain their anonymity. All published information have been verified and approved for distribution by Novo Nordisk.

4 Results

The Results section features a Rich Picture and process sequence illustrating changes in the training process followed by the results of the PACT Analysis. An Affinity Diagram highlights major challenges identified through interviews and observations, categorized into training process and evaluation challenges.

4.1 The Rich Picture

Figure 2 displays the Rich Picture, with internal stakeholders in blue and external stakeholders in white. The following simplified *Process Sequence* explains the actions involved in training process changes and their causes, as shown in the Rich Picture.

Process Sequence

1. (a) Increased consumer demand for a product results in a higher number of doctors requesting the medicine for their patients.
   (b) Changes in regulations or investigation findings may result in modifications to the training process or require training interventions.
2. (a) Upper management sets new production targets for local management and/or informs of regulatory changes or findings.
   (b) Upper management either sets new overall training targets or sends a request for training intervention or changes to global training standards to the training department.
3. (a) Local management communicates the new targets and training requirements to process support and arranges the operators' schedules to accommodate increased production.
   (b) The training department either provides new training standards to process support and 4P trainers (operators) or conducts intervention to enhance the existing training methods at the local production site.
4. (a) Process supporters and certified trainers conduct training for newly hired operators and carry out change-training of existing user groups. Feedback from operators is given primarily to the process support department, but also to local management and the central training department in some cases.
   (b) Process support may request additional training resources from the training department to manage the increased training workload, or to assist with identified problems in the current training process.

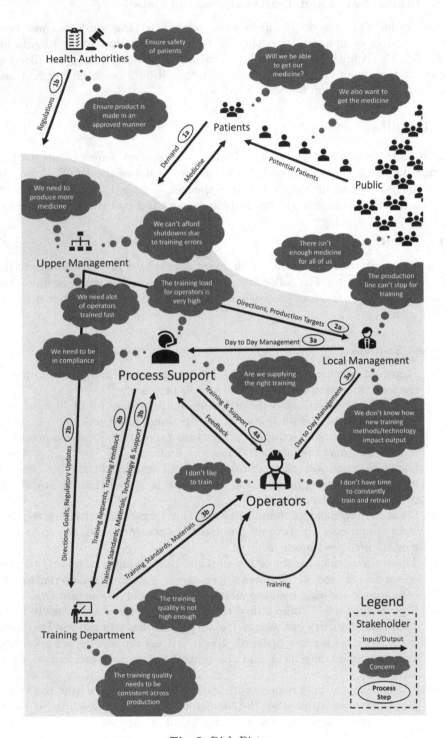

Fig. 2. Rich Picture

4.2   PACT Analysis

The illustration depicts the connection between both human and non-human actors (connected via white lines) who are directly involved in the training interaction between operators and trainers in current up-to-date Danish production sites. The findings of the PACT Analysis is presented below, starting with an analysis of the context.

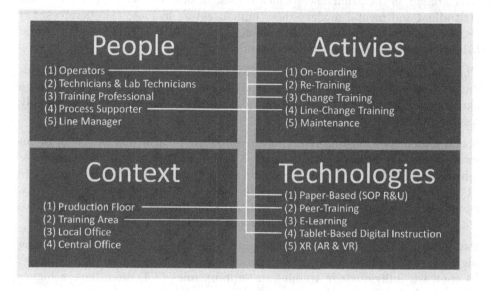

Fig. 3. PACT Analysis

Context. The specific contexts analyzed include: (1) the production floor, (2) the training area, (3) the local office, and (5) the central office, in regards to their physical environment, social context and organizational context.

Physical Enviroment. The production floor (1) is characterized by actively operating machinery, a large number of processes occurring simultaneously, noise, and a sterile environment. In contrast, a training area (2) typically includes a classroom, meeting room, or specific training center, sometimes utilizing mock-ups, and is mostly focused on a single process.

Social Context. On the production floor (1), iPads with manuals are available at most process locations, and there is mostly human-machine interaction. In contrast, the training area (2) is a highly social setting with access to manuals and experts. The office (3,4) provides digital access to all training materials and has a large amount of social interaction available.

Organizational Context. The production floor (1) is a value-producing area, where every second not spent on production results in monetary loss. Novo Nordisk has started investing more in the training area (2) and mockups, as every second spent training in the training area rather than on the production floor results in cost savings.

People. Individuals directly connected to the GxP regulated training were analyzed, based on their differences which consist of physical, social, psychological, attitudinal and mental models. these human actors include: (1) operators, (2) technicians & lab technicians, (3) training professionals, (4) process supporters, (5) line managers (operator team leaders).

Physical Differences: All groups have a BMI/height/gender/age distribution similar to the Danish workforce, line managers (5) tend to be older than the average age of operators however, due to their years of experience. All groups are highly diverse in terms of physical aspects.

Social Differences: Operators (1) have completed Danish middle school or an international equivalent, but often lack a technical background. Technicians & lab technicians (2) have a technical education background. Process supporters (4) & training professionals (3) typically have a tertiary degree in education, communication or engineering. Line managers (5) have an operator background, with additional leadership and management training.

Psychological Differences: Individuals in technical roles (1,2,5) typically having higher spatial abilities and a lower tolerance for reading, but is highly diverse. In contrast, individuals in training or support roles (3,4) often have a higher tolerance for reading but lower spatial abilities.

Attituional Differences: All user groups have an interest in improving training, but only the training professionals (3) and to some extent process supporters (4) are actively seeking to improve training practices on a daily basis. Attitudes towards newer training technologies are highly diverse among operators (1) and technicians (2), with older and more experienced operators being particularly skeptical. line managers (5) prioritize ensuring the production is running smoothly, and any interruption is discouraged.

Mental Model Differences: The majority of user groups have limited technical knowledge of digital training technologies, except for a minority of training professionals (3) and process supporters (4). Younger individuals tend to associate AR & VR with gaming and expect a gamified experience when using them for training. The association contradicts the typical approach to training development at the company, where gamification elements such as the ability to fail a level or restart are actively discouraged due to the nature of the regulated enviroment.

Activities. The specific GxP regulated training activities analyzed include: (1) on-boarding, (2) re-training, (3) change training, (4) line-change training, (5) maintenance (planned & unplanned) along their temporal nature, cooperative nature, complexity & nature of content.

Temporal: On-boarding (1) is a general process that occurs frequently and can last from a few weeks to several months, depending on the process. Re-training (2) and planned maintenance (5a) are performed at specific intervals and are typically flexible and low-pressure in terms of time constraints, allowing them to be done during troughs of work. Other types of training occur at different intervals and are dependent on factors such as regulatory changes, machinery breakdowns, and sickness. These types of training are typically non-flexible and high-pressure in terms of time constraints, as they must be done to ensure production can continue.

Cooperation: On-boarding (1), line change training (4), and some re-training (2) require interaction with a trainer and certifier. Change training (3) is usually introduced by a Change Training Ambassador (Process Support Department), while maintenance (5) is typically carried out independently.

Complexity: Benyon differentiate between the complexity of tasks, based on how well defined they are [5]. On-boarding (1) and line-change training (4) follow a step-by-step process and involve large amounts of information but have low complexity. Re-training (2) is also of low complexity. Change training (3) has medium complexity, while planned maintenance (5a) is typically of low complexity, but requires technical knowledge. In contrast, unplanned maintenance (5b) has high complexity. All activities however are critical to ensure compliance.

Nature of Content: On-boarding (1) consists of a combination of standardized organizational information and process-specific training materials. Re-training (2) and line-change training (4) involve process-specific materials, while change training (3) involves changes to process-specific materials. Maintenance (5), on the other hand, involves machinery-specific materials.

Technologies. The specific technologies analyzed include: (1) paper-based instructions (SOP read and understand), (2) peer-Training (unstructured and structured), (3) e-Learning, (4) tablet-based digital instructions, (5) XR (AR & VR), focusing on how information is communicated and the content. XR technology is currently being tested but not utilized on a large scale. Classroom training is employed in some cases, but mostly for training of trainers and delivery of non job-specific information.

Communication: SOPs (1) can be communicated through tablets, computers, or paper, while peer-training (2) involves physically present individuals. E-learning (3) and digital instructions (4) can be accessed through tablets or computers, and XR-based (5) training utilized head-mounted displays.

Content: Peer-training (2) involves SOPs, instructions, expert knowledge, and experiences. E-learning (3) includes specifically designed training modules, and XR (5) use custom instructions based on existing instructions for the process.

Challenges with the training process

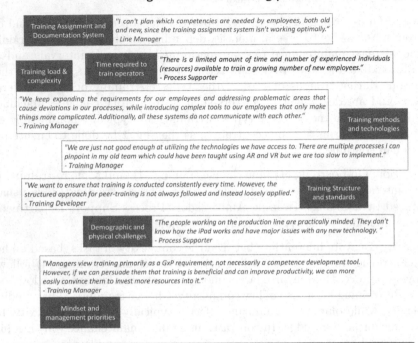

Challenges with evaluating training

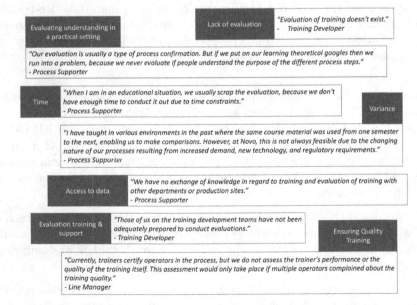

Fig. 4. Affinity Diagrams

4.3 Interview Findings and Observations

The major challenges defined by the different roles are presented in Fig. 4, with representative statements attached. The investigation identified significant challenges in various aspects of the training process at the company. These challenges were classified into categories such as the limited training assignment and documentation system, increased load and complexity of training, limited time for training, utilization (or lack thereof) of training methods and technologies, lack of adherence to training structures and standards, limited digital literacy of users, and a compliance-focused mindset from management regarding training. The challenges related to the evaluation of training were also identified, including historical lack of evaluation, difficulty in evaluating understanding, inadequate time for evaluation, variance in processes and user groups, lack of data sharing and access to baseline data, inadequate training in conducting evaluations, and lack of investigation into the quality of training.

5 Discussion

5.1 Context and Users

The significant size and variability of production settings and output led to the decentralization of training responsibilities in the past. Although there has been a concerted effort to develop global training standards, decentralization has resulted in challenges due to the variations in training approaches, demographics, culture, management style, performance tracking systems, quality of training material and learning management systems across different production lines and locations. Variance exists among people working at different sites due to geographic and cultural differences. The T-PACK Model [28] outlines three types of knowledge required for effective teaching with technology: technological, pedagogical, and content knowledge. Variability in the trainer group, with some lacking in technological or pedagogical knowledge, must also be considered in any training interventions.

5.2 Isolating Training Technology or Method as a Parameter

Research has found that in other settings, factors such as organizational structure or attitudes among employees can make it challenging to isolate technology as the primary cause of performance variance [29]. These findings also holds true in the current context. The current environment at the company is not optimal for implementing training technology, unlike controlled environments such as universities, where XR has shown significant benefits for training [12,25]. Assessing the impact of a training technology implementation is challenging since company training initiatives aren't isolated, and introducing new technology usually involves a larger organizational intervention with management trained in proper standards. The effectiveness of training at the company is influenced by various factors, including the trainer's skills, the quality of digital instruction, the type of process being trained, and the user group. The training should be tailored to the specific needs of the process and the trainees, and designed to accommodate the unique characteristics of the user group. During the interviews, the participants expressed several usability issues. Furthermore, the highly regulated nature of the industry and the advanced maturity level of the existing training process has led to lower levels of innovation, similar to findings from other mature industries [7].

5.3   The Lack of a Baseline

Establishing a baseline is essential when conducting quality impact evaluations [2]. A major problem expressed by the subjects is the current lack of access to training data, and a lack of an established baseline for different training methods. There is no centralized storage of evaluation data at the current time, which means any evaluation of local initiatives is stored at a local level. While reconstruction of baseline data is possible using secondary sources [3], no studies within the pharmaceutical industry have been published which can be utilized, as far as the authors are aware. The absence of baseline data is particularly crucial for emerging technologies like AR and VR. Developers face significant pressure to demonstrate the effectiveness of their products, but local managers may be unwilling to invest resources in large-scale tests due to the pressure to maintain output levels.

5.4   Evaluating Impact

Centralized training initiatives at the company have actively pursued trying to generate baseline data and metrics to show impact, and have recently focused on connecting these more directly to key production metrics such as OEE (Overall Equipment Efficiency). At the case company, the centralized training department uses Kirkpatrick's levels of evaluation as the standard, although its use at local sites throughout the company is still limited. While it is possible to link Benyon's usability evaluation metrics [5] with the assessment of learning outcomes through Kirkpatrick's 4 levels [19] during prototype development and testing, demonstrating long-term impact and behavioral changes necessitates a greater level of engagement and implementation of the technologies. Currently at the company, based on principles of the forgetting curve [31], a follow-up evaluation is supposed to be conducted by the line manager. However, due to personnel time constraints, the follow-up evaluation is frequently neglected.

6   Conclusion and Future Work

6.1   Conclusion

The empirical data collection and synthesis through interviews, observations, PACT analysis, The Rich Picture, and affinity revealed multiple challenges

in various aspects, including: technological challenges, organizational challenges, attitude, lack of required competences, regulatory requirements, increased
demand, and data access. Key challenges in regards to the current training
process include a limited training assignment and management system, lack
of adherence to training standards, and limited resources for training due to
high product demand. Challenges to the adoption of digital training technologies include a lack of documented effect, the limited digital literacy of the user
group, and general usability issues. Evaluating training faces challenges including a lack of available data, limited resources for evaluations, absence of industry
standards, lack of an established evaluation protocol and variance in processes,
contexts, and user groups, hindering any generalized approach.

6.2 Future Work

Based on the outcomes presented, which consisted of a large variety of challenges
connected to the training process, the larger research project will involve the
following steps:

1. Establish measurable indicators for learning that can be linked directly to
   critical production metrics like OEE (Overall Equipment Efficiency).
2. Conduct small-scale experiments in particular production lines that represent
   different processes and user groups to determine the most effective assessment
   techniques that enable the collection and comparison of data across multiple
   sites.
3. Identify contextual factors that may affect the efficacy of different training
   techniques and determine the influence of these variables on the outcomes.
4. Create a general evaluation protocol with the necessary infrastructure to
   enable relevant personnel to store and retrieve data, facilitating knowledge
   exchange and statistical analysis of information from various sites.
5. Expand the evaluation process to encompass additional sites and production
   facilities, enabling researchers to enhance assessment methodologies and optimize training techniques and technologies based on their application context.

6.3 Limitations

There are several limitations which influenced the results of the study and should
be acknowledged, including:

- Restricted access to production facilities, thereby reducing the extend of
  observations, due to the busy schedule of production and the regulated nature
  of the industry.
- Lack of interviews with local personnel from other settings beyond the Danish
  environment. Individuals in the global training department express that significant variations exist in terms of user groups and cultural contexts across
  international production sites.
- Restricted opportunities for longer depth interviews with relevant personnel
  due to their busy schedules.

References

1. Ahadi, S., Jacobs, R.: A review of the literature on structured on-the-job training and directions for future research. Hum. Resour. Dev. Rev. **16**, 153448431772594 (2017). https://doi.org/10.1177/1534484317725945
2. Bamberger, M.: Conducting quality impact evaluations under budget, time and data constraints. World Bank, Independent Evaluation Group/Poverty Analysis, Monitoring and ... (2006)
3. Bamberger, M.: Reconstructing baseline data for impact evaluation and results measurement (2010)
4. Bates, R.: A critical analysis of evaluation practice: the Kirkpatrick model and the principle of beneficence. Eval. Prog. Planning **27**(3), 341–347 (2004). https://doi.org/10.1016/j.evalprogplan.2004.04.011, https://www.sciencedirect.com/science/article/pii/S0149718904000369. Ethics, Evaluation and For-Profit Corporations
5. Benyon, D.: Designing User Experience, 4th edn. Pearson Education Limited, Thousand Oaks (2019). https://pdfuni.com/sample/PoliticsSociology/PS1201-1300/PS1271/sample%EF%BC%8DDesigning%20User%20Experience%204th%204E%20David%20Benyon.pdf
6. Bondin, A., Zammit, J.: A new age for plant maintenance: making use of augmented reality to improve maintenance of production assets. Institute of Electrical and Electronics Engineers Inc. (2022). https://doi.org/10.1109/ICTMOD55867.2022.10041879, https://www.scopus.com/inward/record.uri?eid=2-s2.0-85149549109&doi=10.1109%2fICTMOD55867.2022.10041879&partnerID=40&md5=7e136752752d7f15f93c513af3a40e5b. Cited By 1
7. Bos, J.W., Economidou, C., Sanders, M.W.: Innovation over the industry life-cycle: evidence from EU manufacturing. J. Econ. Behav. Organ. **86**, 78–91 (2013). https://doi.org/10.1016/j.jebo.2012.12.025, https://www.sciencedirect.com/science/article/pii/S0167268112002843
8. Brinkerhoff, R.O.: The success case method: a strategic evaluation approach to increasing the value and effect of training. Adv. Dev. Hum. Resour. **7**(1), 86–101 (2005)
9. Flyvbjerg, B.: Five misunderstandings about case-study research. Qual. Inquiry **12**(2), 219–245 (2006). https://doi.org/10.1177/1077800405284363, http://qix.sagepub.com/cgi/doi/10.1177/1077800405284363
10. Funk, M., Lischke, L., Mayer, S., Shirazi, A., Schmidt, A.: Teach me how! Interactive assembly instructions using demonstration and in-situ projection. In: Cognitive Science and Technology, pp. 49–73 (2018). https://doi.org/10.1007/978-981-10-6404-3_4, https://www.scopus.com/inward/record.uri?eid=2-s2.0-85051706568&doi=10.1007%2f978-981-10-6404-3_4&partnerID=40&md5=91fcc9ea367e75fba2e6c3561895dee3. Cited By 28
11. Grohmann, A., Kauffeld, S.: Evaluating training programs: development and correlates of the questionnaire for professional training evaluation. Int. J. Training Dev. **17** (2013). https://doi.org/10.1111/ijtd.12005
12. Gukwon Koo, N.L., Kwon, O.: Combining object detection and causality mining for efficient development of augmented reality-based on-the-job training systems in hotel management. New Rev. Hypermedia Multimedia **25**(3), 112–136 (2019). https://doi.org/10.1080/13614568.2019.1694594
13. Hammond, J.P.: Four generations of quality-GxP pharmaceutical quality assurance, an alternative track? Spectroscopy Europe (2021)

14. Hanington, B., Martin, B.: Universal Methods of Design Expanded and Revised: 125 Ways to Research Complex Problems, Develop Innovative Ideas, and Design Effective Solutions. Rockport Publishers, Google-Books-ID: SFnBDwAAQBAJ

15. Holtzblatt, K., Beyer, H.: Contextual Design: Evolved. Synthesis Lectures on Human-Centered Informatics. Springer, Cham (2015). https://doi.org/10.1007/978-3-031-02207-4, https://link.springer.com/10.1007/978-3-031-02207-4

16. Ifenthaler, D., Yau, J.: Utilising learning analytics to support study success in higher education: a systematic review. Educ. Technol. Res. Dev. **68**, 1961–1990 (2020). https://doi.org/10.1007/s11423-020-09788-z

17. Kalkan, Ö.K., Karabulut, Ş., Höke, G.: Effect of virtual reality-based training on complex industrial assembly task performance. Arab. J. Sci. Eng. **46**(12), 12697–12708 (2021). https://doi.org/10.1007/s13369-021-06138-w, https://www.scopus.com/inward/record.uri?eid=2-s2.0-85114111546&doi=10.1007%2fs13369-021-06138-w&partnerID=40&md5=a900c21d7277ccc98dabbbfbcfd24272.   Cited By 9

18. Kaufman, R., Keller, J., Watkins, R.: What works and what doesn't: evaluation beyond Kirkpatrick. Performance + Instruction **35**(2), 8–12 (1996). https://doi.org/10.1002/pfi.4170350204, https://onlinelibrary.wiley.com/doi/abs/10.1002/pfi.4170350204

19. Kirkpatrick, D., Kirkpatrick, J.: Evaluating Training Programs: The Four Levels. Berrett-Koehler Publishers (2006)

20. Kochanowska, M., Gagliardi, W.R.: The double diamond model: in pursuit of simplicity and flexibility. In: Perspectives on Design II: Research, Education and Practice, pp. 19–32 (2022)

21. Koumaditis, K., Venckute, S., Jensen, F., Chinello, F.: Immersive training: outcomes from small scale AR/VR pilot-studies, vol. 2019-January, pp. 1894–1898. Institute of Electrical and Electronics Engineers Inc. (2019). https://doi.org/10.1109/VR44988.2019.9044162, https://www.scopus.com/inward/record.uri?eid=2-s2.0-85083372162&doi=10.1109%2fVR44988.2019.9044162&partnerID=40&md5=a8550f1e0e0dd00c9d93da14f248dd68. Cited By 11

22. Kwiatek, C., Sharif, M., Li, S., Haas, C., Walbridge, S.: Impact of augmented reality and spatial cognition on assembly in construction. Autom. Constr. **108**, 102935 (2019). https://doi.org/10.1016/j.autcon.2019.102935, https://www.scopus.com/inward/record.uri?eid=2-s2.0-85074570326&doi=10.1016%2fj.autcon.2019.102935&partnerID=40&md5=2a3012f89f3a6600932e3c7daea0a986. Cited By 52

23. Lavric, T., Bricard, E., Preda, M., Zaharia, T.: An industry-adapted AR training method for manual assembly operations. In: Stephanidis, C., et al. (eds.) HCI International 2021 - Late Breaking Papers: Multimodality, eXtended Reality, and Artificial Intelligence, HCII 2021. LNCS (including subseries Lecture Notes in Artificial Intelligence and Lecture Notes in Bioinformatics), vol. 13095, pp. 282–304. Springer, Cham (2021). https://doi.org/10.1007/978-3-030-90963-5_22, https://www.scopus.com/inward/record.uri?eid=2-s2.0-85119876841&doi=10.1007%2f978-3-030-90963-5_22&partnerID=40&md5=64056f6159b68dc9883aad0897fbb66e. Cited By 4

24. Le, K.D., Azhar, S., Lindh, D., Ziobro, D.: VRQUEST: designing and evaluating a virtual reality system for factory training. LNCS (including subseries Lecture Notes in Artificial Intelligence and Lecture Notes in Bioinformatics), vol. 12936, pp. 300–305. Springer, Cham (2021). https://doi.org/10.1007/978-3-030-85607-6_26, https://www.scopus.com/inward/record.uri?eid=2-s2.0-85115213725&doi=10.100

7%2f978-3-030-85607-6_26&partnerID=40&md5=db82539d96cdbc51ab0c9d68 81f82dff. Cited By 1

25. Loch, F., Quint, F., Brishtel, I.: Comparing video and augmented reality assistance in manual assembly. In: 2016 12th International Conference on Intelligent Environments (IE), pp. 147–150 (2016). https://doi.org/10.1109/IE.2016.31

26. Marino, E., Barbieri, L., Colacino, B., Bruno, F.: User-centered design of an augmented reality tool for smart operator in production environment. In: Rizzi, C., Campana, F., Bici, M., Gherardini, F., Ingrassia, T., Cicconi, P. (eds.) Design Tools and Methods in Industrial Engineering II, ADM 2021. LNME, pp. 125–132. Springer, Cham (2022). https://doi.org/10.1007/978-3-030-91234-5_12, https://www.scopus.com/inward/record.uri?eid=2-s2.0-85121782911&doi=10.1007 %2f978-3-030-91234-5_12&partnerID=40&md5=110ce213c3f609b06a24bc90 0bdccfbc. Cited By 0

27. Marino, E., Barbieri, L., Colacino, B., Fleri, A., Bruno, F.: An augmented reality inspection tool to support workers in industry 4.0 environments. Comput. Ind. **127**, 103412 (2021). https://doi.org/10.1016/j.compind.2021.103412, https://www. scopus.com/inward/record.uri?eid=2-s2.0-85121782911&doi=10.1007%2f978-3-030-91234-5_12&partnerID=40&md5=110ce213c3f609b06a24bc900bdccfbc. Cited By 0

28. Mishra, P., Koehler, M.J.: Technological pedagogical content knowledge: a framework for teacher knowledge. Teach. Coll. Rec. **108**(6), 1017–1054 (2006). https:// doi.org/10.1111/j.1467-9620.2006.00684.x

29. Mollahoseini, A., Farjad, S.: Assessment effectiveness on the job training in higher education (case study: Takestan University). Procedia - Soc. Behav. Sci. **47**, 1310–1314 (2012). https://doi.org/10.1016/j.sbspro.2012.06.817, https:// www.sciencedirect.com/science/article/pii/S1877042812025530. Cyprus International Conference on Educational Research (CY-ICER-2012) North Cyprus, US08-10 February 2012

30. Monk, A., Howard, S.: Methods & tools: the rich picture: a tool for reasoning about work context. Interactions **5**(2), 21–30 (1998). https://doi.org/10.1145/274430. 274434, http://doi.acm.org/10.1145/274430.274434

31. Murre, J.M.J., Dros, J.: Replication and analysis of Ebbinghaus' forgetting curve. PLOS ONE **10**(7), 1–23 (2015). https://doi.org/10.1371/journal.pone.0120644

32. Obermair, F., et al.: Maintenance with augmented reality remote support in comparison to paper-based instructions: experiment and analysis, pp. 942–947. Institute of Electrical and Electronics Engineers Inc. (2020). https:// doi.org/10.1109/ICIEA49774.2020.9102078, https://www.scopus.com/inward/ record.uri?eid=2-s2.0-85086080234&doi=10.1109%2fICIEA49774.2020.9102078& partnerID=40&md5=94c4541928209e733dbcc945dddec018. Cited By 22

33. Phillips, J.J.: Return on Investment in Training and Performance Improvement Programs, 2nd edn. (2012). https://doi.org/10.4324/9780080516257, https:// www.scopus.com/inward/record.uri?eid=2-s2.0-84908957912&doi=10.4324 %2f9780080516257&partnerID=40&md5=b974a690e27bfea67e8a2573a020efc8. Cited By 38

34. Polaine, A., Løvlie, L., Reason, B.: Service design: from insight to implementation. Rosenfeld Media (2013). https://books.google.dk/books?hl=zh-CN&lr=&id=NHo3DwAAQBAJ&oi=fnd&pg=PR1&dq=Service+design: +from+insight+to+implementation.&ots=4BEAJNis8z&sig=s4IE1fg_- CQsWqphbdzWdw14ESI&redir_esc=y#v=onepage&q=Service%20design%3A %20from%20insight%20to%20implementation.&f=false

35. Regulation, G.D.P.: General data protection regulation (GDPR). Intersoft Consulting **24**(1) (2018). Accessed in October
36. Schwarz, S., Regal, G., Kempf, M., Schatz, R.: Learning success in immersive virtual reality training environments: practical evidence from automotive assembly. Association for Computing Machinery (2020). https://doi.org/10.1145/3419249. 3420182, https://www.scopus.com/inward/record.uri?eid=2-s2.0-85117540506& doi=10.1145%2f3419249.3420182&partnerID=40&md5=153fa478563bcc6723edc8 9877237002. Cited By 18
37. Simões, B., Amicis, R., Segura, A., Martín, M., Ipiña, I.: A cross reality wire assembly training system for workers with disabilities. Int. J. Interact. Des. Manuf. **15**(4), 429–440 (2021). https://doi.org/10.1007/s12008-021-00772-2, https://www. scopus.com/inward/record.uri?eid=2-s2.0-85116809131&doi=10.1007%2fs12008-021-00772-2&partnerID=40&md5=419d5e741f406ad808659039b57a8188.   Cited By 1
38. Stoughton, J., Gissel, A., Clark, A., Whelan, T.: Measurement invariance in training evaluation: old question, new context. Comput. Hum. Behav. **27**, 2005–2010 (2011). https://doi.org/10.1016/j.chb.2011.05.007
39. Valentina, D.P., Valentina, D.S., Salvatore, M., Stefano, R.: Smart operators: how industry 4.0 is affecting the worker's performance in manufacturing contexts. Procedia Comput. Sci. **180**, 958–967 (2021). https://doi.org/10.1016/j.procs.2021.01. 347, https://www.sciencedirect.com/science/article/pii/S1877050921004014. Proceedings of the 2nd International Conference on Industry 4.0 and Smart Manufacturing (ISM 2020)
40. de Vaus, D.: Surveys in Social Research. Social Research Today, Taylor & Francis (2013). https://books.google.dk/books?id=VTqdKnhfufMC
41. Wagner, M., Leubner, C., Strunk, J.: Mixed reality or simply mobile? A case study on enabling less skilled workers to perform routine maintenance tasks, vol. 217, pp. 728–736. Elsevier B.V. (2022). https://doi. org/10.1016/j.procs.2022.12.269, https://www.scopus.com/inward/record.uri? eid=2-s2.0-85163809864&doi=10.1016%2fj.procs.2022.12.269&partnerID=40& md5=24cbed138cfa3d607915904146af76e5. Cited By 0
42. Werrlich, S., Daniel, A., Ginger, A., Nguyen, P.A., Notni, G.: Comparing HMD-based and paper-based training, pp. 134–142 (2018). https://doi. org/10.1109/ISMAR.2018.00046, https://www.scopus.com/inward/record.uri? eid=2-s2.0-85062171885&doi=10.1109%2fISMAR.2018.00046&partnerID=40& md5=c206a2dd977504ba7c080ff7a8072a51. Cited By 52
43. Zeisel, J., Eberhard, J.: Inquiry by Design: Environment/Behavior/Neuroscience in Architecture, Interiors, Landscape, and Planning. W.W. Norton, New York (2006). https://books.google.dk/books?id=voeTQgAACAAJ
44. Zolas, N., et al.: Advanced technologies adoption and use by us firms: evidence from the annual business survey. Technical report, National Bureau of Economic Research (2021)

Blended Learning Based on H5P Interactive Exercises: Insights from a Case Study

Michel Noutcha[✉] and Suzanne Kieffer

Université Catholique de Louvain, Institute for Language and Communication,
Louvain-la-Neuve, Belgium
{michel.noutcha,suzanne.kieffer}@uclouvain.be

Abstract. The user experience (UX) in educational settings is crucial, extending beyond academic performance to encompass students' perceptions and responses to teaching methods. Blended learning (BL), integrating online and face-to-face components, including flipped learning (FL), enhances engagement through platforms like the HTML5 package (H5P). Despite these advancements, guidelines for designing and evaluating online learning experiences with H5P are lacking. This paper aims to address this gap by providing recommendations for H5P integration and a methodology for assessing student learning experiences. Key contributions include positioning H5P among comparable tools, offering a detailed process for leveraging H5P, and emphasizing the need for effective assessment methods. The case study, conducted in a master's thesis methodological seminar, involved two rounds of user testing, revealing insights into student preferences and needs. Findings suggest students prioritize content and usability over attractiveness and value H5P interactive features. Future work should replicate this case study with other teaching units, e-learning technologies, or other student groups.

Keywords: Blended learning · H5P · User Experience · Learning experience · Case study · Recommendations

1 Introduction

User experience (UX) encompasses individuals' perceptions and responses resulting from using and/or anticipating the use of a product, system or service [18]. Beyond usability [21], UX requires examination of both pragmatic (e.g. ease of use) and hedonic attributes (e.g., stimulation) [13]. Aligned with UX, the learning experience extends beyond academic performance to include students' perceptions and responses to an educational approach.

Blended learning (BL) merges online and face-to-face components [4,17,23], incorporating flipped learning (FL) where students access learning materials such as videos, tutorials, or documents online before attending classes. Plugins such as HTML5 Package (H5P)[1] enrich learning materials with interactive videos,

---

[1] H5P: https://h5p.org.

P. Zaphiris and A. Ioannou (Eds.): HCII 2024, LNCS 14722, pp. 214–233, 2024.
https://doi.org/10.1007/978-3-031-61672-3_14

fill-in-the-blanks or image sequencing, which empowers students to engage directly with educational content [5,36,41], enhancing the learning experience [7,35].

However, specific guidelines for the design and evaluation of H5P-based learning experiences are lacking, which raises questions such as: How to design online learning experiences that fully leverage the advantages of H5P? To what extent does the integration of H5P exercises into learning materials benefit students' overall learning experience? These are relevant questions to address given the ever-increasing demand for e-learning tools, especially since the successive lockdowns during the covid-19 pandemic. Studying the relevance of these tools is crucial for developing meaningful online learning experiences.

The objective of this paper is twofold: (1) provide recommendations for integrating H5P elements into pedagogical frameworks; (2) provide a methodology for assessing students' learning experience with H5P material in terms of performance, perceptions, and responses. The paper makes the following contributions:

1. The related work section positions H5P among comparable e-learning tools such as Xerte, Storyline, Adapt or eXeLearning, both informing current practices and establishing a foundation for potentially replicating this research, which focuses on H5P, with other e-learning tools.
2. The case study provides a detailed, step-by-step breakdown of how to leverage H5P interactive exercises to flip content. Special emphasis is placed on the critical role of designing H5P exercises that seamlessly integrate into pedagogical frameworks, thereby enhancing the effectiveness of learning.
3. The paper underscores the need for effective assessment methods and tools, using insights from a case study that evaluates students' performance and learning experiences with H5P exercises. It demonstrates the relevance of H5P exercises in fostering student engagement with the learning material.

The case study focuses on the integration of H5P exercises in the instructional design of a course taught at Université catholique de Louvain (UCLouvain). We integrated the H5P exercises in Moodle, an open-source learning management system (LMS) [1]. We conducted two rounds of user testing to evaluate students' academic performance and learning experience with the H5P material. A mixed-method approach allowed us to collect data from multiple data sources, cross-analyze these data, and report an integrated vision of the case. We adopted a case study approach, as scientific literature about the learning experience with H5P is scarce and we have no intent to statistically generalize findings or demonstrate cause-and-effect [29]. Instead, we discuss the proposed assessment methodology and recommendations, and the replication of the case study across other teaching units or e-learning technologies.

2   Background

2.1   Blended Learning (BL)

BL, often used interchangeably with hybrid learning [17], lacks agreement on its definition in the scientific literature [40]. Generally, it refers to the integration of face-to-face (F2F) and online instruction [4,5,17]. Online learning occurs remotely via connected devices, either synchronously or asynchronously [8,10,30]. Two influential BL definitions are offered by Graham [11], emphasizing F2F with computer-mediated instruction, and Garrison [9], focusing on integrating F2F and online experiences. Graham's definition, more inclusive, omits constraints on digital technology spaces, while Garrison's emphasizes spatial, temporal, and human aspects of learning [8,10].

Three meta-analyses consistently report that BL outperforms other teaching modalities, namely F2F [3,39] and online [27,39]. In particular, the authors show positive effects on knowledge outcome, academic performance, and enhancing education. These results can be explained as follows. From the instructor's perspective, BL combines F2F and online modalities to address their respective shortcomings [7]. F2F lectures facilitate direct interaction, fostering a strong connection to the course structure and speakers, while online learning eliminates spatial and temporal barriers, reduces operational costs, and enhances instructors' monitoring capabilities, allowing for personalized educational activities [24]. From the student's perspective, BL cultivates 21st century skills such as creativity, critical thinking, and collaboration [19], while offering greater flexibility [22,35] and student engagement [12].

However, BL remains challenging for both students and instructors. The main challenges for students are related to self-regulation and the use of educational technologies. As for instructors, the challenges are primarily linked to integrating technology for pedagogical purposes [31]. There are also security and privacy issues associated with using the H5P Hub to share and reuse interactive content, as well as physical and time constraints on students and instructors to access and use online resources effectively [5,35].

2.2 Flipped Learning (FL)

FL empowers students with more responsibility [14], by providing them with access to learning materials such as videos, tutorials, or documents online before F2F classes. Therefore, students' initial exposure to new concepts or content occurs through self-directed online learning, allowing class time to be utilized for more interactive and collaborative activities, discussions, or application of knowledge. This approach contrasts with instructor-centered methods where students typically receive instructional content during class time and then work on assignments or activities independently outside of class.

Several tools exist to flip content (Table 1), among which HTML5 Package (H5P) (See Footnote 1). H5P is a free and open-source framework supporting the creation, sharing, and reuse of interactive HTML5 content. The framework includes an editor that allows creation and sharing H5P content, a website, and plugins for integration into learning management systems (LMS). The website contains examples of content types, a guide for authors and developers, and a forum for sharing libraries, applications, and content types. To date, H5P offers 52 content types among which quizzes, puzzles, interactive videos, and branching scenarios.

Table 1. Comparison between H5P, Xerte, Storyline, Adapt, eXeLearning. Analysis conducted in Jan 2024. y stands for yes.

Systems	H5P	Xerte	Storyline	Adapt	eXeLearning
Last version	2024	2023	2023	2019	2013
Open-source	y	y		y	y
SCORM & HTML5	y	y	y	y	y
Other standards	y	y	y	y	limited
Reusable content	y	y	y	y	y
Community support	y	y	y	y	y
Responsiveness	y	y	y		y

In exploring H5P applications in education, we first delved into its positive impacts on student engagement, motivation, and self-regulation. For example, H5P branching scenarios enhance the learning experience within virtual simulations [35], while H5P interactive videos facilitate active engagement, self-paced review, and immediate feedback [22]. Additionally, H5P interactive activities contribute to asynchronous instructor presence [36]. Our exploration then extended to studies leveraging H5P to enhance video-based flipped classes [23,41] or exploring various content types for out-of-class activities, such as branching scenario [37], accordion, image hotspot, and image sequencing [36]. Importantly, none of these works uses the 'column' content type, an H5P feature allowing the grouping of various H5P content types in a column layout. Our analysis reveals an untapped potential in utilizing this 'column' feature for a more integrated and dynamic learning experience. Moreover, to our knowledge, none explicitly investigates the UX with H5P or provides recommendations for flipping a course.

3 Case Study

3.1 Context

We developed H5P resources for the master's thesis methodological seminar in the communication sciences program at UCLouvain. The seminar aims to equip students with essential research skills, including defining a research topic, anticipating methodological developments, evaluating project feasibility, and planning the research steps and formal requirements for completing the master's thesis. The 120-unit, two-year master program involves the seminar (2 units), pre-thesis research (3 units), and a master's thesis (20 units). The seminar assignment focuses on synthesizing future research elements, while pre-thesis research requires a comprehensive paper covering problem statement, literature review, methods, initial data, and research plan.

The shift to FL was prompted in 2018 by the combination of the following observations: students' stress and frustration due to the lack of individual follow-up; poor quality of the research topics submitted by the students at the end of the seminar; course holder's work overload while answering students' individual requests and grading students' research topic. In response, academic staff decided to flip the class about bibliography management, and initiated group tutoring during the seminar. Group tutoring reduced both students' stress and course holder's work overload, and increased the quality of the research topics proposed by students. The resulting instructional design includes F2F lectures and discussions, individual assignments, in-class quizzes, and H5P exercises accessible on Moodle.

3.2 Flipping Content with H5P

We flipped bibliography management for several reasons. First, it is universally applicable across all research topics, catering to the needs of all students. Second, mastering these activities is crucial for scientific and master's thesis writing, offering valuable refreshers for students. Last, flipped content replaces less engaging readings and lectures, optimizing F2F time for more pertinent subjects.

Although BL is often associated with video-based classes, we diverged from the choice of H5P interactive video, the most extensively discussed H5P content type in scientific literature. Instead, we opted for the H5P column for the following three reasons. First, relying solely on interactive videos for FL would have been time-consuming, since video preparation and maintenance is resource-intensive [41]. Second, interactive videos, proven to be most effective within 5–10 min [23,35], could risk losing student interest when dealing with a larger quantity of content to flip. Third, by utilizing H5P columns, we could consolidate the content associated with a specific teaching unit within a single column, adhering to Mayer's segmenting principle [26]. Specifically, we chunked the content into four chapters, database searching (Chap. 1), bibliography (Chap. 2), referencing (Chap. 3) and avoiding plagiarism (Chap. 4). We created a fifth H5P column to introduce students to H5P interaction. For each H5P exercise (i.e., chapter), we followed the same procedure: (1) document the content of the corresponding teaching unit; (2) assign H5P modalities to the written content; (3) implement in H5P; (4) proof-read and check the result as validation.

Table 2. Description of the H5P content used in each H5P column/exercise.

	Chap. 1	Chap. 2	Chap. 3	Chap. 4
https://h5p.org/drag-and-drop	2	11	0	3
https://h5p.org/drag-the-words	4	5	1	2
https://h5p.org/fill-in-the-blanks	0	3	0	0
https://h5p.org/image-hotspot-question	0	4	0	0
https://h5p.org/image-hotspots	1	3	0	0
https://h5p.org/image-slider	0	5	0	0
https://h5p.org/single-choice-set	2	0	4	3
https://h5p.org/true-false	0	3	1	3
https://h5p.org/interactive-video	2	4	2	2

3.3   User Testing

We employed user testing to gather data allowing us to assess participants' UX, academic performance, and attitude toward the H5P exercises. User testing involved questionnaire to measure UX, knowledge test to measure academic performance, and interview or questionnaire to gather data about attitude. This mixed-method approach allowed us to cross-analyze different types of data.

We proceeded in two rounds. Round 1 (R1) was exploratory and took place in distant synchronous mode in June 2021 with $N = 12$ participants, while Round 2 (R2) was descriptive and took place in online asynchronous mode in May 2023 with $N = 27$ participants. Both rounds followed a similar procedure. First, all participants signed an online consent form authorizing the use of their anonymized data for research purposes. Following this, they performed the experimental tasks. Finally, they filled out a questionnaire regarding UX, which was followed by either an interview (R1) or a questionnaire (R2) about their attitude toward the H5P material. There were differences between R1 and R2 regarding the user testing mode, the scope of the experimental task, the pretest questionnaire, and the knowledge tests (Table 3). First, R1 took place synchronously on Teams using links to the different instruments (e.g. consent form, tests, etc.) with a video recording of the participant's screen shared while they performed the experimental task on Moodle. R2 took place completely asynchronously on Moodle. Second, R1 participants completed one or two H5P chapters, while R2 participants completed all four H5P chapters. Third, R2 participants completed a questionnaire assessing their level of expertise with each teaching unit and their level of familiarity with H5P. Finally, R2 participants underwent a pretest and posttest knowledge test, respectively before and after the completion of the experimental task.

Table 3. Overview of the methodology in both rounds. * indicates R1 activities accessed through a link provided by the experimenter in Teams conversation.

Round	R1	R2
Period	June 2021	May 2023
Goal	exploratory	descriptive
Mode	online synchronous	online asynchronous
Participants	$N = 12$	$N = 27$
Online consent form	yes*	yes
Pretest questionnaire	no	yes
Pretest knowledge test	no	yes
Experimental task	1 or 2 chapters	all 4 chapters
Posttest knowledge test	no	yes
UX questionnaire	yes*	yes
Follow-up	interview	questionnaire

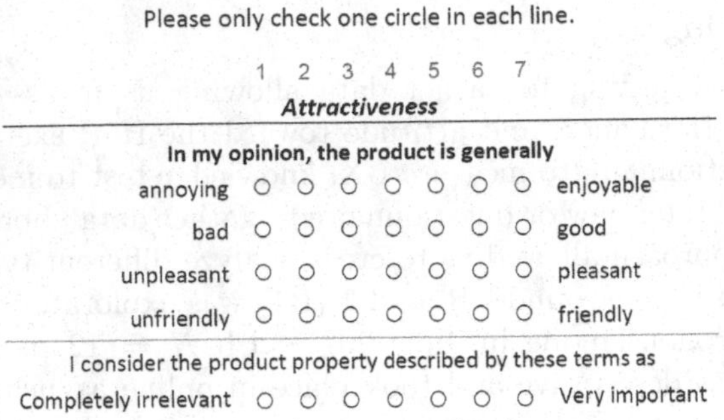

Please only check one circle in each line.

1   2   3   4   5   6   7

Attractiveness

In my opinion, the product is generally

annoying   O   O   O   O   O   O   O   enjoyable

bad   O   O   O   O   O   O   O   good

unpleasant   O   O   O   O   O   O   O   pleasant

unfriendly   O   O   O   O   O   O   O   friendly

I consider the product property described by these terms as

Completely irrelevant   O   O   O   O   O   O   O   Very important

Fig. 1. Attractiveness scale. Template from https://ueqplus.ueq-research.org/

3.4   Data Collection Methods

User Experience. To assess participants' UX with the H5P material, we used the UEQ+, a modular and standardized questionnaire for measuring UX according to up to 26 scales [33]. We used the same nine scales in both rounds. Specifically, we opted for efficiency, usefulness, perspicuity, and intuitive use, as these are recommended by authors for assessing systems designed to help users achieve specific goals. We also included trustworthiness and quality of content, as suggested for products conveying knowledge. We selected attractiveness, stimulation, and novelty as they apply to all products. We chose these scales due to their balanced coverage of task-oriented (e.g. usefulness) and non-task-oriented (e.g. stimulation) attributes of UX [13]. Each scale gathers ratings on a 1 to 7 scale for four related items and the relative importance of the scale (Fig. 1). The ratings for the four related items collected from all participants enable the calculation of a mean UX score for each scale and an overall UX score for the H5P exercises. The mean relative importance of each scale is computed as the average of the importance ratings across all participants.

Academic Performance. To assess R2 participants' academic performance (not assessed in R1), we administered Moodle knowledge tests. A pretest knowledge test measured participants' baseline understanding of each teaching unit, serving as a benchmark for evaluating teaching effectiveness. We then compared the posttest knowledge test results to assess participant progress and the efficacy of H5P exercises. Finally, we cross-analyzed data with participants' scores in each H5P exercise, which were accessible from Moodle gradebook. We developed a Moodle question database consisting of 20 questions in total, with five questions allocated to each H5P chapter. Our design prioritized competencies over knowledge assessment, with four questions on knowledge (i.e., what students know) and 16 questions focusing on competencies (i.e., what students can do with that knowledge) assessment, respectively. Examples of questions are provided in Table 4. Questions were randomly extracted from the Moodle question database for both the pretest and posttest knowledge assessments.

Table 4. Examples of R2 knowledge test questions by question type. Q: questions; A: answers; correct answers in bold; blank indicates no question for that question type.

Knowledge	Competency
Chapter 1: Database searching	
Q: What does bibliographic research entail? A: **identifying previous research conducted on a specific topic**; referencing existing research on the topic; summarizing prior research findings on the topic	Q: What factors should be prioritized in analyzing the relevance of a document found in a scientific article database? A: **abstract**; authors; page count; source
Chapter 2: Bibliography	
	Q: What type of document does "Lallemand, C., Gronier, G., & Dugué, M. (2018). Méthodes de design UX: 30 méthodes fondamentales pour concevoir des expériences optimales (2e éd). Eyrolles." correspond to? A: article; **book**; book chapter; DVD
Chapter 3: Referencing	
Q: Where should all references be found? A: at the end of the text, in footnotes, **in the list of references**	Q: How to cite a source from a single author in parenthesis format? A: **(author's name, publication date)**; (author's name, publication date, page); (publication date, author's name)
Chapter 4: Avoiding plagiarism	
Q: Why cite sources in academic work? (select all that apply) A: **to avoid plagiarism; ; to distinguish personal opinions from others'; to enhance credibility; to provide readers with additional reference**	Q: How to avoid plagiarism when copy-pasting a verbatim excerpt into your own work? A: italicizing; **italicizing, using quotation marks and referencing the source**; using quotation marks

Attitude. To assess R1 participants' attitudes toward H5P exercises, we conducted semi-structured interviews using the following questions: "Which aspects of the H5P exercises positively affected your satisfaction?", "What are the three most positive/negative aspects of the exercises?", and "Which aspects should we improve in the H5P exercises?". Additional interventions, such as "Could you tell us more about [...]?", "Do you have a concrete example of [...]?", or "What does [...] mean to you?", were used when needed to clarify participants' statements. For R2 participants' attitudes toward the H5P-based instructional design, we administered a questionnaire with the following questions: "What do you consider to be the positive aspects of this learning tool?", "What aspects of this learning tool do you believe could be improved?", and "Is there anything else you would like to add?". This approach allowed us to gather comprehensive insights into participants' perceptions and preferences regarding the H5P exercises and instructional design, facilitating informed decision-making for future improvements and enhancements.

3.5   Participants

We recruited all participants from the communication science master's program at UCLouvain, thereby the sample is representative of the targeted user population [20]. Specifically, R1 participants were recruited through the social media of the master's program, while R2 participants were all enrolled and active students in the UX course of the master's program. Analysis of pretest questionnaire revealed varying levels of familiarity with H5P: in R1, 9 out of 12 participants (75%) had never used H5P before the user tests, whereas all R2 participants (100%) had used it at least once.

Proficiency in bibliography management showed consistent patterns among R2 participants (Table 5). Notably, they reported above average proficiency in all teaching units with slight variability ($Mean = 2.77$, $Median = 3$, $SD = .67$). Additionally, they reported a higher proficiency ($Mean = 2.96$) in avoiding plagiarism, presumably due to the severe consequences it carries in academia, while reporting lower proficiency in both database searching and bibliography ($Mean = 2.70$) with a smaller variability ($SD = .67$), suggesting a potential lack of confidence in their computational skills when searching databases and a potential lack of familiarity with tools for automated bibliography creation.

Table 5. Summary of R2 participants' proficiency with chapters. Proficiency expressed on a 4-level scale from not proficient (1) to proficient (4). SD: standard deviation.

Proficiency	Mean	Median	SD
Database searching (Chap. 1)	2.70	3	.67
Bibliography (Chap. 2)	2.70	3	.67
Referencing (Chap. 3)	2.81	3	.62
Avoiding plagiarism (Chap. 4)	2.96	3	.71

3.6   Conducting User Tests

Completing all four chapters typically takes around two hours. Therefore, to ensure that user tests remained within a reasonable duration of under 60 min, we randomized the assignment of R1 participants to different chapters. Participants P1, P4, P7, and P10 completed Chap. 1; participants P2, P5, P8, and P11 completed Chap. 2; and participants P3, P6, P9, and P12 completed both Chap. 3 and Chap. 4. This allocation was based on the number of H5P contents in each chapter (Table 2). We used random assignment to mitigate selection bias [38].

In R2, the user tests were intentionally conducted asynchronously on Moodle, closely mimicking the intended instructional setting. This allowed R2 participants to complete exercises at their own pace, without an experimenter present, promoting greater autonomy and enhancing action fidelity [20]. While R1 participants' behavior may not correspond to the intended behavior due to artificial conditions, R2 participants' behavior may align closely with the behavior expected in the natural instructional context.

We employed conditional access on Moodle to ensure that certain activities remained inaccessible until prerequisites were completed. As depicted in Fig. 2, R2 participants were required to sign the consent form before proceeding to the pretest questionnaire and knowledge test, and to complete pretest activities before accessing the posttest knowledge test and questionnaires. We opted not to implement conditional access to the chapters to maintain action fidelity. This allowed participants the flexibility to skip chapters or complete them in any order they preferred. This choice was also driven by occasional issues where H5P activities are not always recognized as completed in Moodle, despite being so, making it challenging to assess completion.

To collect complete answers, the user test was treated as an assignment in the UX course, contributing to R2 participants' final grade. The user test would not be considered accomplished unless the last questionnaire was answered. The user test had a designated start and end date. We provided an estimated duration to complete each chapter.

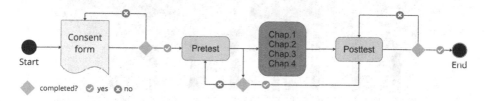

Fig. 2. Conditional access to Moodle activities.

4   Results

We collected both quantitative and qualitative data. R1 being exploratory and R2 descriptive, we limited quantitative data analysis to descriptive statistics. We used content analysis to analyze qualitative data, which consisted in transcribing answers, coding information in an analysis grid, and processing it.

4.1   User Experience

We analyzed participants' UX with H5P exercises by looking at the data collected with the UEQ+. Table 6 presents UX scores for each scale, while Fig. 3 depicts UX scores and relative importance. Altogether, UX scored very high in R1 ($Mean = 2.18$) and high in R2 ($Mean = 1.58$) indicating an overall very good UX with the H5P exercises. However, we observe a consistent decrease in UX scores across all scales between R1 and R2 (mean: $-.60$, range: $-.90$ to $-.36$), likely due to R2 participants' greater familiarity with H5P exercises and their acquired UX expertise from attending UX courses in contrast to R1 participants, and the much longer duration of user tests in R2.

Table 6. UX scores per round. Descending order on R2 means. SD: standard deviation.

UX scale	Mean		SD	
	R1	R2	R1	R2
Efficiency	2.02	1.65	1.01	0.96
Usefulness	2.42	1.73	0.81	1.1
Perspicuity	2.29	1.93	0.82	0.94
Intuitive use	2.17	1.72	0.94	0.88
Trustworthiness of content	2.56	1.94	0.67	0.84
Quality of content	2.42	2.06	0.73	0.81
Attractiveness	2.15	1.3	0.92	1.03
Stimulation	1.88	0.98	1.03	1.14
Novelty	1.75	0.93	1.28	1.1

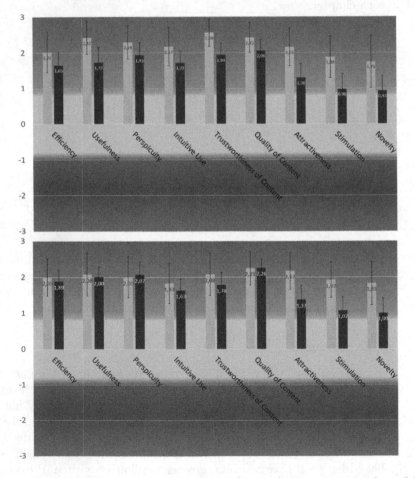

Fig. 3. UX scores (top) and relative importance (bottom). Mean scores with confidence intervals per UX scale on a −3 to +3 range. R1 in light grey, R2 is in dark grey.

UX scores for efficiency, usefulness, perspicuity, and intuitive use are well above average in both rounds (consolidated means: 2.23 in R1, 1.76 in R2), highlighting the effectiveness of the H5P exercises in facilitating goal achievement. In particular, perspicuity scores indicate that learning how to use H5P was easy. In addition, participants in both rounds consistently expressed the high importance of these four UX attributes, especially in R2 compared to attractiveness, stimulation, or novelty.

Throughout both rounds, participants consistently expressed high regard for the trustworthiness and quality of content (consolidated means: 2.49 in R1, 2.00 in R2), as reflected in the respective mean UX scores with significant relative importance. This indicates that the information conveyed through the H5P exercises is reliable, of high quality, up-to-date, and well-prepared. Notably, the relative importance of quality of content did not decrease between rounds, which indicates that participants placed more value on substance than on other system characteristics, such as attractiveness, stimulation, or novelty.

UX scores for attractiveness, stimulation, and novelty exhibit the most notable decrease between R1 and R2 (consolidated means: 1.93 in R1, 1.07 in R2), indicating a significant decline in overall impression regarding the exercises' attractiveness, originality, and enjoyment. This decline could be attributed to R2 participants' increased familiarity with H5P exercises and their acquired UX expertise from attending UX courses, as well as the substantially longer duration of user tests in R2. Unsurprisingly, R2 participants also rated these system characteristics as less important compared to others. Although results demonstrate the usability of the H5P exercises as well as the validity of prioritizing content quality, they suggest that the entire H5P set could benefit from shortening the overall duration to complete the exercises, so as to increase attractiveness.

4.2 Academic Performance

As there was no knowledge test in R1, the entire remainder of this section focuses solely on R2 and its participants. We analyzed R2 participants' academic performance by looking at the scores they obtained at the pre- and posttest knowledge tests (12 questions, 1 point each) and H5P exercises (10 points each). Participants exhibited improved performance in the posttest ($Mean = 10.21$) compared to the pretest ($Mean = 8.47$), with most scores clustered near the maximum ($Median = 10.75$) and a smaller range of scores from 6 to 12 (Table 7), which highlights the effectiveness of H5P exercises in improving knowledge and competencies regarding bibliography management.

Table 7. Comparison of academic performance between pretest and posttest.

Test	Mean	Median	Range	N
Pretest	8.47	8	3.85–11.5	27
Posttest	10.21	10.75	6–12	27

Most participants ($N = 18$, 67%) improved their scores between the pretest and posttest, two (7%) maintained identical scores, seven (26%) experienced decline (Table 8). The group that showed improvement increased performance by 26% (from 62% to 88%), while the group that experienced decline decreased performance by 10% (from 88% to 78%). This suggests H5P exercises are most beneficial for participants who demonstrated the least proficiency in the pretest.

A detailed examination of participants performance and engagement in H5P activities highlights a consistent trend of high scores across all chapters, with

Table 8. Participants scores per chapter, pretest and posttest. Delta: score difference between posttest and pretest.

Participant	Chap. 1	Chap. 2	Chap. 3	Chap. 4	Pretest	Posttest	Delta
P8	10	–	10	–	5.5	11.8	6.30
P6	10	–	10	–	7.5	12	4.50
P20	10	10	10	8.89	7.5	12	4.50
P4	10	10	10	–	7.75	12	4.25
P26	10	–	10	–	8	12	4.00
P25	10	10	10	9.72	7	10.75	3.75
P11	10	–	10	–	7.5	11	3.50
P19	10	–	–	–	7.6	11	3.40
P14	10	–	10	–	7	10	3.00
P1	7.65	–	9.38	6.94	7.5	10.5	3.00
P21	10	–	9.38	–	6.5	9.35	2.85
P27	–	–	–	–	5.5	8	2.50
P3	10	10	10	9.72	9.5	12	2.50
P24	10	–	10	–	3.85	6	2.15
P2	10	10	10	9.72	10	12	2.00
P9	10	–	–	–	9.35	11.1	1.75
P23	10	–	10	–	6	7.25	1.25
P12	10	–	10	–	10	10.6	0.60
P7	10	–	10	–	10	10	0.00
P13	10	–	10	–	11	11	0.00
P5	10	10	10	8.89	11.25	11	−0.25
P16	10	10	10	–	11.50	11	−0.50
P17	10	10	10	10	10	9	−1.00
P22	10	10	8.75	–	11	10	−1.00
P10	6.47	–	8.75	–	10.25	8.50	−1.75
P15	–	–	10	–	10.25	8.25	−2.00
P18	3.53	–	–	–	10	7.75	−2.25
Mean	9.50	10.00	9.84	9.13	8.47	10.21	1.74
N	25	9	23	7	27	27	27

the majority of participants achieving 100% together with a strong engagement in Chap. 1 ($N = 25$) and Chap. 3 ($N = 23$). Chap. 2 and Chap. 4 appear less explored, with a majority of participants (respectively $N = 18$ and $N = 20$) failing to engage with them.

Notably, 88% of participants achieved a score of 10 in Chap. 1, 100% in Chap. 2, 82.60% in Chap. 3, and only 14% in Chap. 4, demonstrating a solid grasp of the material except in Chap. 4. Participants exhibited a strong engagement in Chap. 1 (92.59%) and Chap. 3 (85.19%), indicating interest in the themes, likely because database searching and referencing are areas where they typically encounter the most difficulty. Conversely, participants shown disinterest in both Chap. 2 and Chap. 4, likely overestimating their knowledge and competencies in bibliography and plagiarism.

4.3   Attitudes

Thematic analysis of participants feedback reveals recurring themes, providing insight into positive aspects and areas for improvement in the H5P material. Positive aspects include the richness of H5P contents, their interactive features, and their ability to empower participants. First, participants praised the diversity of content types offering a good user experience, ranging from drag-and-drop exercises to interactive videos. In particular, participants found the combination of video and text beneficial as it enabled them to easily follow along with the text while watching the video (P12 in R1, P25 in R2). In R2, P8 mentioned that the variety of questions helped in retaining the information read. Second, participants enthusiastically welcomed interactive features such as drag-and-drop and interactive videos, despite manipulation slips while placing tiles in drag-and-drop (P9 in R1, P6 and P13 in R2) and some activities exceeding the page size (P6 and P20 in R2). However, interactions kept them engaged (P6 in R1, P2 in R2), focused (P8 in R2), while making exercises enjoyable to use (P5 in R2). Third, participants valued the ability to self-correct thanks to direct feedback after answers, the flexibility to study at their own pace, the ability to access exercises at any time (e.g. P6 in R1 and P8 in R2). Furthermore, P2 in R1 and P25 in R2 judged the possibility to retry as motivating. These results are consistent with the relevant literature regarding testing effect [36], interactivity [22], stimulation [37], and interactive videos [41].

Suggestions for enhancement mainly centered around augmenting the H5P column with new features, such as a progress bar (P8 in R1, P6 in R2), which is beyond our control. P11 in R2 also suggested incorporating accessibility features for students with special needs. Additionally, participants expressed concerns about the excessive length of Chap. 2. Lastly, two participants (P1 in R1, P23 in R2) highlighted the need for additional feedback in H5P activities, regardless of whether they provided correct answers or not. This issue is beyond our control since feedback in H5P is determined by a range of correctness rather than individual items. However, we intend to meet this request in a future version of Moodle pre- and posttest knowledge tests.

5 Discussion

5.1 Cross-Analyzing Data

Participants from R1 and R2 exhibited a high level of satisfaction with the H5P exercises, as evidenced by both UX scores and attitudes. Their satisfaction was particularly pronounced regarding content (trustworthiness, quality, and richness) and they perceived the H5P exercises as beneficial to learning. While usability factors (efficiency, usefulness, perspicuity, and intuitive use) also contributed to their satisfaction, they received less emphasis, especially efficiency and intuitive use. This is likely due to minor difficulties (e.g. placing tiles in drag-and-drop features and content exceeding page size), which required participants to redo their work to achieve their goals. These minor shortcomings are largely balanced out by the fact that H5P interactive features kept participants motivated and focused on the content. These findings demonstrate that the information conveyed in H5P exercises is reliable, well-crafted, and engaging, which is crucial for the effectiveness of online learning [39].

The pronounced decrease between R1 and R2 in attractiveness, stimulation, and novelty UX scores can be attributed to two factors: increased familiarity of R2 participants with H5P and excessive duration of Chap. 2. The duration of Chap. 2 also elucidates the disinterest of R2 participants, as evidenced by their lack of engagement with it. The comparable and simultaneous decrease in relative importance suggests that participants prioritized substance over form, viewing H5P as a task-oriented technology in learning contexts. Task-oriented refers to technologies that users employ to achieve specific goals (here, learning), whereas non-task-oriented refers to technologies where users formulate goals "on the fly" [13]. This finding underscores the importance of crafting H5P exercises that capture students' interest and prompt them to fully engage with them [12].

Moreover, the improvement in academic performance observed between pre- and posttest knowledge tests suggests that the H5P exercises effectively facilitate knowledge and competencies acquisition. This finding corroborates existing literature indicating the efficacy of H5P in promoting deeper understanding and mastery of subject matter [5,22,35]. Chap. 1 and Chap. 3, which elicited higher levels of engagement, exhibited superior academic performance, highlighting the importance of designing engaging and relevant learning materials. The association between R2 participants' engagement and academic performance further supports the notion that active involvement in learning activities contributes to better learning outcomes [12].

Finally, participants' feedback provided valuable insights into the strengths and areas for improvement of the H5P exercises. Positive feedback regarding the variety of content types and user-friendly interactive features underscores the importance of providing diverse and engaging learning experiences [6]. However, suggestions for enhancements, such as accessibility features for students with special needs, indicate areas where further development is needed to meet the evolving needs of users.

5.2   Strengths and Limitations

The improvement in academic performance observed between pre- and posttest knowledge tests supports our initial objective of flipping content to allocate more F2F lecture time to other relevant topics, while addressing the methodological needs of all students regarding a core aspect of completing a master's thesis. By equipping students with a solid foundation in bibliographic management, H5P exercises have brought us closer to achieving this goal.

We did not intend to make statistical generalizations. Case studies typically intend to provide an in-depth understanding of a specific case. Instead, we report an integrated vision of multiple qualitative and quantitative variables regarding students' user experience, academic performance, and attitude toward learning material flipped with H5P. R2 assessment methodology can be replicated with other courses, curricula, and other e-learning tools, such as Xerte, Storyline, Adapt or eXeLearning. Cross-analysis between multiple variables with $N = 39$ participants is a strength rather than a weakness. However, it would be interesting to replicate the case study with student groups in other master's programs.

6   Recommendations

BL requires changing the habits and practices of both students and instructors [34]. Specifically, instructors may face challenges while flipping content for BL. The following recommendations are intended for instructors willing to use H5P to flip content and range from practical tips (1–4) to conceptual advice (5–8), positioned against related work.

1. Start small with existing unflipped resources. The implementation of H5P exercises is resource-intensive [41]: implementing our first H5P exercise took us a hundred times the student time to complete the exercise. We recommend starting with a small chunk [26] of course that will produce a substantial return on investment, e.g. a refresher course.
2. Use one H5P column per teaching unit. Instructors can consolidate content for a teaching unit in one H5P column, aligning with Mayer's segmenting principle [26]. Structuring these elements in a column layout introduces a visually engaging dimension, promoting clear comprehension [26]. This versatile approach optimizes student engagement, elevating the learning experience's overall effectiveness.
3. Be economical with both content and instructions. Superfluous elements can impede learning by requiring excessive cognitive processing, hindering educational objectives [6,26]. Additionally, maintaining video duration of around five minutes is advised to mitigate dropout rates [23,35]. Finally, avoid spending time producing a getting started tutorial, as H5P is intuitive and easy to use.
4. Allow students to manage the pace of their learning by indicating time to complete exercises and providing unconstrained access to material. This promotes self-regulation by creating an opportunity for students to learn how to control their time and to complete exercises in the sequence they choose.

5. Establish instructor-student relationship through feedback in answers [25,32]. Although this recommendation requires a significant resource investment, it is worth the effort, as it is important to provide feedback to guide and motivate underperforming students and to mark the presence of the physically absent instructor.
6. Allow for game-based learning [2,28] through various H5P contents ranging from well-known interactions such as drag-and-drop to lesser-known such as image hotspots. The playfulness of H5P interactions (e.g. earning points and stars) will help maintain students' motivation [22,35].
7. Promote inclusive and accessible teaching by using multiple modalities (e.g. text, images, audio, video) to present the same information. This "efficient redundancy" addresses the specific needs of a wide range of students with diverse abilities and learning styles [6,26].
8. Flip common-ground content that will meet a need encountered by all students. We recommend selecting refresher courses, or a document or a lecture that students typically consider boring, to allocate more F2F lecture time to advanced topics and students' requests.

7 Conclusions

In this paper, we adopted a user-centered approach to flip course content using H5P and delivered an instructional design that meets students' needs [42]. Further, we demonstrated that H5P exercises satisfy the increasing need for active pedagogy aiming at making students actors of their learning [15]. Through user testing of H5P material targeted at bibliography management, we demonstrated that H5P helps maintain students' motivation, and supports self-directed, game-based and trial-and-error learning, which enhances learning experiences [16]. However, ongoing efforts are required to address students' specific needs. The case study provides a detailed, step-by-step breakdown of how to leverage H5P interactive exercises to flip content, as well as a series of recommendations to flip content using H5P. Future work should replicate the case study with student groups in other master's programs.

Acknowledgments. The authors acknowledge the support provided by the LECaaS project (reference 8610), funded by Service public de Wallonie (SPW) and by the Institute for Language and Communication. Appreciation is also extended to the anonymous reviewers for their insightful feedback on an earlier iteration of this work. Lastly, the authors warmly thank all the participants in the user testing, and Mrs. Estelle Pepinster, whose significant contributions as part of her master's research thesis were instrumental in the design and implementation of H5P exercises.

Disclosure of Interests. The authors have no competing interests to declare that are relevant to the content of this article.

References

1. Al-Ajlan, A., Zedan, H.: Why Moodle. In: 2008 12th IEEE International Workshop on Future Trends of Distributed Computing Systems, pp. 58–64. IEEE (2008). https://doi.org/10.1109/FTDCS.2008.22
2. Alsawaier, R.S.: The effect of gamification on motivation and engagement. Int. J. Inf. Learn. Technol. **35**(1), 56–79 (2018). https://doi.org/10.1108/IJILT-02-2017-0009
3. Bernard, R.M., Borokhovski, E., Schmid, R.F., Tamim, R.M., Abrami, P.C.: A meta-analysis of blended learning and technology use in higher education: from the general to the applied. J. Comput. High. Educ. **26**, 87–122 (2014). https://doi.org/10.1007/s12528-013-9077-3
4. Boelens, R., De Wever, B., Voet, M.: Four key challenges to the design of blended learning: a systematic literature review. Educ. Res. Rev. **22**, 1–18 (2017). https://doi.org/10.1016/j.edurev.2017.06.001
5. Chen, L., Manwaring, P., Zakaria, G., Wilkie, S., Loton, D.: Implementing H5P online interactive activities at scale. In: ASCILITE 2021: Back to the Future–ASCILITE 2021 Proceedings ASCILITE 2021 in Armidale (2021). https://doi.org/10.14742/ascilite2021.0112
6. Clark, R.C., Mayer, R.E.: E-learning and the Science of Instruction: Proven Guidelines for Consumers and Designers of Multimedia Learning. Wiley, New York (2016)
7. Dakhi, O., Jama, J., Irfan, D., et al.: Blended learning: a 21st century learning model at college. Int. J. Multi Sci. **1**(08), 50–65 (2020)
8. Dhawan, S.: Online learning: a panacea in the time of COVID-19 crisis. J. Educ. Technol. Syst. **49**(1), 5–22 (2020). https://doi.org/10.1177/0047239520934018
9. Garrison, D.R., Kanuka, H.: Blended learning: uncovering its transformative potential in higher education. Internet High. Educ. **7**(2), 95–105 (2004). https://doi.org/10.1016/j.iheduc.2004.02.001
10. George, P.P., et al.: Online eLearning for undergraduates in health professions: a systematic review of the impact on knowledge, skills, attitudes and satisfaction. J. Global Health **4**(1), 010406 (2014). https://doi.org/10.7189/jogh.04.010406
11. Graham, C.R.: Blended Learning Systems. The Handbook of Blended Learning: Global Perspectives, Local Designs, vol. 1, pp. 3–21 (2006)
12. Halverson, L.R., Graham, C.R.: Learner engagement in blended learning environments: a conceptual framework. Online Learn. **23**(2), 145–178 (2019). https://doi.org/10.24059/olj.v23i2.1481
13. Hassenzahl, M.: The Thing and I: understanding the relationship between user and product. In: Blythe, M.A., Overbeeke, K., Monk, A.F., Wright, P.C. (eds.) Funology 2: From Usability to Enjoyment, pp. 301–313. Springer, Cham (2018). https://doi.org/10.1007/978-3-319-68213-6_19
14. Hew, K.F., Lo, C.K.: Flipped classroom improves student learning in health professions education: a meta-analysis. BMC Med. Educ. **18**, 1–12 (2018). https://doi.org/10.1186/s12909-018-1144-z
15. Hilliard, A., Kargbo, H.F.: Educationally game-based learning encourages learners to be actively engaged in their own learning. Int. J. Educ. Pract. **5**(4), 45–60 (2017). https://doi.org/10.18488/journal.61.2017.54.45.60
16. Homanová, Z., Havlásková, T.: H5P interactive didactic tools in education. In: 11th International Conference on Education and New Learning Technologies, pp. 9266–9275 (2019)

17. Hrastinski, S.: What do we mean by blended learning? TechTrends **63**(5), 564–569 (2019). https://doi.org/10.1007/s11528-019-00375-5

18. ISO 9241-210:2019: Ergonomics of Human-System Interaction – Part 210: Human-Centred Design for Interactive Systems. Standard, International Organization for Standardization, Geneva, CH (2019)

19. Karaca-Atik, A., Meeuwisse, M., Gorgievski, M., Smeets, G.: Uncovering important 21st-century skills for sustainable career development of social sciences graduates: a systematic review. Educ. Res. Rev. **39**, 100528 (2023). https://doi.org/10.1016/j.edurev.2023.100528

20. Kieffer, S.: ECOVAL: ecological validity of cues and representative design in user experience evaluations. AIS Trans. Hum.-Comput. Interact. **9**(2), 149–172 (2017)

21. Kieffer, S., Rukonic, L., Kervyn de Meerendré, V., Vanderdonckt, J.: Specification of a UX process reference model towards the strategic planning of UX activities. In: VISIGRAPP (2: HUCAPP), pp. 74–85 (2019). https://doi.org/10.5220/0007693600740085

22. Killam, L.A., Luctkar-Flude, M.: Virtual simulations to replace clinical hours in a family assessment course: development using H5P, gamification, and student co-creation. Clin. Simul. Nurs. **57**, 59–65 (2021)

23. Kuran, M.Ş., Pedersen, J.M., Elsner, R.: Learning management systems on blended learning courses: an experience-based observation. In: Choraś, M., Choraś, R.S. (eds.) Image Processing and Communications Challenges, vol. 9, pp. 141–148. Springer, Cham (2018). https://doi.org/10.1007/978-3-319-68720-9_17

24. Lhafra, F.Z., Abdoun, O.: Adaptive collaborative learning process in a hybrid model. In: Hassanien, A.E., Snášel, V., Tang, M., Sung, T.W., Chang, K.C. (eds.) Proceedings of the 8th International Conference on Advanced Intelligent Systems and Informatics 2022, pp. 26–38. Springer, Cham (2022). https://doi.org/10.1007/978-3-031-20601-6_3

25. Lucas, G.M.: Initiating student-teacher contact via personalized responses to one-minute papers. Coll. Teach. **58**(2), 39–42 (2010). https://doi.org/10.1080/87567550903245631

26. Mayer, R.E.: Using multimedia for e-learning. J. Comput. Assist. Learn. **33**(5), 403–423 (2017). https://doi.org/10.1111/jcal.12197

27. Means, B., Toyama, Y., Murphy, R., Baki, M.: The effectiveness of online and blended learning: a meta-analysis of the empirical literature. Teach. Coll. Rec. **115**(3), 1–47 (2013). https://doi.org/10.1177/016146811311500307

28. Padilla-Meléndez, A., del Aguila-Obra, A.R., Garrido-Moreno, A.: Perceived playfulness, gender differences and technology acceptance model in a blended learning scenario. Comput. Educ. **63**, 306–317 (2013). https://doi.org/10.1016/j.compedu.2012.12.014

29. Quintão, C., Andrade, P., Almeida, F.: How to improve the validity and reliability of a case study approach? J. Interdisc. Stud. Educ. **9**(2), 264–275 (2020). https://doi.org/10.32674/jise.v9i2.2026

30. Raes, A., Detienne, L., Windey, I., Depaepe, F.: A systematic literature review on synchronous hybrid learning: gaps identified. Learn. Environ. Res. **23**, 269–290 (2020). https://doi.org/10.1007/s10984-019-09303-z

31. Rasheed, R.A., Kamsin, A., Abdullah, N.A.: Challenges in the online component of blended learning: a systematic review. Comput. Educ. **144**, 103701 (2020)

32. Reinholz, D.L., Dounas-Frazer, D.R.: Personalized instructor responses to guided student reflections: analysis of two instructors' perspectives and practices. Am. J. Phys. **85**(11), 850–860 (2017)

33. Schrepp, M., Thomaschewski, J.: Design and validation of a framework for the creation of user experience questionnaires. Int. J. Interact. Multimedia Artif. Intell. **5**(7) (2019). https://doi.org/10.9781/ijimai.2019.06.006

34. Senali, M.G., Iranmanesh, M., Ghobakhloo, M., Gengatharen, D., Tseng, M.L., Nilsashi, M.: Flipped classroom in business and entrepreneurship education: a systematic review and future research agenda. Int. J. Manage. Educ. **20**(1), 100614 (2022)

35. Singh, S., Scholz, K.: Using an e-authoring tool (H5P) to support blended learning: librarians' experience. In: Me, Us, IT! Proceedings ASCILITE2017: 34th International Conference on Innovation, Practice and Research in the Use of Educational Technologies in Tertiary Education, pp. 158–162 (2017)

36. Sinnayah, P., Salcedo, A., Rekhari, S.: Reimagining physiology education with interactive content developed in H5P. Adv. Physiol. Educ. **45**(1), 71–76 (2021). https://doi.org/10.1152/advan.00021.2020

37. Tran, D., Havlásková, T., Homanová, Z.: Encouraging students to take action in developing problem-solving competency. In: 2019 17th International Conference on Emerging eLearning Technologies and Applications (ICETA), pp. 770–776. IEEE (2019). https://doi.org/10.1109/ICETA48886.2019.9039967

38. Tripepi, G., Jager, K.J., Dekker, F.W., Zoccali, C.: Selection bias and information bias in clinical research. Nephron Clin. Pract. **115**(2), c94–c99 (2010). https://doi.org/10.1159/000312871

39. Vallée, A., Blacher, J., Cariou, A., Sorbets, E.: Blended learning compared to traditional learning in medical education: systematic review and meta-analysis. J. Med. Internet Res. **22**(8), e16504 (2020). https://doi.org/10.2196/16504

40. Van der Merwe, A., Bozalek, V., Ivala, E., Peté, M., Vanker, C., Nagel, L.: Blended learning with technology. In: Moving Beyond the Hype: A Contextualised View of Learning Technology in Higher Education, pp. 11–15. Universities South Africa (2015). http://hdl.handle.net/2263/50953

41. Wehling, J., et al.: Fast-track flipping: flipped classroom framework development with open-source H5P interactive tools. BMC Med. Educ. **21**(1), 1–10 (2021). https://doi.org/10.1186/s12909-021-02784-8

42. Wright, G.B.: Student-centered learning in higher education. Int. J. Teach. Learn. High. Educ. **23**(1), 92–97 (2011)

Evaluating the Efficacy of Automated Video Editing in Educational Content Production: A Time Efficiency and Learner Perspective Study

David Nußbaumer⬤, Bettina Mair⬤, Sandra Schön⁽✉⁾ ⬤, Sarah Edelsbrunner⬤, and Martin Ebner⬤

Graz University of Technology, Münzgrabenstraße 36, 8010 Graz, Austria
{sandra.schoen,martin.ebner}@tugraz.at

Abstract. Automated editing technology offers notable efficiencies in educational video production. This study contrasts the time-saving benefits of automated editing against manual professional editing. Raw learning video footage was recorded in a professional studio with a green screen and presented in a frontal lecture style. The raw footage underwent editing by both an automated tool and professional editors. Time comparison results revealed significant savings with the use of automated tools. The paper further investigates the impact of automated editing on the learning video quality from the learners' viewpoint. An online survey with 129 participants evaluated their perceptions of potential learning outcomes after viewing automatically and manually edited versions of two videos. The survey found a statistically significant difference in perceived learning potential from one of the videos, although not for both. Additionally, the study considers how differences in study group characteristics might influence these results. In summary, while automated editing presents a compelling case for production time reduction, its impact on the perceived quality of educational videos remains uncertain, necessitating additional research to understand the subtleties of learner interaction with video content.

Keywords: Automatic editing · learning video · higher education

1 Introduction

Learning with videos has become common practice in different age groups and societies in recent years, although to different degrees. Especially among young people, there is hardly anyone who has not consumed a learning video, such as make-up tutorials, cooking videos, explanations of mathematical functions or how to dance. Online learning videos offer the potential for anyone with internet access to learn at their own pace, regardless of time or place. This potential has also been recognized in the education sector, where learning videos are used to enhance teaching. Many institutions nowadays offer self-produced learning videos on a wide range of topics. These learning videos vary greatly in production effort. Depending on the complexity of the topic, a lot of work must be put into preparation, editing, production, and finally post-production. Due to the constant rise of the number of learning videos, there is a need for smart processes that substitute manual work in the production of learning videos. In this paper, we present an empirical analysis of a comparison of automatically and manually edited learning videos concerning the time needed for production and effects on video quality from the learners' perspective. The work builds upon a master's thesis by the first author.

2 Learning with Videos, Good Learning Videos and Their Automated Editing

Learning videos and their consumption are still on the rise, but of already big importance anywhere in the world with regular broadband Internet access: A study by the German Council for Cultural Education surveyed more than 800 12- to 19-year-olds about their involvement in digital education. Almost 50% of all students who also use YouTube (n = 520) perceive educational YouTube videos as important to very important and use these videos, for instance, to repeat lessons, which they had trouble understanding, or to prepare for exams (Rat für Kulturelle Bildung, 2019). The Pew Research Center surveyed more than 4,500 Americans about their use of YouTube. 51% of respondents identified YouTube as a highly important tool to learn new things (Pew Research Center, 2018). YouTube itself, in a survey of over 1,000 users between the ages of 18 and 54, concluded that about 70 percent of participants use the platform to solve problems in the areas of work, study, or hobbies (2and2/Google, 2017). Nevertheless, the areas of application of learning videos are very diverse: Videos can be part of informal learning, used in online courses or face-to-face settings. Especially when schools and universities were closed due to the Covid-19 pandemic, videos served as a substitute for face-to-face teaching. At Graz University of Technology, for example, the number of users accessing our video portal TU Graz TUbe quadrupled during Austria's first lock-down in March 2020 (Ebner et al., 2020). Furthermore, videos are for a dominant feature of Massive Open Online Courses (MOOCs, see Wedekind, 2013), as on the Austrian national platform iMooX.at (Ebner, 2022).

When using learning videos, the benefits for the learner can be quite significant if a learning video is well prepared: Smyrni and Nikopoulos (2010) examined the use of short video units and the learning process of their recipients in comparison to traditional teaching methods. The results show that the use of videos is at least as effective as traditional teaching methods. In addition, the participating students report increased attention and motivation when watching the videos. Nevertheless, MacHardy and Pardos' study (2015) showed that even after a good learning video, it is important to refer to exercises to be filled out after watching the video, such as a self-assessment. The authors examined MOOCs of Stanford University and Khan Academy and showed that videos with little to no explanation surrounding the following exercises contribute very little to the learning success of the participant. In the study of Carpenter et al. (2013), it was shown that a higher fluency of the instructor can positively influence the impression that something was learned. To sum up, videos alone do not seem to be a recipe for learning success. There is an indication that it is important how they are implemented in terms of structure, content, and technology, and that a didactic concept is necessary.

When focusing on the learning videos, there are of course different aspects to consider. First, there are different typologies of learning videos available. Some authors differentiate learning videos according to their technical production, such as screencast, slide-cast, lecture recording, animation, etc. (e.g. Ebner & Schön, 2017). Guo et al. (2014) distinguish learning videos into the types of slides with voice over, code, Khan.Style, lecture recording, studio, and office desk. Some others try to extract didactic-methodological elements (Honkomp-Wilkens et al., 2022). How features of learning videos – such as production style, structure, duration, design components, and quality of audio – influence (potential) learning results is of interest for research, but it is not an easy investigation. The length of videos is a much "simpler" feature that can be used as a variable in such research. Guo et al. (2014) for example analyzed data of edX courses concerning the watch time of a video vs. the actual video duration, interactivity, or engagement, i.e. whether students paused videos, whether there are certain spots in videos which are paused more often than others. An important result is that the median student engagement time is longest for videos under six minutes in length. A further observation of the study is that in frontal teaching videos, close-ups of the lecturers can have a positive effect on engagement. However, the observation has some limitations and no high reliability, since only two online courses are compared, an aspect also noted by the authors of the study. When comparing the two courses, one course was produced in an "office desk" style, which is characterized by a higher proportion of close-ups of the lecturer. The second course was produced in a "studio" style and is characterized by the fact that the lecturer is standing at a desk and therefore takes up less space in the picture. From these two striking differences and from the observation that the office desk style course has a higher average student interaction time, the authors cautiously conclude that videos with a higher proportion of close-ups of the speaker can have a positive effect on engagement time. Huynh-Thu and Ghanbari introduce the term "head-and-shoulders content" in their publication, which refers to these kinds of videos. However, the authors address videos in general and not just learning videos (Huynh-Thu and Ghanbari, 2008).

Another approach to good learning videos is to focus on "quality" and how it can be measured. There are many ways to define and describe the "quality" of a learning video. For example, a video should have a good image and sound quality; it should be well structured didactically; and it should be retrievable as smoothly and as trouble-freely as possible. To better categorize the different requirements for learning videos in general, there are several interpretations of terms for qualities. Quality can either be described as Quality of Service (QoS; technical factors like an underlying network that delivers a video) and Quality of Perception (QoP; perception of a learner, how the learner experiences the video) (Ghinea and Chen, 2006). The quality of a learning video can also refer to Quality of Experience (QoE) (Akhtar et al., 2019): This term also reflects subjective views of a user from a more technical viewpoint, i.e. how the underlying system enables communication, e.g. the transmission of a video. If a user rates a video in a learning setting poorly, this may be due to the underlying streaming system (QoS, technical factors, frame dropping, buffering), content-related technical factors such as audio quality, image quality (QoE factors) or content-related factors

(QoP factors, content poorly presented, the video content itself is not liked). To sum up, the content of a learning video and its presentation mainly influence the perceived quality (QoP).

Other assumptions that must be considered when talking about the quality of education videos are Mayer's (2005), which form the foundation of the cognitive theory of multimedia learning and are often transferred to learning videos as well (Mayer, 2005). There are three assumptions that are also relevant for learning video production: the assumption that there are two independent channels in a human's memory process (dual channel), a limited capacity, and active processing while memorizing (see p. 36). Building upon this, principles of multimedia design were developed, evaluated and are currently the base of many manuals for learning video production. They include, for example, the principle of signaling – the need to mark important content, and the principle of temporal contiguity, which means that related words and images should be presented simultaneously and not consecutively. Some of these quality factors can already be considered and possible issues eliminated during the creation of a learning video, while other quality factors, such as the QoS problem of frame dropping, only occur when the video is being transmitted. To sum up, a synergy of all quality factors is important to present a good educational video to the user. As users are not always aware of the manifold (technical) influences, it is not very helpful to ask them very differentiated questions when evaluating the quality of a video. In our case, we wanted to know how users generally assess the quality of the learning videos. We did not directly ask about the quality of the video cutting, so as not to draw attention to an issue which might not even be considered important to learners.

With the rise of and possibility to use automatic editing services for video production in the organizational unit "Educational Technology" at Graz University of Technology (TU Graz), we were wondering if and how much this would affect the post-production of videos as well as the assessed quality of learning videos, especially when the videos are part of MOOCs at the iMooX.at platform. Manual video editing processes include digitizing and importing footage onto a PC, removal of unwanted segments of clips, placing the clips onto a timeline (i.e. a multi-track visualization with different layers of audio, videos, and effects), adding effects and video transitions, adding additional optional audio, and rendering the final video (Millerson, 2008, p. 301). Particularly in cutting and transitions, links between scenes matter to give the viewer a sense of continuity (Dancyger, 2018, p. 401) and to avoid jump cuts, which occur when two concatenated shots of a person produce the effect that a person jumps around (Lima et al., 2012).

Currently, several automated editing services for videos are available and have been tested. For narrated videos, i.e. videos where the narrator is not directly visible in the video, the tool QuickCut supports the selection of content-relevant sequences by giving the user the possibility to assign suitable video sequences to the spoken text, which are derived from the narrator's audio. On a timeline, the user can then select suitable video units for each individual sentence segment. Transitions are automatically calculated and inserted (Truong et al., 2016). To show QuickCut's efficiency, Truong et al. (2016) have six short videos (shorter than two minutes) edited with QuickCut by a wide variety of people, with editing effort ranging from 14 to 52 min per video. To determine whether these are efficient times, opinions are sought from professional filmmakers who estimate the time required to create a minute of finished video to be several hours (bid, p. 499). Berthouzoz et al. (2012) provide several tools in their work to help editors cut interview videos in a time-saving way. The raw recordings are translated and transcribed using a paid external crowd-based service (casting-words.com) and linked to the video content using another software (Virage). The cut suitability evaluation is based on several scores. On the one hand, quiet and calm passages are found by comparing audio and transcript, and on the other hand, frame analysis is used to find similar frames where the speaker pauses. The sum is described as the "cut suitability score" (Berthouzoz et al., 2012, p. 4). To evaluate the efficiency of the interface, Berthouzoz et al. gather user feedback from journalists and professional video editors on five exemplary interview-style videos that were edited using the interface. The feedback is generally positive, and the participants can imagine incorporating the interface in their own video editing workflow (ibid., p. 7). Fried et al. present a tailor-made approach for talking-head videos, i.e. videos in which only the upper part of a speaker's body from stomach to head is visible (Fried et al., 2019). Their approach takes text input, e. g. a transcript, and uses an optimization procedure for each desired audio sequence to find the corresponding sequence in the video that most resembles the movements of the mouth (ibid., p. 2). Using 3D face modeling, part of the face can then be masked so that a synergy is created between the spoken word and the expression of the rest of the face. Despite partly unrealistic and incorrect representation of the 3D face model, participants of a user study considered almost 60% of the automated cuts to be made by humans (n = 138, see ibid, p. 11). In addition to editing existing video material, words can be added, rearranged, and deleted with their system.

These examples and related research show that there are some attempts to support or even automate the editing process. All solutions presented are niche solutions for different types of videos. A general automated editing solution for all types of videos has not yet been established and is unlikely to ever exist. Nevertheless, some steps can be partially automated relatively well.

The manual steps necessary to transform uncut raw footage into edited raw footage using screen text can be roughly summarized as follows (see Fig. 1): open a video editing environment, import raw footage, listen to audio, watch video streams, set cut points depending on the content of the screen text, rearrange the found segments, add transitions, if necessary, export the final video. The automated steps for the same desired outcome can be described as following: extract audio stream from video (extraction step), obtain a transcript with timestamps (transcription step), compare the obtained transcript with the provided input text and find the best matching segments (matching step), find cut points, and apply transitions, if necessary (optimization step), concatenate and export the final video (export step).

We considered implementing a set of tools that takes raw footage of learning videos (i.e. videos that contain several takes and errors) and corresponding screen texts and autonomously creates an edited video fitting the screen text (removal of irrelevant segments). This is achieved through a combination of several technologies like speech-to-text translation and command line multimedia processing. Therefore, we use a combination of several tools, including Node.js and Google Cloud services (speech-to-text, cloud storage), Natural, Lodash, and FFmpeg. The automated editing processes are shown in Fig. 1 as well.

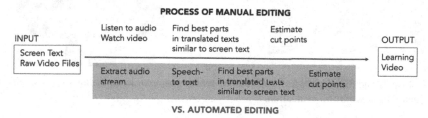

Fig. 1. Automated vs. manual video editing workflow in our research.

The manual workflow differs from the automated one. While humans tend to assess both video and audio to decide, only the audio stream is considered in automated decision-making. Whether a take looks better visually with the same spoken text is up to human judgment. Based on the accuracy of the translation, the best-matching segments are found in the automated workflow.

3 Methodology

The use of tools can improve the video editing process in different aspects. This paper investigates whether the video editing workflow of learning videos with a screen text can be improved in terms of effort while preserving quality by automating certain steps. The hypotheses to be investigated are:

- H1: Raw footage of learning videos can be automatically pre-cut to save time.
- H2: Raw footage of learning videos can be automatically pre-cut while preserving quality.

For the investigation of the stated two hypotheses, two steps are carried out: (a) an evaluation of time consumption of a manual video editing workflow and direct comparison with an automated workflow and (b) an evaluation of the video quality generated in step 1 by performing an online survey. In the following paragraphs, both steps will be described in detail.

3.1 Evaluation of the Workflow

For the workflow evaluation, raw footage of learning videos is needed. Therefore, ten different raw segments of learning videos in frontal lecture style shown in Fig. 2 (table on the left side) with their according screen text serve as input material. The average duration of the raw footage is two minutes, with the longest test video lasting over four minutes and the shortest just under 50 s. Figure 2 also provides an overview of the video thumbnails.

Each input video was recorded in 1920 × 1080 25 fps with professional equipment (high quality camera and microphone). Then, different users with video editing background were asked to perform a simple rough cut on each raw footage provided. For the

Name of the video	Duration	Takes	Language	Gender of lecturer
Video 1	2m39s	3	German	f
Video 2	1m24s	4	English	m
Video 3	1m55s	2	German	f
Video 4	1m17s	4	English	m
Video 5	1m22s	2	German	f
Video 6	1m25s	3	English	m
Video 7	0m49s	1	German	m
Video 8	4m13s	5	English	m
Video 9	2m47s	2	German	m
Video 10	2m55s	4	German	m

Fig. 2. Details and thumbnail gallery of the raw footage of provided learning videos serving as input material for workflow evaluation.

evaluation of the manual video editing workflow, a total of three people with video editing skills took part (two people B and C with self-reported moderate video editing skills and person A with self-reported moderate to expert video editing skills). Each video rough cut was time-tracked with a stopwatch. In addition, the automated workflow was performed on each raw input material and tracked. Finally, tracked times could be compared (time for automated work vs. average duration of manual work). In the tracking of the manual work, all the following steps were included: listening to audio, watching video, clicking through the streams, finding optimal cut points according to screen text and placing transitions (if needed). In contrast to the manual work, the following steps were tracked in the automated workflow: extracting audio from video, transcription of audio, matching the screen text to the transcription, finding cut points, and optimizing and reducing cut points (if possible).

3.2 Evaluation of Video Quality

In designing the study, we wanted to avoid focusing too much on the video editing; we rather wanted to see the (possible) effects. This also meant that we did not want to present two versions of the same video, automatically and manually edited, to the same subjects. Both strategies would have resulted in the editing being highlighted as the issue, but we would not know if the editing was even significant for the learner. Therefore, the following research design was developed:

A short questionnaire was developed, not directly addressing the main topic (automatic/manual editing). Instead, participants were asked to rate general statements about the quality of the learning video as shown in Fig. 3. According to a Likert scale, 1 indicates disagreement and 5 indicates full agreement to the given statement. Q1 to Q3 are questions about pronunciation, how well participants can learn with the video and how they generally like the video. The goal is to measure how participants perceive the videos and content (quality of perception). Q4 to Q6 are more technically oriented questions about subtitles, audio and image quality to measure how participants experience the videos (quality of experience). Additionally, standardized questions concerning sex, age and learning with videos were added as well as two open questions what the participants find good or bad concerning the videos they have seen.

We then selected video 2 and video 3 in its two versions – manually and automatically edited (see Fig. 2) as sample videos for the evaluation, due to different languages and

Question (translated from German)	Likert-Scale
Q_1: The words were pronounced clearly and distinctly.	1-5
Q_2: I can learn well with this learning video.	1-5
Q_3: Generally I like this video.	1-5
Q_4: The content of the video matches the subtitles.	1-5
Q_5: Image quality is good in my opinion.	1-5
Q_6: Sound quality is good in my opinion.	1-5

Fig. 3. Standardized questions used within the questionnaires.

genders of the presenters. Of course, all videos and versions have a similar image quality in terms of resolution. Participants are asked to watch two videos and to answer a set of questions for each video. Each participant is randomly assigned to a group. Group A is asked to evaluate video 2 (manually edited) and video 3 (automatically edited) and group B is asked to evaluate video 2 (automatically edited) and video 3 (manually edited). Figure 4 provides a visualization of the used video versions in both groups, always followed by the questionnaire.

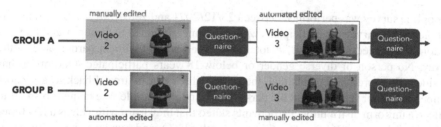

Fig. 4. Research Design: Random assignment to one of two groups and different video versions.

The survey was performed with LimeSurvey. For the analysis of the data, methods of descriptive statistics as well as inferential statistics were used.

4 Results Concerning Video Production

This chapter presents the results of the comparison between manual and automated workflows regarding time saved and the results of the online survey regarding quality. Table 1 provides an overview of the manual workflow evaluation of our three different video editors, their arithmetic average time consumption, standard derivation as well as the duration of the automated workflow. It shows that the automated video editing workflow is on average 76% (SD = 6%) faster than the manual editing workflow.

Table 1. Time for manual editing by three editors, their average and standard derivation, comparison of times of automated and average manual work, and potential time saving with automated editing.

Video	Workflow duration			Rounded		Workflow duration		Time savings
	Person A	Person B	Person C	$\bar{x}$	SD	Automated	Manual $\bar{x}$	
Video 1	110s	310s	160s	193s	104s	44s	193s	77%
Video 2	80s	545s	125s	250s	256s	23s	250s	90%
Video 3	95s	220s	110s	141s	68s	35s	141s	75%
Video 4	50s	180s	75s	101s	68s	19s	101s	81%
Video 5	70s	110s	95s	91s	20s	23s	91s	74%
Video 6	90s	85s	65s	80s	13s	22s	80s	72%
Video 7	40s	45s	95s	60s	30s	19s	60s	68%
Video 8	115s	450s	220s	261s	171s	73s	261s	72%
Video 9	140s	180s	195s	171s	28s	40s	171s	76%
Video 10	255s	320s	245s	273s	40s	48s	273s	82%

5 Results for Preserving Quality

5.1 Survey Participation and Participants

The online survey was performed between 23/12/2021 and 14/01/2022. 129 participants completed the survey. 74 participants were randomly assigned to Group A and 55 were randomly assigned to Group B. A total of 85 men and 44 women participated in the survey. No person of diverse gender or below 18 years participated. One group has considerably more participants than the other, which can be traced back to a random number generator that assigned the participants and the sample size being too small to achieve a uniform distribution. Participants stated that they learn with videos a few times throughout the year (36%), a few times a month (32%), and regularly, i.e. a few times a week (30%). The survey content was watched mostly on smart phones (44%) or with an external monitor (30%). Audio was consumed mainly with built-in audio speakers (61%) or with headphones (27%).

5.2 Differences in Assessment of the Learning Videos Variants

Figure 5 provides details of the results. Overall, most participants assess all videos as generally good in pronunciation, but slightly prefer the speakers from video 3. Also, more participants generally like video 3 than video 2. Sound quality is also rated higher for video 3 than for video 2 (especially in the manually edited versions). Of course, these differences might also influence the perception of the video as a learning resource. Looking systematically at the differences of manually and automatically edited versions, there is no clear tendency; the assessments of the different versions are not uniform. Surprisingly, the automatically edited video 2 received better evaluation results than the manually edited one, except for the relevant statement "I can learn well with this learning video", where the agreement is stronger for the manual version. In video 3, the differences are all minor. Especially the questions about pronunciation, subtitles, image, and sound quality do not show any systematic differences, but of course these statements do not directly address cutting. There are no statistically significant differences for 5 of the 6 statements and their manually and automatically edited versions.

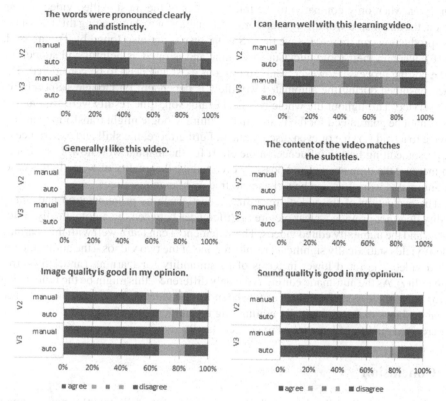

Fig. 5. Results concerning all video version (n = 129; group A n = 74, group B n = 55).

If we focus on the most important statement, whether the participants think they can learn well with the video, the results are as follows: Three versions received similar assessments but the automatically edited version of video 2 obtained worse results. The t-test of video 2, manually and automatically edited, shows a significant difference (0.03).

5.3 Insights from Open Questions

The participants answered the open questions with many different issues, such as the lack of visualization or concerning pronunciation. But again, the comparison of the answers of the automatically edited versions shows no obvious difference to those regarding the manually edited version.

6 Discussion

The automated workflow outperforms the manual workflow in terms of time consumption. Even when only compared to the tracked times of the most skilled video editing person, the automated workflow outperforms the manual one. Automating this part of the post-production can therefore save time. Similar results are also found by Truong et al. (2016), wherein their tool QuickCut saves time and is rated as helpful and supportive to the editing process. However, some limitations exist and need to be considered. The time consumed during the automated workflow is dependent on Google's Speech-To-Text service. Throughout the whole practical evaluation, time results were similar, but this cannot be guaranteed for the future. In the future, Google might transform their free service to a paid service or even discontinue it. Furthermore, the skill and experience of the person editing has an influence on the effort for the manual workflow. Distractions can increase the time needed and possibly even reduce the quality of work. In this case, the automated workflow can be a chance to free up human resources.

The evaluation of the videos regarding aspects such as pronunciation and image quality does not provide a clear picture or differences between the automatically edited videos and the manually edited videos. The statement "I can learn well with this learning video" yields statistically significant results for one of the two videos – the automatically edited video 2 is rated lower in terms of its suitability for learning (under 5% error probability). As the automatic editing is the only difference, this might be the influencing factor. Nevertheless, such an effect cannot be shown for video 3. To sum up, the presented research shows that automatically editing might significantly influence the assessment of perceived quality of learners – but not necessarily.

7 Conclusion

Due to advancing digitalization and the increasing amount of digital information, smart processes are needed to relieve the manual workload on humans. Especially for repetitive tasks, machines can make a significant contribution to relieving the workload. In the field of learning videos and their post-production, machines can also support or even adopt certain workflows. A combination of modern tools can fully automate the workflow of pre-cutting raw footage of frontal lectures with certain limitations. Saving time while preserving quality could be a strong driver towards adopting the presented approach in practice. Our results do not show clear differences in technical quality factors. However, for one of the videos, the perceived quality for learning was assessed as significantly worse. Nevertheless, this is not necessarily always the case for automatically cut videos, as the results of the second video show. We would be pleased if the research design and results presented here stimulated further investigations to be able to make sensible decisions in the future, especially where masses of videos are edited, as is the case at many higher education institutions.

Disclosure of Interests. The authors have no competing interests to declare that are relevant to the content of this article.

References

2and2/Google. The Values of YouTube (2017). https://www.thinkwithgoogle.com/consumer-insights/consumer-trends/self-directed-learning-youtube-work-study-hobbies/. Visited 1 Sept 2022

Akhtar, Z., et al.: Why is multimedia quality of experience assessment a challenging problem? IEEE Access 7, 117897–117915 (2019). https://doi.org/10.1109/access.2019.2936470

Berthouzoz, F., Li, W., Agrawala, M.: Tools for placing cuts and transitions in interview video. ACM Trans. Graph. 31(4), 1–8 (2012). https://doi.org/10.1145/2185520.2185563

Carpenter, S.K., Wilford, M.M., Kornell, N., Mullaney, K.M.: Appearances can be deceiving: instructor fluency increases perceptions of learning without increasing actual learning. Psychon. Bull. Rev. 20(6), 1350–1356 (2013)

Dancyger, K.: The Technique of Film and Video Editing: History, Theory, and Practice. FOCAL PR, p. 1138628395, 28 November 2018. https://www.ebook.de/de/product/28746041/ken_dancyger_the_technique_of_film_and_video_editing_history_theory_and_practice.html

Dror, I.E.: Technology enhanced learning. Pragmatics Cogn. 16(2), 215–223 (2008). https://doi.org/10.1075/pc.16.2.02dro

Ebner, M., et al.: COVID-19 epidemic as e-learning boost? Chronological development and effects at an Austrian University against the background of the concept of "E-Learning Readiness". Future Internet 12, 94 (2020). https://www.mdpi.com/1999-5903/12/6/94

Ebner, M., Schön, S.: Lern-und Lehrvideos: Gestaltung, Produktion, Einsatz. Handbuch E-Learning Erg. Lfg. 71, 1–14 (2017)

Ebner, M.: iMooX - a MOOC platform for all (universities). In: 2021 7th International Conference on Electrical, Electronics and Information Engineering (ICEEIE), pp. 1–5 (2021). https://doi.org/10.1109/ICEEIE52663.2021.9616685

Fried, O., et al.: Text-based editing of talking-head video. ACM Trans. Graph. 38(4), 1–14 (2019). https://doi.org/10.1145/3306346.3323028

Ghinea, G., Chen, S.Y.: Perceived quality of multimedia educational content: a cognitive style approach. Multimedia Syst. 11(3), 271–279 (2019). https://doi.org/10.1007/s00530-005-0007-8

Guo, P.J., Kim, J., Rubin, R.: How video production affects student engagement. In: Proceedings of the First ACM Conference on Learning @ Scale Conference - L@S 2014. ACM Press (2014). https://doi.org/10.1145/2556325.2566239

Honkomp-Wilkens, V., Wolf, K.D., Jung, P., Altmaier, N.: Informelles Lernen auf YouTube: Entwicklung eines Analyseinstruments zur Untersuchung didaktischer und gestalterischer Aspekte von Erklärvideos und Tutorials. MedienPädagogik: Zeitschrift für Theorie und Praxis der Medienbildung, pp. 495–528 (2022)

Huynh-Thu, Q., Ghanbari, M.: Temporal aspect of perceived quality in mobile video broadcasting. IEEE Trans. Broadcasting 54(3), 641–651 (2008). https://doi.org/10.1109/tbc.2008.2001246

de Lima, E.S., et al.: Automatic video editing for video-based interactive storytelling. In: 2012 IEEE International Conference on Multimedia and Expo. IEEE, July 2012. https://doi.org/10.1109/icme.2012.83

MacHardy, Z., Pardos, Z.A.: Evaluating the relevance of educational videos using BKT and Big Data. In: Proceedings of the 8th International Conference on Educational Data Mining, pp. 424–427 (2015)

Mayer, R.E.: Multimedia learning. Annu. Rep. Educ. Psychol. Japan 41, 27–29 (2002)

Mayer, R.E.: Cognitive theory of multimedia learning. In: The Cambridge Handbook of Multimedia Learning, vol. 41, pp. 31–48 (2005)

Millerson, G.: Video Production Handbook. Focal Press, Amsterdam, Boston (2008). ISBN: 9780240520803

Pew Research Center. Many Turn to YouTube for Children's Content, News, How-To Lessons (2018). https://www.pewresearch.org/internet/2018/11/07/many-turn-to-youtube-for-childrens-content-news-how-to-lessons/. Visited 1 Sept 2022

Rat für Kulturelle Bildung. Jugend/Youtube/Kulturelle Bildung - Horizont 2019 Studie: eine repräsentative Umfrage unter 12- bis 19-jährigen zur Nutzung kultureller Bildungsangebote an digitalen Kulturorten. Rat für Kulturelle Bildung e.V., Essen (2019). ISBN: 9783982017365

Smyrni, P., Nikopoulos, C.: Evaluating the impact of video-based versus traditional lectures on student learning. In: Educational Research, pp. 304–311, October 2010

Truong, A., et al.: "QuickCut". In: Proceedings of the 29th Annual Symposium on User Interface Software and Technology. ACM, October 2016. https://doi.org/10.1145/2984511.2984569

Wedekind, J.: MOOCs - eine Herausforderung für die Hochschulen? In: Reinmann, G., Ebner, M., Schön, S. (eds.) Hochschuldidaktik im Zeichen von Heterogenität und Vielfalt. Doppelfestschrift für Peter Baumgärtner und Rolf Schulmeister, pp. 45–62. Books on Demand, Norderstedt (2013). https://www.ebook.de/de/product/20705828/hochschuldidaktik_im_zeichen_von_heterogenitaet_und_vielfalt.html

A Qualitative Case Study of Perceptions and Attitudes Towards Remote Internships and a Model for Their Implementation

Ana María Pinto-Llorente(✉) ⓘ, Sonia Verdugo-Castro ⓘ, Lucía García-Holgado ⓘ, and Francisco José García-Peñalvo ⓘ

Research Institute for Educational Sciences, GRIAL Research Group, Universidad de Salamanca, Salamanca, Spain
{ampintoll,soniavercas,luciagh,fgarcia}@usal.es
https://ror.org/02f40zc51

Abstract. The current study is developed within the framework of the European project *PREVIEW* whose main objective is to promote a model of remote internships to meet the challenges of the digital era and improve educational practice. This paper presents the preliminary results obtained in the semantic and content analyses of a focus group carried out at the University of Salamanca. The results emphasizes that one of the main differences between face-to-face and remote internships in the field of tourism and cultural heritage is the possibility of having face-to-face, contact with clients something that is considered essential in this sector. Tutors consider that it is more difficult to monitor students in remote internships, since they believe that communication is less fluid when students are not physically in the institutions. On the other hand, the results point out that remote internships can be an opportunity to address training aspects that do not require physical presence, to go deeper into others that have been superficially addressed during the degree, to develop certain competencies, especially digital competencies, or to extend the period of internships. The results of the study also highlight that remote internships bring the opportunity of the development of more egalitarian practices, favouring that all students can have these experiences even in international companies. Regarding the PREVIEW Plan, most of the participants consider that it is a very well-structured plan although there is a certain resistance towards the change from traditional face-to-face practices to remote internships that this model proposes.

Keywords: Competences · Remote Internships · Qualitative Research

1 Introduction

The development of digital technologies has led to changes in all areas of life, including the workplace. Digitization and advances in computing and artificial intelligence have brought society into the Fourth Industrial Revolution characterised for hyperconnectivity and efficient collaboration through the network, among others [1, 2]. This has transformed labour markets in many ways, creating new management and organisational models, as well as new jobs and new ways of working.

P. Zaphiris and A. Ioannou (Eds.): HCII 2024, LNCS 14722, pp. 247–259, 2024.
https://doi.org/10.1007/978-3-031-61672-3_16

If we add the unprecedented situation caused by the COVID-19 pandemic to all the technological developments of the last decades, we can say that the digital transformation has accelerated and promoted online work [3]. The adaptation of companies and organisations around the world to a new remote reality has meant the biggest change in working modalities in history, from fully in-person to fully remote. It has also meant that the fully remote modality is seen as the future of work in many areas. Even some authors, such as MacRae and Sawatzky [4], consider it to be the way of working today. In this regard, several studies [5, 6] have shown that organisations have declared that they will build their work around a hybrid-remote policy, so that companies will be able to opt for a hybrid work model, where employees perform part of their work in the office and part of it remotely, or a mixed-work model where companies are composed of a mix of full-time employees, part of whom work remotely and part of whom work in person.

The study carried out by Yang et al. [7] shows that the shift from traditional office work to working from home or anywhere has accelerated due to the global pandemic situation. It also emphasized that even companies that did not maintain a full-time teleworking or teleworking policy after the pandemic ended did not fully return to their pre-pandemic working arrangements [8].

The VALS European initiative developed sustainable approaches and methodologies to forge knowledge-based partnerships between Higher Education (HE) institutions and enterprises [9, 10]. This collaboration aimed to address real-world business challenges through open innovation [11] facilitated by employing open-source software (OSS). OSS serves as a conduit through which HE institutions, students, corporations, and foundations can collectively work towards solving genuine business issues via virtual internships, thereby promoting a collaborative ecosystem for open innovation.

This change or transformation implies the need to develop skills or competences, both in terms of digital competences and soft skills. Several studies [12, 13] have been conducted to identify and explore the core competences of remote work, highlighting digital literacy, communication and collaboration, problem solving or teamwork, among others. The development of these new skills and competences requires a new educational paradigm based on the identification, support, and assessment of the competences needed to work successfully in a virtual and technological environment.

To meet this challenge, educational institutions must train students and graduates to know how to use different technologies, how to work and collaborate in virtual teams, and how to reorganise work activities using new digital and networking tools.

The current research is developed within the framework of the European project PRE-VIEW, whose main objective is to promote an innovative model of remote internships to meet the new societal challenges arising from the digital age and to improve educational practice, learning and teaching activities applied during internships. An initiative that supports the design and development of a student-centred remote model of internship that contributes to the acquisition of the core competences for the remote or hybrid work environment, thereby reducing the mismatch between relevant skills supply and demand for the new remote work environment. An innovative and more inclusive pedagogical and training model of remote internships that aims to broaden the possibilities of work in an increasingly globalised context, and to support the actors of the ecosystem (students, academic supervisors, and company mentors), eliminating the physical, geographical and personal barriers that could hinder their development, widening the possibilities of international projection at both educational and institutional levels, and offering students the opportunity to reconcile their studies and their private lives, providing them with opportunities for training and professional development.

2 Method

2.1 Objective

The aim of the research is to explore the perceptions of remote internships in general and the design of the PREVIEW Remote Internship Blueprint (RIB) in particular among the stakeholders involved in curricular and extra-curricular internships (students, academic tutors, and company mentors).

2.2 Methodology

The methodology used in the research was qualitative, using a phenomenological approach. A method that provides the opportunity to explore key informants' perceptions, opinions and experiences of remote internships, their opportunities, and limitations [14]. In accordance with the research objective, the research design was a descriptive study with a qualitative approach [15]. Once the qualitative data had been collected by means of the focus group technique, there was a reduction and transformation of the data in order to continue the process of analysis and interpretation [16]. Semantic analysis and content analysis were carried out as part of a classic content analysis [17].

2.3 Participants

The strategy used to identify and recruit key informants on the study phenomenon was the expert sampling technique [15, 18]. The participants were students of the degree in Tourism Management who had completed or were completing face-to-face internships; academic tutor from the Faculty of Education and Tourism of Avila, who tutor internships of that degree; and company mentors from the institutions that collaborate with the University of Salamanca and provide internships for the students of this degree. A total of nine people, five women and four men, aged between 21 and 63, participated in the focus group held at the University of Salamanca (see Table 1).

Table 1. Participants

Profile	Code	Age	Gender	Qualification/Studies
Student	USAL_1_1	23	Female	Bachelor's degree in Tourism Management
Students	USAL_1_2	21	Female	Bachelor's degree in Tourism Management
Company mentor	USAL_1_3	40	Female	Bachelor's degree in Tourism Management

(*continued*)

Table 1. (*continued*)

Profile	Code	Age	Gender	Qualification/Studies
Company mentor	USAL_1_4	53	Male	Bachelor's degree in Tourism Management
Company mentor	USAL_1_5	63	Male	Bachelor's degree in Tourism Management
Academic tutor	USAL_1_6	55	Female	PhD in Business Administration
Academic tutor	USAL_1_7	62	Female	PhD in Art History
Academic tutor	USAL_1_8	59	Male	Bachelor's degree in Psychology
Academic tutor	USAL_1_9	43	Male	PhD in Human Motricity Science

2.4 Instrument

The research technique used to collect the data was the focus group, which was developed according to the protocol established in the European project PREVIEW, and after receiving the informed consent form signed by all the participants. Three of the researchers involved in the project participated in the development of the focus group, acting two of them as moderators and another one as an observer.

The focus group was divided into two parts as follows. In the first part, general questions about remote practices were asked to get to know how the participants perceived them. In the second part, the design of the PREVIEW Remote Internship Blueprint (RIB) was presented by one of the moderators and further questions about this model were asked in order to know its strengths and weaknesses. The focus group was held virtually through the Zoom platform on 20 May 2023 and lasted two hours. It was recorded to facilitate subsequent transcription and to increase its fidelity, with the discourse being transcribed verbatim. Once the transcription was completed, content analysis was carried out. This procedure was undertaken with the support of the CAQDAS NVivo12 and included the following steps: (1) importing the file into the created project, (2) creating the category system, (3) axial coding (delimiting of the units of analysis and coding), and (4) data extraction. This strategy allowed us to go deep into the meanings, perceptions, experiences, etc. of the participants.

3 Results

3.1 Semantic Analysis Results

The results of the semantic analysis show the twenty most frequent words in the coded discourse. Figure 1 shows the word cloud obtained. The words that make up the cloud have a size that is directly related to their frequency of occurrence. These words reflect the topics most frequently raised by the participants in the study. The words that stand out the most are technology, remote and internships, terms that are directly related to the objective of the study. The semantic analysis also highlighted the terms digital, skills, protocol, hybrid, system, socialisation, equal or monitoring.

systematized protocol
competences
team **internships** challenge
hybrid system
egalitarian **remote** digital
barriers
loneliness **technology** time
efficient
opportunity socializing customer
monitoring

Fig. 1. Word cloud.

3.2 Content Analysis Results

In terms of content analysis, the results show the categories (1. Self-perception, and 2. PREVIEW Remote Internship Blueprint - RIB) and the subcategories that emerged during coding. Extracts or textual quotations from the participants' discourse are included to illustrate these results. Each of these fragments was given a code according to this structure USAL_1_number assigned to each participant.

Category: Self-perception / Subcategory: Main differences between remote and face-to-face internships. The results that refer to the category self-perception of the participants on the subcategory that refers to the main differences between remote and face-to-face internships in the field of tourism and cultural heritage show that one of the main differences is the possibility to have direct, face-to-face, contact with clients. Something that is considered essential in this sector and, therefore, in a tourism management internship. This opinion is mainly due to the fact that all the participants in the focus group (students, academic supervisors, and company mentors) had previously only experienced face-to-face internships, where customer service was obviously synchronous, direct, and personal. This perception led them to initially reject remote internships without thinking about or exploring other technology-mediated ways of contacting communicating with clients.

"The main difference would obviously be customer service. When we talk about the tourism sector, this is undoubtedly fundamental in order to be prepared for the future work, for the demands of the companies." (USAL_1_2)

"Obviously, the most important thing is customer service, which, strangely enough, I find is often what is most lacking in the training of students. It makes sense that a certain part of the work can be done at home, such as quotations or some previous work, but the important thing in this sector is to develop the work face to face". (USAL_1_5)

"After my experience of many years, I believe and I agree with my colleagues that internships in tourism must be mainly face-to-face, because it is essential to have direct contact with clients, with colleagues, because it is fundamental to work in a team and to have the skills to do so". (USAL_1_7)

The participants also emphasised that another important difference between face-to-face and remote internship is the way in which the students can keep in touch with their own company. They consider that it is necessary to have a continuous and personal contact, as they believe that students who are physically present at the institution are able to get to know the company better and have access to different departments, sensitive documents, sensitive data, etc.

"I think that internships, after completing a part of the studies or after having finished them, must be face-to-face because students need hours of direct learning in a company or institution related to their studies." (USAL_1_4)

"Learners must adapt to companies, they must know them and see how they work. It is quite difficult to have the same opportunities to learn this in a remote internship. I still find it a bit complicated, a bit difficult." (USAL_1_5)

Another important difference that emerges from the content analysis of the differences between face-to-face and remote internships is the contact with company staff. They consider that this contact is more fluid in face-to-face internships, as students can see their colleagues' reactions in specific situations from which they can learn, etc. They think that it is impossible to achieve the same involvement and treatment in remote internships, where the direct contact is basically reduced to the company mentor.

"Another thing I would like to highlight is the contact with the team. I think that one of the most important aspect of internships is the opportunity to be part of a working team, to be with colleagues, to see how they work, what they do, how they manage or how they solve problems; and to learn from that working environment." (USAL_1_5)

"One of the main differences can be the lack of social interactions or the lack of fluidity in those interactions in remote internships. I think that the relationships that can be built in face-to-face internships are closer and deeper, and it is very, very important to have the opportunity to interact with peers." (USAL_1_6)

Finally, the results of the subcategory related to the differences between face-to-face and remote internships show that the participants think that the support and supervision of the students in remote internships is more complicated or, at least, not as fluid as in face-to-face internships, since when the learners are physically in the company, they can get immediate feedback, and also the company mentors can share this task with other colleagues because when the learners are in a certain department, any member of that department can solve their doubts.

"Face-to-face internships allow for direct observation and immediate feedback, which allows for constant monitoring that helps students to develop different skills." (USAL_1_7)

"Of course, it is possible to monitor students in remote internships, but it is more difficult than in face-to-face ones. In face-to-face internships, the person in charge of the students can immediately correct any mistakes that occur or resolve any doubts that the students may have. This is not the case with remote internships. In addition, company mentors cannot share the support or monitoring with other colleagues." (USAL_1_5)

Category: Self-perception/Subcategory: Opportunities. The results of the participants' self-perception of the subcategory that refers to the opportunities offered by remote internships emphasise the possibility to address aspects related to companies that do not require physical presence or to deepen those aspects that have been superficially addressed during the degree. They consider that a remote internship can be a prelude to a face-to-face internship or a way of dealing with aspects of the sector that do not require physical presence, such as those related to management, planning, technological systems, etc.

"Technology is still a challenge. I think it is very complicated to know how to use the administration or management programmes that companies use. When we graduate, we think that we know them, but when you do an internship, you realise that you really don't know how to use them. Remote internships could encourage this lack of knowledge by providing specific training on these aspects or content that does not require physical presence." (USAL_1_2)

"The first contact with the world of work cannot be reduced only to customer service, although it is very important, or to teamwork, although it is also fundamental. There are other areas of knowledge that can be put into practice in remote internships. I do not know, I am thinking for example of everything related to management, planning, back office, front office, technology applied to marketing, etc." (USAL_1_6)

"There is a part of tourism management that does not require direct and continuous contact with clients, but it can be developed remotely." (USAL_1_7)

"Anything that has to do with systems can be dealt with in remote practices, as students need to know it better before the start the face-to-face internship period. It is more complex than it seems. It is not a question of being familiar with technologies, networks or the web, but with the knowledge related to management systems, which is very dense and is something that I think could be addressed in remote practices." (USAL_1_2)

As well as appreciating the potential of remote placements to deepen the theoretical and practical content covered during the degree, participants also feel that remote internships facilitate the development of certain competences. Skills that are necessary to perform specific tasks in an effective and efficient way. In particular, they highlight technological skills, digital skills, skills directly linked to the cultural transformation and digitalisation of companies, in order to improve both the processes and the achievement of the objectives of organisations or institutions.

"I think that we must differentiate according to areas. There is a part that has to do with technology, with remote work that can be developed in remote internships. Specifically, aspects related to the development of the digital skills needed for the world of work, where students have to put into practice what they have learned." (USAL_1_6)

According to the participants, remote internship can also be an opportunity to have a first contact with the world of work, with companies, with the sector for which the students are being trained, and, on the other hand, an opportunity to extend or spread out the internships. Regarding the last aspect, the participants opted for hybrid internships (face-to-face & remote). This would eliminate the barriers identified for remote internships such as direct customer service and would offer the possibility of extending the duration of practices, since students could do part of the work remotely and gain experience in different departments that did not require physical presence in the company.

"I think they can work as a first contact with the working world. There are departments in which they could work online. Obviously, it would not be possible in a department likes reception, where you have to be present all the time, but there are some departments where it is possible." (USAL_1_3)

"There may be a problem of viewpoints. In any case, it could be a hybrid model, but it depends on the area of work." (USAL_1_8)

"It offers new opportunities to explore other departments, for example, marketing, that do not require or do not need 100% face-to-face attendance. I think the best thing would be a hybrid internship that would be longer, not as rigid as it is now with only three months and eight hours a day. They would be longer, more flexible and extended in time." (USAL_1_3)

"We focus on the tourism sector as if it was only the hotel industry or only customer service. I think that there are many areas that are not just the intermediary and the public part of tourism management. There are other jobs that have to do with planning that do not require a hundred per cent presence in the company." (USAL_1_6)

Finally, regarding the results of the subcategory that refers to the opportunities offered by remote internships, the participants see them as practices that can be more equal and bring more opportunities to do internships, to be in contact with companies regardless of where the students are or their personal situation. They value remote internships as a way of breaking down any spatial, temporal, or personal barriers that might exist, and that could prevent students from doing them.

"They also offer more equal opportunities to do internships. New opportunities for those students who may not have the opportunity to do them or to do them in an international company because they live in a small city or town. This gives them the opportunity to have contact with leading companies that are in Barcelona or Paris" (USAL_1_6).

"Remote internships can be an attractive offer for many students who may not have access to them because of infrastructure issues. They bring opportunities in different areas in many degrees." (USAL_1_2).

"I think it is a brilliant idea, the idea of equality, the idea of access to companies that some students might not have access to. If we think in more international contexts or international companies, there is something that remote internships could encourage, working in international teams." (USAL_1_6)

Category: Self-perception/Subcategory: Disadvantages. On the other hand, the results of the participants' self-perception category for the subcategory that refers to the disadvantages of remote internships indicate that one of the main disadvantages is that remote internships prevent face-to-face and direct contact with clients and colleagues in the company. This aspect has already been mentioned when referring to the main differences between face-to-face and remote internships.

"The internships are the first contact with work and a period where learners can put into practice what they have learned at university. It is a learning that happens in contact with clients." (USAL_1_4)

"The students really learn when we are there, in the company, when we can see how our colleagues act. We acquire new knowledge, I don't know, I learned a lot during my internship, and I don't think that I would have learned the same through a computer." (USAL_1_1)

"Those of us who work in hotels know the importance of direct contact with customers. It is important to have face-to-face contact with them. I work in a hotel and can say that physical contact with customers is the basis of my business." (USAL_1_3)

The results also emphasised that a possible disadvantage is that students cannot be adequately supported and monitored. The participants felt that the continuous, direct, and immediate monitoring that students receive in face-to-face internships cannot be transferred to remote internships as the feedback somehow loses its immediacy.

"Remote internships require greater involvement of company mentors and academic tutors. It is difficult to provide good supervision in this type of internships and it cannot be the same as in face-to-face internships. I think it is practically impossible because in face-to-face internships it is continuous and immediate, and although in remote internships we can use different technological tools that can help us to monitor learners, it is clear that the immediacy is lost." (USAL_1_3)

Category: Self-perception/Subcategory: Challenges. One of the main challenges highlighted in the results obtained in the category of self-perception of the participants in the subcategory related to the challenges of remote internships is that the university should rethink these internships, their organisation, their duration, and, above all, the roles that all the actors involved (students, academic tutors, and company mentors) have to play. The participants believe that the way internships are currently planned cannot be transferred to remote internships.

"It is important that universities and companies adapt their internship programmes to optimise the benefits of remote internships and to address the challenges that may arise." (USAL_1_7)

"It is necessary to redefine how internships, and especially remote internships, need to be approached." (USAL_1_8)

"Internships should be re-planned. The tasks and roles of academic tutors, company mentors and students need to be clearly defined. If this is properly defined, remote internships can be feasible and can help students to work better during internships." (USAL_1_6)

In terms of results, another of the main challenges of remote internships is to achieve a continuous and adequate monitoring of the trainees, so that they really acquire the content, develop the competences, and feel the support of the academic tutors and company mentors when they perform a task, or when they have doubts that might arise. This challenge implies the need to use different technological systems, especially on the part of the company mentors, and to communicate constantly with the learners to avoid the isolation or loneliness that they might feel in remote internships.

"Remote internships would require, on the one hand, constant contact between the academic tutor and the students doing the internships, but above all, constant contact between the company mentor and them." (USAL_1_6)

"It is necessary that the tutors carry out a good monitoring of the tasks performed by the learners. It would be essential to have a monitoring programme to which academic tutors, company mentors and students have access. A monitoring programme that would allow them to know the progress of the students and to resolve doubts when necessary." (USAL_1_8)

Category: PREVIEW Remote Internship Blueprint (RIB)/Subcategory: Phases. Concerning the results of the category PREVIEW Remote Internship Blueprint (RIB) and the subcategory Phases, it is relevant to highlight that despite the initial reluctance of the participants towards remote internships, most of them consider that the PREVIEW Remote Internship Blueprint is a very well-structured plan. They believe that it is a well-structured plan that specifies all the phases that need to be considered in remote internships. It is emphasised that the proposal presents a very well-defined methodology for the supervision of remote internships, taking into account all the key moments, tasks, roles, and obligations of all the actors involved, etc. The model presents the necessary information about the participating institutions and the remote internships they offer. These aspects were highlighted by the students and the academic tutors who participated in the focus group. Specifically, the students mentioned that they would be able to find out about all the possibilities that exist for remote internships, by simply visiting a web or a virtual platform where they could consult all the information directly, so that they would not have to ask different people or even contact companies to know whether or not they could do an internship or not, as is currently the case with face-to-face internships. They also added that they would know in advance the objectives of each of the remote internships offered and could choose the one that best suited their interests.

"As a model for the supervision of remote internships, I find it exceptional, very well structured at all times, with all the necessary phases and the actors that will participate in each phase." (USAL_1_9)

"It is made up of well-defined phases that contain the necessary information for successful remote internships." (USAL_1_7)

"It allows us to get to know the participating companies and the internships they offer. This is the most difficult phase in the current face-to-face internships for the students because we have to contact the companies. Sometimes they respond very quickly, sometimes very close to the start of the internship and sometimes they do not respond at all. We never know what kind of internships they are going to offer before we start, or what the tasks are going to be. The fact that there is a model with all the phases and the commitment of all the actors is very positive." (USAL_1_2)

Category: PREVIEW Remote Internship Blueprint (RIB)/Subcategory: Systematisation of Processes. Regarding the results of the category PREVIEW Remote Internship Blueprint (RIB) and the subcategory Systematisation of processes, the academic tutors consider that the model designed is an effective model mainly because it presents a very systematic structure, with a well-defined protocol that details the processes, the roles of the different actor involved, the phases to be developed, the means of communication, the tools available, etc. This allows students and tutors to know from the beginning what their roles and obligations are, what the workload is, how the whole process unfolds, etc. They appreciate that the process is well-defined and that it requires a commitment on their part to carry it out.

"Everything is very systematic, detailed and concrete. We can know from the beginning how much time you are going to spend on it, what tasks we have to do, what tools we can use, etc." (USAL_1_6)

"The model defines the minimums, the meetings and their frequency, etc. We know from the beginning what we have to do. The work is totally systematised." (USAL_1_6)

"I insist that as a model for monitoring remote internships, it is very well organised, very well structured, and it could be very useful". (USAL_1_6)

"The more detailed it is, the more useful it will be. If we know what is expected of us, what our duties are, it is easier for us to do it, to do it properly."(USAL_1_6)

"It gives us the timetable, our functions, our tasks, etc., in a very systematic way." (USAL_1_8)

Company mentors feel that the PREVIEW RIB could increase their workload. They appreciate the fact that the tasks and phases are clearly defined, but they think that the monitoring of the students will increase the time that they have to devote to internships, a monitoring that has to be continuous and cannot be shared with their colleagues as it is currently the case with the face-to-face Internships. On the other hand, they appreciate that the proposal will allow them to have a clearer offer of the internships, they find it very positive because it is much more systematic, and the students will make a greater commitment to the companies as they will choose the internships that really match their preferences.

"It is quite difficult to have more time. This proposal means that we as company mentors will have to invest more time, exponentially more than the time we currently spend on face-to-face internships. It is a big commitment that if the companies take on, then, of course, the tutors will take it on and do it as well as they can, but it will be difficult." (USAL_1_4)

"This proposal would also force companies to have a clearer offer of what the internships are. This could be very good because the students would be better able to choose what they want." (USAL_1_3)

"This also forces students to commit to companies, and companies to commit to the training of students. I think it is a good proposal. It is true that it requires more time from us, time in the workplace, and time in the preparation of the internships, but it is all about commitment." (USAL_1_3)

Category: PREVIEW Remote Internship Blueprint (RIB)/Subcategory: Technological Ecosystem. Finally, regarding the results of the category PREVIEW Remote Internship Blueprint (RIB) and the subcategory Technological Ecosystem, the participants describe it as an essential environment, a useful environment for remote internships, an environment where it is possible to access information and where it favours the participation of all the actors involved in internships. A good proposal to reduce the lengthy processes involved in the management and planning of internships. In this sense, the academic tutors and company mentors underline that this proposal will help to reduce the management work before to the start of internships and during their development. They point out that the current model of face-to-face internships implies signing a large number of agreements, most of them for only one student, with different entities according to the preferences of the students and the willingness of the companies. However, this proposal provides an environment where all the actors involved in remote internships will have access to the agreements already signed. The participants see this as a significant step forward in terms of management. On the other hand, the participants believe that the technological ecosystem and the available tools can allow them to establish a continuous communication between students and tutors and to monitor continuously and properly the process of remote internships in order to achieve the learning objectives.

"I think that this technological ecosystem, in general, improves and reduces the process of managing agreements, which is one of the most stressful parts of internships. I think that this is also a fundamental part, and it is easier for students, for academic tutors, and company mentors." (USAL_1_2)

"Well, for me, it is the necessary tool to carry out an adequate monitoring of the students and to establish a fluid communication between all the actors involved in the remote internships". (USAL_1_8)

4 Conclusion

In relation to the results obtained, we can highlight a certain resistance to the change from traditional face-to-face internships to a hundred percent remote internships, mainly on the part of company mentors. However, the students and academic tutors see them as an opportunity because they can increase equity by responding to the training needs of those people who are unable to attend in person, as well as those groups that may be in a disadvantaged or difficult situation in a rural environment or one that is difficult to access. In addition, remote internships can be developed in companies and institutions that would not be possible in person, as they may be international entities located in different cities and countries.

There are doubts about the feasibility of implementing remote internships, since they imply important and relevant changes in their organisation and duration, as well as in the tasks and functions of all the actors involved. In this sense, it is considered that it would be more feasible to try to implement a model of hybrid internships, which would eliminate some of the barriers and disadvantages of remote internships mentioned by the participants.

Regarding the PREVIEW Remote Internship Blueprint (RIB), we can generally conclude that it is well systematised, protocolled and contains all the key aspects (phases, key moments, functions, tasks, obligations, etc.) for the successful implementation of remote internships. However, there are again two different perspectives on the design of the model. On the one hand, students and academic tutors appreciate its systematisation and believe that it will benefit the development of remote internships as well as the communication between all actors involved in remote internships. On the other hand, company mentors perceive a significant increase of their workload in remote internships, and they do not know if it will be feasible. They think that this proposal would allow them to define their internship offer more clearly and that students would be committed to the company as everything is so protocolised, but they have doubts about its implementation. The design of the technological ecosystem and its tools is key for success of the development of remote internships. However, we can conclude that it seems more appropriate to carry out hybrid internships in the field of tourism and cultural heritage. Internships in which the support of technology must be a constant in order to facilitate communication, student monitoring, evaluation, etc.

Acknowledgments. This project was undertaken with the support of the Erasmus+ Programme of the European Union: "KA2 - Cooperation partnership in higher education." Promoting Resilience and Employability in university (PREVIEW) (Reference number 2022-1-IT02-KA220-HED-000088742). Views and opinions expressed are those of the author(s) only and do not necessarily reflect those of the European Union or the European Education and Culture Executive Agency (EACEA). Neither the European Union nor EACEA can be held responsible for them.

Disclosure of Interests. The authors have no competing interests to declare that are relevant to the content of this article.

References

1. González-Perez, L.I., Rodríguez-Montoya, M.S.: Components of Education 4.0 in 21st century skills frameworks: systematic review. Sustainability **14**, 1493 (2022). https://doi.org/10.3390/su14031493
2. García-Peñalvo, F.J., Llorens-Largo, F., Vidal, J.: The new reality of education in the face of advances in generative artificial intelligence. RIED: Revista Iberoamericana de Educación a Distancia **27**, 9–39 (2024). https://doi.org/10.5944/ried.27.1.37716
3. García-Peñalvo, F.J., Corell, A., Abella-García, V., Grande-de-Prado, M.: Recommendations for mandatory online assessment in higher education during the COVID-19 pandemic. In: Burgos, D., Tlili, A., Tabacco, A. (eds.) Radical Solutions for Education in a Crisis Context. COVID-19 as an Opportunity for Global Learning, pp. 85–98. Springer, Singapore (2021). https://doi.org/10.1007/978-981-15-7869-4_6
4. MacRae, I., Sawatzky, R.: Trabajo remoto: Personalidad y rendimiento Resultados de la investigación (2020). https://bit.ly/42Gkwcs
5. OECD: Teleworking in the COVID-19 pandemic: Trends and prospects. OECD Policy Responses to Coronavirus (COVID-19) (2021). https://www.oecd.org/coronavirus/policy-responses/teleworking-in-the-covid-19-pandemic-trends-and-prospects-72a416b6/
6. Steward, J.: The Ultimate List of Remote Work Statistics for 2022 (2022). https://findstack.com/remote-work-statistics/
7. Yang, L., Holtz, D., Jaffe, S., et al.: The effects of remote work on collaboration among information workers. Nat. Hum. Behav. **6**, 43–54 (2022)
8. Lund, S., Cheng, W.L., André Dua, A.D.S., Robinson, O., Sanghvi, S.: What 800 executives envision for the postpandemic workforce. McKinsey Global Institute (2020)
9. García-Peñalvo, F.J., Cruz-Benito, J., Griffiths, D., Achilleos, A.P.: Virtual placements management process supported by technology: proposal and firsts results of the Semester of Code. IEEE Revista Iberoamericana de Tecnologías del Aprendizaje (IEEE RITA) **11**, 47–54 (2016). https://doi.org/10.1109/RITA.2016.2518461
10. García-Peñalvo, F.J., Cruz-Benito, J., Conde, M.Á., Griffiths, D.: Virtual placements for informatics students in open source business across Europe. In: 2014 IEEE Frontiers in Education Conference Proceedings (22–25 October 2014 Madrid, Spain), pp. 2551–2555. IEEE, USA (2014). https://doi.org/10.1109/FIE.2014.7044411
11. Chesbrough, H.W.: Open Innovation: The New Imperative for Creating and Profiting from Technology. Harvard Business School Press, Boston (2003)
12. Bersin, J., Spratt, M., Enderes, K.: Big Reset Playbook: Human-Centered Leadership. Josh Bersin (2021)
13. Sawatzky, R., Sawatzky, N.: Competences for Success in remote and hybrid working context (2022). https://bit.ly/3N8uTjy
14. Sarrado, J.J., Cléries, X., Ferrer, M., Kronfly, E.: Evidencia científica en medicina: ¿única alternativa? Gac. Sanit. **18**, 13 (2004)
15. Hernández Sampieri, R., Fernández Collado, C., Baptista Lucio, P.: Metodología de la investigación. McGraw-Hill Education, México (2014)
16. Miles, M., Huberman, A.M.: Qualitative Data Analysis. A Source Book of New Methods. SAGE, Beverly Hills (1984)
17. Andréu Abela, J.: Las técnicas de Análisis de Contenido: Una revisión actualizada. Fundación Centro Estudios Andaluces, Universidad de Granada **10**, 1–34 (2000)
18. Mendenhall, W., Scheaffer, R.L., Ott, R.L.: Elementos de muestreo. Paraninfo, Barcelona (2006)

Integrating Individual and Collective Skills: A Rubric-Based Model for Teamwork Competence Assessment

María Luisa Sein-Echaluce[1][(✉)] [iD], Ángel Fidalgo-Blanco[2] [iD],
Francisco José García-Peñalvo[3] [iD], and David Fonseca Escudero[4] [iD]

[1] Departamento de Matemática Aplicada, Escuela de Ingeniería y Arquitectura, Universidad de Zaragoza, Zaragoza, Spain
mlsein@unizar.es
[2] LITI Laboratorio, Universidad Politécnica de Madrid, Madrid, Spain
angel.fidalgo@upm.es
[3] Departamento de Informática y Automática, Grupo de Investigación GRIAL, Instituto Universitario de Ciencias de la Educación, Universidad de Salamanca, Salamanca, Spain
fgarcia@usal.es
[4] La Salle, Universitat Ramon Llull, Barcelona, Spain
david.fonseca@salle.url.edu
https://ror.org/012a91z28, https://ror.org/03n6nwv02,
https://ror.org/02f40zc51, https://ror.org/04p9k2z50

Abstract. The competence of teamwork comprises a set of skills that enable the assessment of teamwork evolution (collective skills) and the involvement of each team member (individual skills). In most research works, these skills are grouped without making this distinction between collective and individual skills. In this study, collective skills are associated with the different phases that constitute the evolution of teamwork, allowing for the identification of the precise moment when such a skill should be applied. Individual skills are applied in all phases of teamwork, as they measure individual involvement and responsibility, along with the competencies necessary at an individual level to develop teamwork. This work presents a rubric that associates phases, evidence, technology, and indicators and allows educators to measure the degree of acquisition of each and collective skill. The method used for the development of teamwork has been the Comprehensive Training Model of the Teamwork Competence, which supports both the continuous and transparent creation of evidence of teamwork development by the teams and each of their members, as well as the continuous monitoring of this development by educators.

Keywords: Teamwork Competence · Rubric-Based Assessment · Individual Skills · Collective Skills · Comprehensive Training Model · CTMTC

P. Zaphiris and A. Ioannou (Eds.): HCII 2024, LNCS 14722, pp. 260–274, 2024.
https://doi.org/10.1007/978-3-031-61672-3_17

1 Introduction

Teamwork is a cross-cutting competence highly demanded in the labor [1] and academic sectors [2]. In both contexts, teamwork is considered a tool that enhances cooperation [3] to solve complex problems [4] and leads to greater efficacy in outcomes [5–7]. However, in the educational sector, additional objectives include training, assessing, and improving the motivation of students on teamwork competence [8, 9].

This competence presents a set of intrinsic problems to the method itself, among which the difficulty in coordinating team members [10], measuring individual workload [11], individual responsibility [12], and even the team's own identity [10] stand out. In the academic context, all these factors complicate the training and evaluation of this competence.

In this latter aspect, in traditional evaluation, the entire team usually receives the same grade after completing the teamwork, leading to unfair situations among its members. Having evidence that can show the teaching staff the individual workload, responsibilities, and cooperation among team members, along with a rubric that analyzes such evidence, would be a way to assess teamwork and improve the learning outcomes of the competence itself [13].

Other research works have highlighted the need to apply rubrics that allow measuring team formation, planning, communication, coordination, mediation, contribution, meeting management, and assumption of responsibilities [14–17]. Some of these skills are associated with a specific stage in the evolution of teamwork [18]. For example, team formation and planning are applied in the early phases of teamwork.

Other skills are vertical, as they are applied throughout all phases of teamwork [19], such as coordination, mediation, and assumption of responsibilities. Moreover, although these skills are used throughout the development of the work team, they are used in different ways in each phase. For example, in the initial stages, coordination is greater and more complex than in the final stages of teamwork.

Based on this approach, this research identifies the following terms:

- *Phases*: Stages of the evolution of teamwork.
- *Skills:* Capacities that make up the teamwork competence.
- *Indicators:* Allow measuring the degree of skill acquisition.
- *Evidence*: Resource generated by the work team members during their participation in the work. The evidence can be of two types: associated with the team (such as a timeline) and those associated with the individual (such as individual responsibility).

Evidence is an essential part of this research work as it is the resource that allows measuring competence acquisition. Associated with it are two factors: the temporality with which they are generated and the type of evaluation of the skill analyzed. If evidence is only obtained at the end of the teamwork, for example, with a peer evaluation, a knowledge questionnaire, a satisfaction survey, or by analyzing the final results, then only a final summative evaluation would be taking place (which is the traditional method).

Suppose evidence is generated and analyzed during the development of the teamwork, without waiting for its completion; a diagnostic and formative evaluation can be carried out throughout the development. In addition, a summative evaluation at the end of the process might be developed.

In this context, it is vital to apply a teamwork model that allows monitoring the progress of each team member to report on the degree of task compliance [20] and thus regulate learning [21]. That is, the method must generate individual evidence from the beginning of the teamwork until it ends. This type of method is called "open box," as opposed to "closed box" methods that do not show continuous evidence during the development of the teamwork. On the contrary, once the teamwork is finished, the evaluation is based on the final result and sometimes on a peer evaluation among team members or on questionnaires of perception of the use of such teamwork skills by each team member. This research aims to design a rubric that can measure the acquisition of teamwork competence through skills via measurable indicators associated with the phases of teamwork, the continuous generation of evidence, and the type of evidence (collective or individual).

The following sections will describe the evidence model used, the developed rubric, and the connection between the components. The last section includes the conclusions of this work.

2   Comprehensive Training Model Description

This section describes the various components used to contrast the rubric indicators: the phases, evidence generation, technologies, and the proposed final evidence model.

2.1   Phases

The development of teamwork progresses through phases: Forming, Storming, Norming, Performing [22], and Delivering [23, 24]. The primary objective of each phase is:

1. *Forming*: Formation of the work team and leader selection. Definition of the work team's common vision, mission, and objectives.
2. *Storming*: Distribution and assignment of tasks, responsibilities, selection, and handling of technologies. Reinforcement of the team's common vision.
3. *Norming*: Establishing norms to regulate conflicts, decision-making, communication, and overall planning.
4. *Performing*: Development of teamwork based on individual responsibilities and tasks. Coordination, monitoring, and meeting management. Monitoring of individual and group progress.
5. *Delivering/Conclusion*: Final work results, reports on the resources used to carry out the work, conclusions, and lessons learned.

This model, initiated by Tuckman, consisted of five phases, with the last one called "Adjourning" (team disbanding). However, the application of the IPMA [23], along with the application of Tuckman's model in universities conducted by Stein [25], adapted Tuckman's last phase, "Adjourning," to emphasize the idea that teamwork does not end when the final product is delivered. Instead, other resources can be managed for the organization to retain the experience of the completed teamwork and leverage resources in future teamwork. This phase was named "Conclusion and deliverables." Therefore, the modified Tuckman model consists of the following phases: Forming, Storming, Norming, Performing, and Conclusion and deliverables.

This model is applied in both universities and professional environments. Notably, the International Project Management Association (IPMA) based in Switzerland stands out in professional settings. This association comprises 59 national associations from over 30 countries and certifies the acquisition of teamwork competence.

2.2   A Method for Evidence Generation

In this research work, the "Comprehensive Training Model of the Teamwork Competence" (CTMTC) [26] is utilized to generate both individual and collective evidence [19] and to monitor them continuously and progressively. This method has been validated through various scientific publications and allows for the continuous and transparent validation of both types of evidence. The transparency in evidence generation allows the team to verify the work's evolution [27], besides enabling the assessment of skill acquisition. Transparency in individual evidence enables the verification of the involvement and responsibility of the work team members.

2.3   Technologies

The use of technological platforms by students generates a set of evidence resulting from their interaction. This evidence originates from two sources: the technology itself through student interaction (such as logins on the platform) and the evidence provided by the students using technological tools (for example, messages in a forum). In this work, the open-source e-learning platform Moodle and other tools provided by educational institutions, such as those from Google and Microsoft, have been used.

2.4   Evidence Model

Throughout the development of this teamwork method, the team progresses through the various phases. To demonstrate that a phase has been completed the CTMTC method presents a set of evidence [28] displayed in Table 1. The first column indicates the phase, and the second column shows the evidence that the phase has been completed. In the CTMTC method, these are referred to as collective evidence.

In the evidence column of Table 1, some of the competencies identified in the literature review are reflected, such as team formation, meeting management, planning, and assumption of responsibilities. In this work, these competencies are called collective competencies, as each corresponds to a specific phase in the evolution of teamwork. Their measurement is carried out through the collective evidence in Table 1, which is generated by the team.

However, other competencies, such as communication, coordination, shared leadership, and contribution, apply in all phases of the method and must be present throughout the development. These competencies have been termed individual competencies, as each team member must maintain them throughout their development. Their measurement is carried out through the individual evidence generated by everyone. Therefore,

Table 1. Phases and associated evidence

Phase	Collective evidence
Forming	Team formation Leader selection Common vision of mission and objectives Identification of achievements to be accomplished as a team
Storming	Tasks of shared leadership to be exercised by different team members Identification of technologies and their functionality within the management of teamwork Development tasks leading to the final product that each team member must undertake
Norming	Norms governing the behavior of the work team Planning of tasks assigning products to be achieved and completion dates Work schedule
Performing	Monitoring of individual work Monitoring of group work
Conclusion and deliverables	Final results. The outcome of the work Resources and technologies used in some part of the work, indicating their utility within the team Documentation of partial results, consulted reports, meeting minutes… Lessons learned: experience where the team reflects on certain tasks, what needed to be done, what was done, and how it was done

teamwork competence is defined by both individual and collective competencies, and each member must acquire them during teamwork [19]. In the case of collective competencies, interaction among team members is necessary to achieve them, and individual competencies are associated with the person's involvement.

Competencies are measured through indicators from evidence produced by individuals and the team. Collective evidence indicates that the team is evolving correctly. However, these pieces of evidence are insufficient to guarantee that individuals have acquired teamwork competence. For example, a piece of collective evidence is the regulations, which can be well formulated; however, how can it be ensured that all team members have participated in their creation? To guarantee this, individual evidence must be used, thus ensuring the acquisition of collective competence. All this must be done transparently for the entire work team [29]. Thus, the rubric must measure both collective and individual competencies and be able to contrast them. Table 2 shows the individual evidence to be applied during all phases of teamwork.

As mentioned, the CTMTC method [30] is an academic adaptation of the professional method used in IPMA. However, in the academic context, applying all phases is only sometimes necessary. For example, in the following cases:

Table 2. Individual evidence applicable throughout the evolution of teamwork

Individual evidence
Coordination
Shared leadership tasks
Fulfillment of assigned tasks
Technology management
Contribution

- The teaching staff or an automatic system forms the teams.
- The work's outcome mission, and objectives are defined by the teaching staff and, therefore, not chosen by the team.
- The work is simple, applying very specific contents of the subject, or it is a task whose development involves a short period (e.g. a few weeks within a semester).

For these situations, the phases of the method present some restrictions. In the Storming phase, the evidence of mission and objectives is not used, and in the Norming phase, planning and the schedule are not utilized. For these cases, a version of CTMTC called Agile CTMTC [26] is applied, where the evidence for each phase is restricted, (the table of collective competencies vs. individual competencies is defined as shown in Table 3.

Table 3. Relationship between phases, collective competence, and individual competence

Phase	Collective competence	Individual competence
Forming	- Team formation - Leader selection	- Coordination - Shared leadership tasks - Fulfillment of assigned tasks - Technology management - Contributions
Storming	- Tasks of shared leadership to be exercised by different team members - Identification of technologies and their functionality within the management of teamwork - Development tasks leading to the final product that each team member must undertake	
Norming	- Norms governing the behavior of the team	
Performing	- Monitoring of individual work - Monitoring of group work	

(continued)

Table 3. (*continued*)

Phase	Collective competence	Individual competence
Conclusion and deliverables	- Final results. The outcome of the work - Resources and technologies used in some part of the work, indicating their utility within the team - Documentation of partial results, consulted reports, meeting minutes - Lessons learned. Experience where the team reflects on certain tasks what needed to be done, what was done, and how it was done	

This work presents a rubric based on the above method to assess individual skills, workload, commitment, and individual responsibility. Likewise, it enables the contrasting of such evidence in each teamwork phase. This assessment can be carried out progressively and finally. Doing it progressively allows the teaching staff to make decisions, introduce corrective actions, and conduct training in teamwork competence. Having a final assessment will enable the teaching staff to make an individual assessment of the teamwork based on each individual's commitment, responsibility, and workload.

The following section defines the indicators associated with collective evidence (associated with the phases of the evolution of teamwork) and individual evidence (associated with each team member). This includes the technology used to conclude with the proposed rubric model for assessing collective and individual skills.

3   A Rubric Model for Assessing Collective and Individual Skills

The rubric described below was applied in the Mathematics II subject of the Chemical Engineering degree at the University of Zaragoza (Spain) during the first semester of the 2023–24 academic year. The sample comprises 93 students grouped into 16 teams (5–6 members/team).

This section will present the results related to the indicators associated with the evidence that allows measuring the skills, the technology that helps to follow these indicators, and finally, the designed rubric.

3.1 Indicators

The design of the rubric focuses on four critical aspects of skills, which are the following collective evidence:

- *Norms (Norming)*. The norms are evidence that the team designs a set of rules and standards that affect the behavior of members during the development of teamwork.
- *Responsibilities (Storming)*. This is expressed through a consensual table where the responsibilities and tasks associated with shared leadership, the commitment to handling ICT, and the tasks associated with the academic development of the final work are indicated. All for each team member.
- *Execution of Work (Performing)*. It is a table that reflects the evolution of the tasks and responsibilities included in the responsibilities table for each team member and the generation of their collective evidence.
- *Results (Delivering/Conclusion)*. The different resources that make up the outcome of the work are in the various required formats (text, audiovisuals, etc.).

A list of indicators has been designed to confirm the expected results for each piece of evidence. Table 4 shows these pieces of evidence and the indicators that have been identified to validate the acquisition of the evidence.

Table 4. Collective evidence and indicators

Collective evidence	Collective indicator
Norms	Consensual and accepted elaboration of norms including rules affecting: - Meeting management - Conflict resolution - Consequences of compliance with norms - Internal communication (among team members) and external (with teachers, other teams, and other entities) - Decision making - Ethics and values - Organization - Coordination
Responsibilities	Creation of a table indicating responsibilities of three types: - *Technological* (handling of technologies associated both with the development of the teamwork and the outcomes to be obtained) - *Academic* (tasks of knowledge creation to perform the final product of the teamwork) - *Shared leadership* (tasks of coordination, monitoring, and micro-planning for the proper functioning of the teamwork)
Execution	- Calendar with the responsibilities of the three types carried out by each team member Communication among team members Use of technologies to share what is being done, in a transparent and continuous way - Sharing of partial results
Results	- Achievement of the work objectives - Organization and communication of the work results

Each piece of evidence is measured in two aspects: the collective, that is, the evidence demonstrating that the team has achieved competence, and the individual, which is the involvement of each team member in acquiring the competence.

3.2 Technology

Below are some technological tools used during the application of the teamwork method:

- *Moodle forums.* Students communicate, coordinate, and indicate the tasks each member performs continuously (like a work diary). Communication is organized into well-defined threads: one for each discussion around the evidence (Norms, Responsibility Map, Execution, and Results), a thread to include meeting minutes, an individual thread for each team member's diary, and other threads considered by the team.
- *Moodle Wiki.* Students cooperatively build knowledge, share, and disseminate to all team members (and the teaching staff) the operating norms, the responsibility tables (the three types), and the monitoring table (where individual contributions, dates, incidents, and their resolution, as well as collective achievements are specified). In the Wiki, useful Forum threads (discussions, minutes, individual threads, etc.) are linked, and all information is organized so that the teaching staff can consult and access the information easily.
- *Moodle polls.* To conduct self-assessment polls of the process and co-assessment among team members halfway through and at the end of the development.
- Google Drive. For storing and sharing intermediate documents among members and with the teaching staff.
- *Word Processor, Video Creation and Editing Applications, and YouTube.* To create and publish the final work in different formats.

3.3 Final Rubric

Table 5 presents the final rubric for collective evidence and reflects the evidence (first column), the location where the evidence is stored (second column), and the learning outcomes of the competence (third column). It contains the key aspects that allow assigning values to the indicators.

Each learning outcome is evaluated between 0- None, 1- Somewhat, 2- Quite, and 3- A lot. Except for points 1.1.4, 1.2.4, 1.3.1, and 1.3.4, the values are 0- Never, 1- Somewhat, 2- Quite, and 3- Always.

Table 6 shows the same evidence as Table 5, but the indicators are individual and allow for the verification of student participation in achieving them. Each learning outcome is evaluated between 0- None, 1- Somewhat, 2- Quite, and 3- A lot. Except for points 2.1.2, 2.1.3, 2.1.4, 2.2.2, and 2.2.4, the values given are 0- Never, 1- Somewhat, 2- Quite, and 3- Always.

To carry out the final grading of the teamwork, both collective and individual indicators are considered, and a grade is assigned to each indicator as indicated. The weight of each indicator in the grading is the same. However, a grade of 4 out of 10 is not achieved in the total of the individual indicators; in that case, it is impossible to average it with the grade obtained in the collective indicators. This way, it prevents a team member from passing the competence without working because the rest of the members did, and the

Table 5. Rubric for collective evidence

Evidence	Source of evidence	Learning outcome
Norms of operation and behavior	Wiki and Forum	1.1.1 The team has adapted the normative from the example (where the types of norms expressed in Table 4 are indicated) with the contributions of its members 1.1.2 The team has correctly included its norms in the Wiki 1.1.3 The norms developed include the necessary aspects for the good functioning of the team 1.1.4. The team has applied its norms to resolve conflicts
Responsibility map (roles and functions of each member, shared leadership)	Wiki and Forum	1.2.1 The team has created its responsibility map adapting the given example with their contributions 1.2.2 The team has correctly included its responsibility map in the Wiki 1.2.3 The team's responsibility map includes balanced tasks (in time and effort) among its members 1.2.4 The team has considered its responsibility map in each phase to execute the work
Execution of work	Wiki and Forum: Meeting minutes s	1.3.1 The team has met the schedule of partial deliveries to carry out the final work jointly 1.3.2 The team has communicated following the instructions of the teacher through the Moodle course forum 1.3.3 The team has used in each phase the Moodle course wiki and the shared drive folder to follow the teachers' instructions 1.3.4 The team has created a final version of the work that has been agreed upon by all members
Results	Wiki and Forum	1.4.1 The team has correctly solved the proposed work 1.4.2 The team has presented the work in an appropriate digital/audiovisual format 1.4.3 The team has correctly used mathematical language 1.4.4 The team has respected the ethical norms of knowledge creation not to copy, plagiarize, etc.

collective grade is high. The final grade is distinguished in qualitative (quantitative):

Table 6. Rubric for individual evidence

Evidence	Source of evidence	Learning outcome
Norms of operation and behavior	Forum: Meeting minutes and individual threads Co-evaluation	2.1.1 The team member has contributed ideas to create the norms 2.1.2 The team member has behaved consistently with the team's norms and has not caused conflicts 2.1.3 The team member has behaved respectfully towards the opinions of other members 2.1.4. The team member has participated in resolving conflicts within the team
Responsibility map (roles and functions of each member, shared leadership)	Wiki and Forum (thread, meeting minutes, individual threads) Co-evaluation	2.2.1 The team member has made contributions to create the team's responsibility map 2.2.2 The team member has fulfilled his/her responsibilities established in the team (tasks and times), including surveys 2.2.3 The team member has assisted other team members upon request 2.2.4 The team member knows how to share leadership responsibilities with another member
Execution of work	Wiki and Forum (thread, meeting minutes, individual threads) Co-evaluation	2.3.1 The team member has sent useful messages to the forum 2.3.2 The team member has used the technologies needed to perform their tasks 2.3.3 The team member has had a good attitude towards meeting with other members 2.3.4 The team member has asked for help from other members if needed to complete their tasks
Results	Forum In-person sessions with the teachers	2.4.1 The team member knows how to solve the work 2.4.2 The team member has sought correct solutions to solve the work 2.4.3 The team member has expressed himself/herself correctly in the presentation of the work in-person/audiovisual

Excellent ($x \geq 9$), Adequate ($7 \leq x < 9$), Developing ($5 \leq x < 7$), Not achieved ($x < 5$). The qualitative grade is reflected in an individual certificate issued by the educational center and signed by the teaching staff. The quantitative grade accounts for a maximum of 15% of the overall grade of the subject for each team member.

4 Conclusions

Teamwork methods that generate evidence continuously allow the team to understand the evolution of their work [27]. From this evidence, the teaching staff can collectively and individually evaluate the development of teamwork. Such evidence can be analyzed to assess the acquisition of teamwork. However, it is necessary to establish indicators that measure not only the evolution of the work but also the degree of competence acquisition.

Teamwork competence can be measured through a set of indicators. Individual indicators [31] measure the individual acquisition of the competence; however, this is not sufficient to guarantee its acquisition, as it must be endorsed by overcoming achievements that allow measuring the team's evolution, that is, the results generated both during the work's development and in the final product.

In this work, an open-box model is applied where, continuously and progressively, students generate evidence through interaction with technologies. This evidence shows both individual involvement (responsibility, commitment, contributions, participation in communication, coordination, involvement in conflict resolution, and respect) and the result of individuals' involvement in group work (collective evidence) through the development of norms, the responsibility map, monitoring tables, and the final result of teamwork.

One of the main contributions of this work is that it distinguishes between collective evidence, which measures the team's evolution as a group, and individual evidence, which measures the involvement of individuals in achieving collective competencies. The joint analysis of such evidence defines teamwork competence.

The rubric relates collective evidence to individual evidence through measurable indicators. Likewise, its application is supported by technologies commonly used in universities, such as Moodle e-learning platform [32, 33].

In this research work, the rubric was applied once the teamwork was completed. Future studies will examine the grades obtained when applying the rubric. As future work, it could be used in the Storming, Norming, and Performing phases of teamwork, thus allowing for formative evaluation at each phase and measuring the competence's evolution progressively, taking formative actions based on the degree of competence acquisition.

Acknowledgments. This research has been partially funded by the Ministry of Economy and Competitiveness of Spain with the project AVisSA PID2020-118345RBI00, the University of Zaragoza through the innovation projects PICT-4667 and PICT-4851, and the Polytechnic University of Madrid through the innovation project IE24.0602. The authors would like to thank the support of the research groups EtnoEdu of the University of Zaragoza, GRIAL of the University of Salamanca and LITI of the Polytechnic University of Madrid and to the line of TEL (Technology Enhanced Learning) of the Human Environment Research Group (HER) of La Salle, Ramon Llull University, recognized by Agaur 2022 call.

References

1. Nyarko, S.C., Petcovic, H.L.: Do students develop teamwork skills during geoscience field-work? A case study of a hydrogeology field course. J. Geosci. Educ. **71**, 145–157 (2023). https://doi.org/10.1080/10899995.2022.2107368
2. Belanger, E., Moller, J., She, J.: Challenges to engineering design teamwork in a remote learning environment. Educ. Sci. (Basel) **12**, 741 (2022). https://doi.org/10.3390/educsci12 110741
3. Conde-González, M.A., Colomo-Palacios, R., García-Peñalvo, F.J., Larrucea, X.: Teamwork assessment in the educational web of data: a learning analytics approach towards ISO 10018. Telematics Inform. **35**, 551–563 (2018). https://doi.org/10.1016/j.tele.2017.02.001
4. Schuster, N.: Coordinating Service Compositions: Model and Infrastructure for Collaborative Creation of Electronic Documents, pp. 1–179. KIT Scientific Publishing (2013). https://doi.org/10.5445/KSP/1000035097
5. Peña, E., Fonseca, D., Marti, N., Ferrándiz, J.: Relationship between specific professional competences and learning activities of the building and construction engineering degree final project. Int. J. Eng. Educ. **34**(3), 924–939 (2018)
6. Labrador, E., Villegas, E., Contreras, R.S., Canaleta, X., Fonseca, D.: Teaching teamwork in logistics engineering through a board game. Int. J. Eng. Educ. **36**(1B), 510–520 (2020)
7. Necchi, S., Peña, E., Fonseca, D., Arnal, M.: Improving teamwork competence applied in the building and construction engineering final degree project. Int. J. Eng. Educ. **36**(1B), 328–340 (2020)
8. Fonseca, D., Necchi, S., Alaez, M., Romero, S.: Improving the motivation of first-year under-graduate students through transversal activities and teamwork. In: García-Peñalvo, F.J., Sein-Echaluce, M.L., Fidalgo-Blanco, Á. (eds.) Trends on Active Learning Methods and Emerging Learning Technologies. LNET, pp. 9–28. Springer, Cham (2022). https://doi.org/10.1007/978-981-19-7431-1_2/COVER
9. Romero-Yesa, S., Fonseca, D., Aláez, M., Amo-Filva, D.: Qualitative assessment of a challenge-based learning and teamwork applied in electronics program. Heliyon **9**, e22739 (2023). https://doi.org/10.1016/J.HELIYON.2023.E22739
10. Kazemitabar, M., Lajoie, S.P., Doleck, T.: Emotion regulation in teamwork during a challeng-ing hackathon: comparison of best and worst teams. J. Comput. Educ. (2023). https://doi.org/10.1007/s40692-023-00282-y
11. Friess, W.A., Goupee, A.J.: Using continuous peer evaluation in team-based engineering capstone projects: a case study. IEEE Trans. Educ. **63**, 82–87 (2020). https://doi.org/10.1109/TE.2020.2970549
12. Lencioni, P.: The Five Dysfunctions of a Team: A Leadership Fable. Jossey-Bass, San Francisco (2002)
13. Cebrian-De-La-Serna, M., Serrano-Angulo, J., Ruiz-Torres, M.: ERubrics in cooperative assessment of learning at university (Las eRúbricas en la evaluación cooperativa del apren-dizaje en la Universidad). Comunicar **43**, 153–161 (2014). https://doi.org/10.3916/C43-201 4-15
14. Chhabria, K., Black, E., Giordano, C., Blue, A.: Measuring health professions students' teamwork behavior using peer assessment: validation of an online tool. J. Interprof. Educ. Pract. **16**, 100271 (2019). https://doi.org/10.1016/J.XJEP.2019.100271
15. Singh, M., et al.: The development of an assessment rubric for the core and contingency team interaction among rapid response teams. Simul. Healthc. **17**, 149–155 (2022). https://doi.org/10.1097/SIH.0000000000000602
16. Hiscox, T.J., Papakonstantinou, T., Rayner, G.M.: Written reflection influences science stu-dents' perceptions of their own and their peers' teamwork and related employability skills. Int. J. Innov. Sci. Math. Educ. **30**, 15–28 (2022). https://doi.org/10.30722/IJISME.30.04.002

17. Andrés, A.I., Petrón, M.J., Carrapiso, A.I., Morales, S., Timón, M.L.: Development of team-work skills using ICTs in undergraduate students of food industry engineering degree. Int. J. Eng. Pedagogy (iJEP) **13**, 66–78 (2023). https://doi.org/10.3991/IJEP.V13I4.36971
18. Alaez, M., Romero, S., Fonseca, D., Amo, D., Peña, E., Necchi, S.: Auto-assessment of teamwork and communication competences improvement applying active methodologies. Comparing results between students of first academic year in architecture, economics and engineering degrees. In: Zaphiris, P., Ioannou, A. (eds.) Learning and Collaboration Technologies: New Challenges and Learning Experiences, HCII 2021. LNCS, pp. 193–209. Springer, Cham (2021). https://doi.org/10.1007/978-3-030-77889-7_13
19. Sein-Echaluce Lacleta, M.L., Fidalgo-Blanco, Á., García-Peñalvo, F.J.: Identificación de competencias grupales e individuales en el trabajo en equipo. In: Innovación educativa en los tiempos de la inteligencia artificial, pp. 484–487. Servicio de publicaciones de Universidad de Zaragoza, Madrid (2023)
20. Winne, P.H.: Students' calibration of knowledge and learning processes: implications for designing powerful software learning environments. Int. J. Educ. Res. **41**, 466–488 (2004). https://doi.org/10.1016/j.ijer.2005.08.012
21. Järvelä, S., Nguyen, A., Vuorenmaa, E., Malmberg, J., Järvenoja, H.: Predicting regulatory activities for socially shared regulation to optimize collaborative learning. Comput. Human Behav. **144**, 107737 (2023). https://doi.org/10.1016/j.chb.2023.107737
22. Tuckman, B.W., Ann, M., Jensen, C.: Stages of small-group development revisited. Group Organ. Stud. **2**, 419–427 (1977). https://doi.org/10.1177/105960117700200404
23. IPMA: ICB - IPMA Competence Baseline Version 3.0. International Project Management Association, Nijkerk (NL) (2006)
24. Han, K.: Measuring Long-Term Success. Evaluation of MIT OCW Depends on Articulation of Clear Goals. http://web.mit.edu/fnl/vol/155/han.htm. Accessed 6 Feb 2024
25. Stein, J.: Using the Stages of Team Development. https://hr.mit.edu/learning-topics/teams/articles/stages-development. Accessed 14 Feb 2023
26. Sein-Echaluce, M.L., Fidalgo-Blanco, Á., García-Peñalvo, F.J.: Agile CTMTC: adapting stages for a shorter application of the teamwork method. In: Zaphiris, P., Ioannou, A. (eds.) Learning and Collaboration Technologies: Designing the Learner and Teacher Experience. 9th International Conference, LCT 2022, Held as Part of the 24th HCI International Conference, HCII 2022. Virtual Event, 26 June–1 July 2022, Proceedings, Part II, pp. 274–286. Springer, Cham (2022). https://doi.org/10.1007/978-3-031-05675-8_21
27. Sedlmayer, M.: Individual Competence Baseline for Project Management, 4th edn., Zurich (2015)
28. Conde, M.Á., Hernández-García, Á., García-Peñalvo, F.J., Fidalgo, Á., Sein-Echaluce, M.: Evaluation of the CTMTC methodology for assessment of teamwork competence development and acquisition in higher education. In: Zaphiris, P., Ioannou, A. (eds.) Learning and Collaboration Technologies, LCT 2016. LNCS, vol. 9753, pp. 1–12. Springer, Cham (2016). https://doi.org/10.1007/978-3-319-39483-1_19
29. Sein-Echaluce, M.L., Fidalgo-Blanco, Á., García-Peñalvo, F.J., Fonseca, D.: Impact of transparency in the teamwork development through Cloud Computing. Appl. Sci. **11**(9), 3887 (2021). https://doi.org/10.3390/app11093887
30. Fidalgo-Blanco, Á., Leris, D., Sein-Echaluce, M.L., García-Peñalvo, F.J.: Monitoring indicators for CTMTC: comprehensive training model of the teamwork competence in engineering domain. Int. J. Eng. Educ. (IJEE). **31**, 829–838 (2015)
31. IPMA: IPMA Reference Guide ICB4 in an Agile World. International Project Management Association, Zurich (2018)

32. Sein-Echaluce, M.L.: Moodle de la Universidad de Zaragoza: plataforma de aprendizaje en línea de software libre (2022). https://doi.org/10.5281/ZENODO.7097366
33. Fidalgo-Blanco, Á., Sein-Echaluce Lacleta, M.L., García-Peñalvo, F.J.: Seguimiento y monitorización del trabajo en equipo con Moodle. In: Innovación educativa en los tiempos de la inteligencia artificial, pp. 480–483. Universidad de Zaragoza, Madrid (2023)

Screen Media Usage and Adolescent Learning: Unraveling the Timing and Content-Related Factors Influencing Academic Performance and Motivation

Yingrui Wu[✉] [iD]

Department of Psychology, University of Pittsburgh, Pittsburgh, PA 15260, USA
Yiw157@pitt.edu

Abstract. Screen media has witnessed extensive utilization in classrooms and educational settings. Among this widespread usage, researchers have extensively investigated the influence of screen media usage (SMU). The impact of SMU on adolescents has been the subject of extensive empirical research by scholars. Yet there is limited focus on the association between the content and duration of SMU and students' academic performance. The current study endeavor undertook an examination of the impact of SMU on academic performance and learning motivation, delving into two distinct dimensions, time and content-related aspects. Data were gathered from adolescents ($N = 69$) aged 14–18 from an international high school in Guangzhou, China. Findings demonstrated that various contents of SMU have an impact on academic performance and motivation. Notably, non-academic SMU is negatively correlated with the academic performance and motivation of adolescents, affirming the second hypothesis. Evidence indicated that adolescents should be advised to limit their screen media usage, particularly non-academic content, to ensure that their academic performance and learning motivation remain unaffected. Parents and educators can develop clear guidelines recommending appropriate screen time for adolescents, balancing their academic and recreational usage. The research findings can assist education policymakers and practitioners in formulating more effective educational strategies in the future.

Keywords: Screen media · Adolescents · Learning motivation · Academic performance · PSQI · MSMT

1 Introduction

Screen media has witnessed extensive utilization in classrooms and educational settings. Data from a recent survey indicates that among 1,453 13- to 17-year-old adolescents, approximately 95% of the population use smartphones, and 90% of them have access to laptop computers or desktops [2]. Additionally, teenagers aged 13 to 18, as reported by Rideout et al. [13], spend around eight and a half hours per day on screen media. Among this widespread usage, researchers have extensively investigated the influence of screen media usage (SMU). The impact of SMU on adolescents has been the subject of extensive empirical research by scholars.

© The Author(s), under exclusive license to Springer Nature Switzerland AG 2024
P. Zaphiris and A. Ioannou (Eds.): HCII 2024, LNCS 14722, pp. 275–287, 2024.
https://doi.org/10.1007/978-3-031-61672-3_18

1.1   Effect of SMU on Academic Performance

Advantages. The favorable effects of screen media revealed its potential advantages across diverse domains. Lambic [8] identified the positive influence of Facebook on academic performance. Students leverage the communal aspect of Facebook to engage in academic discussions, share scholarly information, and assist their peers, all while recognizing and addressing their own areas of improvement. Moreover, Facebook facilitates the accessibility of information. When a student seeks clarification from a teacher, the obtained answer can be shared with the entire class, aiding other students and making information retrieval more accessible. Even computer games have been found to be applicable in education. In Yeşilbağ's experiment [20], educational computer games were utilized as a teaching activity, allowing students to learn through gaming. The results demonstrated that students in the group using computer games as an educational tool outperformed those in the traditional teaching group in English grades.

Disadvantages. Various studies affirmed a notable negative relationship between prolonged SMU and academic performance. Anatsui and Adekanye [1] explored the impact of television on adolescents and discovered that excessive TV watching has adverse effects on youths, including obesity, impaired social development, and negative impacts on hearing and vision. More importantly, it significantly weakens reading skills, influencing academic performance. This is because TV watching is a passive activity, and the electronic imagery it provides does not require focused attention, unlike reading, which demands concentrated focus, imagination, and deep thinking. Similarly, cell phone usage was observed to be significantly negatively associated with actual college GPA, especially with the extensive use of social media like Facebook, leading adolescents to spend less time on their studies [5, 7, 9, 16]. Distinct time limit of SMU has been investigated by research, showing that screen time higher than 2 h is adversely associated with poor academic performance [6, 10, 11, 14, 15]. These findings provide compelling evidence for that excessive use of screen media is associated with diminished academic performance.

1.2   Effect of SMU on Learning Motivation

Advantages. SMU has demonstrated positive impacts on students' learning motivation through various avenues. Prabandari and Yuliati [12] found that the duration of social media use positively influenced both intrinsic and extrinsic academic motivation. The longer students engage with social media and the more active their social accounts, the stronger their learning motivation becomes. Similarly, experiments conducted by Syaparuddin and Elihami [18] indicated that students' motivation increased when teachers used video media as a supplementary tool for teaching. Another study revealed that the influence of social media use on students' learning motivation increased from 66% to 81% [17]. This data further corroborates that the use of screen media can significantly impact learning motivation.

Disadvantages. While the positive impacts of SMU on learning motivation are evident, it is crucial to acknowledge the potential disadvantages that can arise from its extensive utilization. The study conducted by Evers et al. [4] revealed a close association between the utilization of social media and sleep disturbances. The induced sleep disturbances were found to be associated with heightened fatigue among students towards school activities and a decline in learning motivation, consequently leading to a decrease in academic performance. Furthermore, there was a negative association found between problematic internet use and learning motivation, with a positive relationship with test anxiety [19].

These studies suggest that prolonged SMU is associated with decreased academic performance. Simultaneously, diverse content in screen media exhibits distinctive effects on both factors. However, there is limited focus on the connection between the content and duration of SMU and its impacts. This study aims to address this gap by concurrently exploring the impact of SMU on academic performance and learning motivation, considering both time and content-related dimensions. This research explores the hypotheses that (a) SMU exceeding 1 h per day on weekdays and surpassing 2 h per day on weekends is negatively associated with the academic performance and motivation of adolescents, and (b) when the non-academic content of SMU is greater than academic content, it is negatively correlated with the academic performance and motivation of adolescents. By delving into these dimensions, the study endeavors to provide a comprehensive understanding of how both the duration and content of SMU collectively impact the academic experiences and motivation of adolescents.

2 Methodology

Participants ($N = 69$; 29 boys; 40 girls) aged 14–18 ($Mage = 16.21$; $SDage = 0.90$) from an international high school in Guangzhou, China were recruited to fill out the questionnaire. A total of 100 paper-based questionnaires were sent out and 84 were returned. There were 69 valid questionnaires, 12 invalid questionnaires, and 3 blank questionnaires. There was no compensation provided for participants in the study. One hundred questionnaires were printed out and delivered to the international high school, where they were distributed by the monitor teachers to students for completion. Subsequently, the completed questionnaires were collected, and data were input into a computer for further analysis.

2.1 Measures

Data were gathered from a self-designed questionnaire investigated screen media usage, integrating the Pittsburgh Sleep Quality Index (PSQI) [3] and Middle School Students' Motivation to Learn Scale (MSMT) [21]. It's important to note that screen media, in this context, refers to the use of mobile phones, computers, iPads, video games, and televisions. Demographic information including age, gender, and grade were collected. Participants were also requested to self-report their subject grades (e.g., Chinese, Math, English, and Overall), measured on a 5-point Likert scales (1 = Very poor; 2 = Below average; 3 = Average; 4 = Above average; 5 = Excellent).

Screen Media Usage. Screen media usage (SMU) was measured by a series of self-designed questions, investigating two dimensions: time and content-related aspects. Taking into consideration the disparity in students' screen media exposure during school days and weekends, the questionnaire categorized the overall question into two distinct time periods: weekdays and weekends (e.g., "On a typical weekday in the past month, how many hours of screen media did you usually use in a day?"). Participants were queried about their screen media usage in relation to academic, non-academic, and interpersonal activities (e.g., "On a typical weekend in the past month, when using screen media, how many hours did you usually use for leisure activities such as watching TV, watching movies, playing games, listening to music, and surfing the Internet?"). To capture the nuanced details of their screen time, participants provided responses in the form of hours and minutes dedicated to screen media usage, filling in the blanks with the format "x hours x minutes."

Sleep Quality. Sleep quality was measured by the introduced Pittsburgh Sleep Quality Index (PSQI), containing 19 self-rated items and 5 informant-rated items. Item 10 does not contribute to the PSQI score, thus deleting the question in the questionnaire. Items on the scale are categorized into seven components: subjective sleep quality, sleep latency, sleep duration, sleep efficiency, sleep disturbance, use of sleep medication, and daytime dysfunction. The chart presented in Table 1 illustrates detailed questions of the sleep efficiency component of the PSQI. Each component scored 0 (no difficulty) to 3 (severe difficulty). Summing the scores for each components yields the total score for the global PSQI score, which falls within the range of 0 to 21 points. A higher total score on the PSQI signifies diminished sleep quality and surpassing a total score of 7 on the PSQI serves as an indicator of potential sleep quality issues. The global PSQI score excluded the 19th self-rated item and 5 informant-rated items.

Table 1. Adapted Pittsburgh Sleep Quality Index (PSQI) component.

Component	Questions
Sleep Efficiency	1. During the past month, what time have you usually gone to bed at night? _____
	3. During the past month, what time have you usually gotten up in the morning? _____
	4. During the past month, how many hours of actual sleep did you get at night? (This may be different than the number of hours you spent in bed.) _____

Learning Motivation. Learning motivation was measured by Middle School Students' Motivation to Learn Scale (MSMT). The scale comprises 20 items, each assessed with a "Agree" or "Disagree" rating. It includes four subscales: weak learning motivation, strong learning motivation, learning interest disturbance, and learning goals disturbance. Refer to Table 2 for further details. Each subscale consists of five items, with a scoring range from 0 to 5. If the score of any subscales was 3 or above, it is considered that there might some misconceptions or a certain level of disturbance in the corresponding aspect of learning motivation.

Table 2. Adapted Middle School Students' Motivation to Learn Scale (MSMT) subscale.

Subscale	Items
Weak Learning Motivation	1. You rarely take the initiative to learn if others don't push you
	2. It takes a long time to refresh yourself when you read
	3. Whenever you read, you feel tired and bored and want to sleep
	4. You don't want to read any more than the homework your teacher assigns
	5. If you don't understand something, you don't even try to understand it
Strong Learning Motivation	6. You often think you can outperform others without spending too much time
	7. You are eager to improve your academic performance in a short period of time
	……
Learning Interest Disturbance	11. You find studying boring and want to find a job
	12. You often think that the basic knowledge of textbooks is nothing to learn, only read advanced theories, read big works can be exciting
	……
Learning Goal Disturbance	16. Most of the learning goals you set for yourself have to be abandoned because you can't achieve them
	17. Most of the learning goals you set for yourself are not easy to achieve
	……

2.2 Statistical Analysis

All data were collected through paper-based questionnaire distributed to participants, and subsequently analyzed using SPSS (Statistical Package for the Social Science). Data preprocessing was used to transform raw data. The Pearson correlation coefficient was used to determine whether there was a correlation between different variables. Additionally, analysis of variance (ANOVA) and t-tests were conducted to examine group differences and associations between specific variables.

3 Results

3.1 Overview of SMU by Gender and Grade

Table 3 shown below presents key statistics for the sample of participants ($n = 69$), highlighting key patterns and variations in SMU, sleep, academic performance, and learning motivation. The distribution across gender and grade levels, including freshmen

(Grade 10), sophomores (Grade 11), and seniors (Grade 12), ensures representation from various demographic groups. For weekdays, the average overall SMU duration is 273.62 min ($SD = 314.41$) for males and 297.25 min ($SD = 265.31$) for females. Interpersonal SMU is the predominant usage type for female ($M = 178.00, SD = 211.46$) while males exhibit a prevalence of non-academic SMU ($M = 146.72, SD = 238.77$). Notably, seniors exhibit a higher mean SMU duration compared to freshmen and sophomores during weekdays. During weekends, the mean SMU duration increases to 555.52 min ($SD = 224.59$) for males and 460.63 min ($SD = 256.47$) for females, with non-academic use becoming more prominent. Specifically, males demonstrate higher non-academic SMU ($M = 351.72, SD = 238.78$), while females exhibit a mean of 237.88 min ($SD = 179.55$) for non-academic SMU. During weekdays, 66% of males engaged in SMU for more than 1 h, and on weekends, 97% exceeded 2 h. Females followed a comparable pattern, with 70% using SMU for over 1 h on weekdays, and on weekends, 90% extended beyond 2 h.

Regarding sleep, within the entire sample, no participant obtained a global PSQI score exceeding 7, indicating none of the participants reported experiencing any sleep-related issues. Specifically, for male students, the mean score is 4.93 ($SD = 3.78$), while for female students, it is 6.10 ($SD = 3.70$). When categorized by grade, Grade 10 (G10) students have an average global PSQI score of 5.96 ($SD = 4.01$), Grade 11 (G11) students have a mean score of 5.91 ($SD = 3.64$), and Grade 12 (G12) students have a score of 3.91 ($SD = 3.27$).

On the motivational aspect, female students exhibit stronger learning motivation ($M = 2.58, SD = 1.84$) compared to males, and the score in learning interest disturbance ($M = 1.69, SD = 1.29$) of males tend to slightly surpass females. When analyzed by grade, G10 students display a mean score of 1.58 ($SD = 1.36$), G11 students show a mean of 2.13 ($SD = 1.16$), and G12 students exhibit a mean of 2.36 ($SD = 1.21$). In G10, students had the lowest mean score of learning goal disturbance ($M = 2.58, SD = 1.68$) among the four motivation subscales, a trend that persists in Grade 11 students ($M = 2.72, SD = 1.76$).

3.2 SMU Effects on Academic Performance and Learning Motivation

The results revealed a statistically significant correlation between the time and content of SMU and students' academic performance and learning motivation, aligning with the anticipated outcomes as posited in previous research hypotheses. Specifically, there was a significant negative correlation between overall SMU > 2 h/day on weekends and Chinese grade ($r = -.313, p < .05$). This suggests that higher screen media usage during weekends is associated with lower Chinese grade. Additionally, there was a significant positive correlation observed between learning interest disturbance and overall SMU > 1 h/day on weekdays ($r = .354, p < .05$), as well as overall SMU > 2 h/day on weekends ($r = .281, p < .05$). This implies that increased screen media usage, beyond 1 h per day on weekdays and 2 h per day on weekends, is positively correlated with disturbances in learning interest. These results suggested that screen media usage beyond 1 h/day on weekdays and 2 h/day on weekends is inversely related to learning motivation of adolescents, providing substantial evidence to support the hypothesis. See Table 4.

Table 3. Overall Descriptive Statistics Data for the Sample.

	Gender		Grade		
	Male	Female	G10	G11	G12
	M (SD)	M (SD)	M (SD)	M (SD)	M (SD)
SMU1	273.62 (314.41)	297.25 (265.31)	198.08 (272.85)	322.50 (306.83)	366.82 (200.25)
SMU2	77.97 (137.438)	178.00 (211.46)	61.15 (94.29)	138.66 (210.81)	304.91 (234.57)
SMU3	107.45 (164.74)	131.88 (116.95)	56.73 (80.21)	139.72 (155.50)	222.27 (127.07)
SMU4	146.72 (238.77)	144.13 (173.03)	120.96 (170.09)	131.56 (214.97)	242.27 (219.83)
SMU5	555.52 (224.59)	460.63 (256.47)	431.54 (230.99)	528.91 (246.68)	580.91 (262.32)
SMU6	165.52 (134.31)	214.00 (210.15)	140.77 (83.04)	238.13 (244.19)	189.09 (104.83)
SMU7	110.52 (127.80)	171.38 (177.10)	125.00 (187.00)	141.09 (150.90)	208.64 (103.59)
SMU8	351.72 (238.78)	237.88 (179.55)	280.58 (198.07)	263.44 (210.32)	362.73 (252.51)
Chinese Grade	2.90 (1.18)	3.40 (1.08)	3.08 (1.09)	3.44 (1.13)	2.73 (1.19)
Math Grade	2.93 (1.41)	2.50 (1.34)	2.62 (1.36)	2.81 (1.47)	2.45 (1.21)
English Grade	2.52 (1.43)	3.00 (1.32)	2.58 (1.50)	2.84 (1.32)	3.18 (1.25)
Overall Grade	2.72 (1.16)	2.78 (1.12)	2.69 (1.29)	3.00 (1.05)	2.91 (0.94)
S1	0.86 (0.95)	0.83 (0.96)	0.92 (0.98)	0.94 (0.98)	0.36 (0.67)
S2	2.03 (1.70)	2.93 (1.97)	2.81 (2.02)	2.53 (1.78)	2.00 (2.00)
S3	0.86 (1.09)	0.93 (0.94)	0.88 (1.03)	1.00 (1.02)	0.64 (0.92)
S4	0.17 (0.60)	0.30 (0.69)	0.27 (0.72)	0.28 (0.68)	0.09 (0.30)
S5	1.00 (0.71)	1.13 (0.61)	1.08 (0.63)	1.16 (0.68)	0.82 (0.60)
S6	4.93 (3.78)	6.10 (3.70)	5.96 (4.01)	5.91 (3.64)	3.91 (3.27)
M1	2.14 (1.92)	2.58 (1.84)	2.27 (1.80)	2.50 (1.92)	2.36 (2.06)
M2	1.55 (1.24)	2.25 (1.21)	1.58 (1.36)	2.13 (1.16)	2.36 (1.21)
M3	1.69 (1.29)	1.58 (1.28)	1.31 (1.12)	1.72 (1.28)	2.09 (1.51)
M4	2.55 (1.92)	2.65 (1.64)	2.58 (1.68)	2.72 (1.76)	2.36 (2.01)

Note. SMU1 = Overall SMU on Weekdays, SMU2 = Interpersonal SMU on Weekdays, SMU3 = Academic SMU on Weekdays, SMU4 = Non-Academic SMU on Weekdays, SMU5 = Overall SMU on Weekends, SMU6 = Interpersonal SMU on Weekends, SMU7 = Academic SMU on Weekends, SMU8 = Non-Academic SMU on Weekends, S1 = Sleep Quality, S2 = Sleep Latency, S3 = Sleep Duration, S4 = Sleep Efficiency, S5 = Sleep Disturbance, S6 = Global PSQI Score, M1 = Weak Learning Motivation, M2 = Strong Learning Motivation, M3 = Learning Interest Disturbance, and M4 = Learning Goal Disturbance

Results also showed a significant positive correlation between interpersonal SMU on weekdays and weak learning motivation ($r = .260$, $p < .05$), as well as learning interest disturbance ($r = .244$, $p < .05$). This suggests that increased interpersonal SMU during weekdays is associated with lower learning motivation and disturbances in learning interest. Moreover, there were significant positive correlations between academic SMU on weekends and strong learning motivation ($r = .267$, $p < .05$) and overall grades ($r = .277$, $p < .05$). This implies that engaging in academic-related SMU during weekends is

Table 4. Impacts of Overall SMU on Learning Motivation.

	M3	Overall SMU on Weekends (>2 h)	Overall SMU on Weekdays (>1 h)
Overall SMU on Weekends (>2 h)	.281*		
Overall SMU on Weekdays (>1 h)	.354*	.658**	
Chinese Grade	−0.021	−.313*	−0.084

Note. M3 = Learning Interest Disturbance
** Correlation is significant at the 0.01 level (2-tailed)
* Correlation is significant at the 0.05 level (2-tailed)

positively linked to higher learning motivation and overall grades. A significant negative correlation was identified between interpersonal SMU on weekends and math grades (r = −.264, p < .05). This indicates that increased interpersonal SMU during weekends is associated with lower math grades. These findings demonstrated that various contents of SMU have an impact on academic performance and motivation. Notably, non-academic SMU displayed a negative correlation with the academic performance and motivation of adolescents, affirming the second hypothesis. See Table 5.

Table 5. Impacts of SMU Contents on Learning Motivation.

	M1	M2	M3	Math Grade	Overall Grade	SMU2	SMU6
M2	0.212						
M3	0.217	.264*					
Math Grade	−.356**	−0.076	0.073				
Overall Grade	−.339**	0.079	0.017	0.762**			
SMU2	.260*	.300*	.244*	−0.216	−0.115		
SMU6	0.179	0.019	0.038	−.264*	−0.157	.563**	
SMU7	0.012	.267*	0.085	0.081	.277*	0.161	0.223

Note. M1 = Weak Learning Motivation, M2 = Strong Motivation, M3 = Learning Interest Disturbance, SMU2 = Interpersonal SMU on Weekdays, SMU6 = Interpersonal SMU on Weekends, and SMU7 = Academic SMU on Weekends
** Correlation is significant at the 0.01 level (2-tailed)
* Correlation is significant at the 0.05 level (2-tailed)

3.3 Sleep

Although prior hypothesis did not mention the interplay between sleep and SMU, it yielded noteworthy correlations, refer to Table 6. A negative correlation emerged between sleep quality and interpersonal SMU on weekdays ($r = -.250, p < .05$), suggesting that prolonged interpersonal SMU during weekdays is linked to poorer sleep quality. Furthermore, a negative correlation was found between sleep latency and non-academic SMU on weekdays ($r = -.276, p < .05$), indicating that increased non-academic SMU during weekdays is associated with shorter sleep latency. Sleep latency also exhibited a negative correlation with overall SMU > 2 h/day on weekends ($r = -.294, p < .05$), revealing that participants with prolonged sleep latency tend to engage in higher overall SMU during weekends. Similarly, sleep efficiency demonstrated a negative correlation with overall SMU > 2 h/day on weekends ($r = -.269, p < .05$), suggesting that lower sleep efficiency is associated with increased overall SMU during weekends. Notably, the global Pittsburgh Sleep Quality Index (PSQI) score displayed a negative correlation with overall SMU > 2 h/day on weekends ($r = -.274, p < .05$). Higher global PSQI scores were linked to heightened overall SMU exceeding 2 h during weekends. These findings collectively underscore the complex relationships between sleep, specific dimensions of SMU, and various facets of sleep patterns.

Table 6. Correlation of SMU and Sleep

	SMU2	SMU4	Overall SMU on Weekends (>2 h)	S1	S2	S
SMU4	.492**					
Overall SMU on Weekends (>2 h)	.624**	.534**				
S1	−.250*	−0.1	−0.203			
S2	−0.15	−.276*	−.294*	.515**		
S4	−0.13	−0.107	−.269*	.422**	.626**	
S6	−0.23	−0.165	−.274*	.825**	.842**	.685**

Note. SMU2 = Interpersonal SMU on Weekdays, SMU4 = Non-academic SMU on Weekdays, S1 = Sleep Quality, S2 = Sleep Latency, S4 = Sleep Efficiency, and S6 = Global PSQI Score
** Correlation is significant at the 0.01 level (2-tailed)
* Correlation is significant at the 0.05 level (2-tailed)

3.4 Gender and Grade on SMU

The results of the analysis of variance (ANOVA) indicate a significant difference in interpersonal SMU on weekdays among different grade levels. Subsequent post-hoc multiple comparisons revealed significant differences between G10 and G12, with a notable difference of −243.76 min ($p < 0.05$). The average SMU for G12 was significantly lower than that of G10. Significant differences were also observed between G11 and G12 with a difference of −166.25 min ($p < 0.05$), indicating that the average SMU for G12 was significantly lower than that of G11. Similarly, the results for academic SMU on weekdays show significant differences among different grade levels. Specifically, significant mean differences were observed in the comparisons between G10 and G11 (-82.99, p = 0.016, 95% CI [-150.17, -15.81]), G10 and G12 (-165.54 min, Sig. <0.001, 95% CI [-257.06, -74.02]), and G11) and G12) (-82.55, $p = 0.068$, 95% CI [-171.49, 6.38]). See Tables 7 and 8.

Table 7. ANOVA Results for Interpersonal SMU on Weekdays by Grade.

Source of Variation	df	Mean Square	F	Sig. (two-tailed)
Grade	2	229854.679	7.056	0.002*

* Correlation is significant at the 0.05 level (2-tailed).

Table 8. ANOVA Results for Academic SMU on Weekdays by Grade.

Source of Variation	df	Mean Square	F	Sig. (two-tailed)
Grade	2	115699.334	7.124	0.002*

* Correlation is significant at the 0.05 level (2-tailed).

The study employed an independent samples t-test to assess the influence of gender on SMU. The results revealed a significant difference in interpersonal SMU (on both weekdays and weekends) between genders at a significance level of 0.05. Further examination of the mean values indicated that female students exhibited higher levels of interpersonal SMU compared to male students. For detailed information, refer to Table 9.

Table 9. T-test Results of Gender Differences in SMU.

	Group	Mean	t	Sig. (two-sided)
SMU2	Male	77.97	-2.309	0.024*
	Female	178.00		
SMU6	Male	165.52	-1.167	0.124*
	Female	214.00		

Note. SMU2 = Interpersonal SMU on Weekdays and SMU6 = Interpersonal SMU on Weekends
* Correlation is significant at the 0.05 level (2-tailed)

4   General Discussion

The findings of this study contribute valuable insights into the multifaceted impact of screen media usage (SMU) on academic performance and learning motivation among adolescents. The widespread use of screen media in educational settings has prompted extensive research, yet this study sought to address a specific gap by examining the nuanced relationship between the content and duration of SMU and its effects on students' academic outcomes.

The results indicated a significant influence of various contents of SMU on academic performance and motivation. Particularly noteworthy was the negative correlation observed between non-academic SMU and both academic performance and motivation, confirming the research hypothesis. This underscores the importance of considering not only the time spent on screen media but also the nature of the content consumed. Adolescents, as the primary users of screen media, may benefit from clear guidelines and recommendations to optimize their academic performance and learning motivation. The evidence suggests that limiting non-academic content in screen media usage can positively impact adolescents' educational outcomes.

4.1 Limitation

While the study contributes insights into the relationship between SMU and adolescences' academic performance and motivation, several limitations should be considered. First, data were gathered through a paper-based questionnaire distributed to students from one international high school. This collected sample may not be representative enough for two reasons: (a) the population size was too small, (b) the total participant for each sample had a significant difference, and (c) the targeted population had too much exclusive characteristics, thus weakening the generalizability of the result. Second, the use of self-report methods to gather data limits the accuracy, as the challenge to retrospective memory and modification of individuals' answers to align with parents' and teachers' expectations.

4.2 Implication

This study offered valuable insights into understanding the impact of SMU on the academic performance and learning motivation of adolescents. Evidence indicated that adolescents should be advised to limit their screen media usage, particularly non-academic content, to ensure that their academic performance and learning motivation remain unaffected. Parents and educators can develop clear guidelines recommending appropriate screen time for adolescents, balancing their academic and recreational usage. On the other hand, encouragement of academic content prioritization could be essential to enhance adolescents' academic performance and motivation. In the educational setting, apart from integrating digital platforms for teaching, teachers can establish clear, approachable learning objectives for students, enabling them to derive a sense of achievement and foster their learning motivation. The research findings can assist education policymakers and practitioners in formulating more effective educational strategies in the future.

Disclosure of Interests.   The author has no competing interests to declare that are relevant to the content of this article.

References

1. Anatsui, T.C., Adekanye, E.A.: Television and academic performance of Nigerian youths: implications for national development. J. Econ. Sustain. Dev. 5(10), 58–66 (2014)

2. Anderson, M., Faverio, M., Gottfried, J.: Teens, Social media and technology 2023: YouTube, TikTok, Snapchat and Instagram remain the most widely used online platforms among U.S. teens. Pew Research Center (2023)

3. Buysse, D.J., Reynolds, C.F., III., Monk, T.H., Berman, S.R., Kupfer, D.J.: The Pittsburgh sleep quality index: a new instrument for psychiatric practice and research. Psychiatry Res. **28**(2), 193–213 (1989)

4. Evers, K., Chen, S., Rothmann, S., Dhir, A., Pallesen, S.: Investigating the relation among disturbed sleep due to social media use, school burnout, and academic performance. J. Adolesc. **84**, 156–164 (2020). https://doi.org/10.1016/j.adolescence.2020.08.011

5. Jamal, A.M.: Social media use, engagement and addiction as predictors of academic performance. Int. J. Psychol. Stud. **7**(4), 86–94 (2015). https://doi.org/10.5539/ijps.v7n4p86

6. Khan, A., Gomersall, S., Stylianou, M.: Associations of passive and mentally active screen time with perceived school performance of 197,439 adolescents across 38 countries. Acad. Pediatr. **23**, 651–658 (2023). https://doi.org/10.1016/j.acap.2022.07.024

7. Kirschne, P.A., Karpinski, A.C.: Facebook® and academic performance. Comput. Hum. Behav. **26**, 1237–1245 (2010). https://doi.org/10.1016/j.chb.2010.03.024

8. Lambic, D.: Correlation between Facebook use for educational purposes and academic performance of students. Comput. Hum. Behav. **61**, 313–320 (2016). https://doi.org/10.1016/j.chb.2016.03.052

9. Lepp, A., Barkley, J.E., Karpinski, A.C.: The relationship between cell phone use and academic performance in a sample of U.S. college students. SAGE Open **5**(1), 215824401557316 (2015). https://doi.org/10.1177/2158244015573169

10. Liu, X., Luo, Y., Liu, Z.Z., Yang, Y., Liu, J., Jia, C.X.: Prolonged mobile phone use is associated with poor academic performance in adolescents. Cyberpsychol. Behav. Soc. Netw. **23**, 303–311 (2020). https://doi.org/10.1089/cyber.2019.0591

11. Neophytou, E., Manwell, L.A., Eikelboom, R.: Effects of excessive screen time on neurodevelopment, learning, memory, mental health, and neurodegeneration: a scoping review. Int. J. Ment. Health Addiction **19**, 724–744 (2021). https://doi.org/10.1007/s11469-019-00182-2

12. Prabandari, K., Yuliati, L.N.: The influence of social media use and parenting style on teenagers' academic motivation and academic achievement. J. Child Dev. Stud. **1**(1), 40–54 (2016). https://doi.org/10.29244/jcds.1.01.39-53

13. Rideout, V., Peebles, A., Mann, S., Robb, M.B.: The common sense census: media use by tweens and teens, 2021. In: Common Sense, p. 3 (2022)

14. Sampasa-Kanyinga, H., Chaput, J.P., Hamilton, H.A.: Social media use, school connectedness, and academic performance among adolescents. J. Primary Prevent. **40**, 189–211 (2019). https://doi.org/10.1007/s10935-019-00543-6

15. Sanders, T., Parker, P.D., del Pozo-Cruz, B., Noetel, M., Lonsdale, C.: Type of screen time moderates effects on outcomes in 4013 children: evidence from the longitudinal study of Australian children. Int. J. Behav. Nutr. Phys. Act. **16**, 177 (2019). https://doi.org/10.1186/s12966-019-0881-7

16. Simuforosa, M.: The impact of modern technology on the educational attainment of adolescents. Int. J. Educ. Res. **1**(9), 1–8 (2013)

17. Sopian, A., Nandiyanto, A.B.D., Kurniawan, T., Muhammad, R.B.: The influence use of social media on the learning motivation of junior high school students. Indonesian J. Multidisciplinary Res. **2**(1), 137–142 (2021)

18. Syaparuddin, S., Elihami, E.: Improving student learning motivation through the utilization of video media in education students. Jurnal Edukasi Nonformal **1**(1), 228–235 (2020)

19. Truzoli, R., Viganò, C., Galmozzi, P.G., Reed, P.: Problematic internet use and study motivation in higher education. J. Comput. Assist. Learn. **36**(4), 480–486 (2020). https://doi.org/10.1111/jcal.12414

20. Yeşilbağ, S., Korkmaz, Ö., Çakir, R.: The effect of educational computer games on students' academic achievements and attitudes towards English lesson. Educ. Inf. Technol. **25**, 5339–5356 (2020). https://doi.org/10.1007/s10639-020-10216-1
21. Zheng, R.C.: Psychological Counseling for Middle School Students, pp. 200–207. Shandong Education Press (1994). (in Chinese)

Exploring the Influence of Shared Learning Logs in the e-Book Utilization

Juan Zhou[1]([📧])[ID], Kae Nakaya[2][ID], Yuichi Ono[3][ID], Hui-Chun Chu[4][ID], and Chengjiu Yin[5][ID]

[1] Tokyo Institute of Technology, 3-3-6 Shibaura, Minato-ku, Tokyo 108-0023, Japan
juan.z.kt@gmail.com
[2] Center for Student Success Research and Practice, Osaka University, Suita, Japan
[3] Institute of Humanities and Social Sciences, University of Tsukuba, Tsukuba, Japan
[4] Department of Computer Science and Information Management,
Soochow University, Taipei, Taiwan
[5] Research Institute for Information Technology, Kyushu University, Fukuoka, Japan

Abstract. Some researchers suggest that when students engage in knowledge-sharing behaviors while learning e-book materials online, it can enhance their interactions and support their individual learning processes. Whether teachers should organize annotation content based on their expertise, or whether learners should share annotations with their peers during learning remains an unresolved research issue. This study aims to address this question by designing two groups: reading the materials with annotations by an instructor and reading by other students (peers) to explore the effects on learning achievement, learning attitude, and mental load. As a result, the students who read the instructor's annotation performed better results on the delayed test and strengthened their attitude toward the importance of learning materials.

Keywords: E-book · Annotation · Share learning logs · Peer · Instructor

1 Introduction

Owing to the rapid growth of digital learning management systems, the resources available to learners online are becoming increasingly diverse, and the interaction between learners and the learning materials is becoming more critical. When reading e-books for personalized learning, students may wish to receive some notes or terminology explanations to help them understand if they find something difficult. Therefore, designing the annotation content when students read e-books online alone has become an important issue [7].

Some researchers have pointed out that in the process of learning e-book materials if students engage in knowledge-sharing behaviors when reading online, it may allow students to have more interaction and support in the process of personal learning [3]. Therefore, whether the content of annotations should be better arranged by teachers according to their professionalism, or whether learners should share their annotations with their peers during the learning process remains an unknown research issue. Therefore, this study aims to explore this issue using a research design.

Note-taking and making markers (e.g., underlining) or annotations in the book can be useful methods to support people in remembering and promoting reading comprehension and learning, as well as skimming the text and using the context to identify unfamiliar words [5]. In a face-to-face environment, students share the notes they have taken in textbooks and discuss their content.

The research questions that this study aims to address are whether there is any benefit for students in sharing notes in an online learning environment, and what kind of annotation sharing is helpful for their study and achievement. This study set two kinds of annotation sharing: one is the notes of peers with the same learning position, and the other is the annotation of an instructor with professional knowledge and experience. We used these two kinds of annotations as two environments for students to study and test the effects of their grades, learning attitude, learning burden, and mental burden.

2   Literature Review

2.1   Annotation Share

Annotation research has progressed from paper and digital comparison to annotation-sharing studies, such as the web-based collaborative reading annotation system (WCRAS) with gamification mechanisms developed by Chen [1]. GroupNotes which is a smartphone-based real-time collaborative note-taking application used to encourage students to proactively engage in student interaction [9]. EduNotes which allows students to write notes associated with a specific lecture slide and share them with peers [8].

In the aforementioned research, it is evident that annotation sharing brings advantages, such as fostering better collaborative learning and increasing students' engagement with the learning materials. Simultaneously, a crucial issue arises in the process of sharing annotations: How to organize and structure these annotations effectively?

A previous study suggested that when multiple learners annotate or underline the same materials, the corresponding sections on other learners' tablet devices can be highlighted in color [11].

From a purely learning-effectiveness perspective, a key question emerges: Are annotations provided by teachers more beneficial, or do annotations generated by students hold greater utility? This study delves into this research question to explore the impact of these two types of annotations on students.

2.2   E-Book System

DITel utilized in this study was developed to support the students' reading behaviors and collect data in class [10]. Teachers upload lecture content including texts and pictures, and the users navigate it by clicking the "Prev" and

"Next" buttons. Further, users can take notes, highlight, underline, and bookmark the pages as needed. All actions performed using the system are recorded in a database that includes "Log ID," "User Number," "Process Code," "Operation Date," "Device Code," "Page Number," and "Pages."

This e-book is used in various learning and educational situations to collect and analyze data, contributing to the understanding of students' learning behaviors and learning styles [12]. Additionally, Zhou et al. developed a group method for e-book learning to reduce information avoidance in practical activities [13].

3   Experiment

3.1   Research Purpose

This study aimed to explore the type of annotation that has a positive effect on students. We prepared two types of e-book annotations: one made by their peers and the other made by an instructor. The study examined the impact of the study performance, students' study attitudes, and mental burdens when reading these two types of e-books.

3.2   Reading Contents

The e-book platform used in this experiment was DITel as described previously, with page truing, marking (highlights and underlines), and note-taking functions. The annotations shared in this study included highlighting, underlining, and notes. The reading content used in this study was extracted from a Python book (Column Edition) [6] about character code error, as shown in Fig. 1.

3.3   Experiment Design

There are 61 graduate students from two classes on "mobile application development" and "tourism design" who participated in this activity. The classes were conducted online using the Zoom platform. All the students were foreign students, and the language used in the class, textbooks, and material was Japanese. The materials used in this study were also Japanese.

To summarize, basic experiment information is presented in the Table 1. A preliminary experiment and an evaluation experiment were conducted. Students of the mobile application development class participated in the preliminary experiment. In the preliminary experiment, the annotation log data of the students were collected. Students of the tourism design class participated in the evaluative experiment, the students were assigned to the experimental or control groups.

Preliminary Experiment. Students read the e-book materials without any annotations. The preliminary experiment collected the annotation log data of these students. These annotation log data were provided to the control group. During the experiment, the reading logs of the students' including reading time, page-turning, underlining, highlighting, and notes, were recorded. The annotations used in this study included highlighting, underlining, and notes.

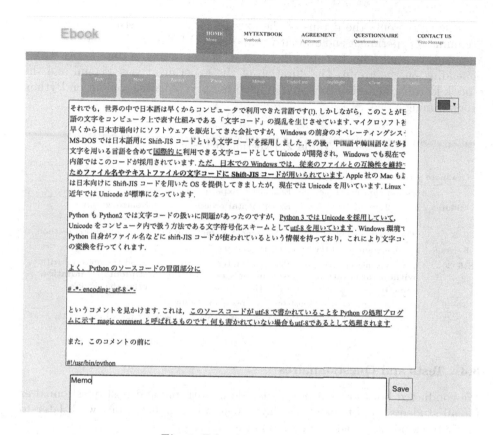

Fig. 1. E-book system interface

Table 1. Experiment Design

Experiment name	Date	Participating class	Participants	Log Data
Preliminary experiment	13/01/2021	Mobile application development class	21	696
Evaluation experiment (Control Group)	19/01/2021	Half students of tourism design class	20	380
Evaluate experiment (Experimental Group)	19/01/2021	Half students of tourism design class	20	485

Evaluative Experiment. Student participants from the tourism design class were assigned to either the experimental group or the control group. In the experimental group, students read the e-book materials with annotations made by the instructor. In the control group, students read the materials with the annotations made by the students who participated in the preliminary experiment.

Table 2 presents the details of the experiment. All the students (both the preliminary experiment and evaluative experiment) followed the same procedure and read the same e-book content; however, the annotations of the e-books varied depending on the group. The duration of the experiment was 45 min, and the e-book learning materials consisted of introductory Japanese content on Python programming.

Table 2. Experiment Design

Graduate students of a university in Japan (N = 61)		
	Preliminary experiment	Evaluation experiment	
Minutes	(N = 21)	Experimental group (N = 20)	Control group (N = 20)
0–5	The instructor explained the experiment details and the e-book operation method.		
6–15	Students answered the pretest and pre-questionnaire.		
16–30	Read the material **without annotation** using the e-book	Read the material with **instructor's annotation** using the e-book	Read the material with **students' annotation** using the e-book
31–40	Students answered the post-test and post-questionnaire.		
41–45	The instructor explained the material and gave feedback for tests to students.		

3.4   Tests and Questionnaires

We conducted both pre-and post-tests, along with pre-and post-questionnaires for all students. Additionally, a delayed test was conducted one week later to verify the students' academic performance.

Pre-test. The pre-test comprised four questions about basic computer knowledge, measuring differences in students' prior knowledge of computer basics.

Example 1. Select all the OS from below. (Multiple responses)
A. Office B. Windows C. au D. iOS E. Android F. Microsoft

Post-test. The post-test, administered after the students had read the instructional materials in the e-book, also included four questions derived from the materials: one multiple-choice question and three free description questions. The delayed test replicated the post-test questions.

Example 2. What does "# -*- encoding: utf-8 -*- " mean? (Free description question example)

Pre-questionnaire. The pre-questionnaire comprised twenty-three questions on a 5-point agreement scale (Strongly Disagree, Disagree, Neutral, Agree, Strongly Agree). It included five questions on the learning attitude of teaching materials, eight questions on self-efficacy for learning and performance, and ten questions on the Japanese anxiety scale [4]. Because the participants were all foreigners, it was necessary to test their anxiety about learning foreign language materials.

Example 3. I believe I will receive excellent grades in this class.
1. Strongly Disagree   2. Disagree   3. Neutral   4. Agree   5. Strongly Agree

Post-questionnaire. The post-questionnaire comprised thirty-nine questions on a 5-point agreement scale and one free description question. It included five questions on the learning attitude of Japanese teaching materials, eight questions on self-efficacy for learning and performance, six questions on satisfaction with learning activities, eight questions on mental Load and mental efforts, twelve questions on system usefulness and usability, and one question for comments.

Example 4. The learning system helped me learn more effectively.
1. Strongly Disagree   2. Disagree   3. Neutral   4. Agree   5. Strongly Agree

4   Results

4.1   Preliminary Experiment

Table 3 lists the annotation results from the preliminary experiment and annotation information used in the experimental group. The e-book materials comprised two pages.

4.2   Data Cleaning

Due to reasons such as not submitting questionnaires or tests or not having log data on the e-book, the final statistics were based on the number of students in each group shown in Table 3.

Table 3. annotation information used in evaluation experiment

		annotation times		Notes
		A word or phrase	Sentence	
From Students	page 1	10	2	4
	page 2	3	2	0
From Instructor	page 1	2	2	0
	page 2	3	2	0

4.3   Analysis of Learning Achievement

The Shapiro-Wilk test was used to check the normality of the data was employed. The value of the test was 0.56, $p = 7.736e\text{-}07$ (pre-test), 0.90, $p = 0.03$ (post-test), 0.77, $p = 0.00$ (delayed post), indicating that the sample of this study had no normal distribution. However, we used a missing value processing method to substitute missing values in the pre-test results with the average value.

The Mann-Whitney U test was employed and Table 4 shows the results for the three test scores, both for annotation by instructor and annotation by peer groups. A significant difference was observed between the two groups only in the delayed test ($w = 22$, $p < 0.05$). The experimental group scored higher than the control group on the post-test and delayed test, although there was no difference on the pre-test.

Table 4. T-test results of the scores for the tests

Test name	Group	N	Mean	S.D	W	p
Pre-test	(E)Annotation by instructor	11	0.48	0.11	72.5	0.164
	(C)Annotation by peer	10	0.49	0.16		
Post-test	(E)Annotation by instructor	11	0.61	0.32	42.5	0.387
	(C)Annotation by peer	10	0.48	0.36		
Delayed test	(E)Annotation by instructor	11	0.32	0.28	22	0.017*
	(C)Annotation by peer	10	0.10	0.10		

*$p < 0.05$

The Levene's of determining the homogeneity of the variance was not violated ($F = 1.30$, $p > 0.05$), indicating that the null hypothesis is tenable, and the variance is equal across groups.

The adjusted means and standard errors were 0.311 and 0.065 for the experimental group, and 0.10 and 0.103 for the control group, respectively. The delayed test scores of the two groups were significantly different ($F(1, 17) = 5.46$ ($p < 0.05$)). The delay test scores of the experimental group were significantly higher than those of the control group. Furthermore, the effect size (η^2) of the learning material was -1.06 indicating a large effect size [2] (Table 5).

Table 5. ANCOVA results of the delayed test scores in both groups

Group	N	Mean	S.D.	Adjusted mean	Adjusted SE	F	η^2
(E)Annotation by instructor	11	0.32	0.28	0.311	0.065	5.46*	-1.06
(C)Annotation by peer	10	0.10	0.10	0.103	0.068		

*$p < 0.05$

4.4 Analysis of Learning Attitude and Self-efficacy

The self-evaluation of the learning attitude and self-efficacy were investigated using a questionnaire, and there was no significant difference between the experimental and control groups (W = 66, W = 55, W = 79, $p > 0.05$) (Table 6).

Table 6 presents the Mann-Whitney U test results of differences in learning attitude and self-efficacy before and after the experiment both in both groups. There was a significant difference between the pre-questionnaire and post-questionnaire in the environmental group on the question item which are "It is important for me to learn this Japanese teaching material" (V = 0, $p < 0.05$) and "I am certain I can understand the difficult material presented in this course" (V = 3.5, $p < 0.05$). In the control group, there was no significant difference in the question items above, in the question of "I will actively search for more Japanese information about my course" (V = 0, $p < 0.05$), there was a significant difference between the pre-questionnaire and post-questionnaire.

4.5 Analysis of Students' Anxiety

Table 7 presents the test results for students' anxiety before the experiment and their mental load after the experiment in the environmental and control groups. The students of the control group showed higher scores than in the experimental group on the responses to questions "I tremble when I know that I'm going to be called on in language class" (C > E, 4.1 3.1, W = 89.5 $p < 0.05$) and "During language class, I find myself thinking about things that have nothing to do with the course" (C > E, 3.8, 2.6. W = 82, $p < 0.05$). However, the response to the question "During the learning activity, the way of presentation of the system (e-book in this study) caused me a lot of mental effort" in the control group had a higher score than in the experimental group after the experiment.

Table 6. Mann-Whitney U test results of learning attitude and self-efficacy between the pre-test and post-test

Questionnaire items	(E) & (C) N	Pre-test		Post-test			
		W Mean	p S.D.	W Mean	p S.D	V	p
Important for me to learn	(E) & (C)	66	0.42	50.5	0.77		
(E)Annotation by instructor	11	4.1	0.83	4.5	0.52	0*	0.04
(C)Annotation by peers	10	4.4	0.52	4.5	0.53	2	0.77
Actively search for more information	(E) & (C)	55	1	71	0.25		
(E)Annotation by instructor	11	3.8	1.08	3.9	0.83	2	0.77
(C)Annotation by peers	10	3.8	0.92	4.3	1.06	0*	0.04
Can understand the difficult material	(E) & (C)	79	0.08	52.5	0.87		
(E)Annotation by instructor	11	3.7	1.08	3.6	1.03	3.5*	0.04
(C)Annotation by peers	10	3.7	1.06	3.5	1.08	7.5	0.42

*$p < 0.05$

Table 7. Mann-Whitney U test results of anxiety between environmental and control groups

Questionnaire items	N	Mean	S.D.	W	p
Pre-questionnaire					
Tremble when I know that I'm going to be called on					
(E)Annotation by instructor	11	3.1	0.83	89.5*	0.010
(C)Annotation by peers	10	4.1	0.74		
Thinking about things that have nothing to do with the course					
(E)Annotation by instructor	11	2.6	0.92	87*	0.022
(C)Annotation by peers	10	3.8	1.03		
Post-questionnaire					
Caused me a lot of mental effort					
(E)Annotation by instructor	11	3	0.77	82*	0.049
(C)Annotation by peers	10	3.8	0.92		

*$p < 0.05$

5   Discussion and Conclusions

In this study, two groups were designed to explore the effect of the shared annotation data, with one reading e-book materials annotated by an instructor and the other by other students. A preliminary experiment and an evaluation experiment were conducted in a mobile application development learning course and a tourism design course, respectively.

The results revealed that annotations made by the instructor were more concise compared to those made by their peers. Although there were no significant differences in the pre-test or the post-test between the two groups, students who read the instructor's annotations achieved better learning performance on the delayed test than the students who read their peers' annotations.

In the pre-questionnaire before the experiment, no differences in learning attitudes or self-efficacy were found between the two groups. However, in the post-questionnaire, students in the experimental group showed improved answers about the importance of learning and reduced answers regarding confidence in understanding difficult materials. This was also reflected in the free-response question, where some students mentioned finding certain concepts challenging. On the contrary, students in the control group increased their scores on questions related to actively searching for more relevant materials.

This indicates that the experiment affected the learning attitude and self-efficacy of the students in the experimental group. They perceived the learning activity as somewhat challenging but also recognized its importance. For the students in the control group, the experiment did not affect their self-efficacy but prompted them to take the initiative in finding relevant materials.

Before the experiment, anxiety was tested in the pre-question, with students in the control group presenting higher scores. Additionally, in the post-questionnaire, students in the control group evaluated themselves and found that the presentation of the e-book made it more challenging to read and understand. The number of annotations on the e-book by peers was greater than that by the instructor, and most of the annotations by peers were underlined words, not sentences. Therefore, excessive annotations cause more conformity among students and affect their understanding and reading.

6   Limitation

Due to the COVID-19 pandemic, the number of students participating in the experiment was small, and individual differences may have had a greater impact on the experimental results. The experiment was conducted as part of an actual class, and because the pretest and questionnaire were loosely related to the class content, we explained that they were optional to submit. As a result, the submission rates for both the pretest and questionnaire were low, leading to a limited sample size for data analysis.

Acknowledgments. This work was partially supported by the Grants-in-Aid for Scientific Research Nos. 21H00905 and 22K13752 from the Ministry of Education, Culture, Sports, Science and Technology (MEXT) of Japan.

Disclosure of Interests. The authors have no competing interests to declare relevant to this article's content.

References

1. Chen, C.M., Li, M.C., Chen, T.C.: A web-based collaborative reading annotation system with gamification mechanisms to improve reading performance. Comput. Educ. **144**, 103697 (2020). https://doi.org/10.1016/j.compedu.2019.103697, https://www.sciencedirect.com/science/article/pii/S0360131519302507
2. Cohen, J.: Statistical power analysis for the behavioral sciences. Academic press (2013)
3. Dennis, A.R., Abaci, S., Morrone, A.S., Plaskoff, J., Hilmer, K.M.: Effects of e-textbook instructor annotations on learner performance. J. Comput. High. Educ. **28**, 221–235 (2016). https://api.semanticscholar.org/CorpusID:28848886
4. Horwitz, E.K., Horwitz, M.B., Cope, J.: Foreign language classroom anxiety. Modern Lang. J. **70**(2), 125–132 (1986). http://www.jstor.org/stable/327317
5. Jensen, M., Scharff, L.: Improving critical reading with e-texts: a controlled study in a collegiate philosophy course. J. Scholarship Teach. Learn. **19**(3) (2019). https://doi.org/10.14434/josotl.v19i2.23978, https://scholarworks.iu.edu/journals/index.php/josotl/article/view/23978
6. Kita, H., Morimura, Y., Okamoto, M.: Programming practice Python 2021 (2021). http://hdl.handle.net/2433/265459

7. Lim, E.L., Hew, K.F.: Students' perceptions of the usefulness of an e-book with annotative and sharing capabilities as a tool for learning: a case study. Innov. Educ. Teach. Int. **51**(1), 34–45 (2014). https://doi.org/10.1080/14703297.2013.771969

8. Popescu, E., Stefan, C., Ilie, S., Ivanović, M.: EduNotes – a mobile learning application for collaborative note-taking in lecture settings. In: Chiu, D.K.W., Marenzi, I., Nanni, U., Spaniol, M., Temperini, M. (eds.) ICWL 2016. LNCS, vol. 10013, pp. 131–140. Springer, Cham (2016). https://doi.org/10.1007/978-3-319-47440-3_15

9. Reilly, M., Shen, H.: Groupnotes: encouraging proactive student engagement in lectures through collaborative note-taking on smartphones (2011)

10. Yin, C., Hwang, G.J.: Roles and strategies of learning analytics in the e-publication era. Knowl. Manage. E-Learn. **10**(4), 455–468 (2018)

11. Yokoyama, K., Misono, T., Inaba, R., Watanabe, Y.: Development of nudge system: to nudge other students through their tablet. In: Stephanidis, C., Antona, M. (eds.) HCII 2020. CCIS, vol. 1225, pp. 372–380. Springer, Cham (2020). https://doi.org/10.1007/978-3-030-50729-9_53

12. Zhao, F., Liu, G.Z., Zhou, J., Yin, C.: A learning analytics framework based on human-centered artificial intelligence for identifying the optimal learning strategy to intervene in learning behavior. Educ. Technol. Society **26**(1), pp. 132–146 (2023). https://www.jstor.org/stable/48707972

13. Zhou, J.,Wang, S., Xu, L., Yin, C.: Using the grouping function of machine learning algorithm to reduce the influence of information avoidance tendency during reading behavior. Smart Learn. Environ. **10**(1), 62 (2023)

Author Index

P. Zaphiris and A. Ioannou (Eds.): HCII 2024, LNCS 14722, pp. 299–301, 2024.
https://doi.org/10.1007/978-3-031-61672-3

Printed in the United States
by Baker & Taylor Publisher Services